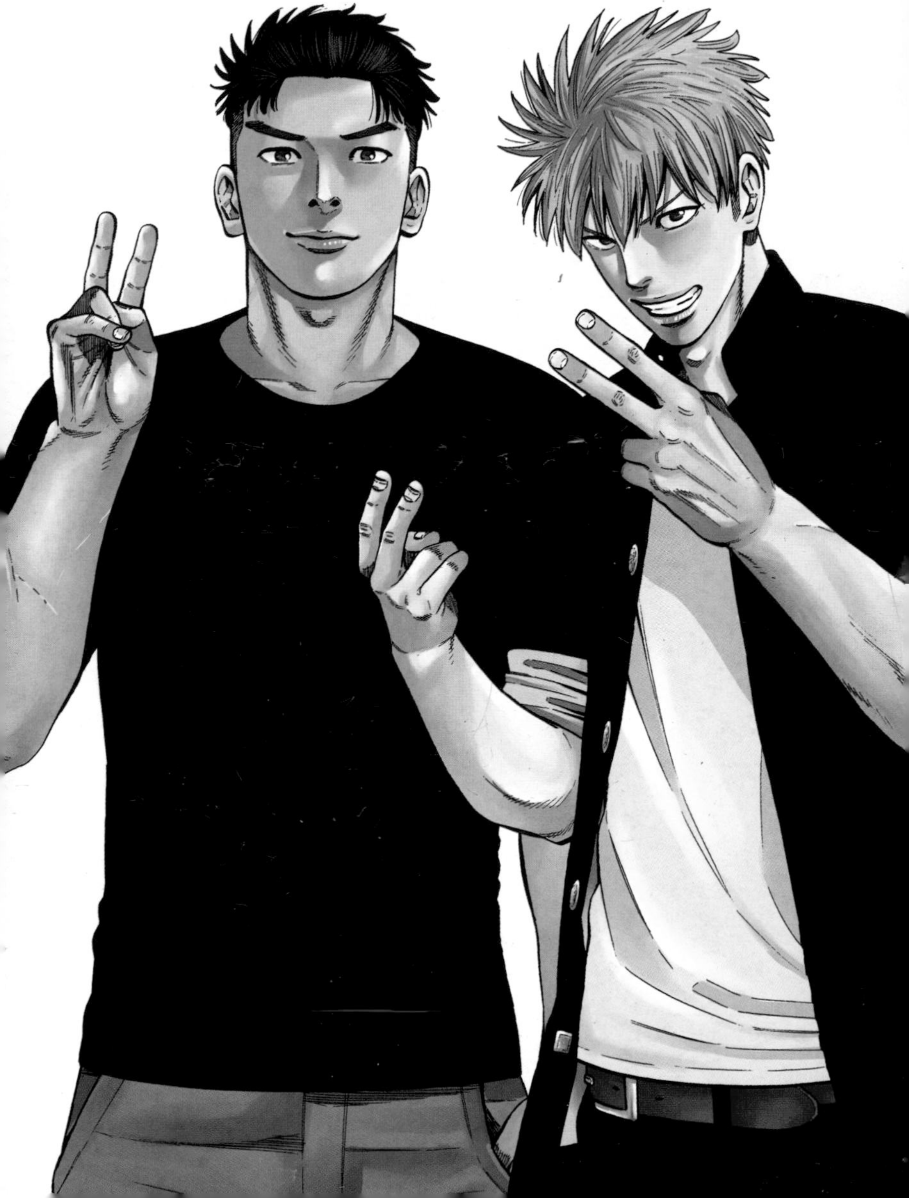

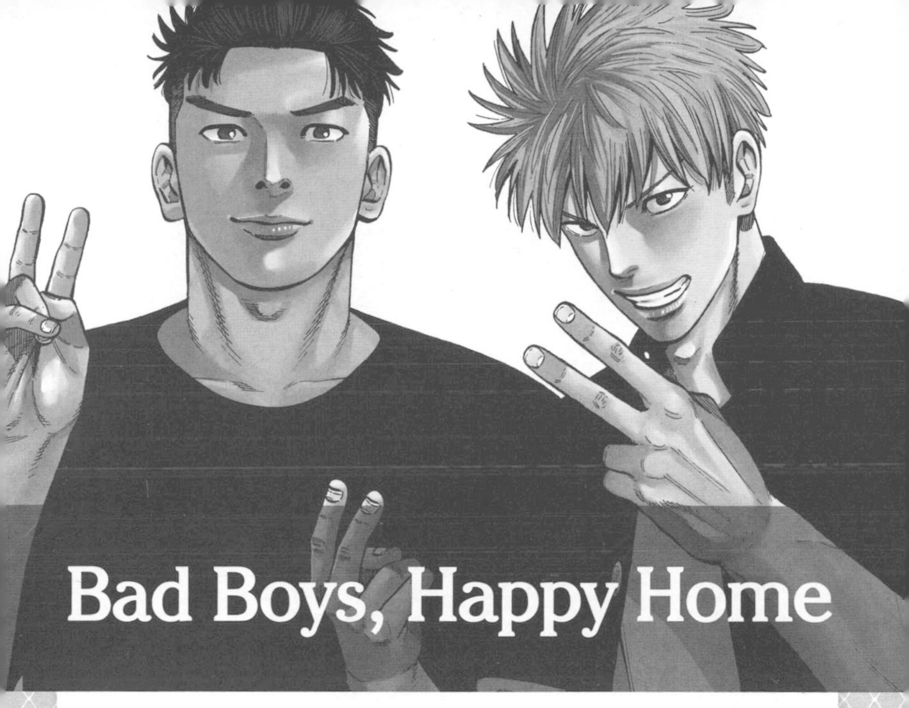

Bad Boys, Happy Home

Story by SHOOWA Art by Hiromasa Okujima volume 3

CONTENTS

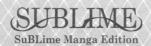

SUBLIME
SuBLime Manga Edition

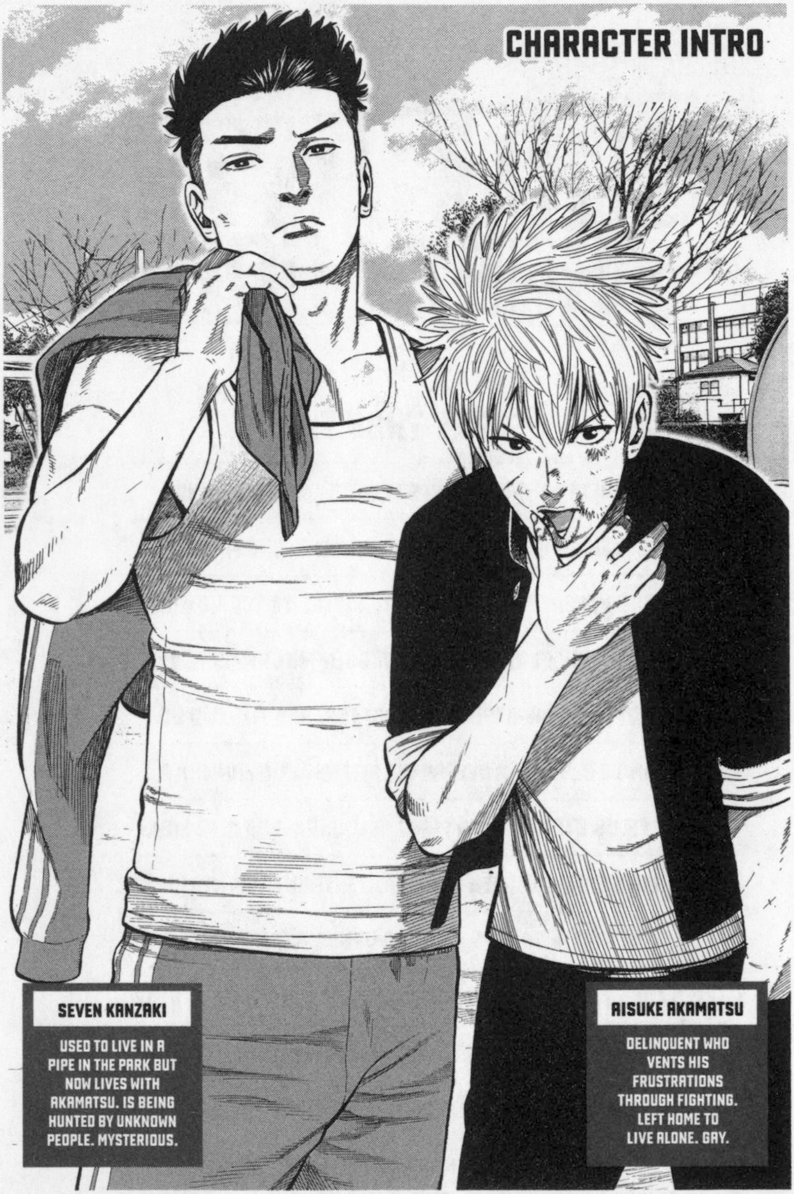
CHARACTER INTRO
AISUKE AKAMATSU
DELINQUENT WHO VENTS HIS FRUSTRATIONS THROUGH FIGHTING. LEFT HOME TO LIVE ALONE. GAY.
SEVEN KANZAKI
USED TO LIVE IN A PIPE IN THE PARK BUT NOW LIVES WITH AKAMATSU. IS BEING HUNTED BY UNKNOWN PEOPLE. MYSTERIOUS.

BAD BOYS
HAPPY HOME

STORY THUS FAR

RANDOM STREET FIGHTS LEAD TO AKAMATSU AND
SEVEN SHARING A SMALL APARTMENT, AND IT'S NOT
LONG BEFORE THEY BECOME ATTRACTED TO EACH OTHER.
ALTHOUGH SURPRISED BY A SUDDEN FIRST KISS FROM
SEVEN, AKAMATSU RECIPROCATES, AND THE TWO GO
ON TO DEVELOP A DEEPER RELATIONSHIP. MEANWHILE,
SEVEN'S STEPBROTHER EIGHT IS LOOKING FOR HIM. EIGHT
GETS FRIENDLY WITH AKAMATSU WITHOUT LETTING HIM
KNOW WHO HE IS. ONE NIGHT HE DRUGS AKAMATSU AND IS
CLOSE TO ASSAULTING HIM WHEN SEVEN ARRIVES TO STOP
HIM. SEVEN THREATENS EIGHT BEFORE TAKING AKAMATSU
HOME. BUT WHEN AKAMATSU WAKES UP THE NEXT
MORNING, SEVEN IS NOWHERE TO BE SEEN.

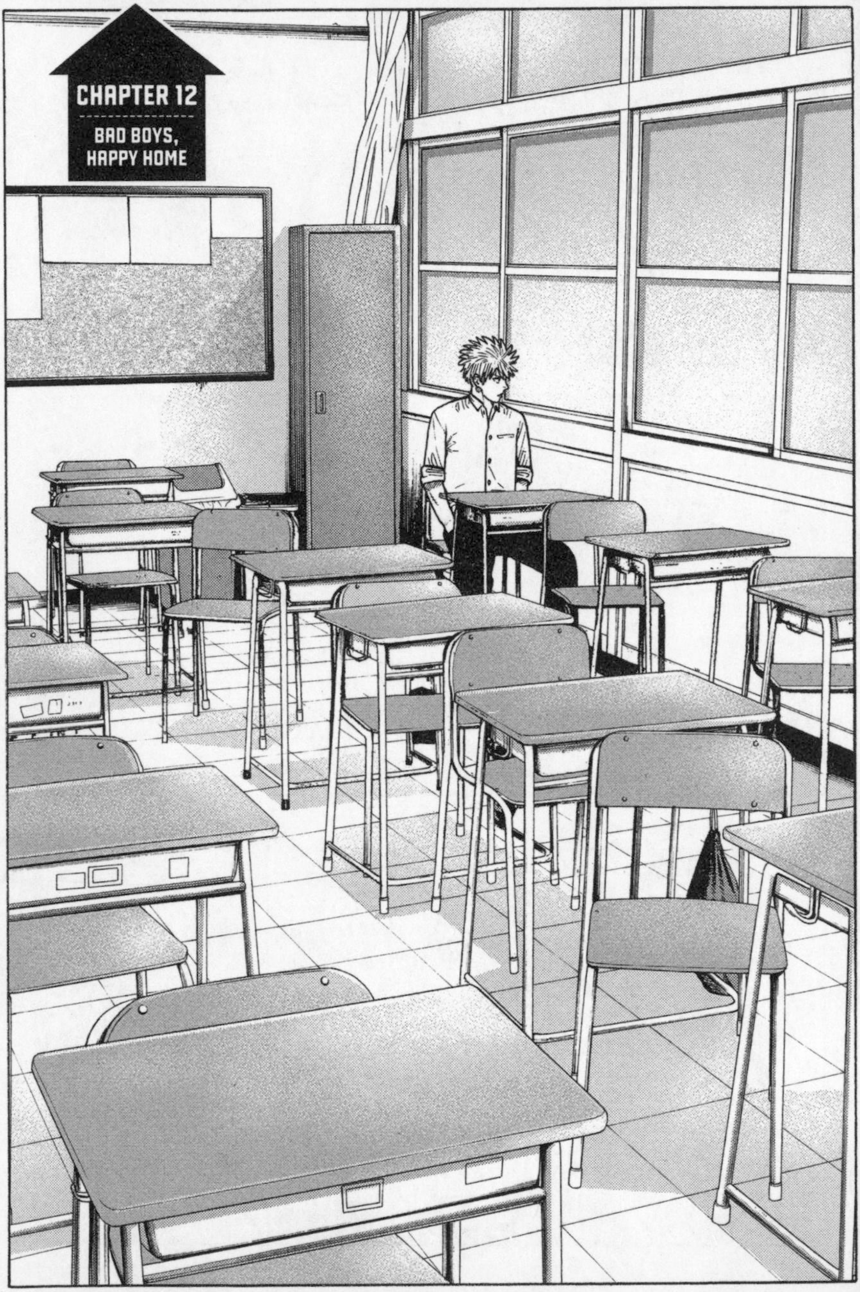
CHAPTER 12
BAD BOYS,
HAPPY HOME

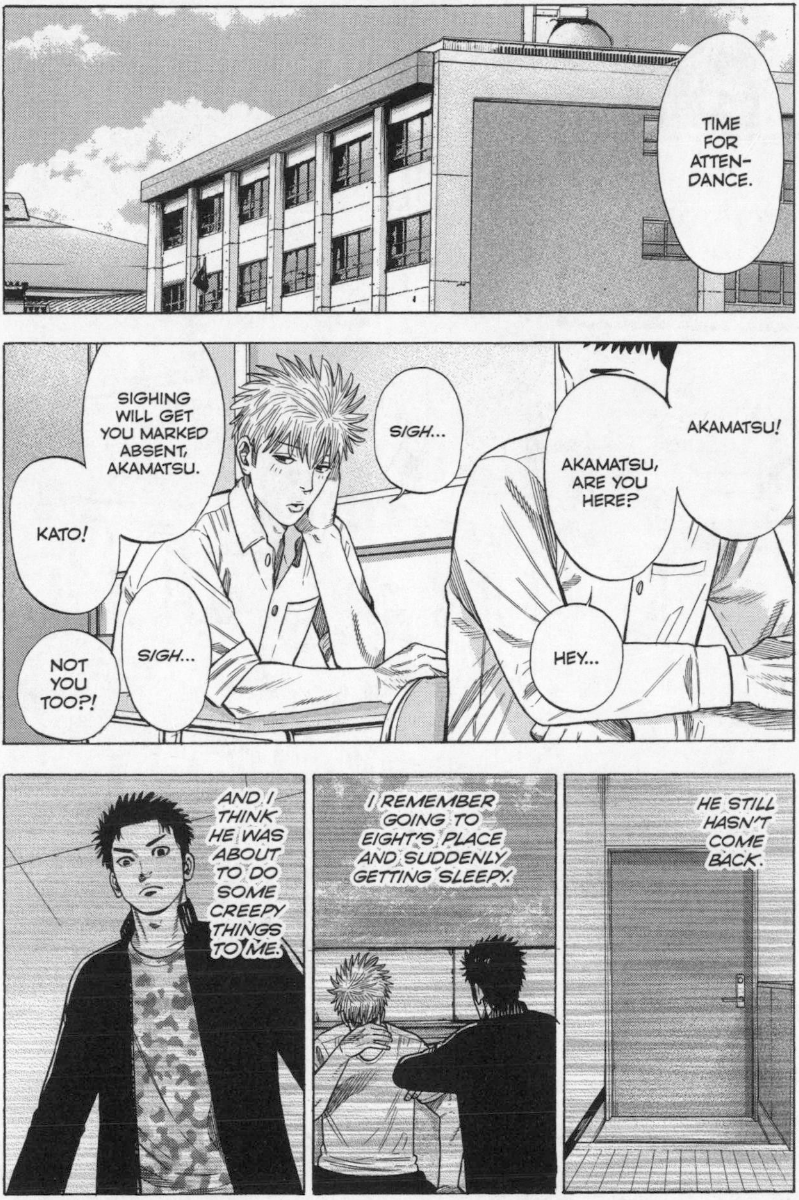
TIME FOR ATTENDANCE.
AKAMATSU!
AKAMATSU, ARE YOU HERE?
SIGH...
SIGHING WILL GET YOU MARKED ABSENT, AKAMATSU.
KATO!
HEY...
SIGH...
NOT YOU TOO?!
HE STILL HASN'T COME BACK.
I REMEMBER GOING TO EIGHT'S PLACE AND SUDDENLY GETTING SLEEPY.
AND I THINK HE WAS ABOUT TO DO SOME CREEPY THINGS TO ME.

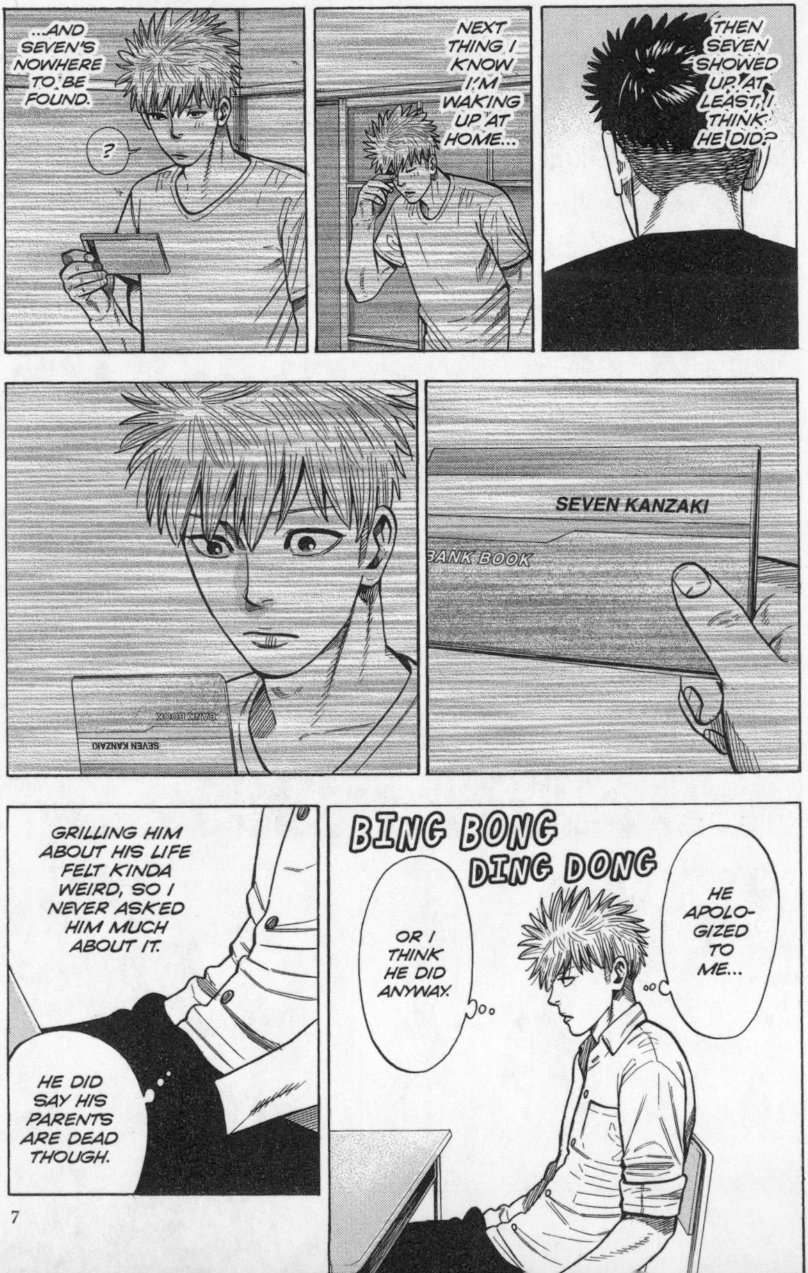
THEN SEVEN SHOWED UP. AT LEAST, I THINK HE DID?
NEXT THING I KNOW I'M WAKING UP AT HOME...
...AND SEVEN'S NOWHERE TO BE FOUND.
?
SEVEN KANZAKI
BANK BOOK
BING BONG
DING DONG
HE APOLO-GIZED TO ME...
OR I THINK HE DID ANYWAY.
GRILLING HIM ABOUT HIS LIFE FELT KINDA WEIRD, SO I NEVER ASKED HIM MUCH ABOUT IT.
HE DID SAY HIS PARENTS ARE DEAD THOUGH.

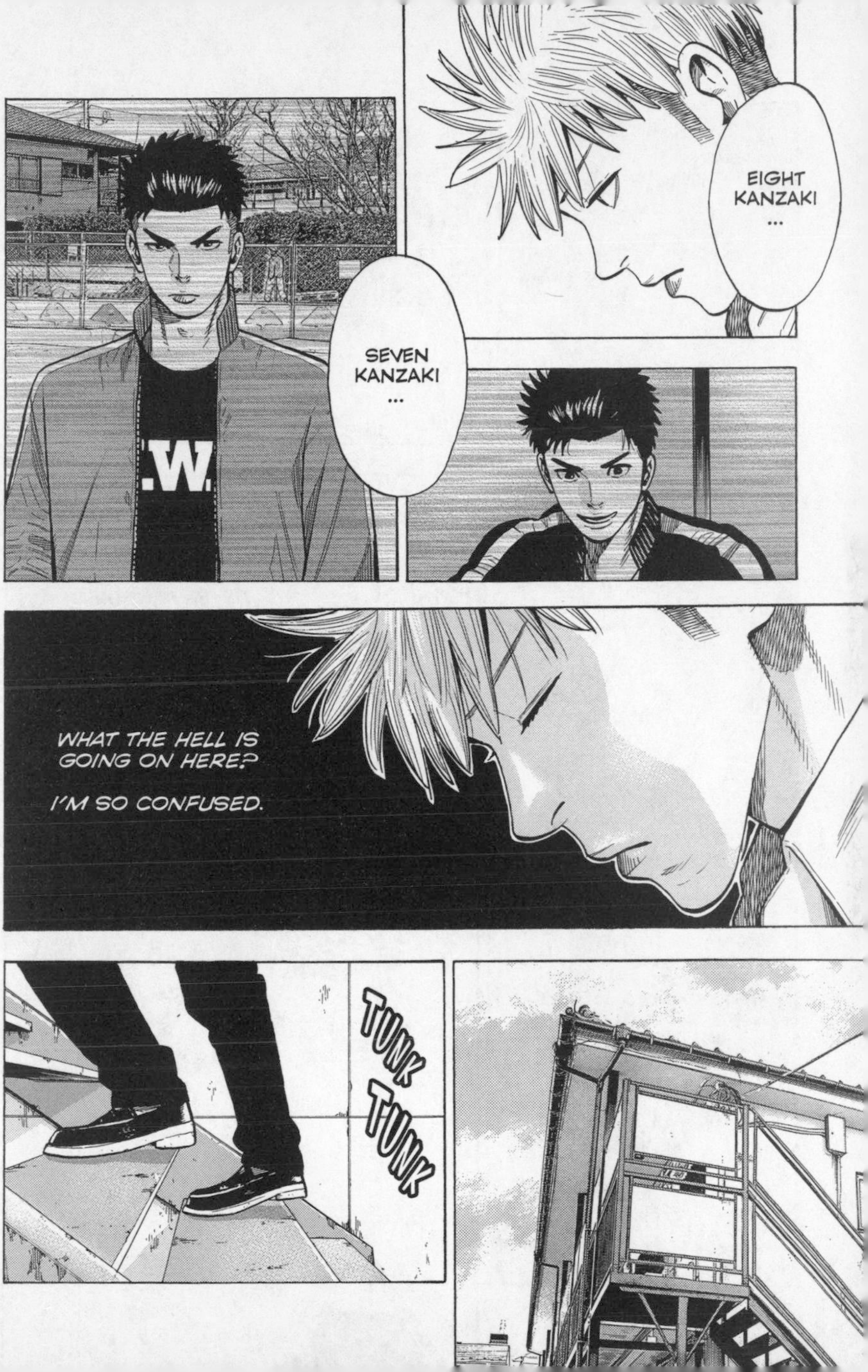
EIGHT KANZAKI ...
SEVEN KANZAKI ...
WHAT THE HELL IS GOING ON HERE?
I'M SO CONFUSED.
TUNK TUNK

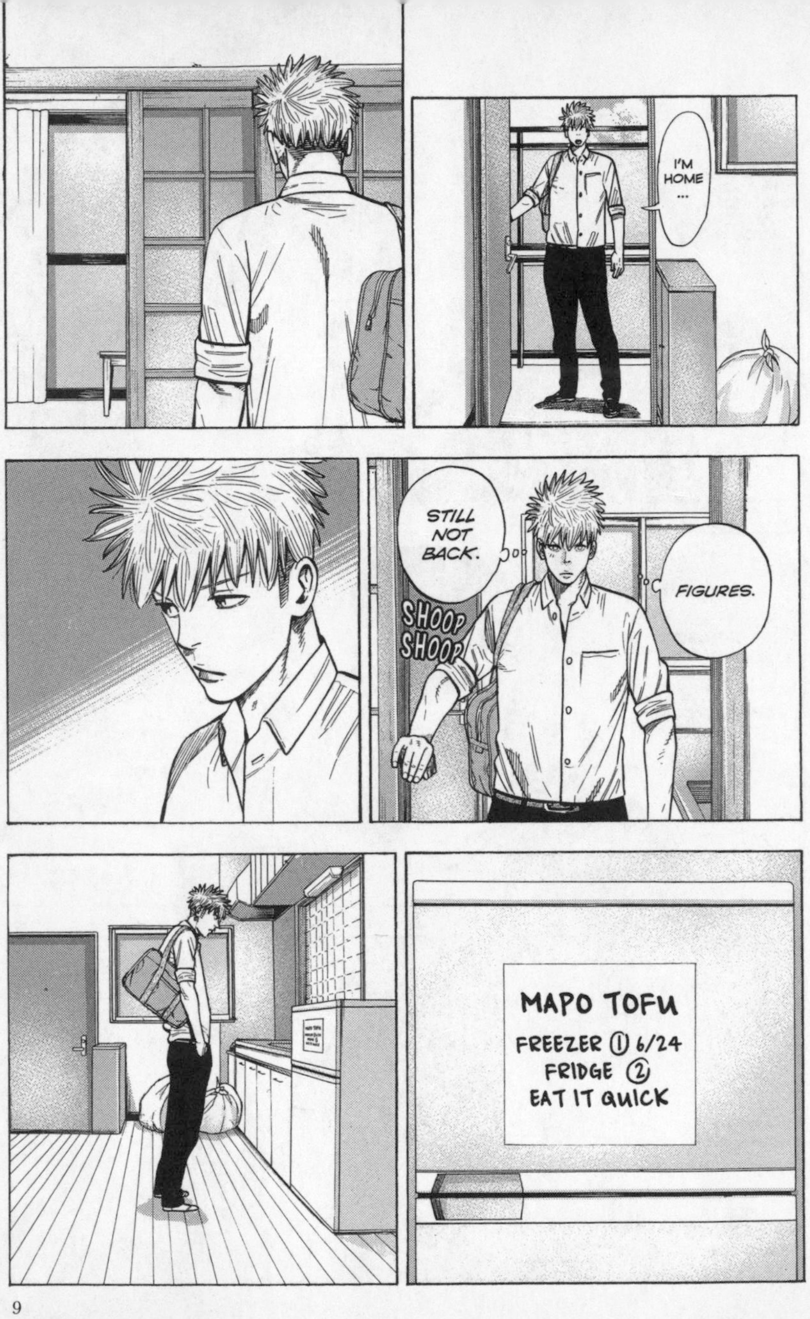
I'M HOME ...
STILL NOT BACK.
FIGURES.
SHOOP SHOOP
MAPO TOFU
FREEZER ① 6/24
FRIDGE ②
EAT IT QUICK

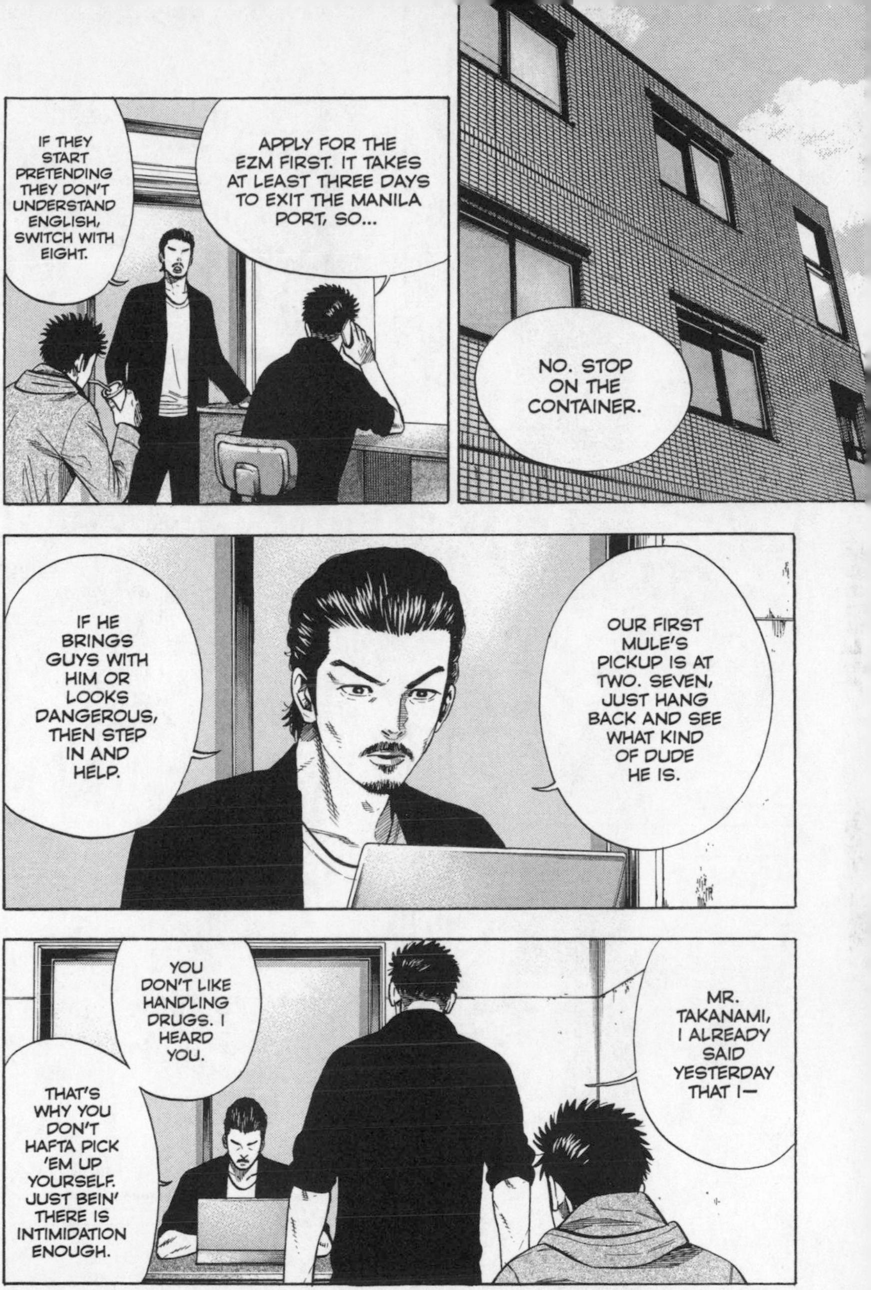
NO. STOP ON THE CONTAINER.
APPLY FOR THE EZM FIRST. IT TAKES AT LEAST THREE DAYS TO EXIT THE MANILA PORT, SO...
IF THEY START PRETENDING THEY DON'T UNDERSTAND ENGLISH, SWITCH WITH EIGHT.
OUR FIRST MULE'S PICKUP IS AT TWO. SEVEN, JUST HANG BACK AND SEE WHAT KIND OF DUDE HE IS.
IF HE BRINGS GUYS WITH HIM OR LOOKS DANGEROUS, THEN STEP IN AND HELP.
MR. TAKANAMI, I ALREADY SAID YESTERDAY THAT I—
YOU DON'T LIKE HANDLING DRUGS. I HEARD YOU.
THAT'S WHY YOU DON'T HAFTA PICK 'EM UP YOURSELF. JUST BEIN' THERE IS INTIMIDATION ENOUGH.

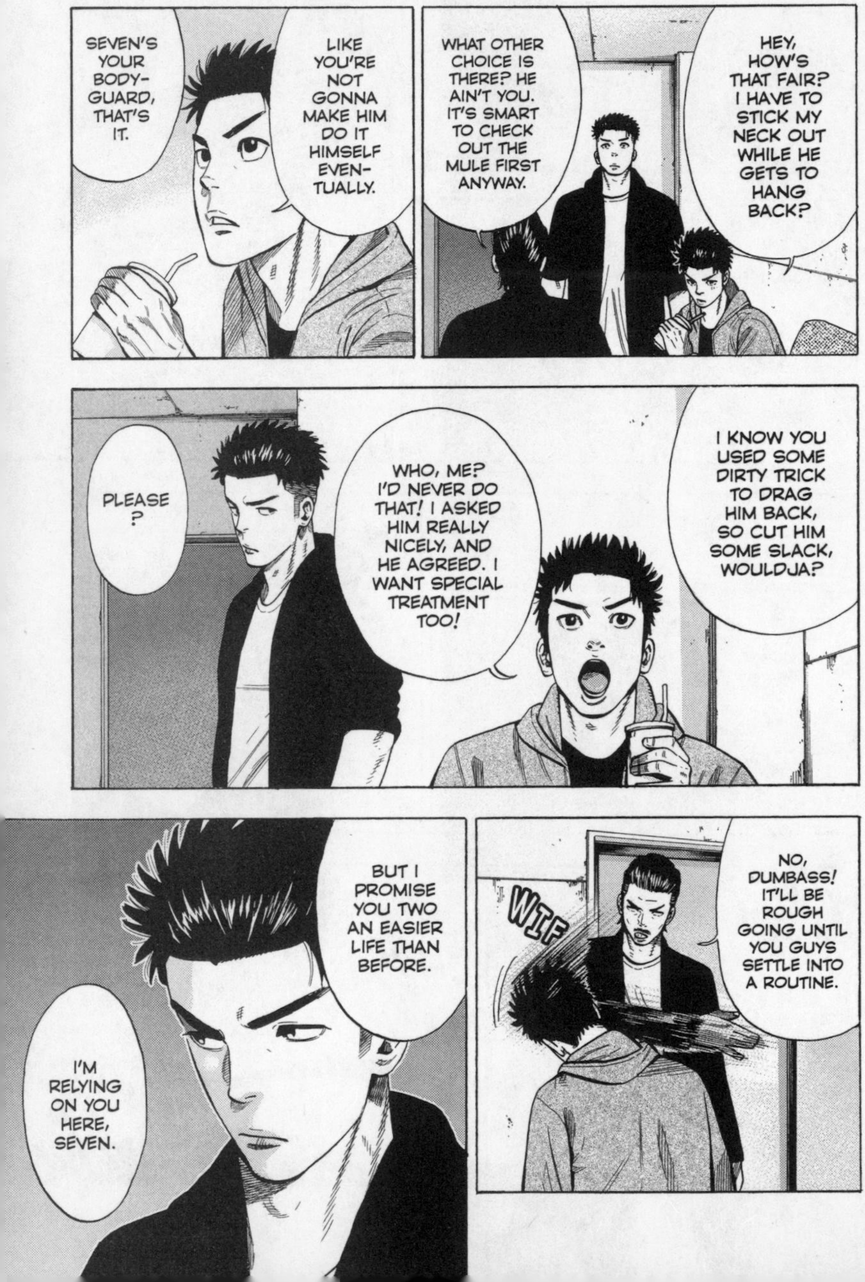
HEY, HOW'S THAT FAIR? I HAVE TO STICK MY NECK OUT WHILE HE GETS TO HANG BACK?
WHAT OTHER CHOICE IS THERE? HE AIN'T YOU. IT'S SMART TO CHECK OUT THE MULE FIRST ANYWAY.
LIKE YOU'RE NOT GONNA MAKE HIM DO IT HIMSELF EVEN-TUALLY.
SEVEN'S YOUR BODY-GUARD, THAT'S IT.
I KNOW YOU USED SOME DIRTY TRICK TO DRAG HIM BACK, SO CUT HIM SOME SLACK, WOULDJA?
WHO, ME? I'D NEVER DO THAT! I ASKED HIM REALLY NICELY, AND HE AGREED. I WANT SPECIAL TREATMENT TOO!
PLEASE?
NO, DUMBASS! IT'LL BE ROUGH GOING UNTIL YOU GUYS SETTLE INTO A ROUTINE.
WIF
BUT I PROMISE YOU TWO AN EASIER LIFE THAN BEFORE.
I'M RELYING ON YOU HERE, SEVEN.

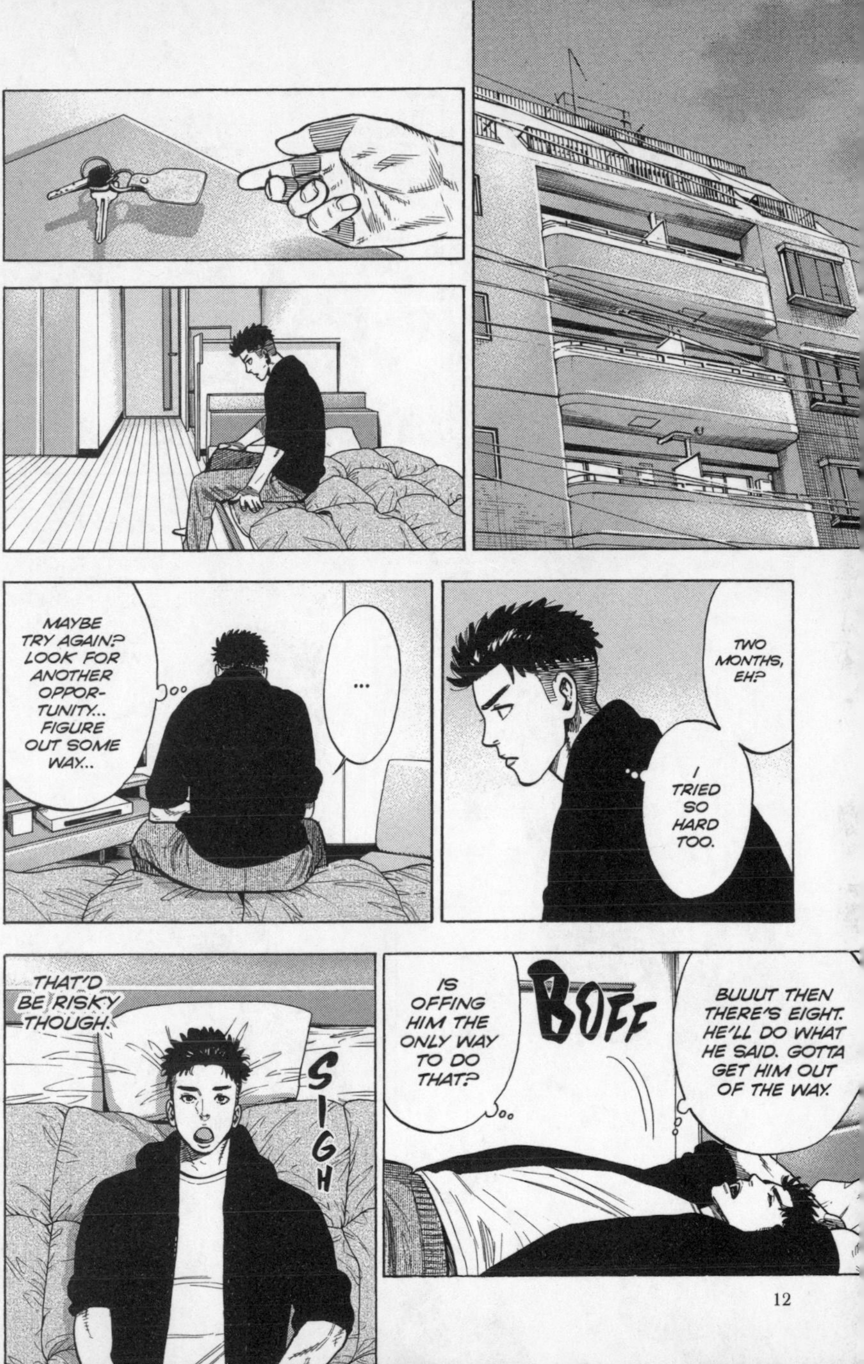
TWO MONTHS, EH?
I TRIED SO HARD TOO.
...
MAYBE TRY AGAIN? LOOK FOR ANOTHER OPPORTUNITY... FIGURE OUT SOME WAY...
BUUUT THEN THERE'S EIGHT. HE'LL DO WHAT HE SAID. GOTTA GET HIM OUT OF THE WAY.
BOFF
IS OFFING HIM THE ONLY WAY TO DO THAT?
THAT'D BE RISKY THOUGH.
SIGH

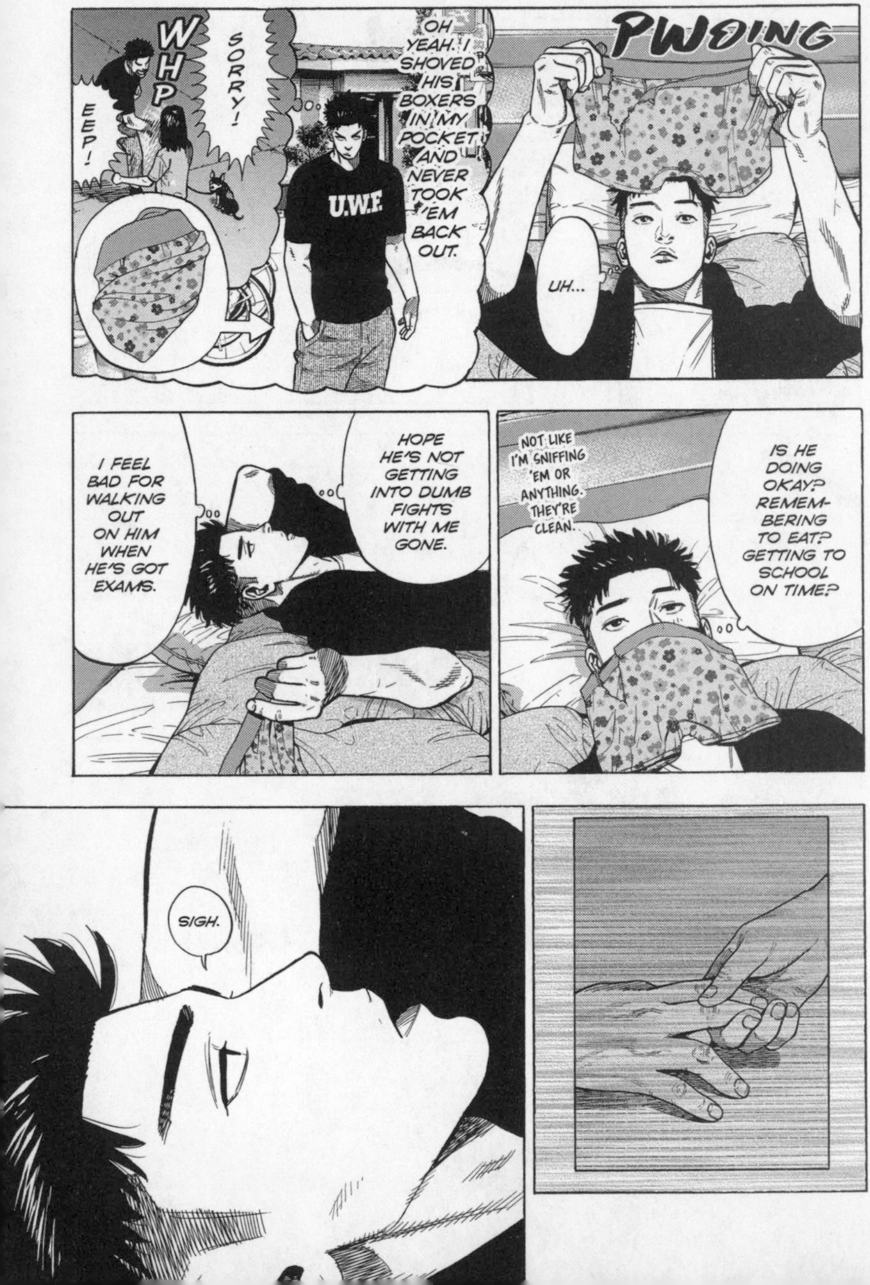
PWOING
UH...
OH YEAH. I SHOVED HIS BOXERS IN MY POCKET AND NEVER TOOK 'EM BACK OUT.
SORRY!
WHP
EEP!
IS HE DOING OKAY? REMEMBERING TO EAT? GETTING TO SCHOOL ON TIME?
NOT LIKE I'M SNIFFING 'EM OR ANYTHING. THEY'RE CLEAN.
HOPE HE'S NOT GETTING INTO DUMB FIGHTS WITH ME GONE.
I FEEL BAD FOR WALKING OUT ON HIM WHEN HE'S GOT EXAMS.
SIGH.

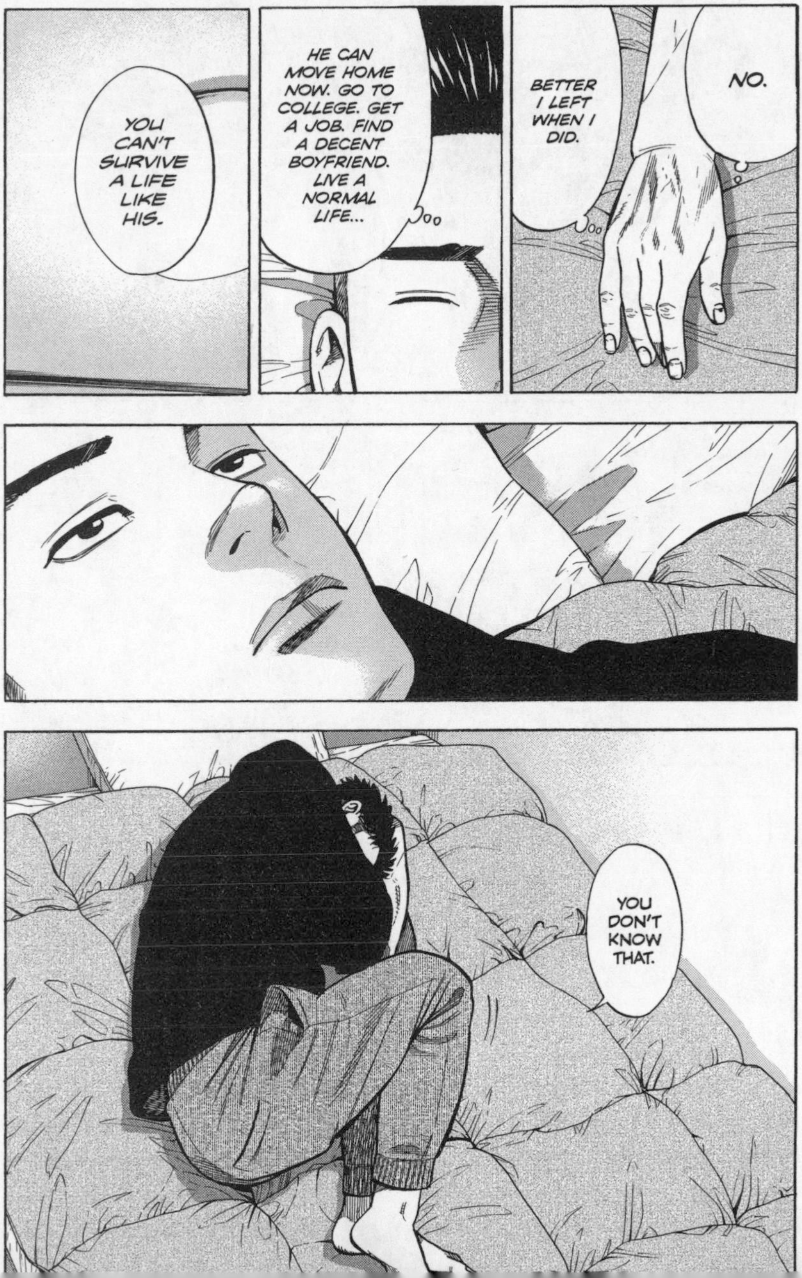
NO.
BETTER I LEFT WHEN I DID.
HE CAN MOVE HOME NOW. GO TO COLLEGE. GET A JOB. FIND A DECENT BOYFRIEND. LIVE A NORMAL LIFE...
YOU CAN'T SURVIVE A LIFE LIKE HIS.
YOU DON'T KNOW THAT.

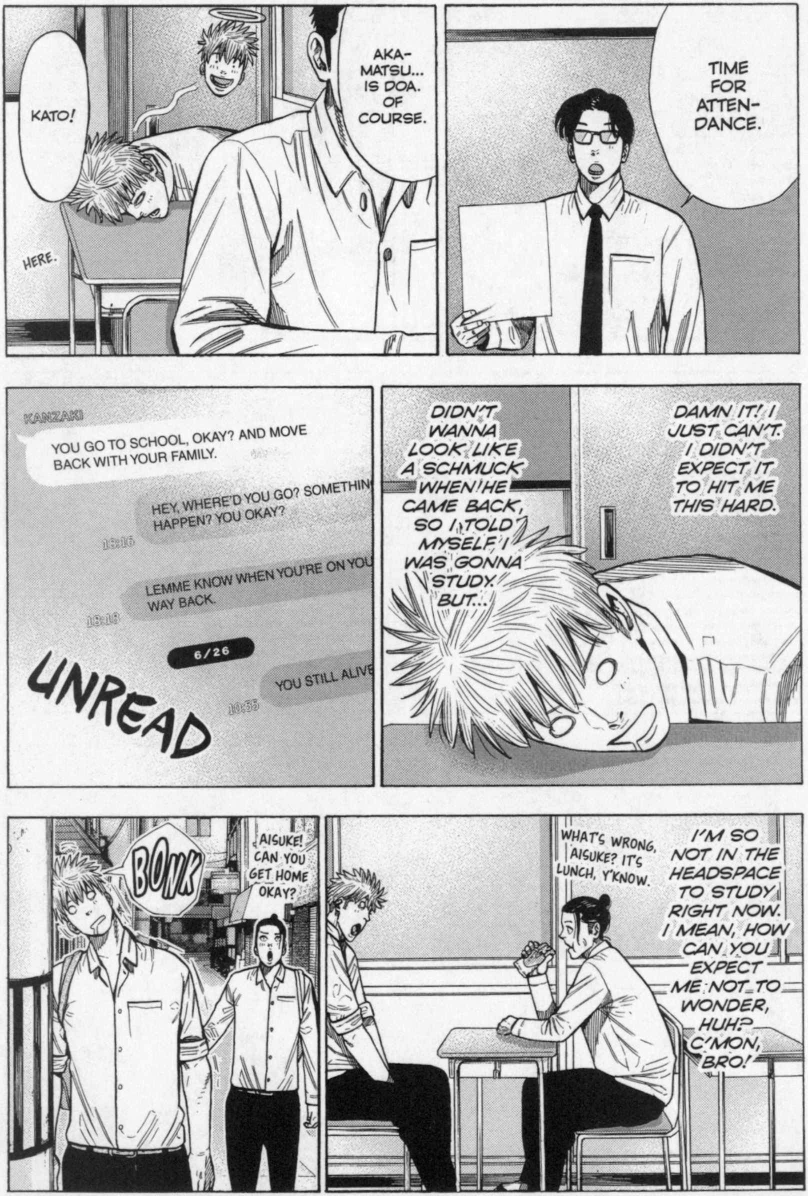
TIME FOR ATTEN- DANCE.
AKA- MATSU... IS DOA. OF COURSE.
KATO!
HERE.
DAMN IT! I JUST CAN'T. I DIDN'T EXPECT IT TO HIT ME THIS HARD.
DIDN'T WANNA LOOK LIKE A SCHMUCK WHEN HE CAME BACK, SO I TOLD MYSELF I WAS GONNA STUDY. BUT...
KANZAKI
YOU GO TO SCHOOL, OKAY? AND MOVE BACK WITH YOUR FAMILY.
HEY, WHERE'D YOU GO? SOMETHIN HAPPEN? YOU OKAY?
18:16
LEMME KNOW WHEN YOU'RE ON YOU WAY BACK.
18:18
6/26
YOU STILL ALIVE
10:55
UNREAD
I'M SO NOT IN THE HEADSPACE TO STUDY RIGHT NOW. I MEAN, HOW CAN YOU EXPECT ME NOT TO WONDER, HUH? C'MON, BRO!
WHAT'S WRONG, AISUKE? IT'S LUNCH, Y'KNOW.
AISUKE! CAN YOU GET HOME OKAY?
BONK

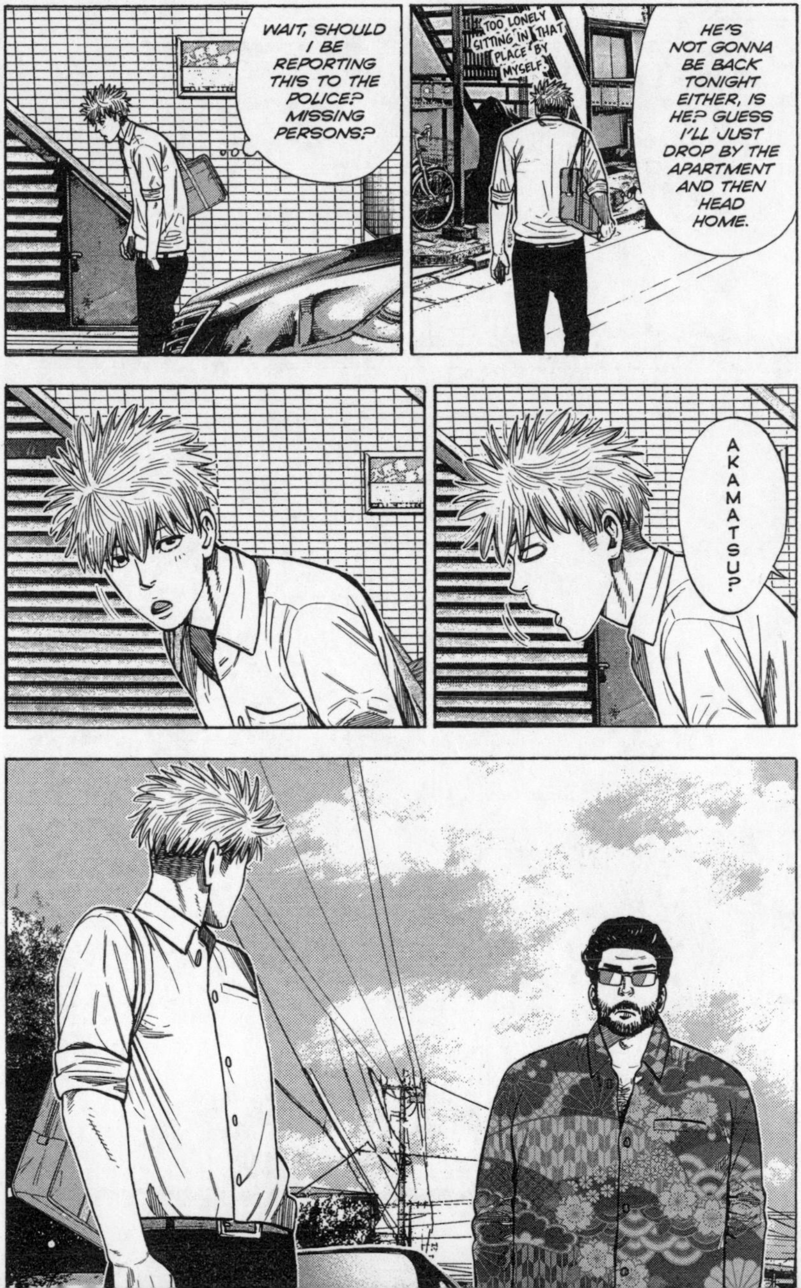
HE'S NOT GONNA BE BACK TONIGHT EITHER, IS HE? GUESS I'LL JUST DROP BY THE APARTMENT AND THEN HEAD HOME.
TOO LONELY SITTING IN THAT PLACE BY MYSELF.
WAIT, SHOULD I BE REPORTING THIS TO THE POLICE? MISSING PERSONS?
AKAMATSU?

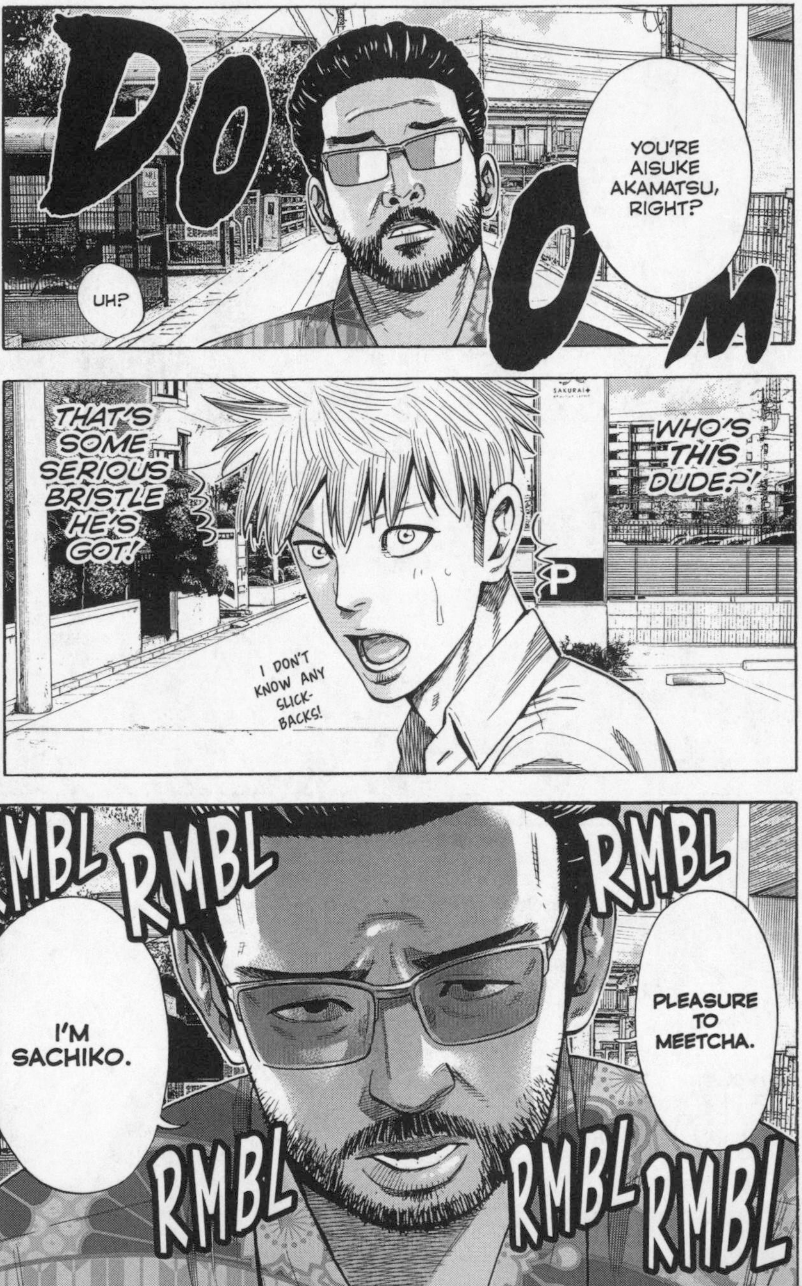
YOU'RE AISUKE AKAMATSU, RIGHT?
DOOOM
UH?
SAKURAI+
WHO'S THIS DUDE?!
P
THAT'S SOME SERIOUS BRISTLE HE'S GOT!
I DON'T KNOW ANY SLICK-BACKS!
RMBL RMBL RMBL
PLEASURE TO MEETCHA.
I'M SACHIKO.
RMBL RMBL RMBL

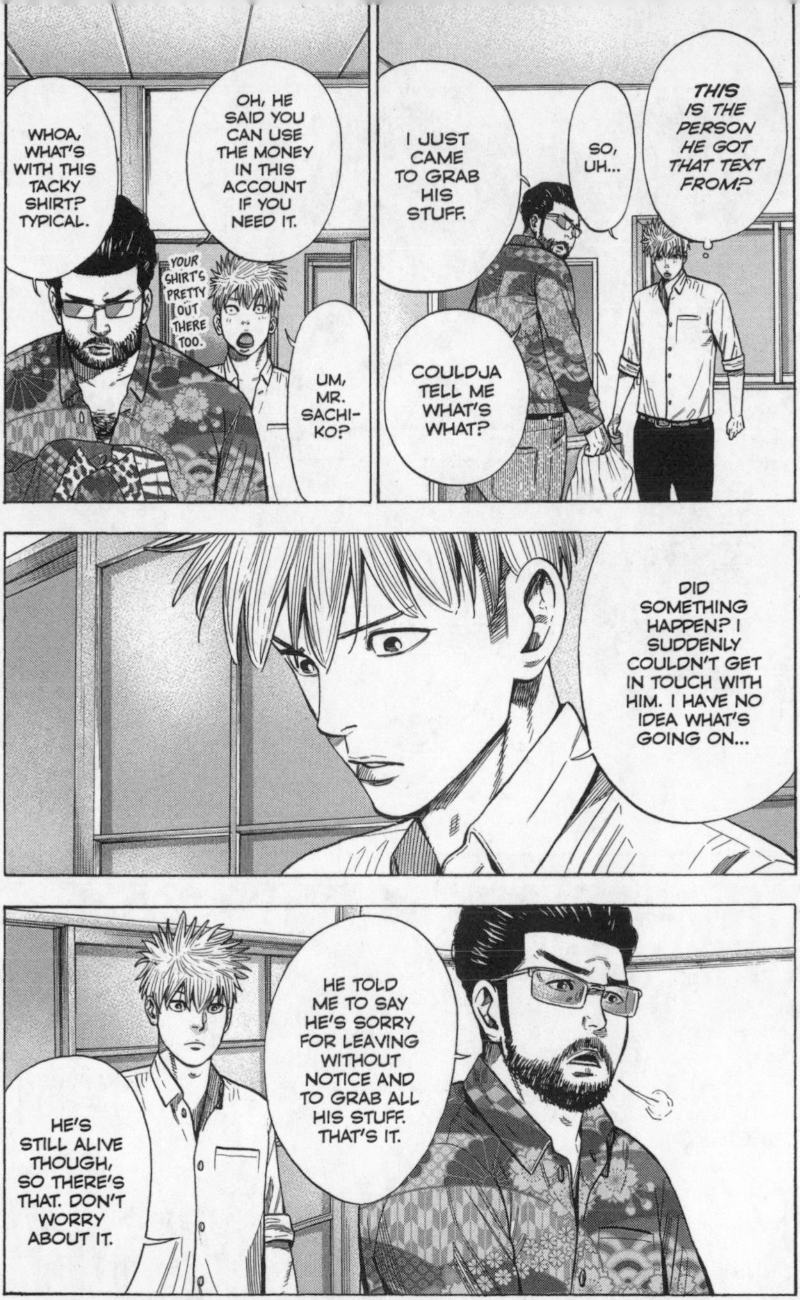
THIS IS THE PERSON HE GOT THAT TEXT FROM?
SO, UH...
I JUST CAME TO GRAB HIS STUFF.
COULDJA TELL ME WHAT'S WHAT?
OH, HE SAID YOU CAN USE THE MONEY IN THIS ACCOUNT IF YOU NEED IT.
WHOA, WHAT'S WITH THIS TACKY SHIRT? TYPICAL.
YOUR SHIRT'S PRETTY OUT THERE TOO.
UM, MR. SACHIKO?
DID SOMETHING HAPPEN? I SUDDENLY COULDN'T GET IN TOUCH WITH HIM. I HAVE NO IDEA WHAT'S GOING ON...
HE TOLD ME TO SAY HE'S SORRY FOR LEAVING WITHOUT NOTICE AND TO GRAB ALL HIS STUFF. THAT'S IT.
HE'S STILL ALIVE THOUGH, SO THERE'S THAT. DON'T WORRY ABOUT IT.

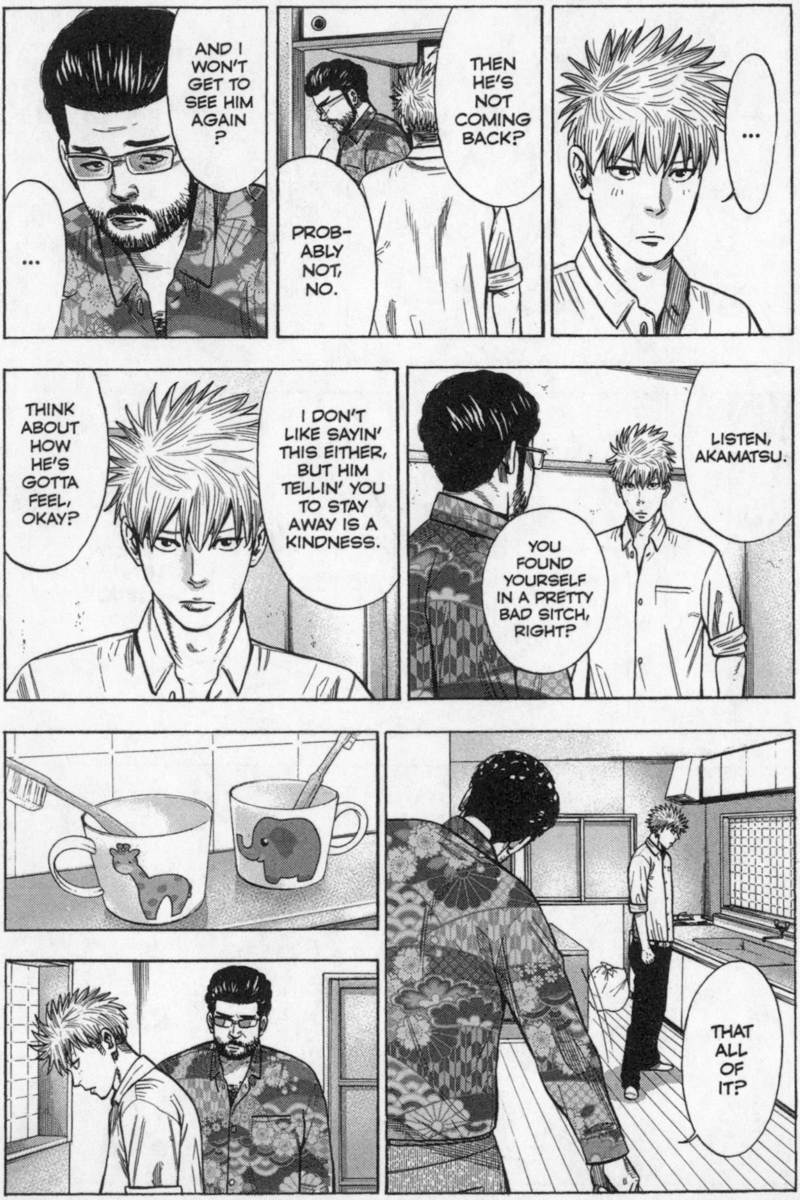
...
THEN HE'S NOT COMING BACK?
PROBABLY NOT, NO.
AND I WON'T GET TO SEE HIM AGAIN ?
...
LISTEN, AKAMATSU.
YOU FOUND YOURSELF IN A PRETTY BAD SITCH, RIGHT?
I DON'T LIKE SAYIN' THIS EITHER, BUT HIM TELLIN' YOU TO STAY AWAY IS A KINDNESS.
THINK ABOUT HOW HE'S GOTTA FEEL, OKAY?
THAT ALL OF IT?

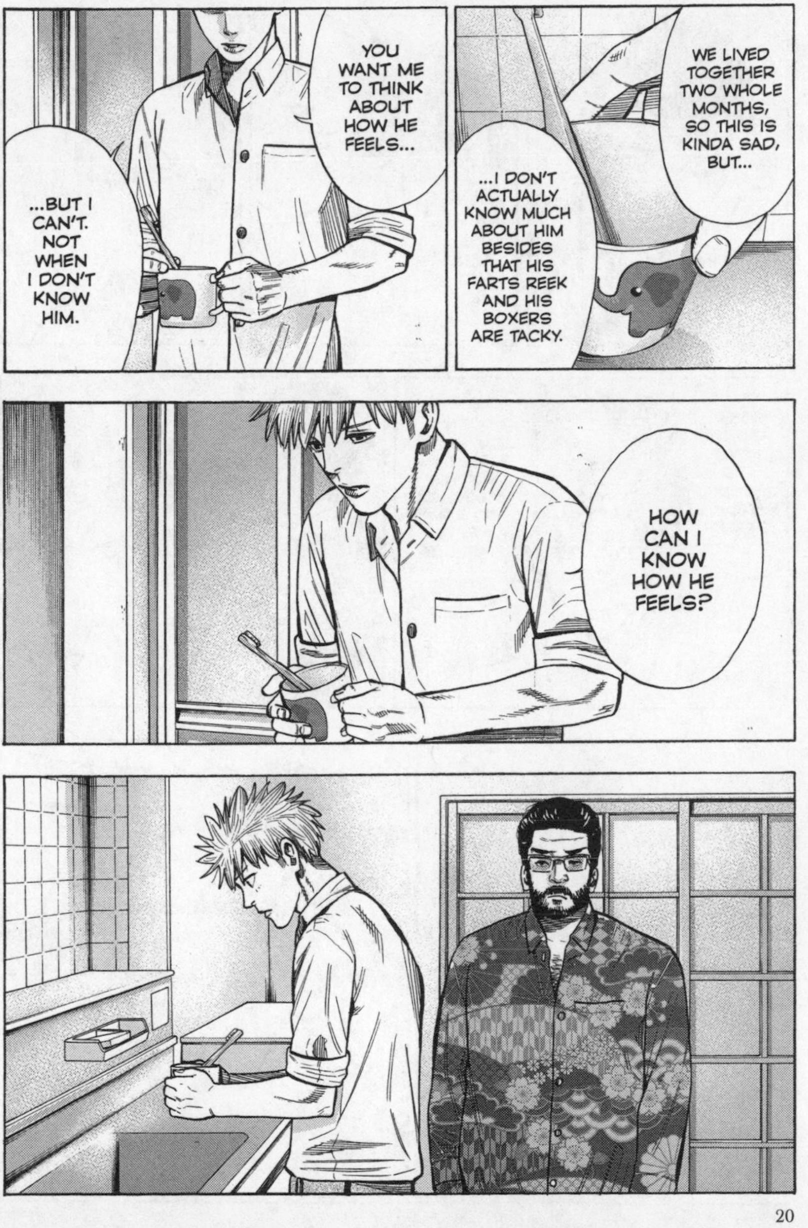
WE LIVED TOGETHER TWO WHOLE MONTHS, SO THIS IS KINDA SAD, BUT...
...I DON'T ACTUALLY KNOW MUCH ABOUT HIM BESIDES THAT HIS FARTS REEK AND HIS BOXERS ARE TACKY.
YOU WANT ME TO THINK ABOUT HOW HE FEELS...
...BUT I CAN'T. NOT WHEN I DON'T KNOW HIM.
HOW CAN I KNOW HOW HE FEELS?

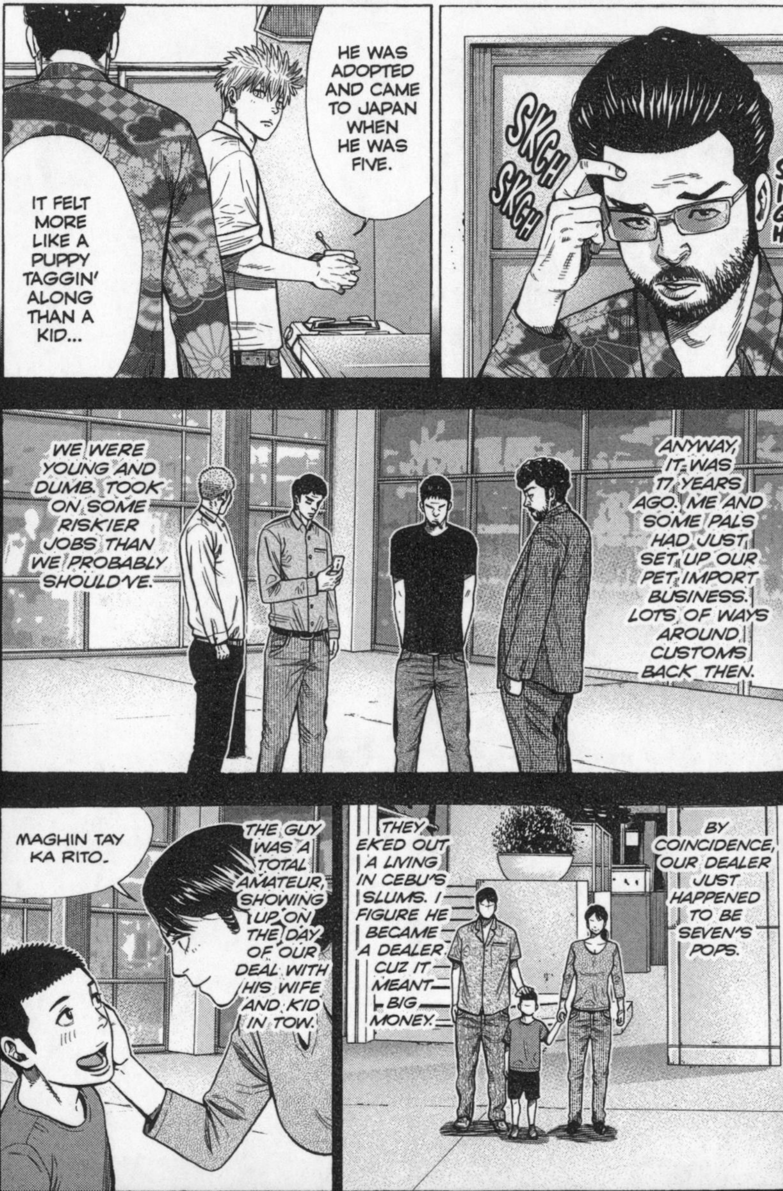
SKGH SKGH
SIGH
HE WAS ADOPTED AND CAME TO JAPAN WHEN HE WAS FIVE.
IT FELT MORE LIKE A PUPPY TAGGIN' ALONG THAN A KID...
ANYWAY, IT WAS 17 YEARS AGO. ME AND SOME PALS HAD JUST SET UP OUR PET IMPORT BUSINESS. LOTS OF WAYS AROUND CUSTOMS BACK THEN.
WE WERE YOUNG AND DUMB. TOOK ON SOME RISKIER JOBS THAN WE PROBABLY SHOULD'VE.
BY COINCIDENCE, OUR DEALER JUST HAPPENED TO BE SEVEN'S POPS.
THEY EKED OUT A LIVING IN CEBU'S SLUMS. I FIGURE HE BECAME A DEALER CUZ IT MEANT BIG MONEY.
THE GUY WAS A TOTAL AMATEUR, SHOWING UP ON THE DAY OF OUR DEAL WITH HIS WIFE AND KID IN TOW.
MAGHIN TAY KA RITO.

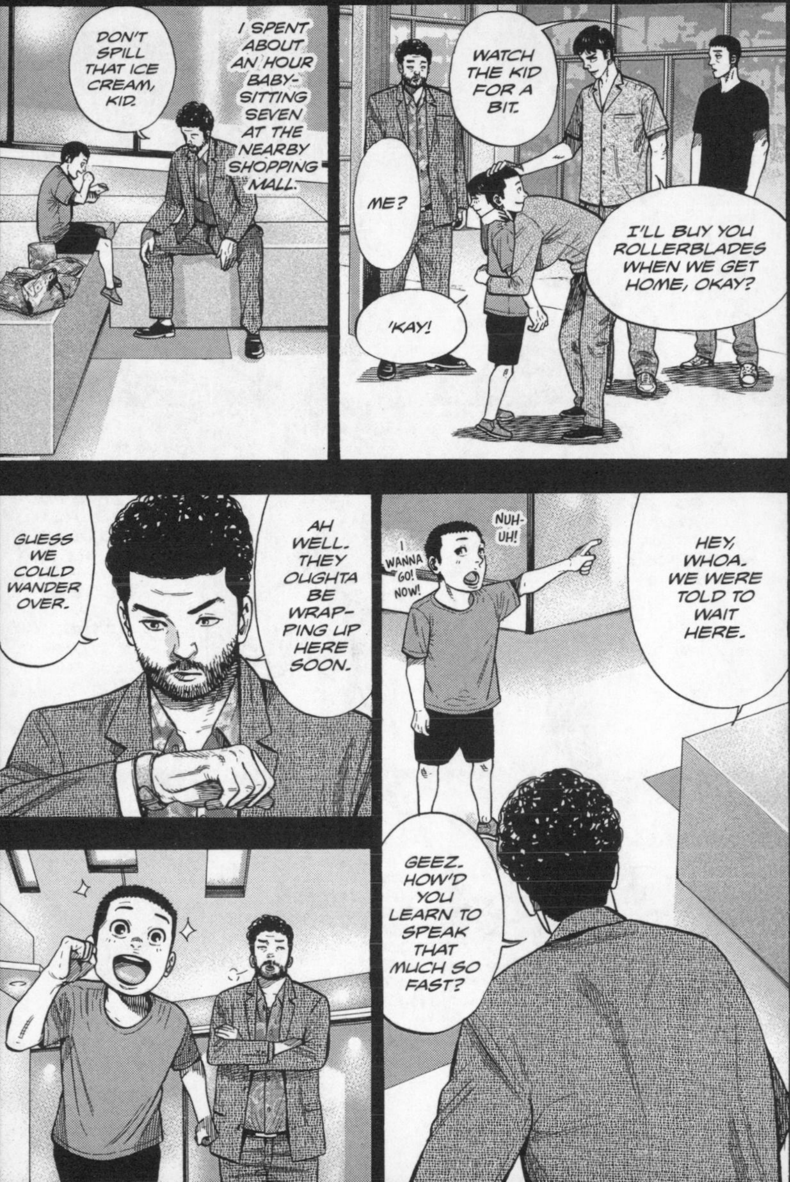
WATCH THE KID FOR A BIT.
ME?
I'LL BUY YOU ROLLERBLADES WHEN WE GET HOME, OKAY?
'KAY!
I SPENT ABOUT AN HOUR BABY-SITTING SEVEN AT THE NEARBY SHOPPING MALL.
DON'T SPILL THAT ICE CREAM, KID.
HEY, WHOA. WE WERE TOLD TO WAIT HERE.
NUH-UH!
I WANNA GO! NOW!
GEEZ. HOW'D YOU LEARN TO SPEAK THAT MUCH SO FAST?
AH WELL. THEY OUGHTA BE WRAP-PING UP HERE SOON.
GUESS WE COULD WANDER OVER.

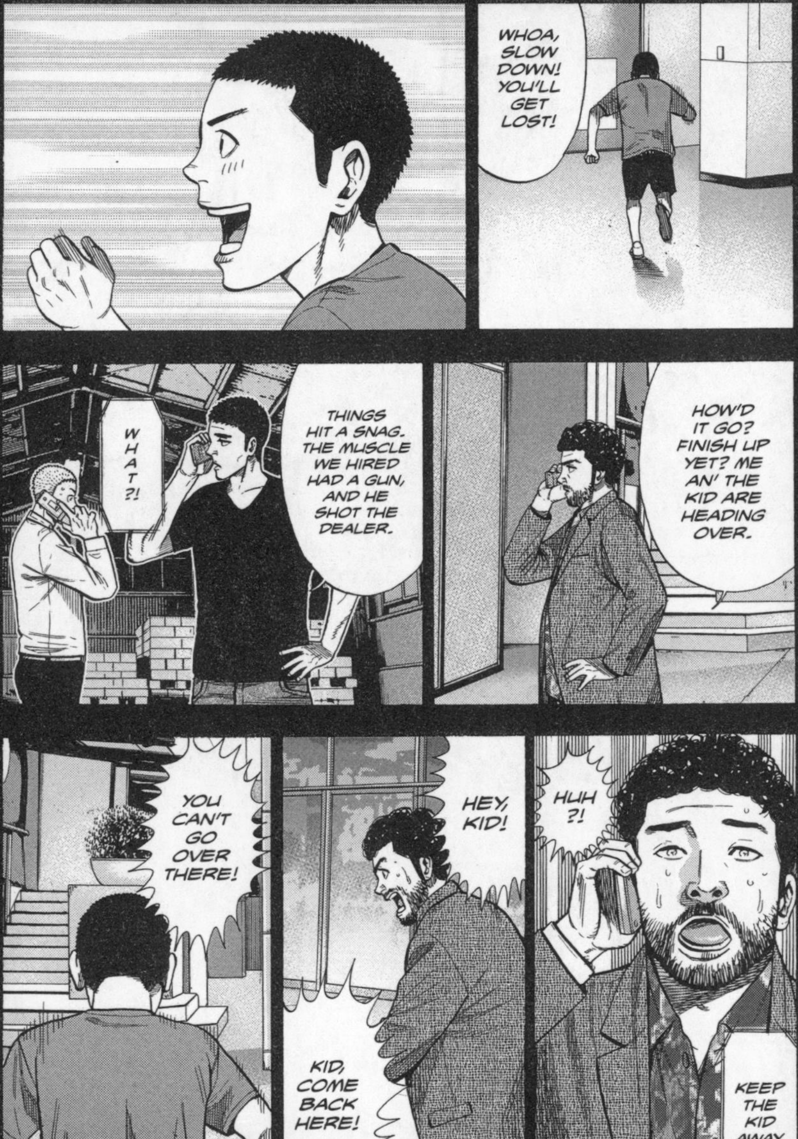
WHOA, SLOW DOWN! YOU'LL GET LOST!
HOW'D IT GO? FINISH UP YET? ME AN' THE KID ARE HEADING OVER.
THINGS HIT A SNAG. THE MUSCLE WE HIRED HAD A GUN, AND HE SHOT THE DEALER.
WHAT?!
HUH?!
KEEP THE KID AWAY.
HEY, KID!
KID, COME BACK HERE!
YOU CAN'T GO OVER THERE!

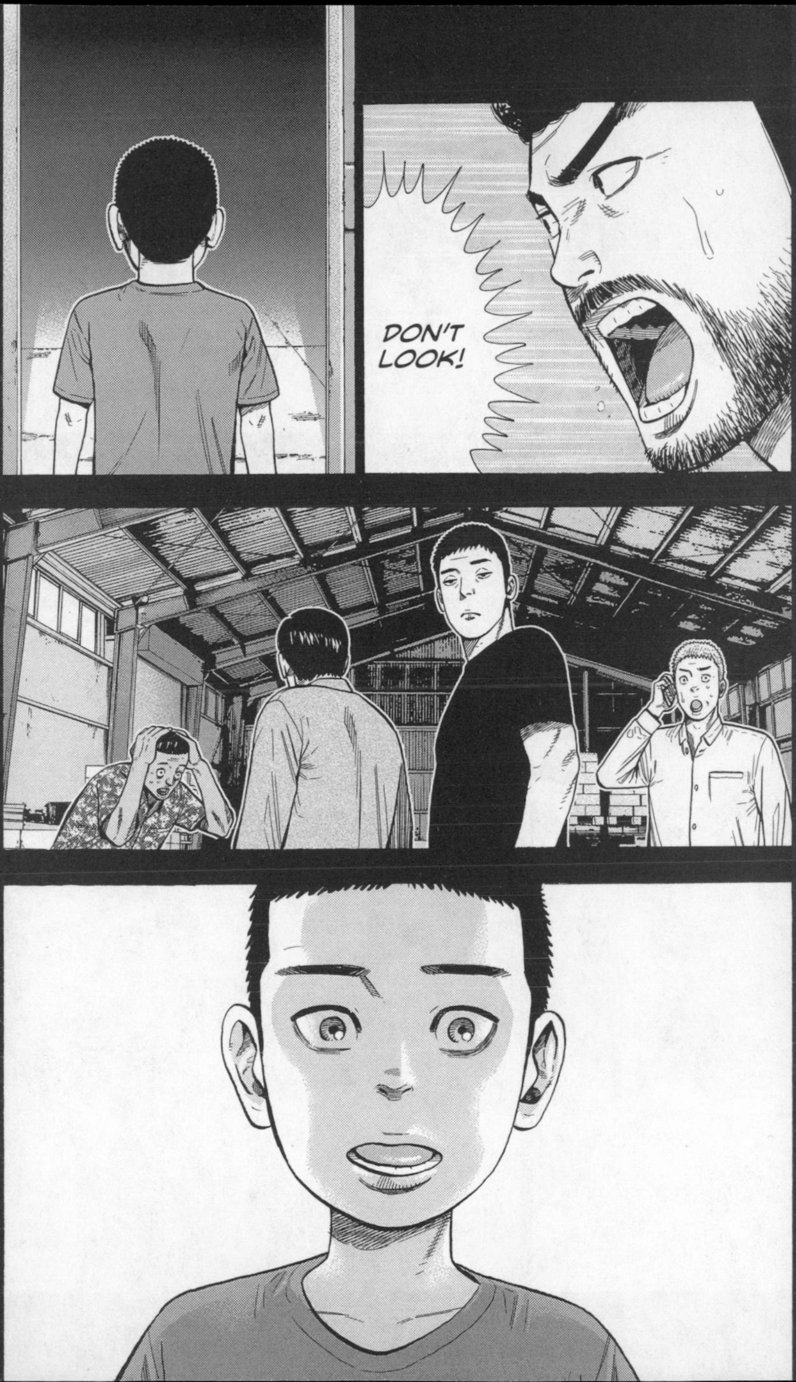
DON'T LOOK!

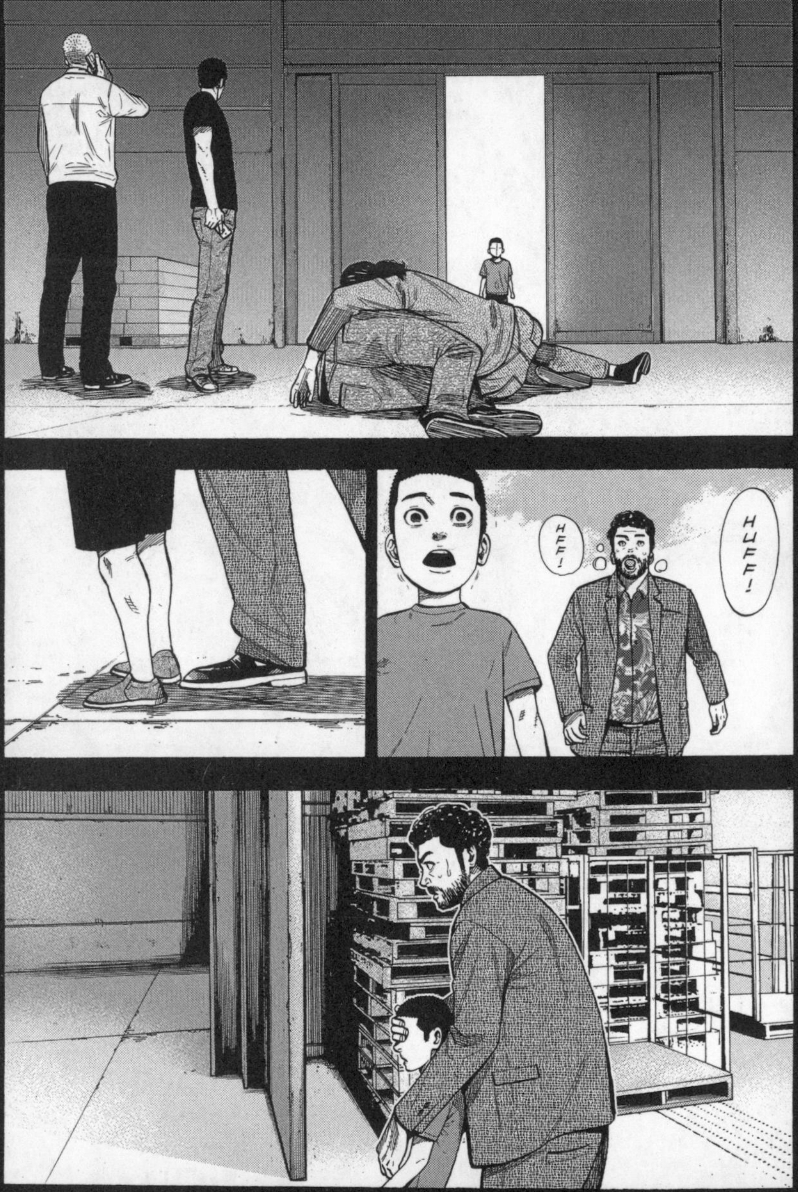
HUFF!
HFF!

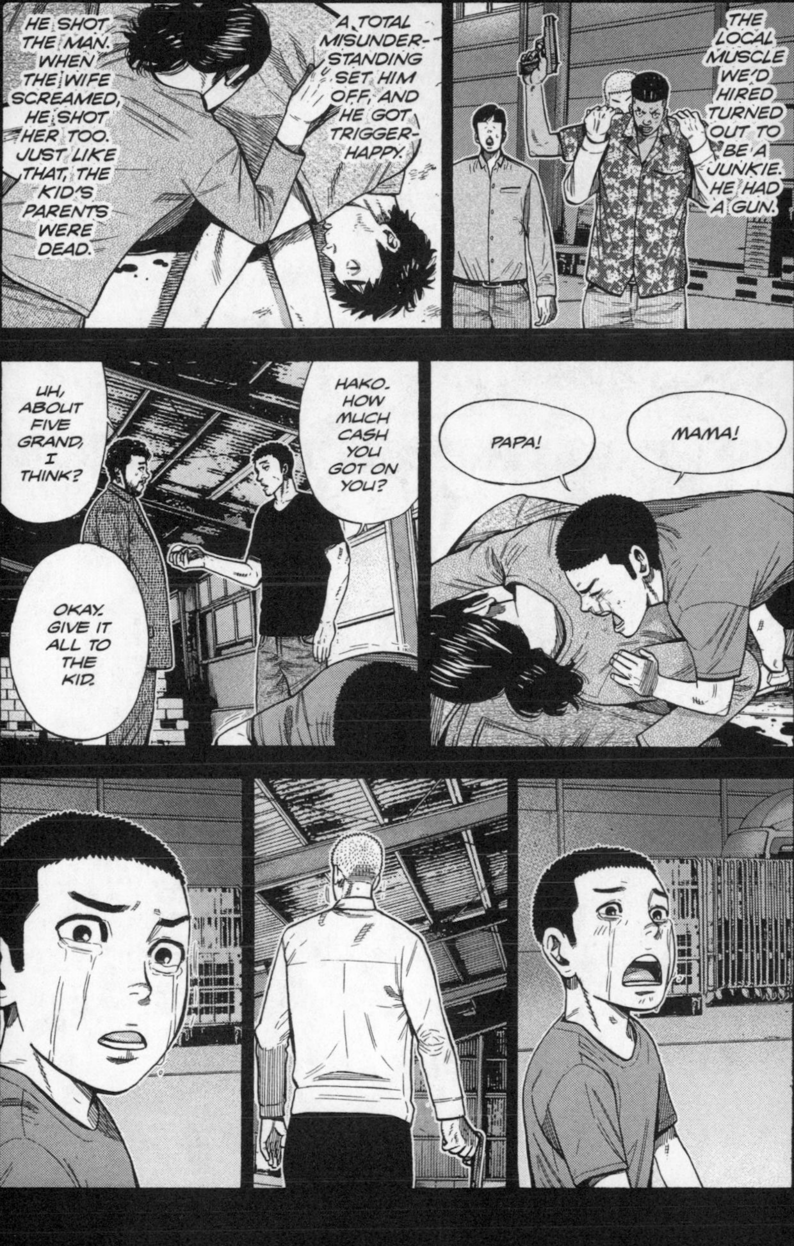
THE LOCAL MUSCLE WE'D HIRED TURNED OUT TO BE A JUNKIE. HE HAD A GUN.
A TOTAL MISUNDERSTANDING SET HIM OFF, AND HE GOT TRIGGER-HAPPY.
HE SHOT THE MAN. WHEN THE WIFE SCREAMED, HE SHOT HER TOO. JUST LIKE THAT, THE KID'S PARENTS WERE DEAD.
MAMA!
PAPA!
HAKO. HOW MUCH CASH YOU GOT ON YOU?
UH, ABOUT FIVE GRAND, I THINK?
OKAY. GIVE IT ALL TO THE KID.

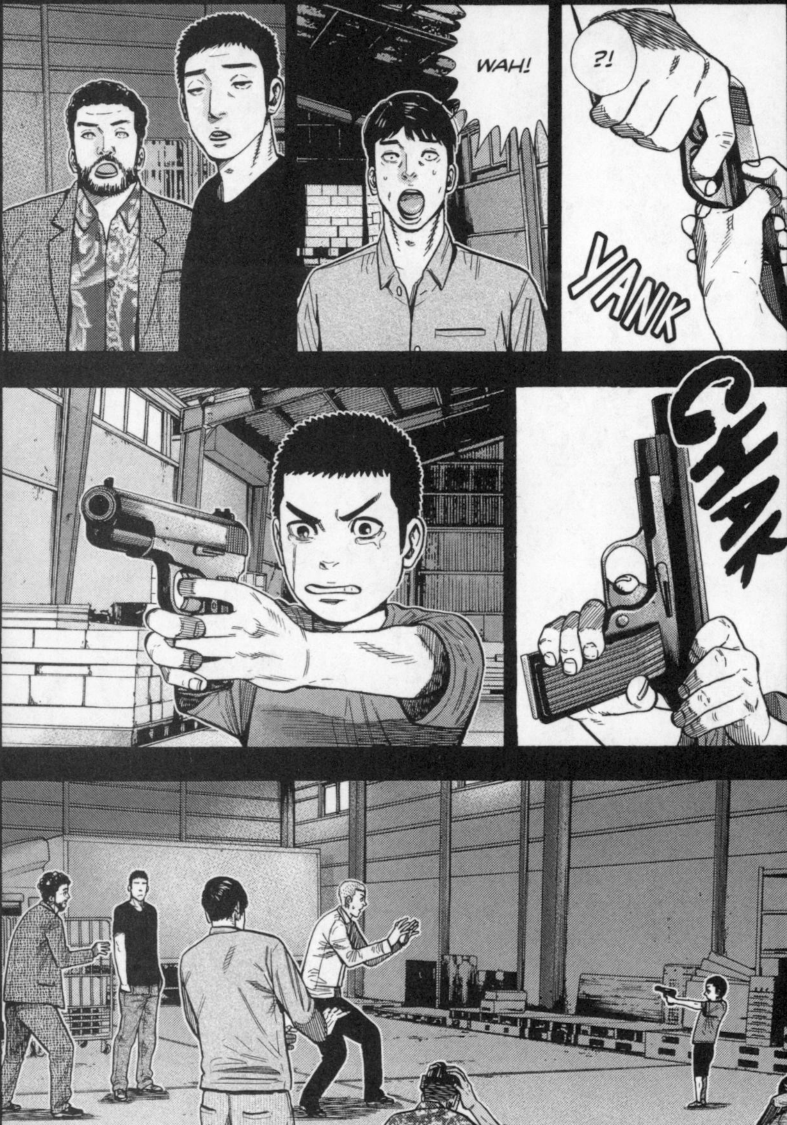
?!
YANK
WAH!
CHAK

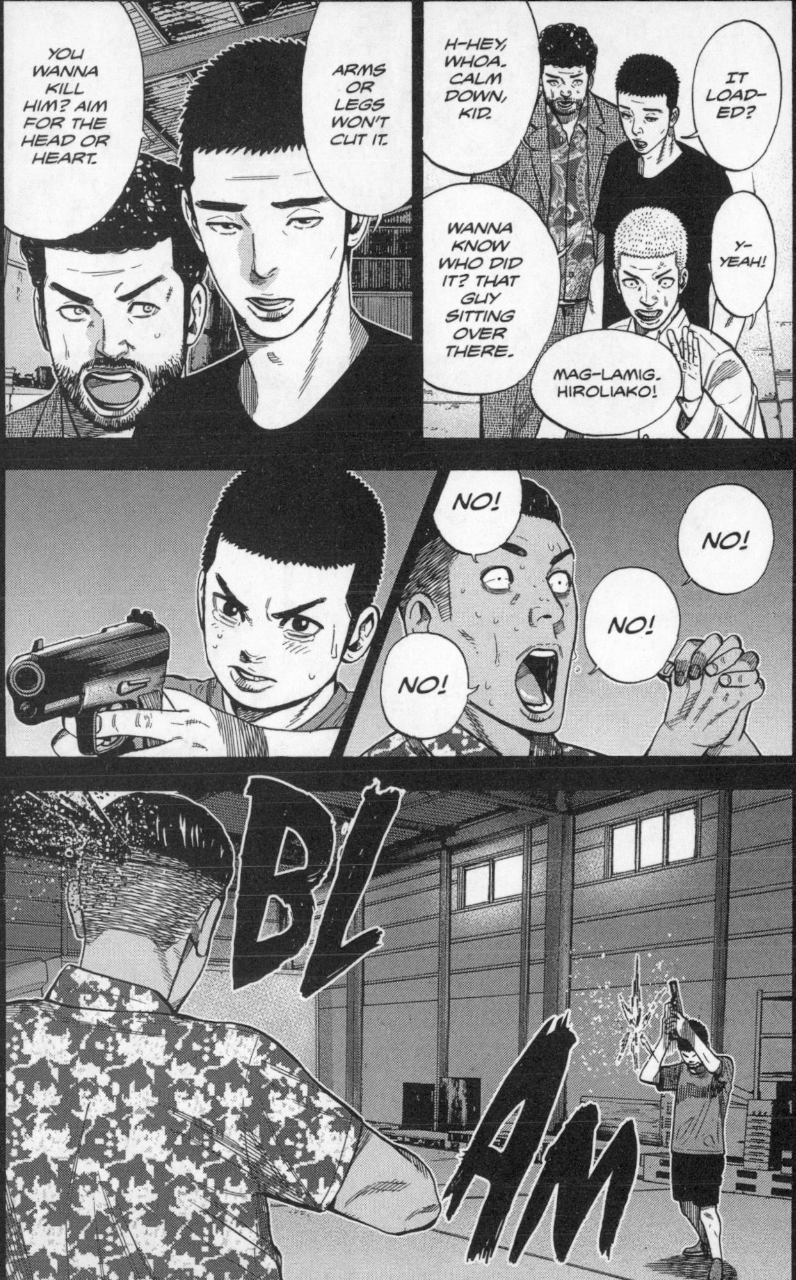
IT LOADED-ED?
H-HEY, WHOA. CALM DOWN, KID.
Y-YEAH!
WANNA KNOW WHO DID IT? THAT GUY SITTING OVER THERE.
MAG-LAMIG. HIROLIAKO!
ARMS OR LEGS WON'T CUT IT.
YOU WANNA KILL HIM? AIM FOR THE HEAD OR HEART.
NO!
NO!
NO!
NO!
BLAM

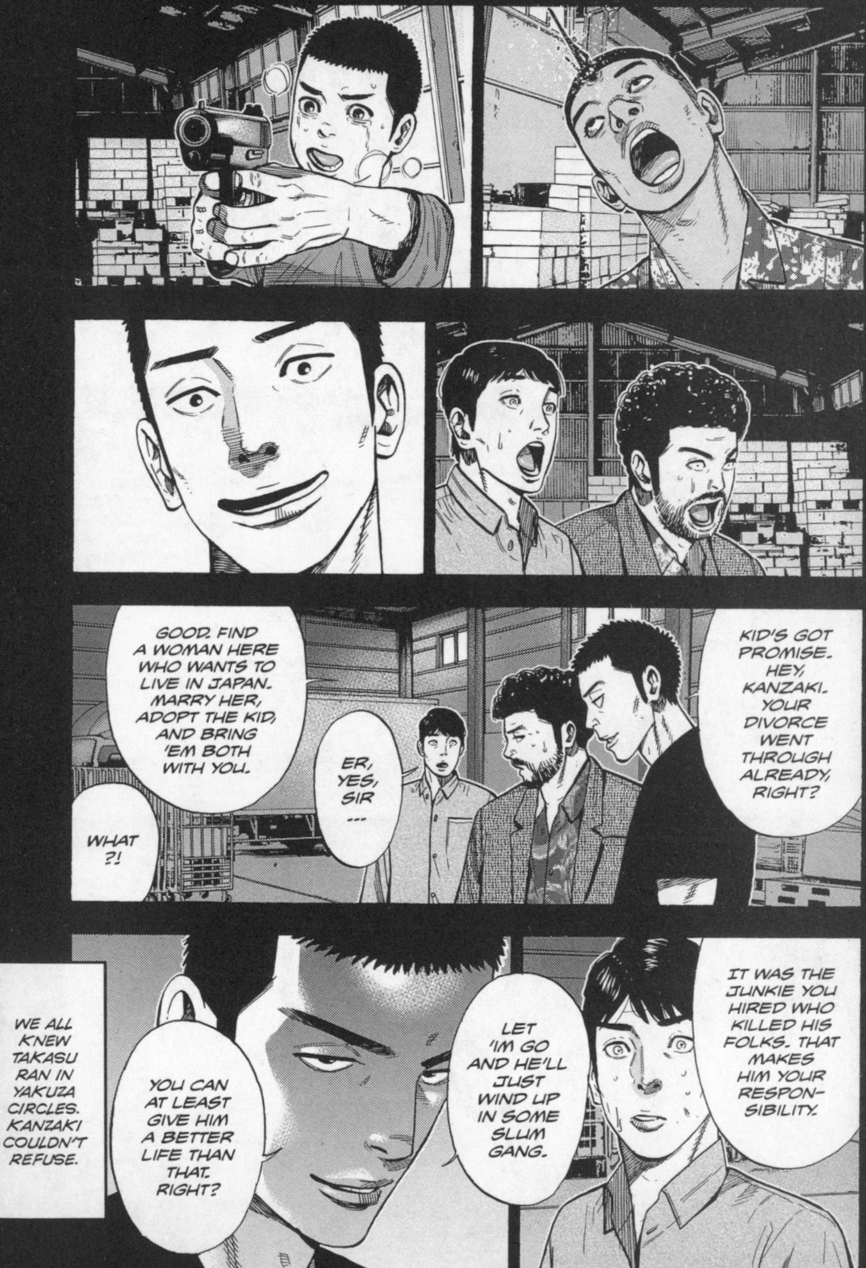
KID'S GOT PROMISE. HEY, KANZAKI. YOUR DIVORCE WENT THROUGH ALREADY, RIGHT?
ER, YES, SIR...
GOOD. FIND A WOMAN HERE WHO WANTS TO LIVE IN JAPAN. MARRY HER, ADOPT THE KID, AND BRING 'EM BOTH WITH YOU.
WHAT ?!
IT WAS THE JUNKIE YOU HIRED WHO KILLED HIS FOLKS. THAT MAKES HIM YOUR RESPON-SIBILITY.
LET 'IM GO AND HE'LL JUST WIND UP IN SOME SLUM GANG.
YOU CAN AT LEAST GIVE HIM A BETTER LIFE THAN THAT. RIGHT?
WE ALL KNEW TAKASU RAN IN YAKUZA CIRCLES. KANZAKI COULDN'T REFUSE.

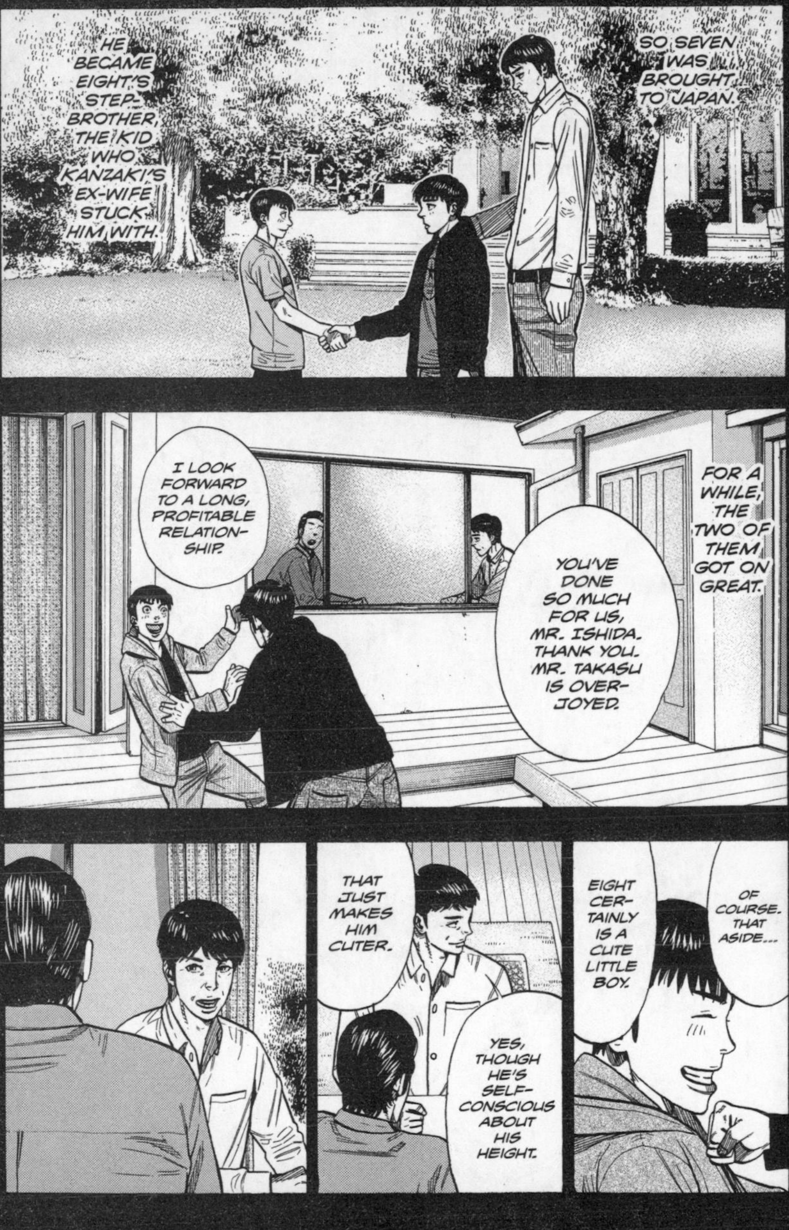
SO SEVEN WAS BROUGHT TO JAPAN.
HE BECAME EIGHT'S STEP-BROTHER, THE KID WHO KANZAKI'S EX-WIFE STUCK HIM WITH.
FOR A WHILE, THE TWO OF THEM GOT ON GREAT.
YOU'VE DONE SO MUCH FOR US, MR. ISHIDA. THANK YOU. MR. TAKASU IS OVER-JOYED.
I LOOK FORWARD TO A LONG, PROFITABLE RELATION-SHIP.
OF COURSE. THAT ASIDE...
EIGHT CER-TAINLY IS A CUTE LITTLE BOY.
YES, THOUGH HE'S SELF-CONSCIOUS ABOUT HIS HEIGHT.
THAT JUST MAKES HIM CUTER.

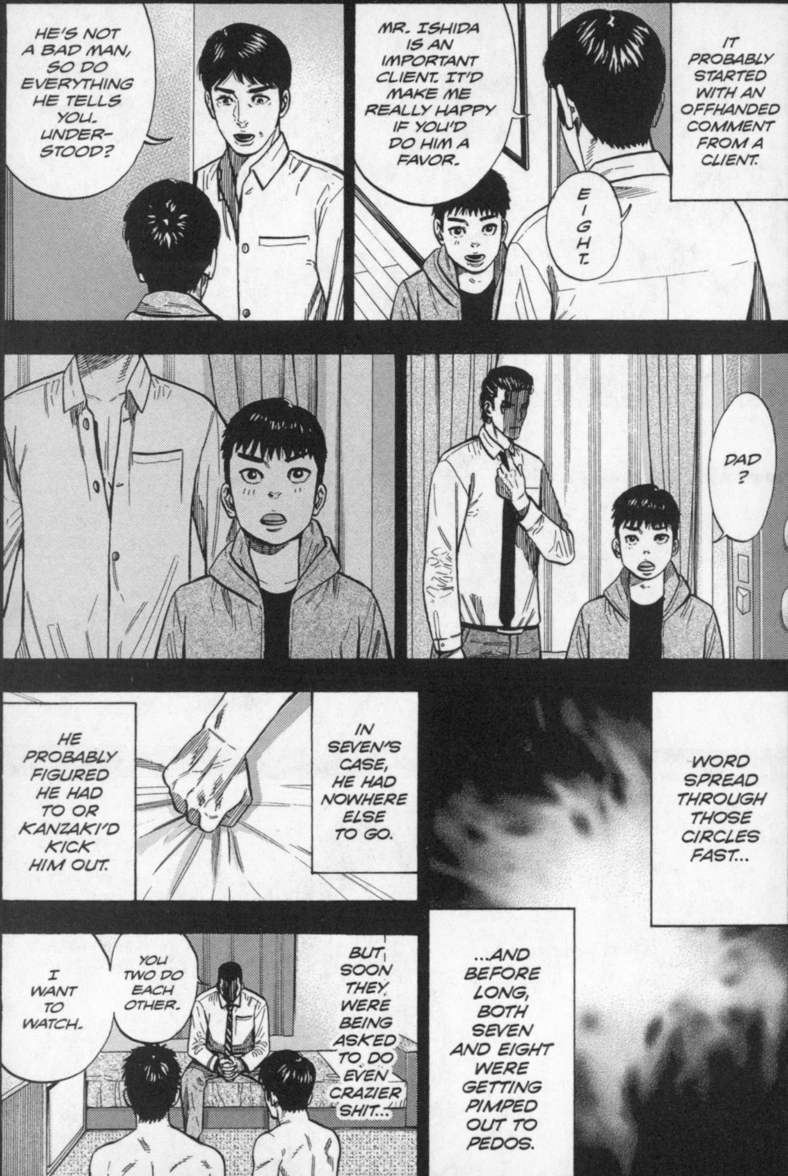
IT PROBABLY STARTED WITH AN OFFHANDED COMMENT FROM A CLIENT.
MR. ISHIDA IS AN IMPORTANT CLIENT. IT'D MAKE ME REALLY HAPPY IF YOU'D DO HIM A FAVOR.
EIGHT.
HE'S NOT A BAD MAN, SO DO EVERYTHING HE TELLS YOU. UNDER-STOOD?
DAD?
WORD SPREAD THROUGH THOSE CIRCLES FAST...
...AND BEFORE LONG, BOTH SEVEN AND EIGHT WERE GETTING PIMPED OUT TO PEDOS.
IN SEVEN'S CASE, HE HAD NOWHERE ELSE TO GO.
HE PROBABLY FIGURED HE HAD TO OR KANZAKI'D KICK HIM OUT.
BUT SOON THEY WERE BEING ASKED TO DO EVEN CRAZIER SHIT...
YOU TWO DO EACH OTHER.
I WANT TO WATCH.

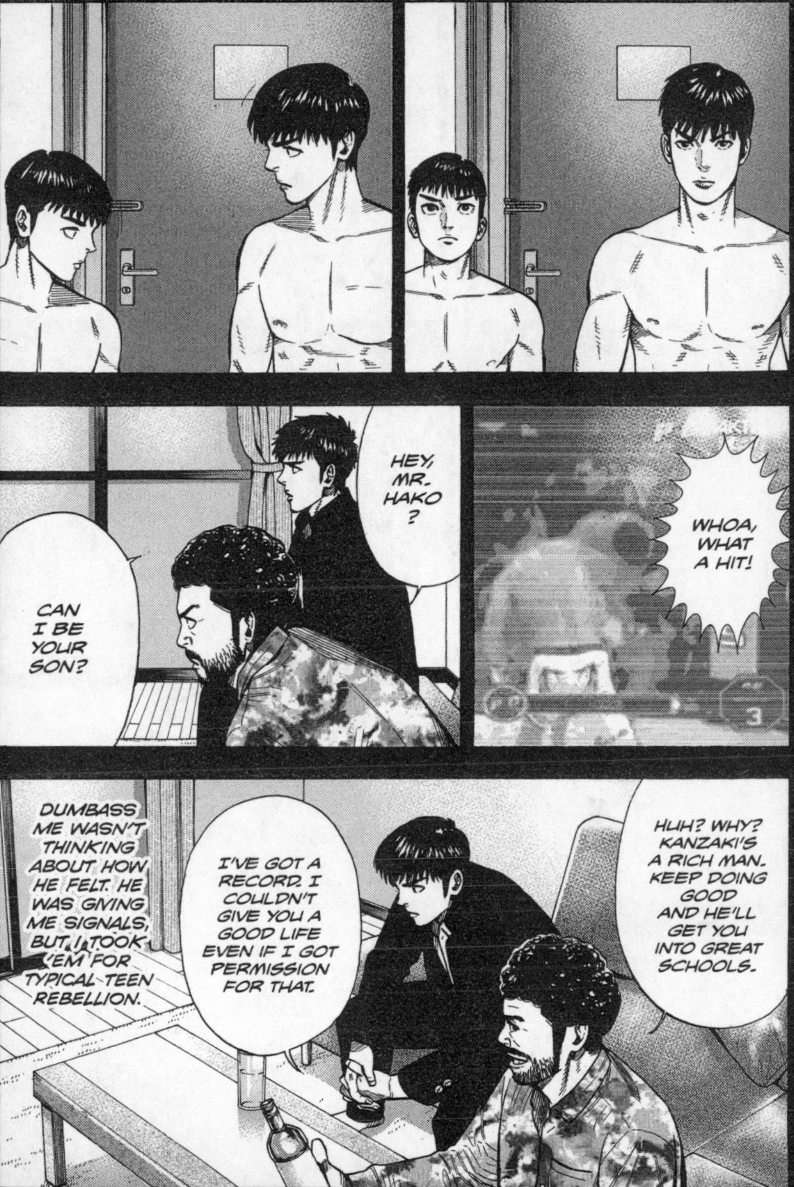
WHOA, WHAT A HIT!
HEY, MR. HAKO?
CAN I BE YOUR SON?
HUH? WHY? KANZAKI'S A RICH MAN. KEEP DOING GOOD AND HE'LL GET YOU INTO GREAT SCHOOLS.
I'VE GOT A RECORD. I COULDN'T GIVE YOU A GOOD LIFE EVEN IF I GOT PERMISSION FOR THAT.
DUMBASS ME WASN'T THINKING ABOUT HOW HE FELT. HE WAS GIVING ME SIGNALS, BUT I TOOK 'EM FOR TYPICAL TEEN REBELLION.

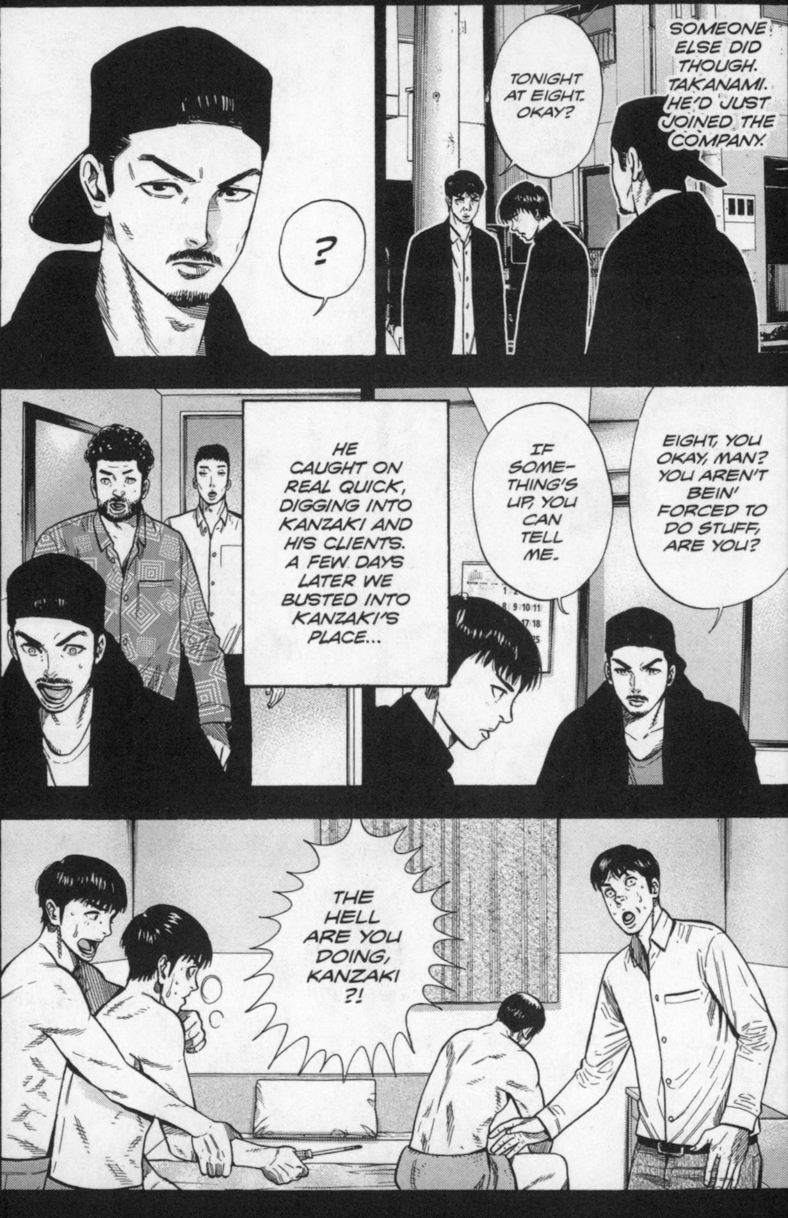
SOMEONE ELSE DID THOUGH. TAKANAMI. HE'D JUST JOINED THE COMPANY.
TONIGHT AT EIGHT. OKAY?
?
EIGHT, YOU OKAY, MAN? YOU AREN'T BEIN' FORCED TO DO STUFF, ARE YOU?
IF SOMETHING'S UP, YOU CAN TELL ME.
HE CAUGHT ON REAL QUICK, DIGGING INTO KANZAKI AND HIS CLIENTS. A FEW DAYS LATER WE BUSTED INTO KANZAKI'S PLACE...
THE HELL ARE YOU DOING, KANZAKI?!

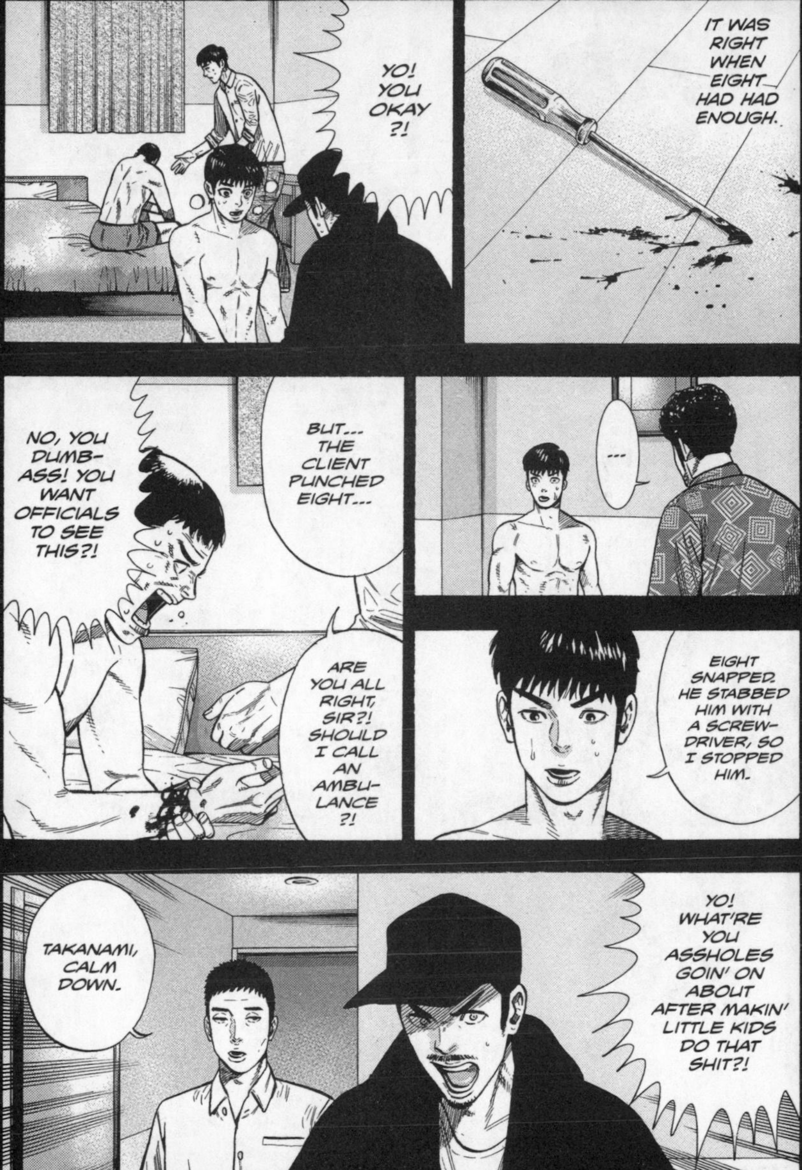
IT WAS RIGHT WHEN EIGHT HAD HAD ENOUGH.
YO! YOU OKAY?!
...
EIGHT SNAPPED. HE STABBED HIM WITH A SCREW-DRIVER, SO I STOPPED HIM.
BUT... THE CLIENT PUNCHED EIGHT...
NO, YOU DUMB-ASS! YOU WANT OFFICIALS TO SEE THIS?!
ARE YOU ALL RIGHT, SIR?! SHOULD I CALL AN AMBU-LANCE?!
YO! WHAT'RE YOU ASSHOLES GOIN' ON ABOUT AFTER MAKIN' LITTLE KIDS DO THAT SHIT?!
TAKANAMI, CALM DOWN.

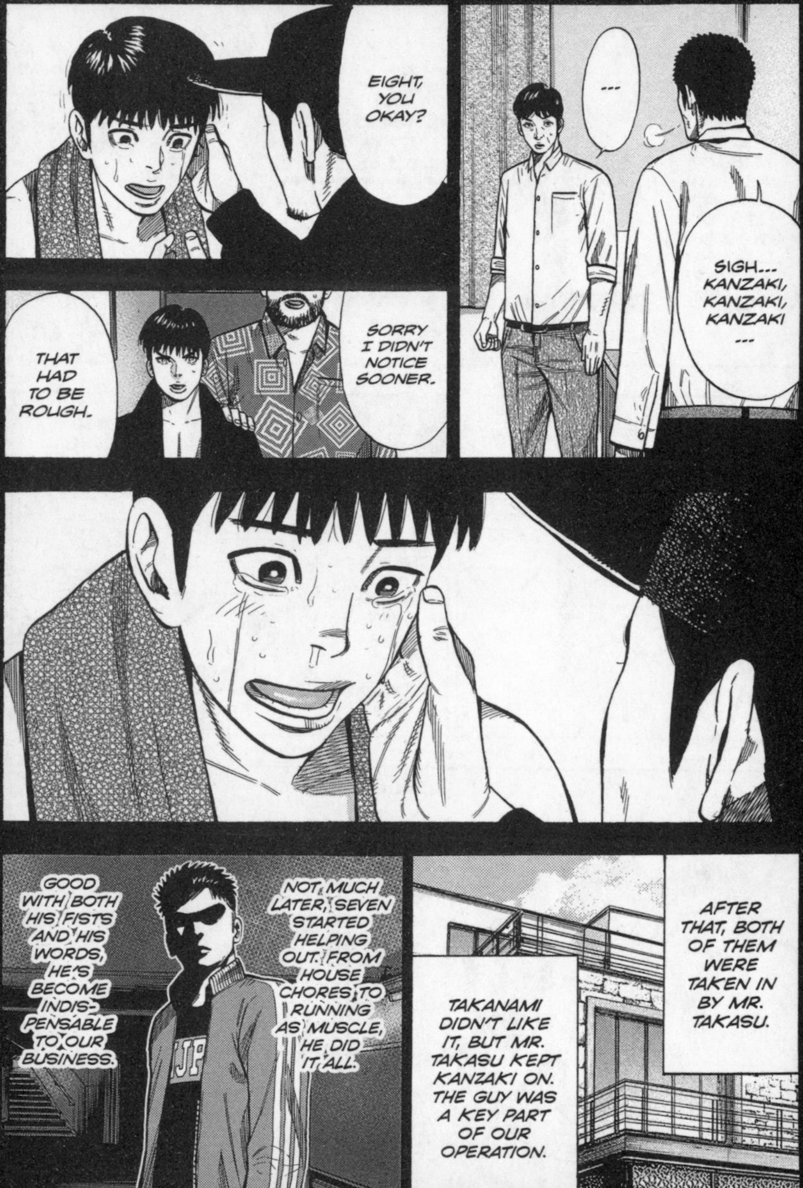
...
SIGH... KANZAKI, KANZAKI, KANZAKI ...
EIGHT, YOU OKAY?
SORRY I DIDN'T NOTICE SOONER.
THAT HAD TO BE ROUGH.
AFTER THAT, BOTH OF THEM WERE TAKEN IN BY MR. TAKASU.
TAKANAMI DIDN'T LIKE IT, BUT MR. TAKASU KEPT KANZAKI ON. THE GUY WAS A KEY PART OF OUR OPERATION.
NOT MUCH LATER, SEVEN STARTED HELPING OUT. FROM HOUSE CHORES TO RUNNING AS MUSCLE, HE DID IT ALL.
GOOD WITH BOTH HIS FISTS AND HIS WORDS, HE'S BECOME INDIS-PENSABLE TO OUR BUSINESS.

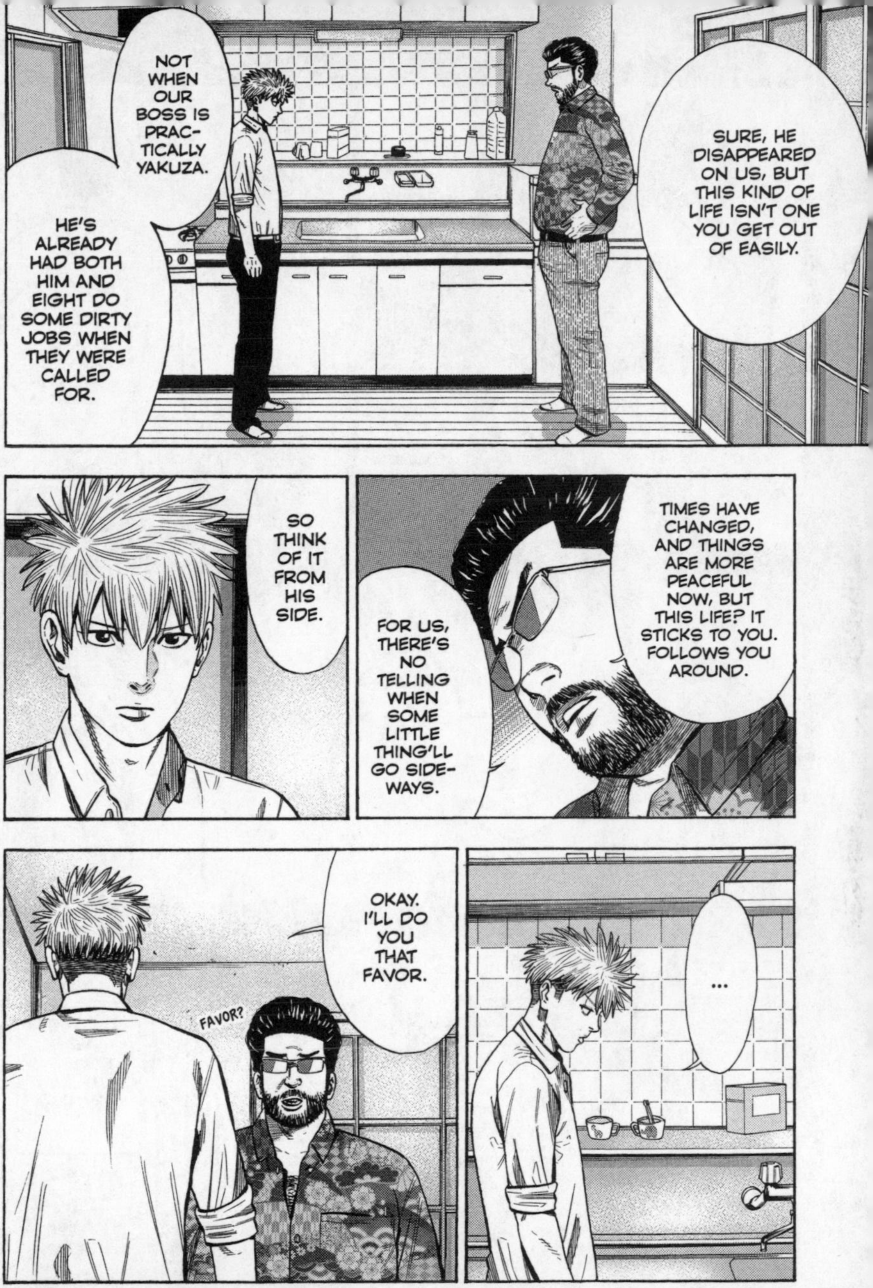
SURE, HE DISAPPEARED ON US, BUT THIS KIND OF LIFE ISN'T ONE YOU GET OUT OF EASILY.
NOT WHEN OUR BOSS IS PRAC-TICALLY YAKUZA.
HE'S ALREADY HAD BOTH HIM AND EIGHT DO SOME DIRTY JOBS WHEN THEY WERE CALLED FOR.
TIMES HAVE CHANGED, AND THINGS ARE MORE PEACEFUL NOW, BUT THIS LIFE? IT STICKS TO YOU. FOLLOWS YOU AROUND.
FOR US, THERE'S NO TELLING WHEN SOME LITTLE THING'LL GO SIDE-WAYS.
SO THINK OF IT FROM HIS SIDE.
...
OKAY. I'LL DO YOU THAT FAVOR.
FAVOR?

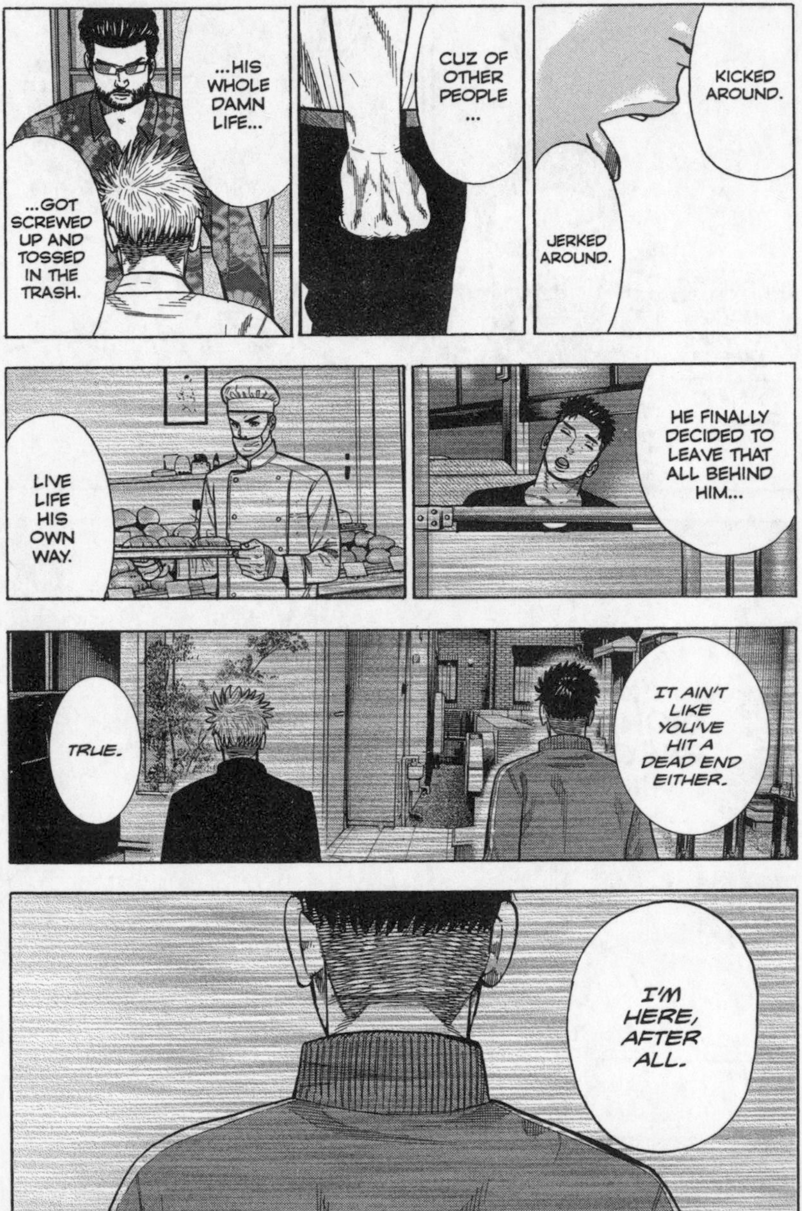
KICKED AROUND.
JERKED AROUND.
CUZ OF OTHER PEOPLE ...
...HIS WHOLE DAMN LIFE...
...GOT SCREWED UP AND TOSSED IN THE TRASH.
HE FINALLY DECIDED TO LEAVE THAT ALL BEHIND HIM...
LIVE LIFE HIS OWN WAY.
IT AIN'T LIKE YOU'VE HIT A DEAD END EITHER.
TRUE.
I'M HERE, AFTER ALL.

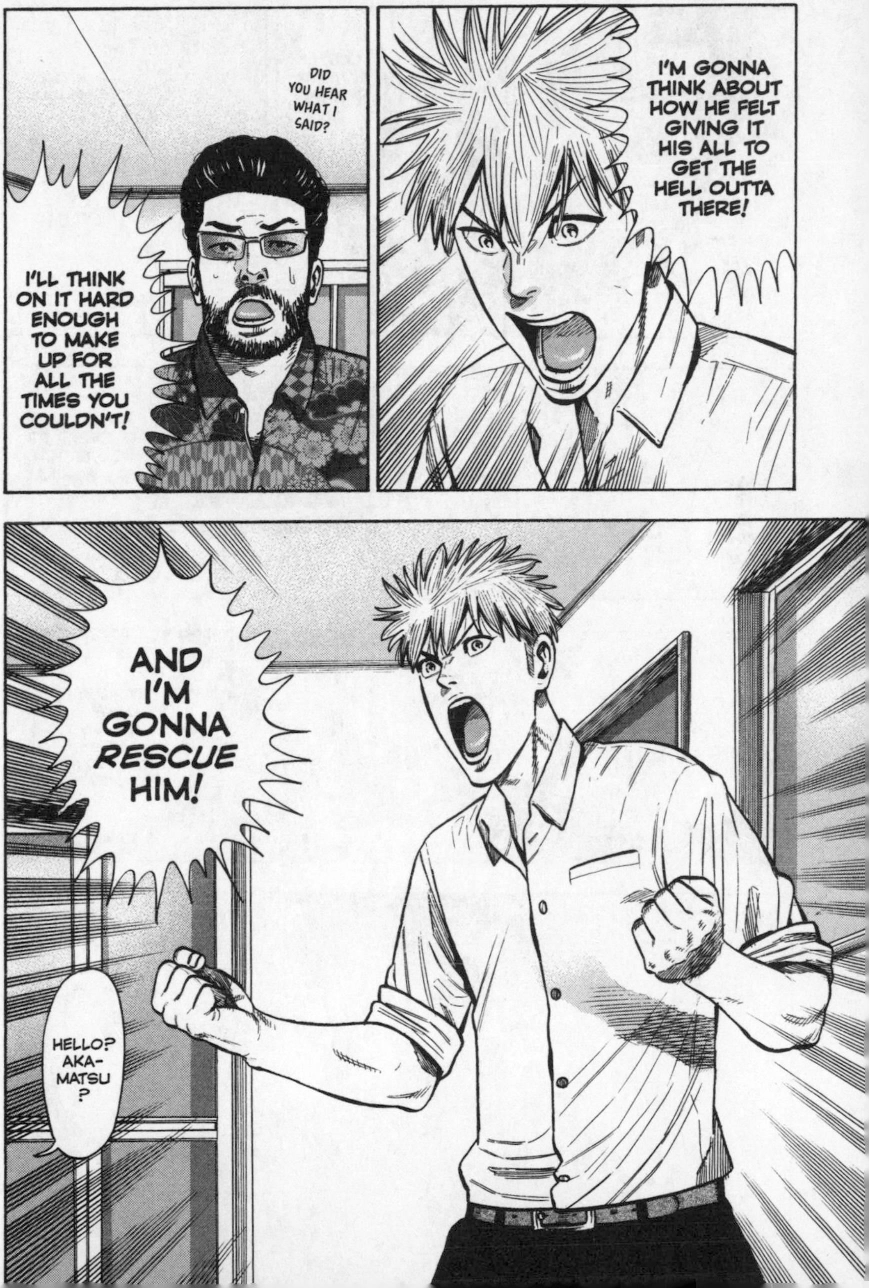
I'M GONNA THINK ABOUT HOW HE FELT GIVING IT HIS ALL TO GET THE HELL OUTTA THERE!
DID YOU HEAR WHAT I SAID?
I'LL THINK ON IT HARD ENOUGH TO MAKE UP FOR ALL THE TIMES YOU COULDN'T!
AND I'M GONNA *RESCUE* HIM!
HELLO? AKAMATSU?

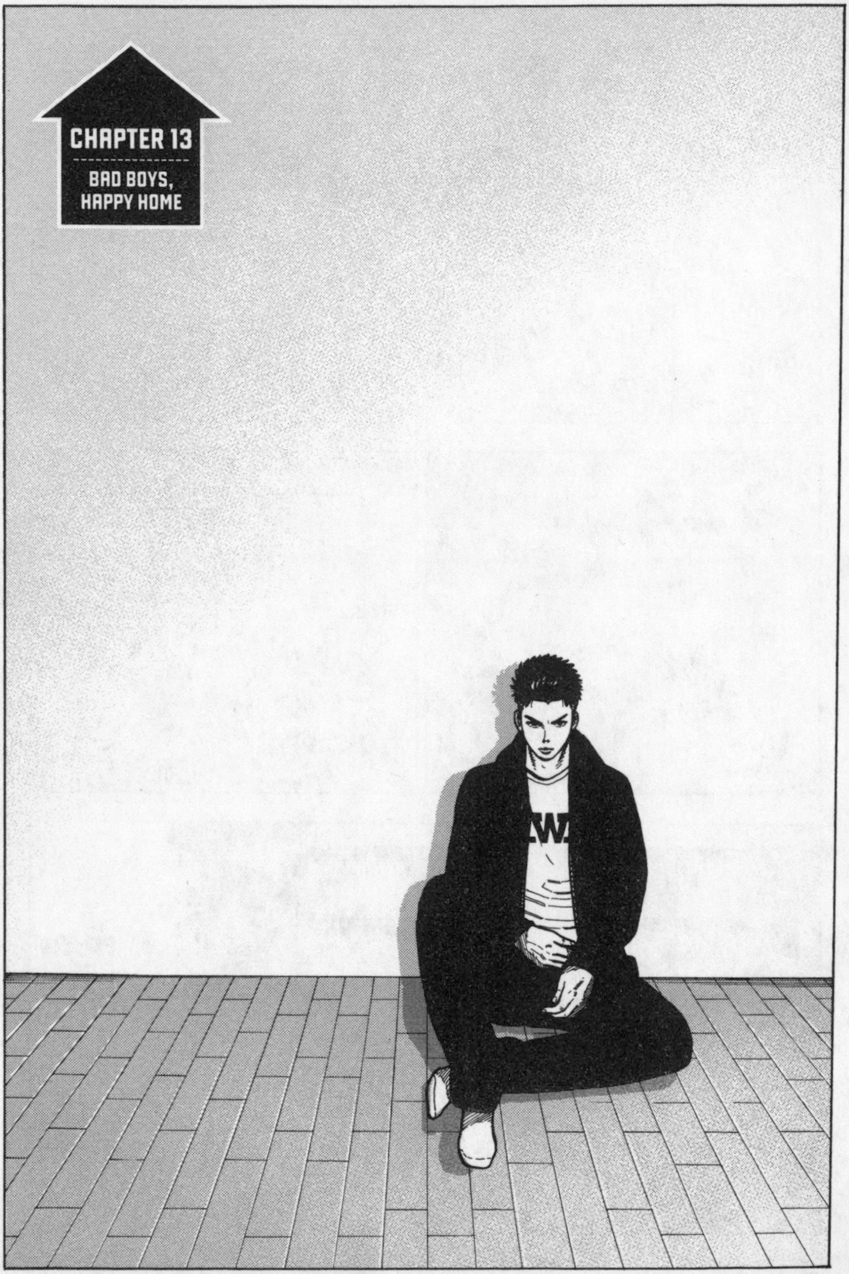
CHAPTER 13
BAD BOYS,
HAPPY HOME

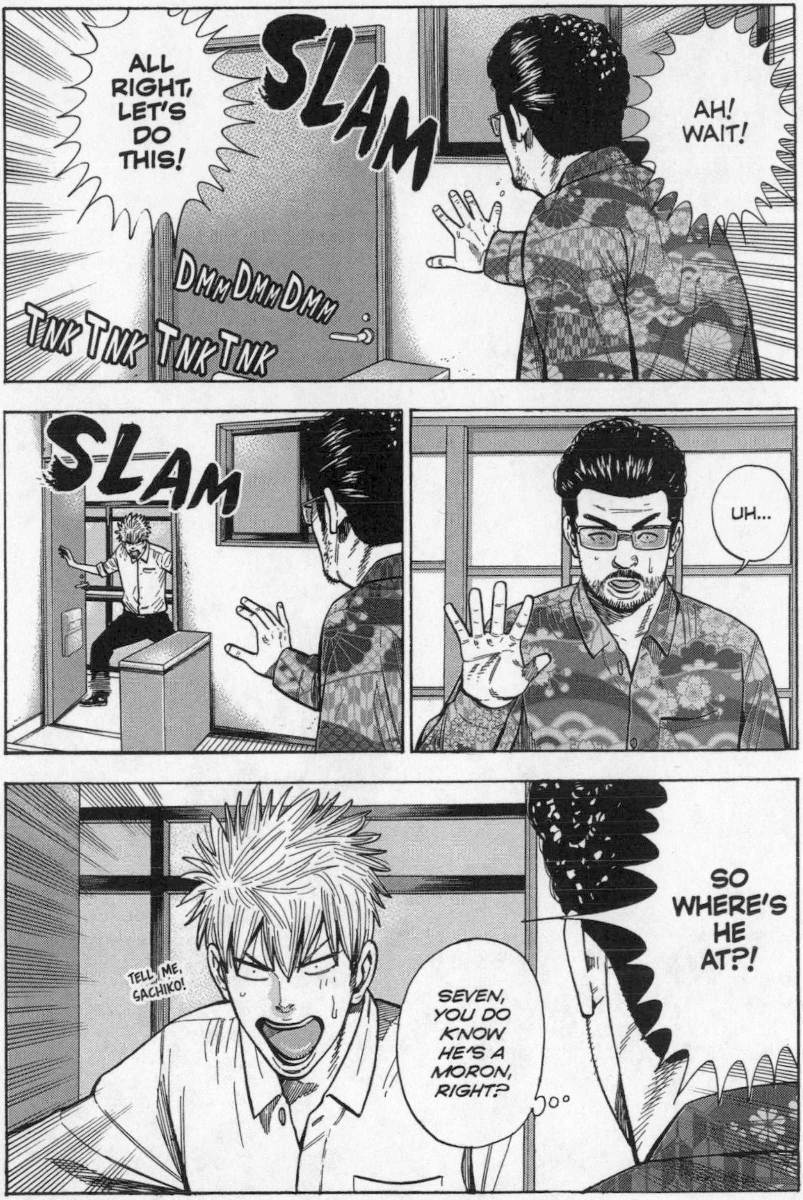
AH! WAIT!
SLAM
ALL RIGHT, LET'S DO THIS!
DMM DMM DMM
TNK TNK TNK TNK
UH...
SLAM
SO WHERE'S HE AT?!
SEVEN, YOU DO KNOW HE'S A MORON, RIGHT?
TELL ME, SACHIKO!

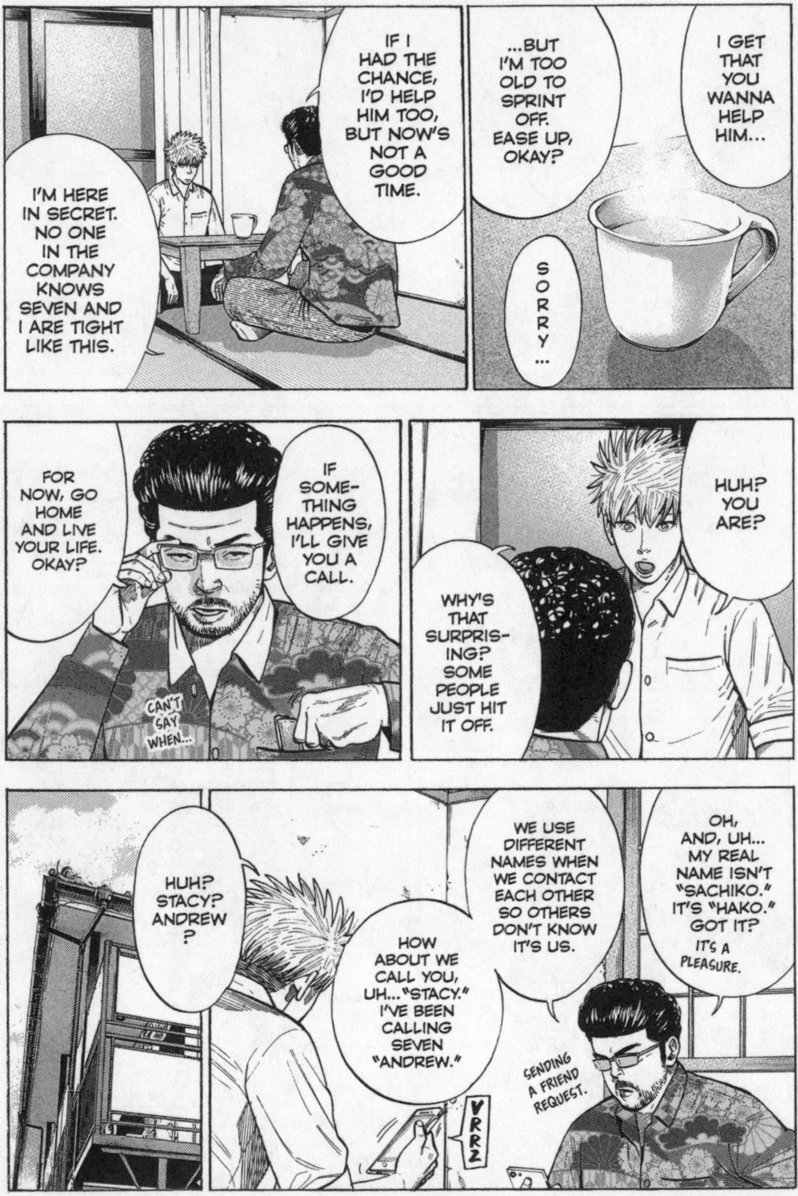
I GET THAT YOU WANNA HELP HIM...
...BUT I'M TOO OLD TO SPRINT OFF. EASE UP, OKAY?
SORRY...
IF I HAD THE CHANCE, I'D HELP HIM TOO, BUT NOW'S NOT A GOOD TIME.
I'M HERE IN SECRET. NO ONE IN THE COMPANY KNOWS SEVEN AND I ARE TIGHT LIKE THIS.
HUH? YOU ARE?
WHY'S THAT SURPRISING? SOME PEOPLE JUST HIT IT OFF.
IF SOMETHING HAPPENS, I'LL GIVE YOU A CALL.
FOR NOW, GO HOME AND LIVE YOUR LIFE. OKAY?
CAN'T SAY WHEN...
OH, AND, UH... MY REAL NAME ISN'T "SACHIKO." IT'S "HAKO." GOT IT?
IT'S A PLEASURE.
WE USE DIFFERENT NAMES WHEN WE CONTACT EACH OTHER SO OTHERS DON'T KNOW IT'S US.
HOW ABOUT WE CALL YOU, UH..."STACY." I'VE BEEN CALLING SEVEN "ANDREW."
SENDING A FRIEND REQUEST.
VRRZ
HUH? STACY? ANDREW?

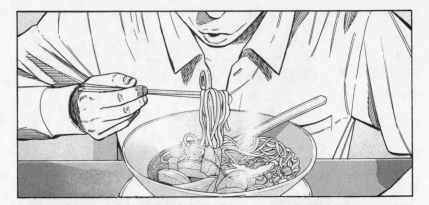

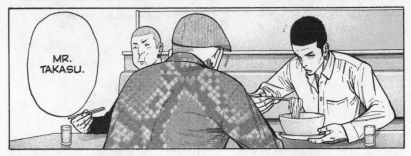

MR. TAKASU.
AH, MR. HATA. IT'S BEEN A WHILE.
HOW'VE YOU BEEN? MISS, ONE VEGGIE *TAN-MEN* PLEASE!
NOT BAD, NOT BAD.
COMIN' UP!
I HEAR THERE WAS A SURPRISE INSPECTION THE OTHER DAY.
ONE OF MY BOYS SAID HE GOT THAT FROM TAKANAMI.
MAY I?
PLEASE.
YEAH. I GOT WORD HE STRUCK OUT ON HIS OWN DOING SOMETHING SIMILAR, SO I FIGURED I'D KEEP HIM IN THE LOOP.

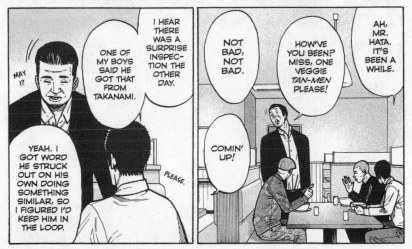

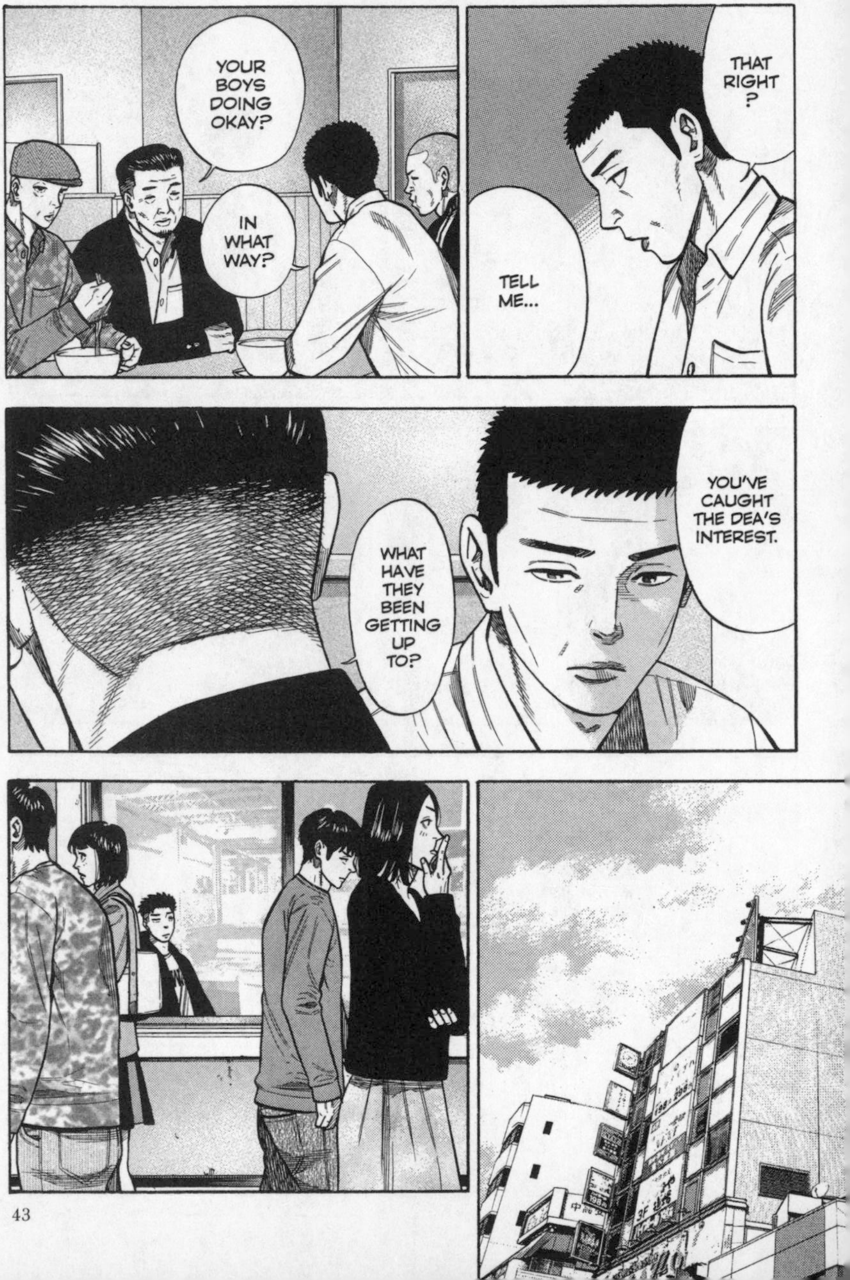
THAT RIGHT?
TELL ME...
YOUR BOYS DOING OKAY?
IN WHAT WAY?
YOU'VE CAUGHT THE DEA'S INTEREST.
WHAT HAVE THEY BEEN GETTING UP TO?

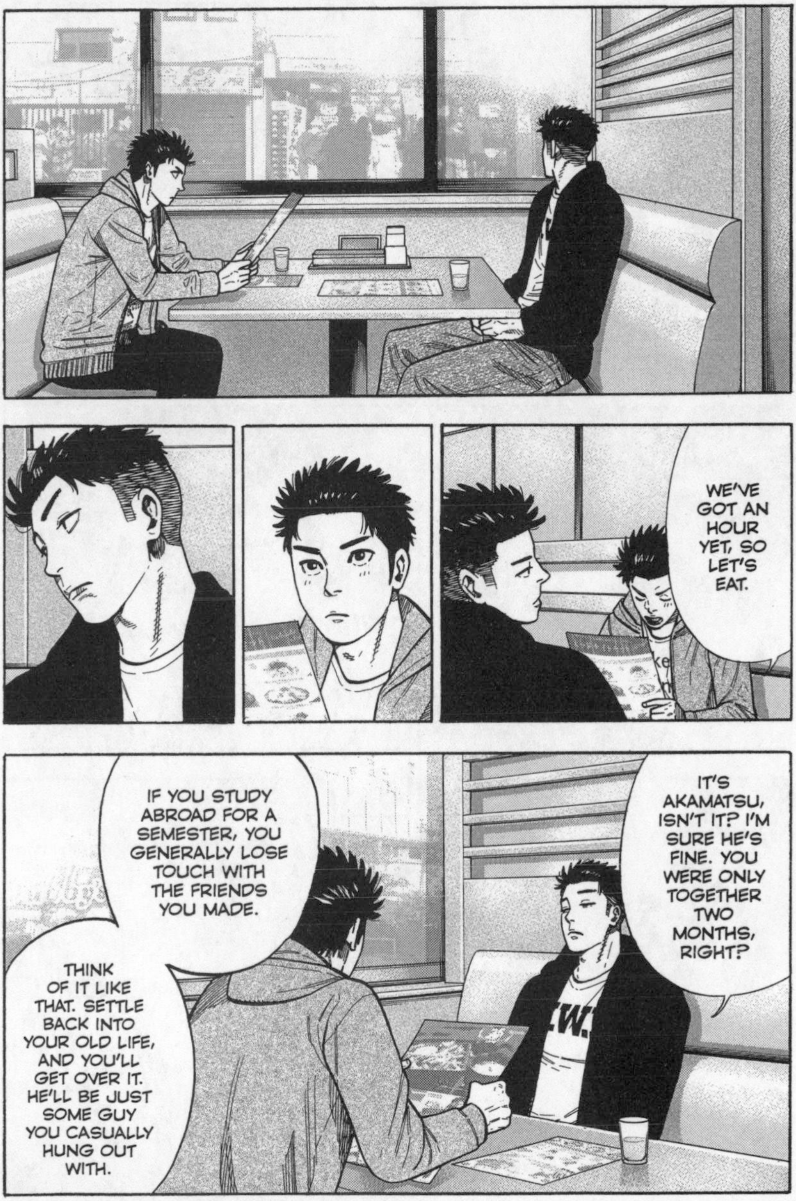
WE'VE GOT AN HOUR YET, SO LET'S EAT.
IT'S AKAMATSU, ISN'T IT? I'M SURE HE'S FINE. YOU WERE ONLY TOGETHER TWO MONTHS, RIGHT?
IF YOU STUDY ABROAD FOR A SEMESTER, YOU GENERALLY LOSE TOUCH WITH THE FRIENDS YOU MADE.
THINK OF IT LIKE THAT. SETTLE BACK INTO YOUR OLD LIFE, AND YOU'LL GET OVER IT. HE'LL BE JUST SOME GUY YOU CASUALLY HUNG OUT WITH.

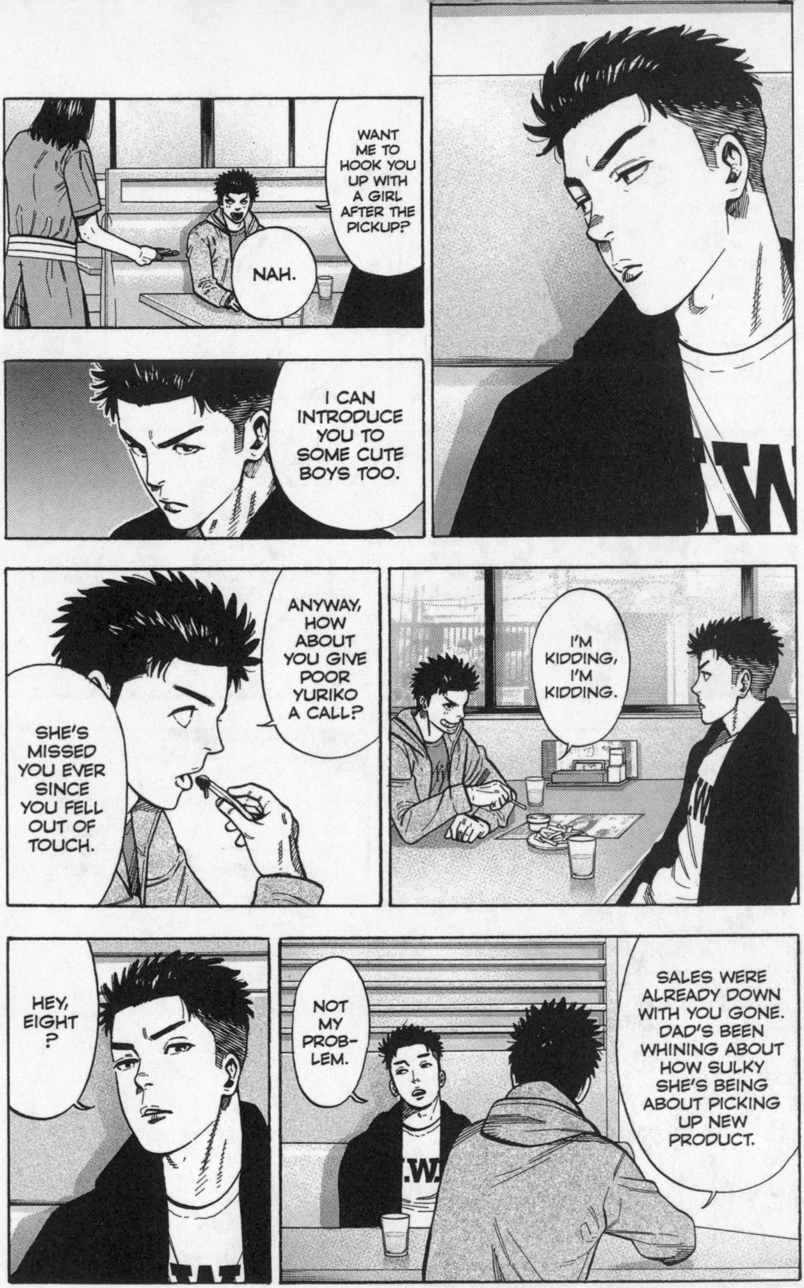
WANT ME TO HOOK YOU UP WITH A GIRL AFTER THE PICKUP?
NAH.
I CAN INTRODUCE YOU TO SOME CUTE BOYS TOO.
I'M KIDDING, I'M KIDDING.
ANYWAY, HOW ABOUT YOU GIVE POOR YURIKO A CALL?
SHE'S MISSED YOU EVER SINCE YOU FELL OUT OF TOUCH.
SALES WERE ALREADY DOWN WITH YOU GONE. DAD'S BEEN WHINING ABOUT HOW SULKY SHE'S BEING ABOUT PICKING UP NEW PRODUCT.
NOT MY PROBLEM.
HEY, EIGHT ?

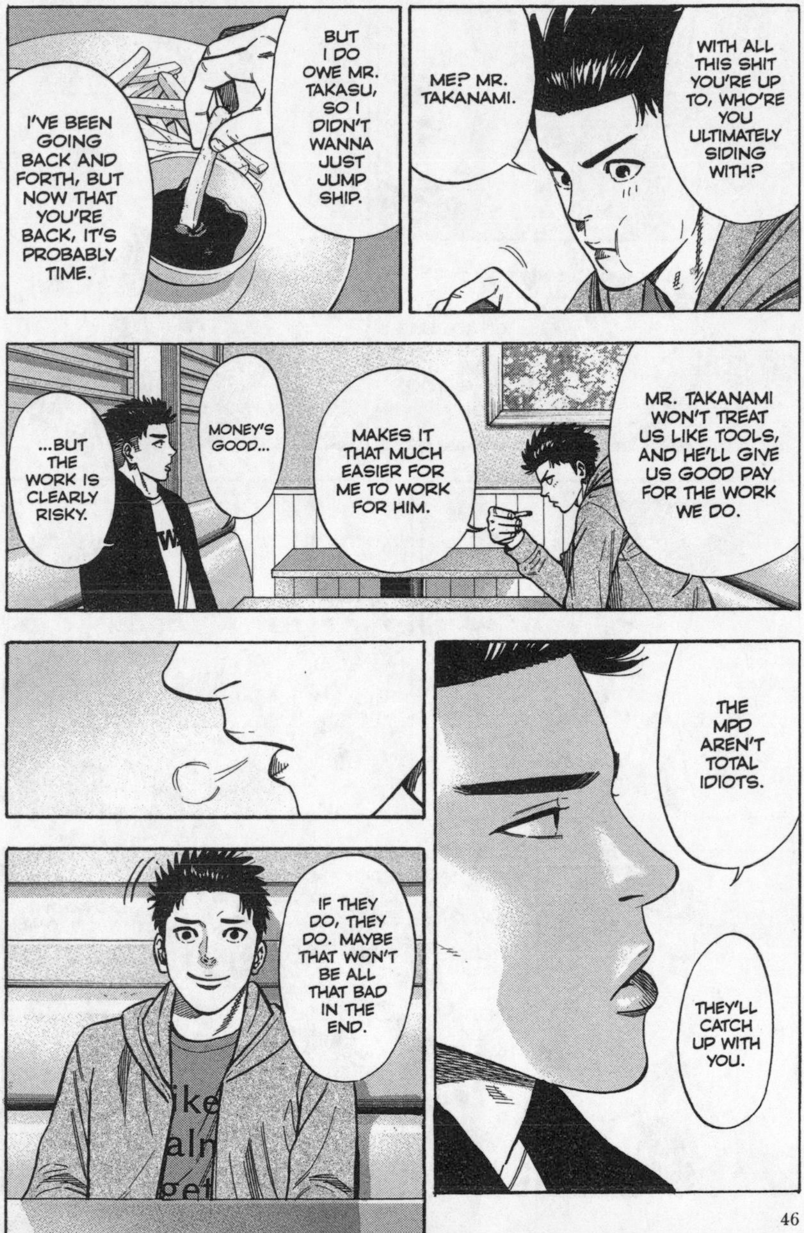
WITH ALL THIS SHIT YOU'RE UP TO, WHO'RE YOU ULTIMATELY SIDING WITH?
ME? MR. TAKANAMI.
BUT I DO OWE MR. TAKASU, SO I DIDN'T WANNA JUST JUMP SHIP.
I'VE BEEN GOING BACK AND FORTH, BUT NOW THAT YOU'RE BACK, IT'S PROBABLY TIME.
MR. TAKANAMI WON'T TREAT US LIKE TOOLS, AND HE'LL GIVE US GOOD PAY FOR THE WORK WE DO.
MAKES IT THAT MUCH EASIER FOR ME TO WORK FOR HIM.
MONEY'S GOOD...
...BUT THE WORK IS CLEARLY RISKY.
THE MPD AREN'T TOTAL IDIOTS.
THEY'LL CATCH UP WITH YOU.
IF THEY DO, THEY DO. MAYBE THAT WON'T BE ALL THAT BAD IN THE END.

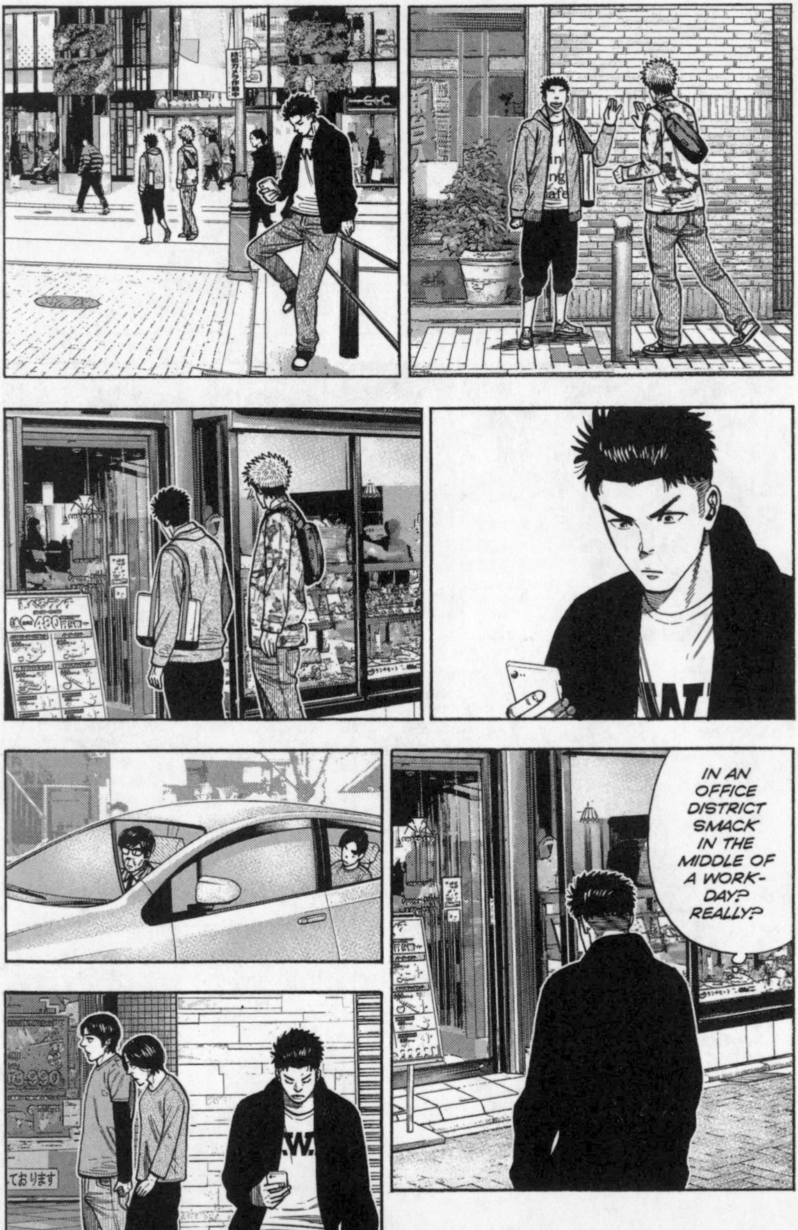
IN AN OFFICE DISTRICT SMACK IN THE MIDDLE OF A WORK-DAY? REALLY?

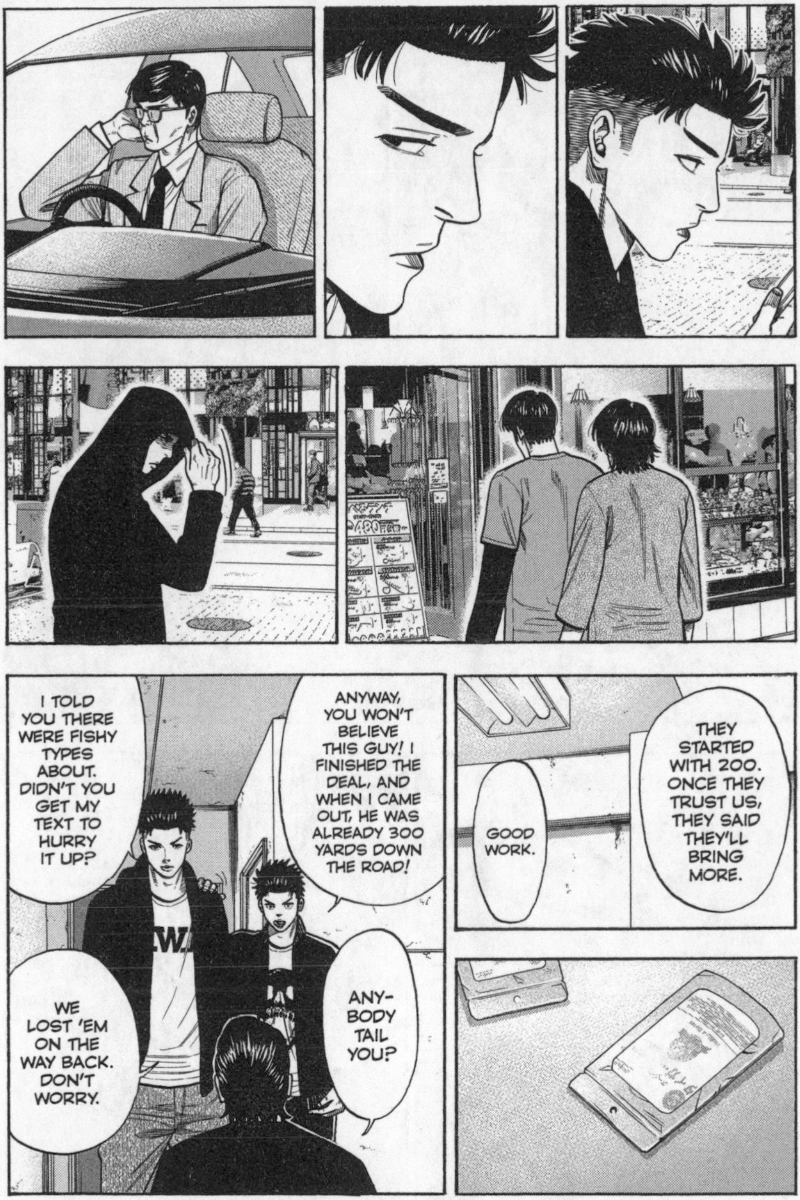
THEY STARTED WITH 200. ONCE THEY TRUST US, THEY SAID THEY'LL BRING MORE.
GOOD WORK.
ANYWAY, YOU WON'T BELIEVE THIS GUY! I FINISHED THE DEAL, AND WHEN I CAME OUT, HE WAS ALREADY 300 YARDS DOWN THE ROAD!
I TOLD YOU THERE WERE FISHY TYPES ABOUT. DIDN'T YOU GET MY TEXT TO HURRY IT UP?
ANY-BODY TAIL YOU?
WE LOST 'EM ON THE WAY BACK. DON'T WORRY.

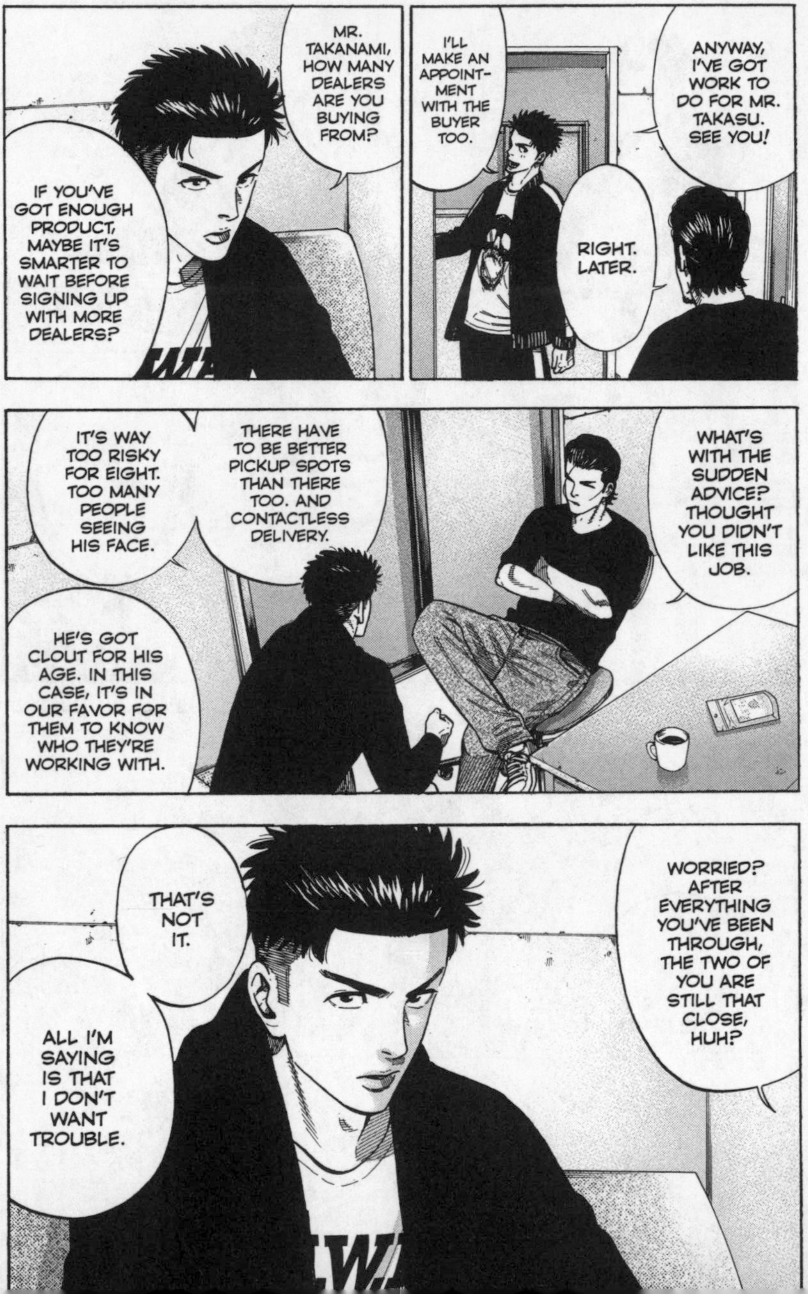
ANYWAY, I'VE GOT WORK TO DO FOR MR. TAKASU. SEE YOU!
I'LL MAKE AN APPOINTMENT WITH THE BUYER TOO.
RIGHT. LATER.
MR. TAKANAMI, HOW MANY DEALERS ARE YOU BUYING FROM?
IF YOU'VE GOT ENOUGH PRODUCT, MAYBE IT'S SMARTER TO WAIT BEFORE SIGNING UP WITH MORE DEALERS?
WHAT'S WITH THE SUDDEN ADVICE? THOUGHT YOU DIDN'T LIKE THIS JOB.
THERE HAVE TO BE BETTER PICKUP SPOTS THAN THERE TOO. AND CONTACTLESS DELIVERY.
IT'S WAY TOO RISKY FOR EIGHT. TOO MANY PEOPLE SEEING HIS FACE.
HE'S GOT CLOUT FOR HIS AGE. IN THIS CASE, IT'S IN OUR FAVOR FOR THEM TO KNOW WHO THEY'RE WORKING WITH.
WORRIED? AFTER EVERYTHING YOU'VE BEEN THROUGH, THE TWO OF YOU ARE STILL THAT CLOSE, HUH?
THAT'S NOT IT.
ALL I'M SAYING IS THAT I DON'T WANT TROUBLE.

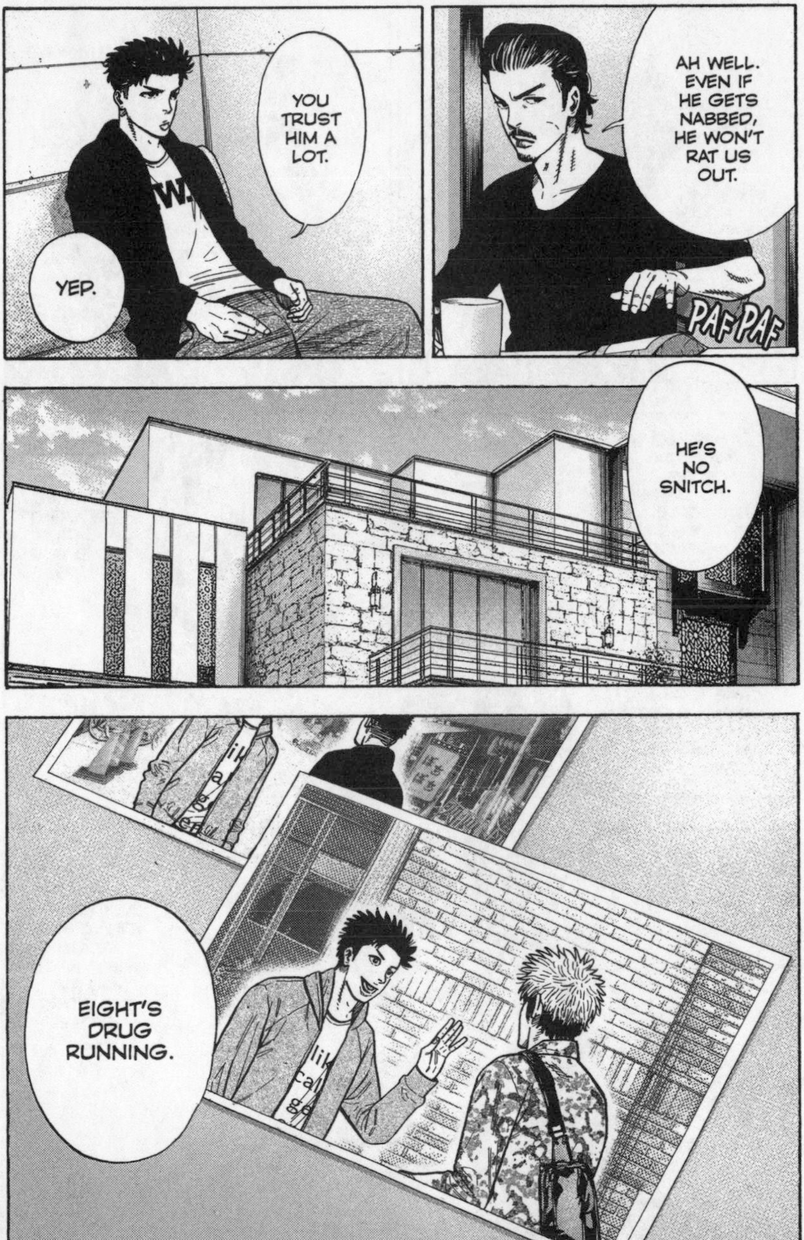
AH WELL. EVEN IF HE GETS NABBED, HE WON'T RAT US OUT.
PAF PAF
YOU TRUST HIM A LOT.
YEP.
HE'S NO SNITCH.
EIGHT'S DRUG RUNNING.

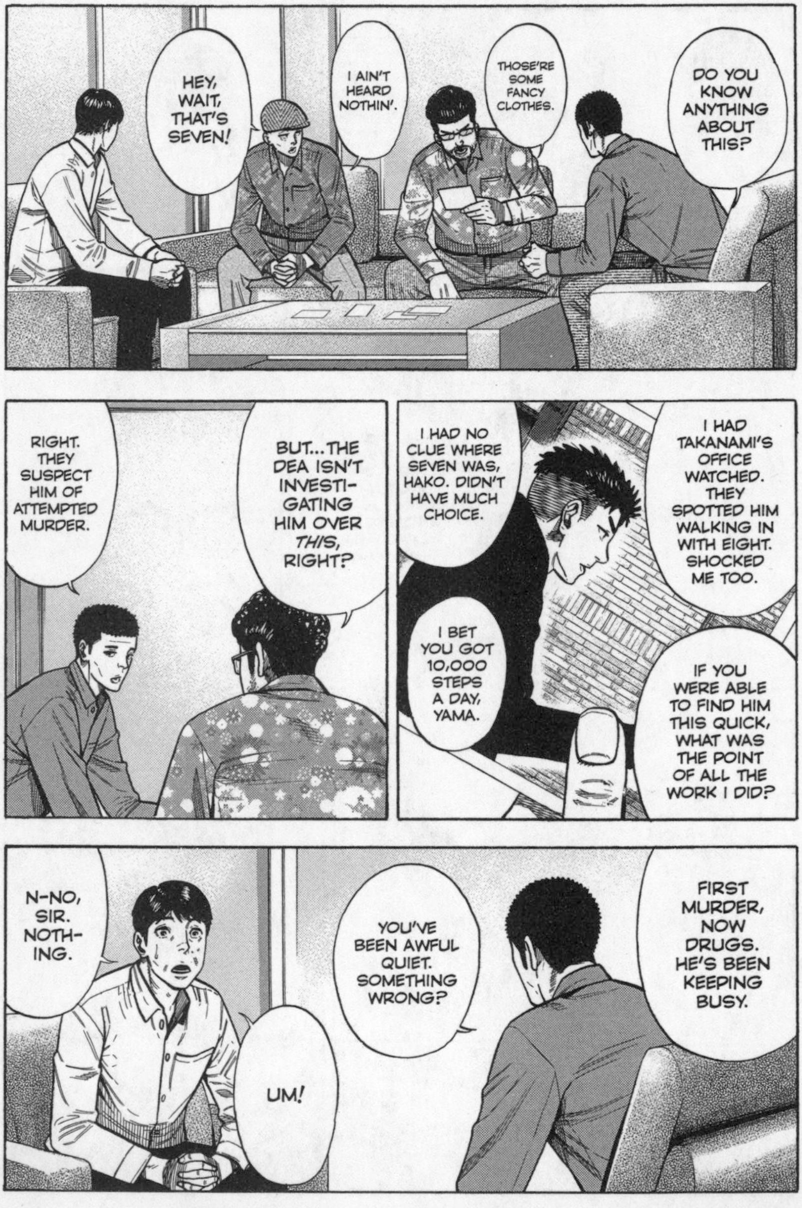
DO YOU KNOW ANYTHING ABOUT THIS?
THOSE'RE SOME FANCY CLOTHES.
I AIN'T HEARD NOTHIN'.
HEY, WAIT, THAT'S SEVEN!
I HAD TAKANAMI'S OFFICE WATCHED. THEY SPOTTED HIM WALKING IN WITH EIGHT. SHOCKED ME TOO.
I HAD NO CLUE WHERE SEVEN WAS, HAKO. DIDN'T HAVE MUCH CHOICE.
IF YOU WERE ABLE TO FIND HIM THIS QUICK, WHAT WAS THE POINT OF ALL THE WORK I DID?
I BET YOU GOT 10,000 STEPS A DAY, YAMA.
BUT...THE DEA ISN'T INVESTI-GATING HIM OVER *THIS*, RIGHT?
RIGHT. THEY SUSPECT HIM OF ATTEMPTED MURDER.
FIRST MURDER, NOW DRUGS. HE'S BEEN KEEPING BUSY.
YOU'VE BEEN AWFUL QUIET. SOMETHING WRONG?
UM!
N-NO, SIR. NOTH-ING.

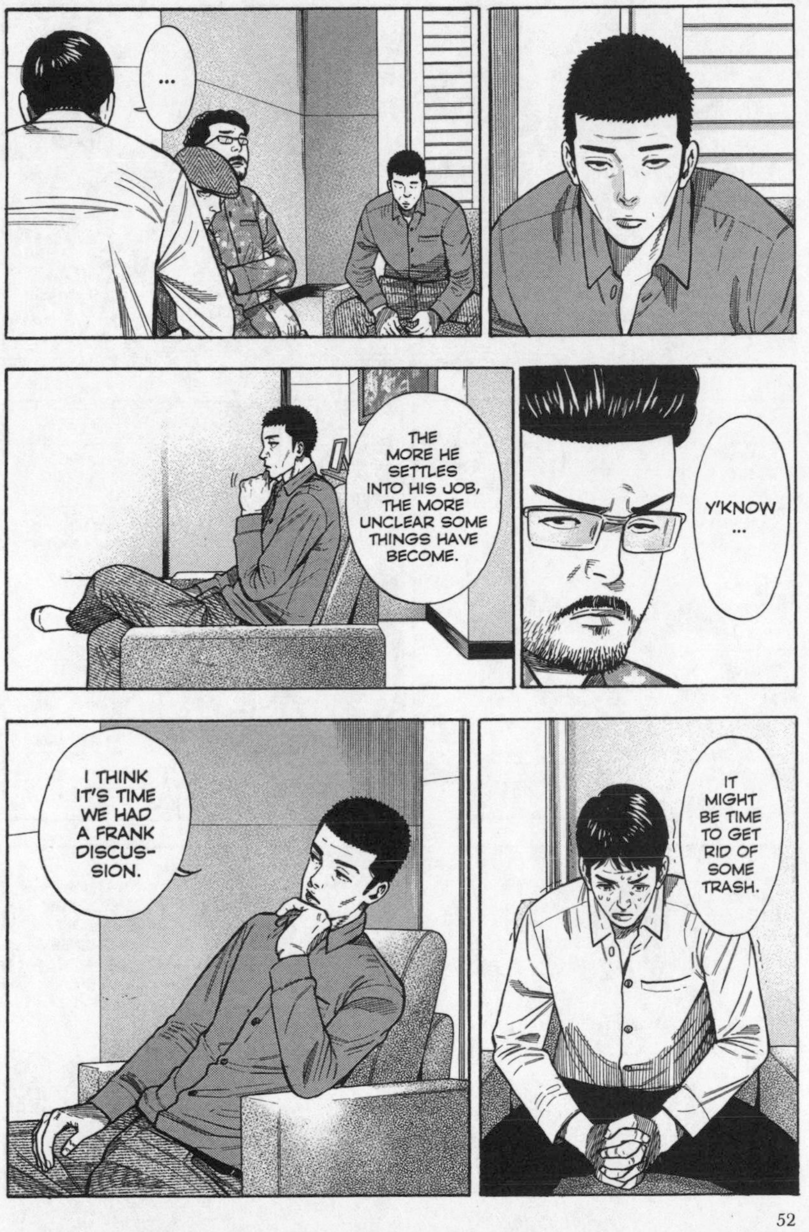
...
Y'KNOW ...
THE MORE HE SETTLES INTO HIS JOB, THE MORE UNCLEAR SOME THINGS HAVE BECOME.
IT MIGHT BE TIME TO GET RID OF SOME TRASH.
I THINK IT'S TIME WE HAD A FRANK DISCUS-SION.

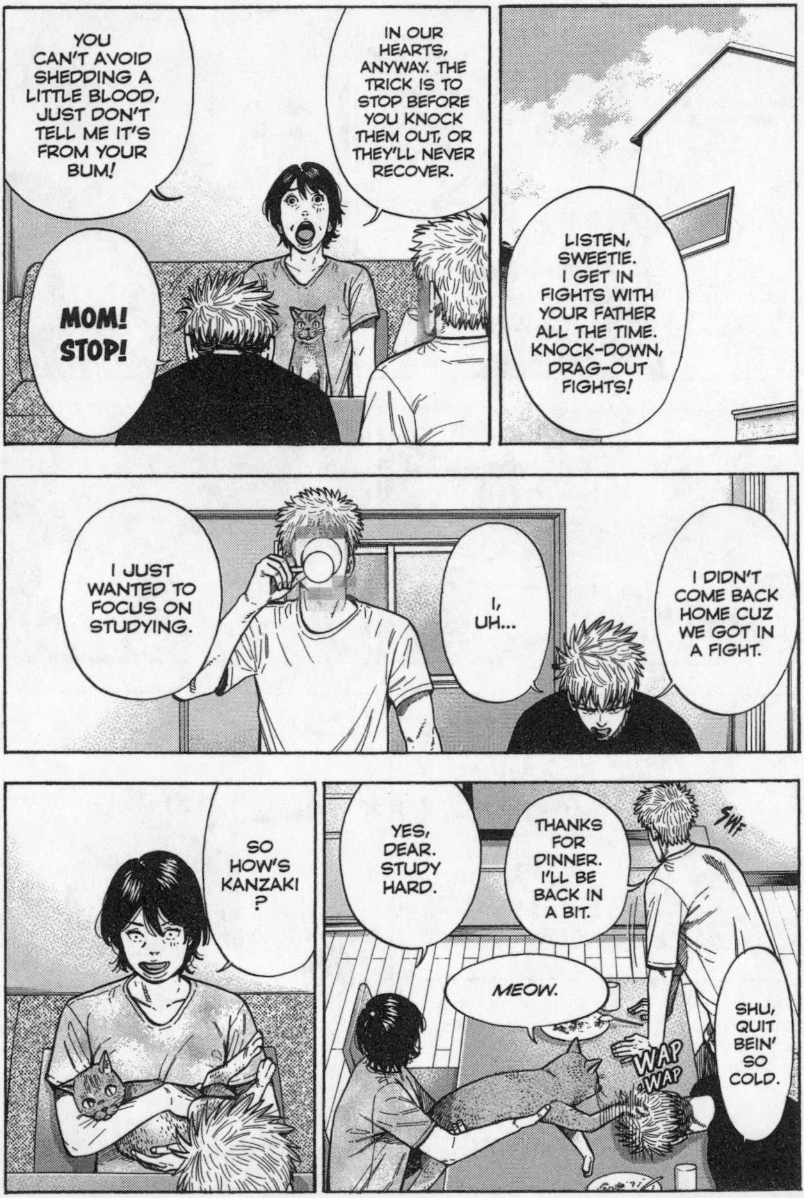
LISTEN, SWEETIE. I GET IN FIGHTS WITH YOUR FATHER ALL THE TIME. KNOCK-DOWN, DRAG-OUT FIGHTS!
IN OUR HEARTS, ANYWAY. THE TRICK IS TO STOP BEFORE YOU KNOCK THEM OUT, OR THEY'LL NEVER RECOVER.
YOU CAN'T AVOID SHEDDING A LITTLE BLOOD, JUST DON'T TELL ME IT'S FROM YOUR BUM!
MOM! STOP!
I DIDN'T COME BACK HOME CUZ WE GOT IN A FIGHT.
I, UH...
I JUST WANTED TO FOCUS ON STUDYING.
SWF
THANKS FOR DINNER. I'LL BE BACK IN A BIT.
YES, DEAR. STUDY HARD.
SHU, QUIT BEIN' SO COLD.
WAP WAP
MEOW.
SO HOW'S KANZAKI?

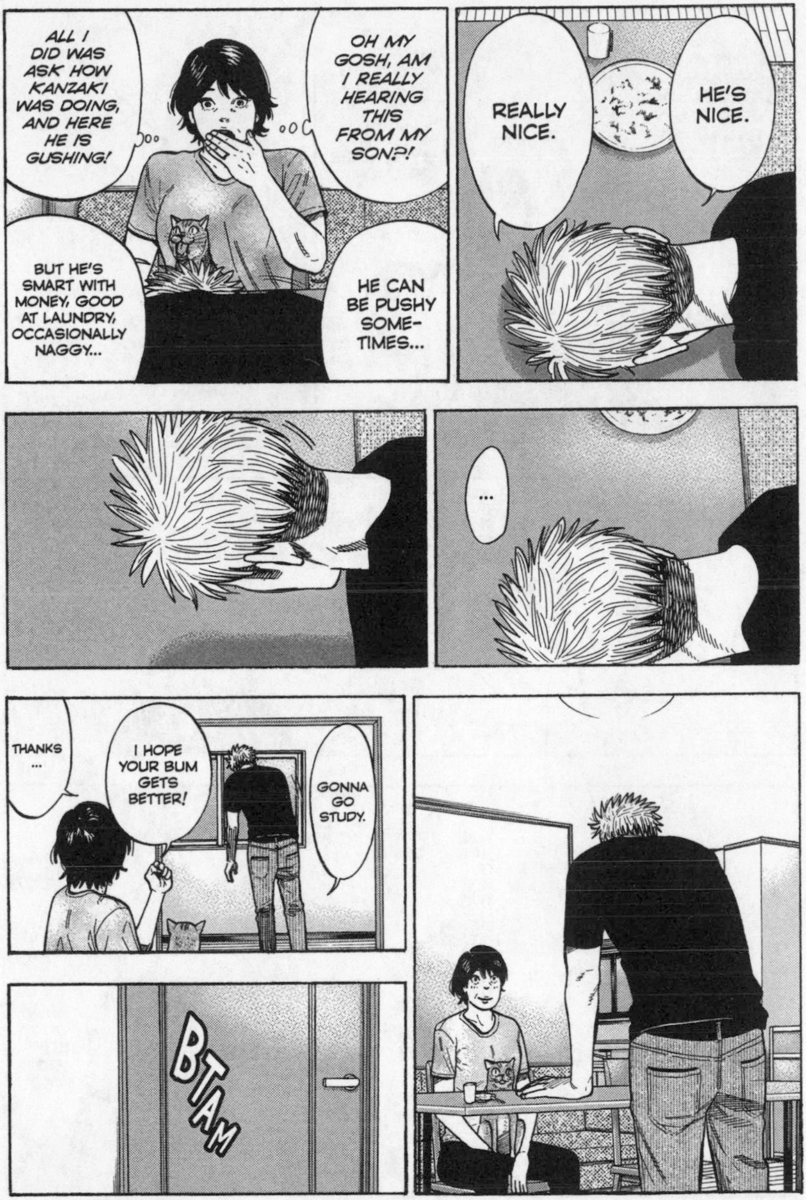
HE'S NICE.
REALLY NICE.
OH MY GOSH, AM I REALLY HEARING THIS FROM MY SON?!
ALL I DID WAS ASK HOW KANZAKI WAS DOING, AND HERE HE IS GUSHING!
HE CAN BE PUSHY SOME-TIMES...
BUT HE'S SMART WITH MONEY, GOOD AT LAUNDRY, OCCASIONALLY NAGGY...
...
GONNA GO STUDY.
I HOPE YOUR BUM GETS BETTER!
THANKS ...
BTAM

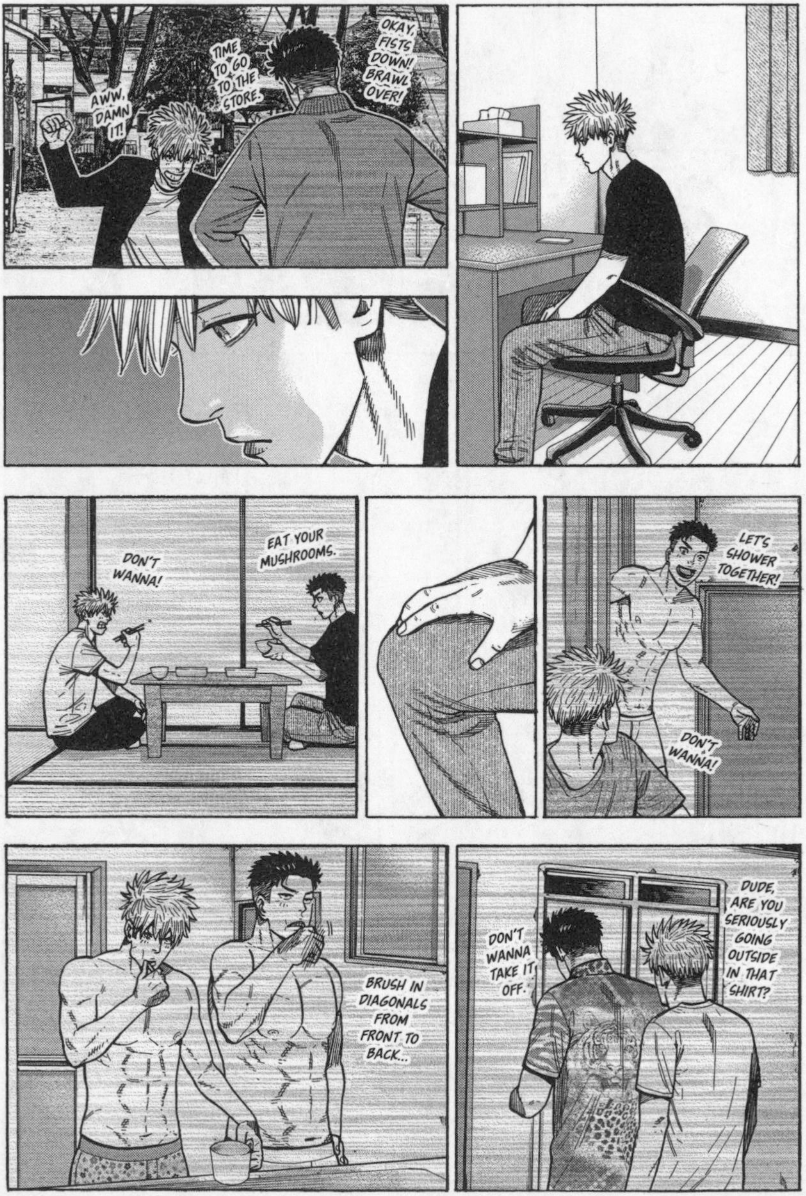
OKAY, FISTS DOWN! BRAWL OVER!
TIME TO GO TO THE STORE.
AWW, DAMN IT!
LET'S SHOWER TOGETHER!
DON'T WANNA!
EAT YOUR MUSHROOMS.
DON'T WANNA!
DUDE, ARE YOU SERIOUSLY GOING OUTSIDE IN THAT SHIRT?
DON'T WANNA TAKE IT OFF.
BRUSH IN DIAGONALS FROM FRONT TO BACK...

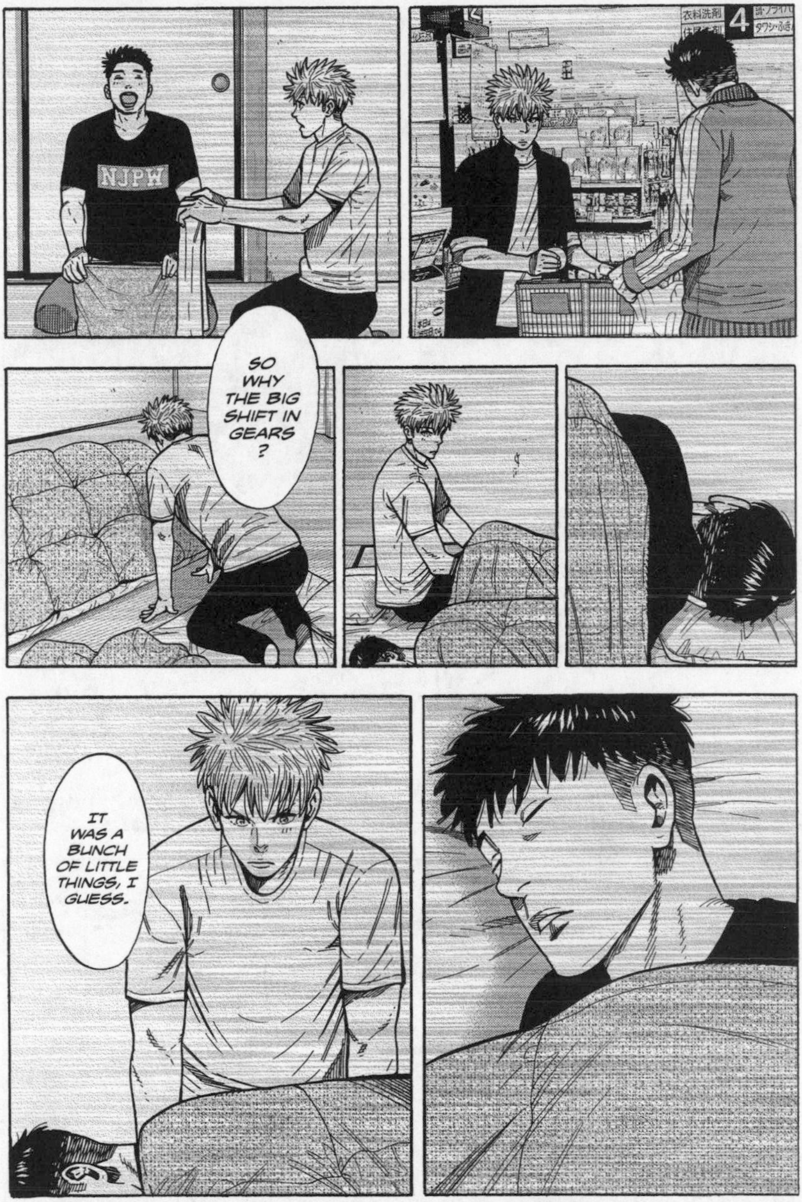
衣料洗剤
4
SO WHY THE BIG SHIFT IN GEARS?
IT WAS A BUNCH OF LITTLE THINGS, I GUESS.

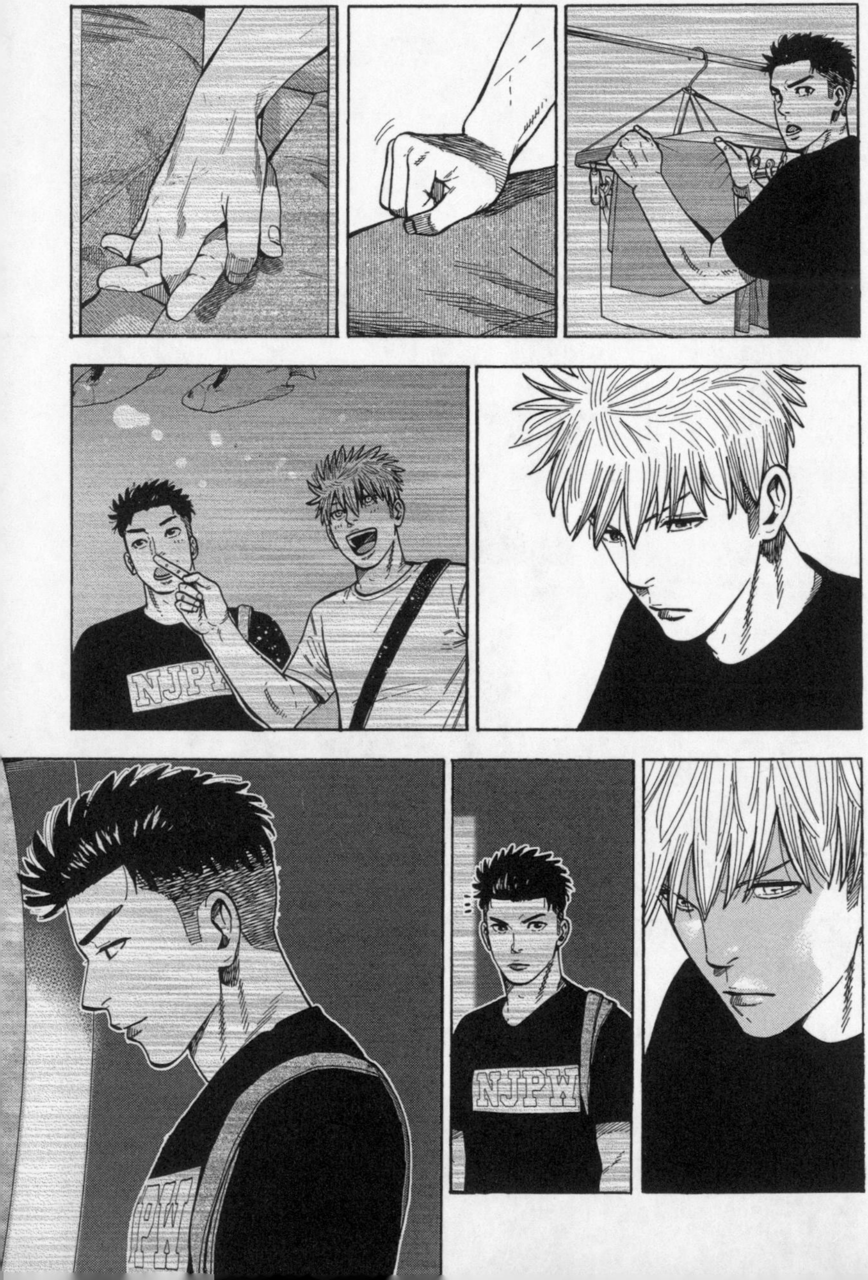
NJPW
NJPW

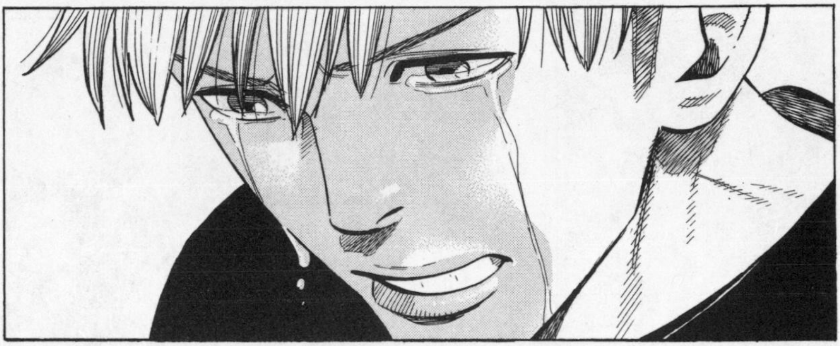
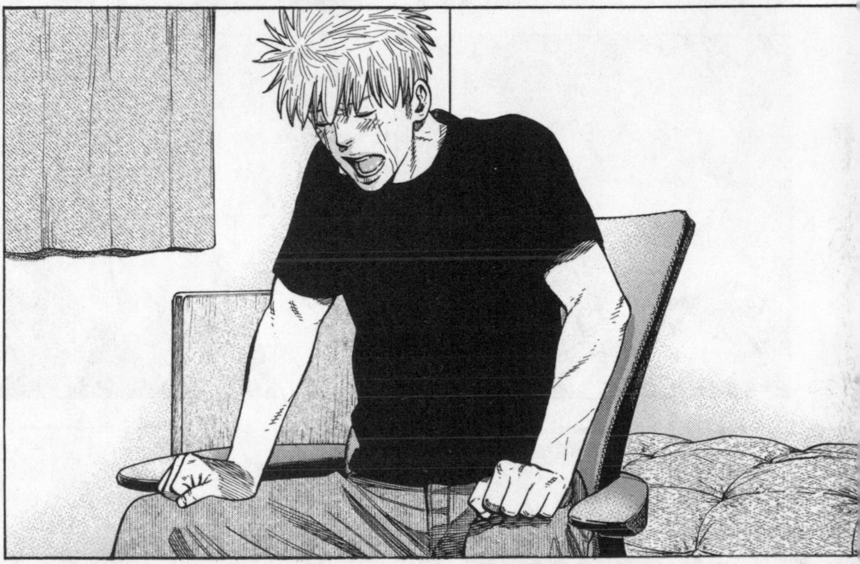
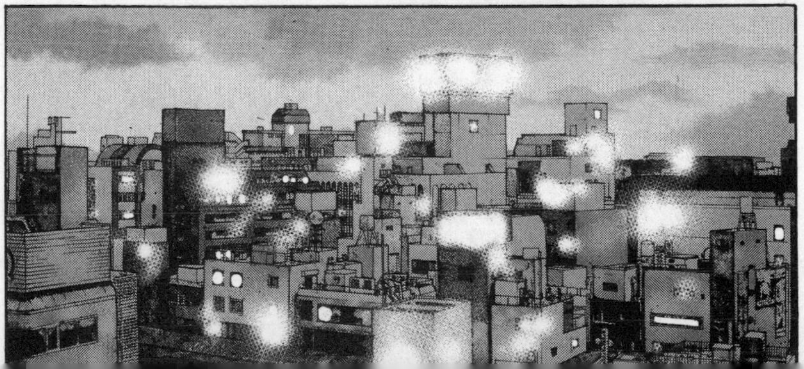

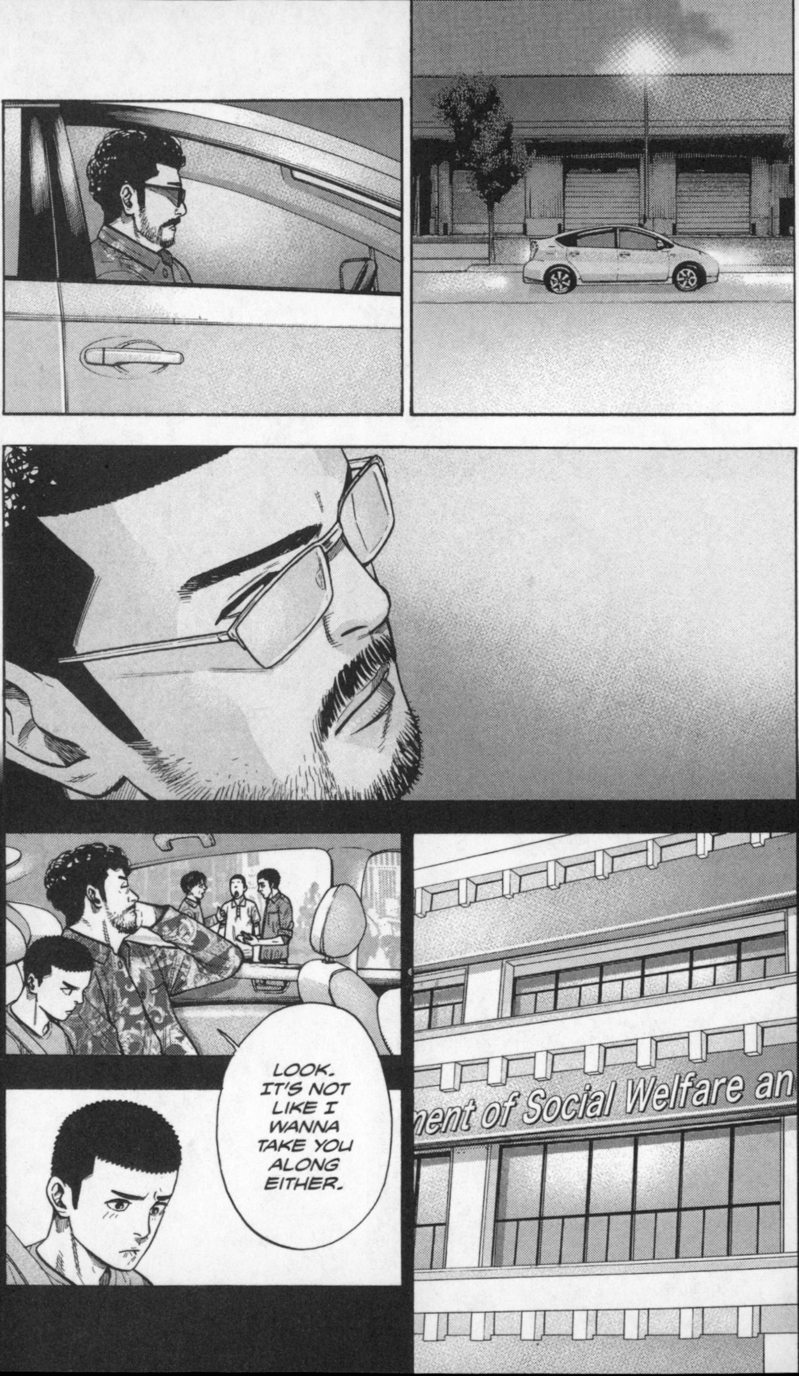
ment of Social Welfare an
LOOK. IT'S NOT LIKE I WANNA TAKE YOU ALONG EITHER.

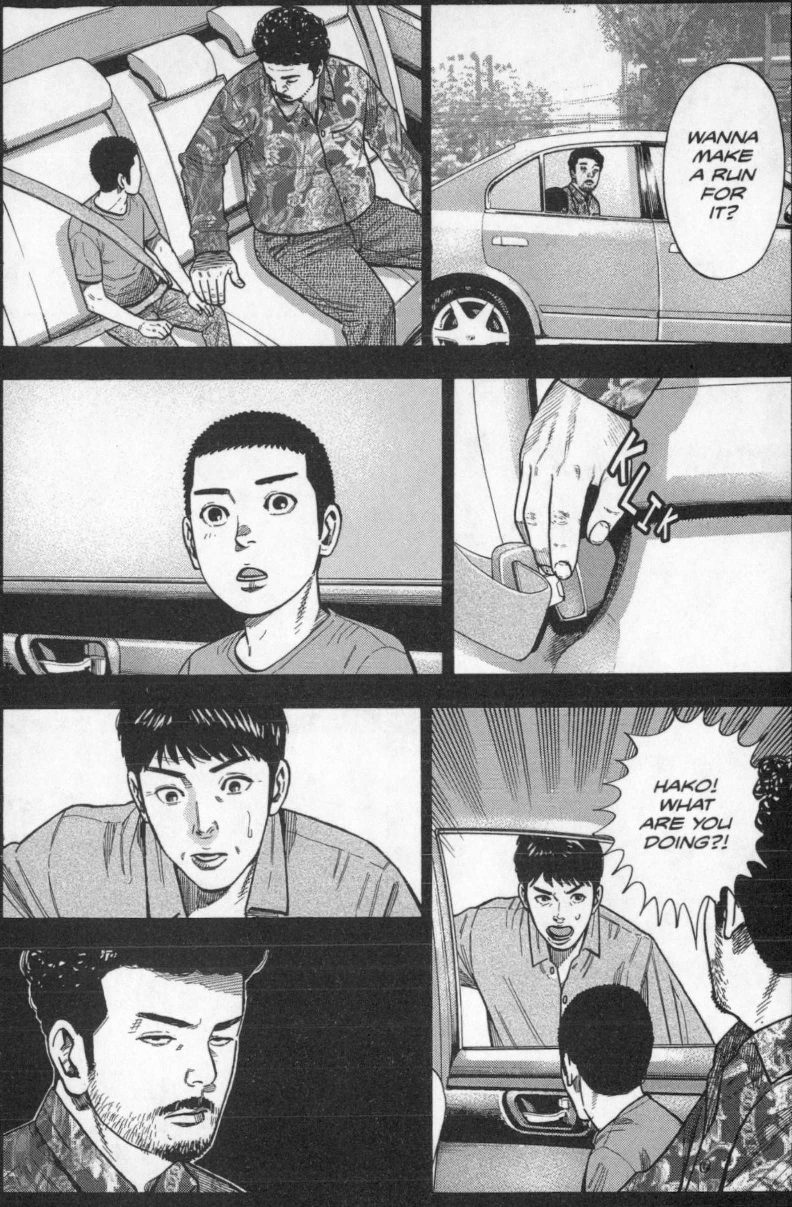
WANNA MAKE A RUN FOR IT?
KLIK
HAKO! WHAT ARE YOU DOING?!

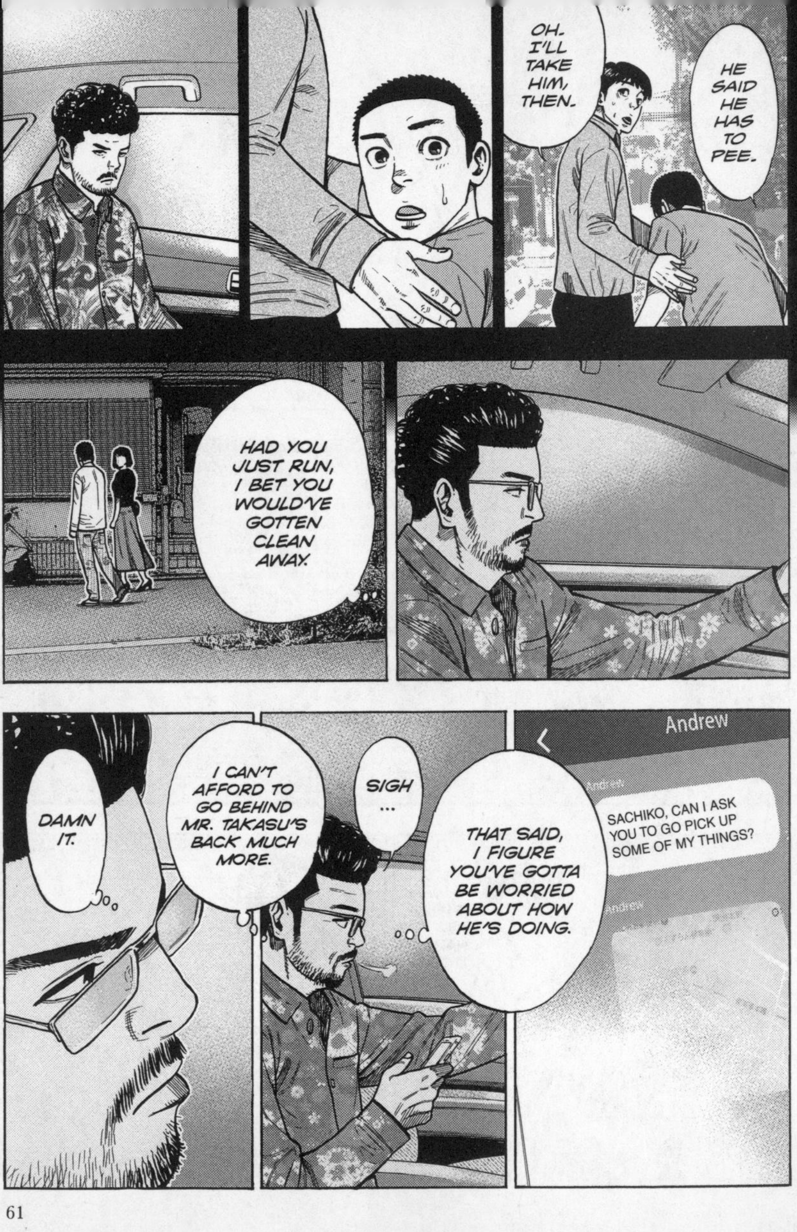
HE SAID HE HAS TO PEE.
OH. I'LL TAKE HIM, THEN.
HAD YOU JUST RUN, I BET YOU WOULD'VE GOTTEN CLEAN AWAY.
Andrew
SACHIKO, CAN I ASK YOU TO GO PICK UP SOME OF MY THINGS?
SIGH ...
I CAN'T AFFORD TO GO BEHIND MR. TAKASU'S BACK MUCH MORE.
THAT SAID, I FIGURE YOU'VE GOTTA BE WORRIED ABOUT HOW HE'S DOING.
DAMN IT.

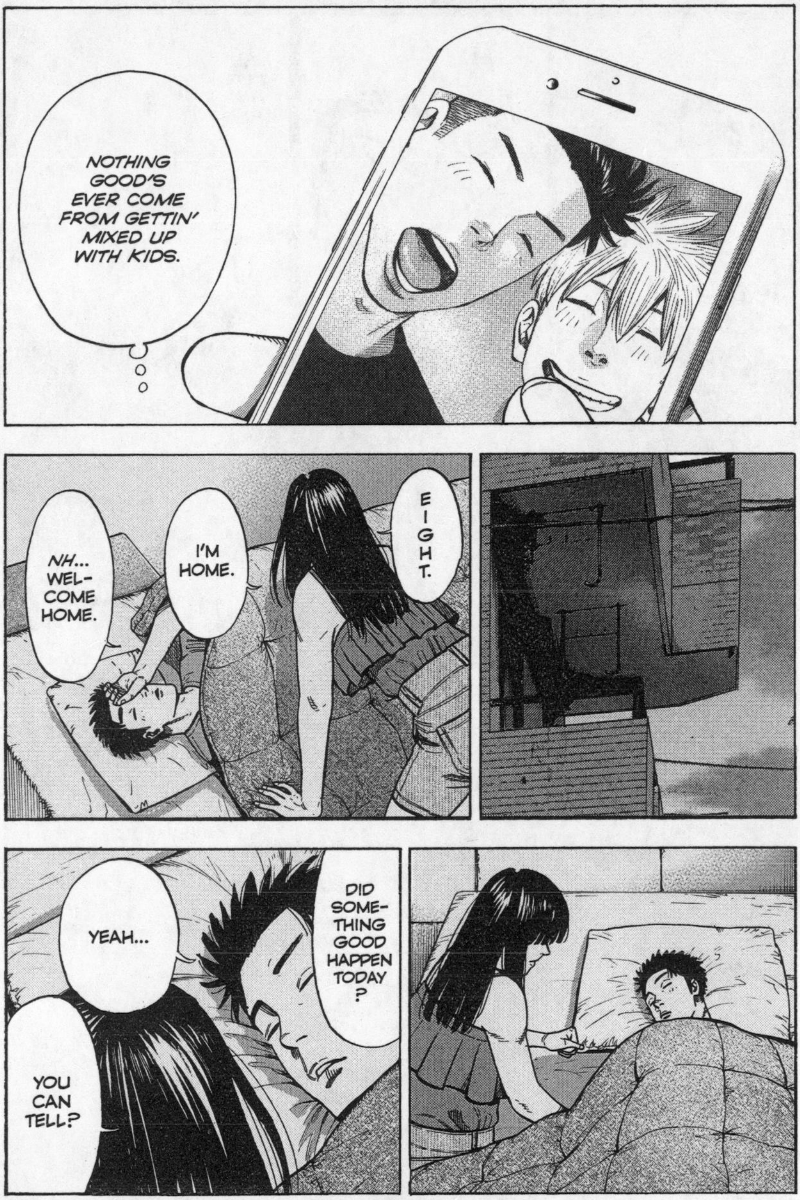
NOTHING GOOD'S EVER COME FROM GETTIN' MIXED UP WITH KIDS.
EIGHT.
I'M HOME.
NH... WEL-COME HOME.
DID SOME-THING GOOD HAPPEN TODAY?
YEAH...
YOU CAN TELL?

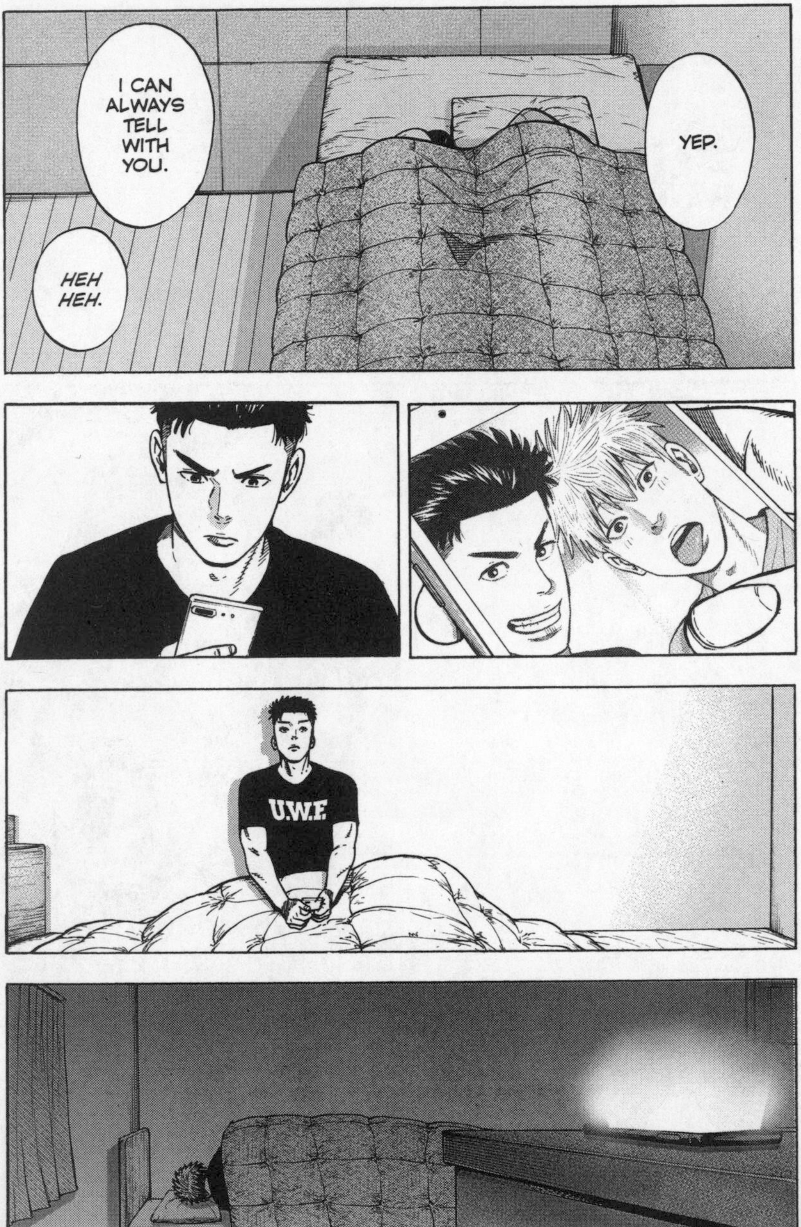
YEP.
I CAN ALWAYS TELL WITH YOU.
HEH HEH.
U.W.F.

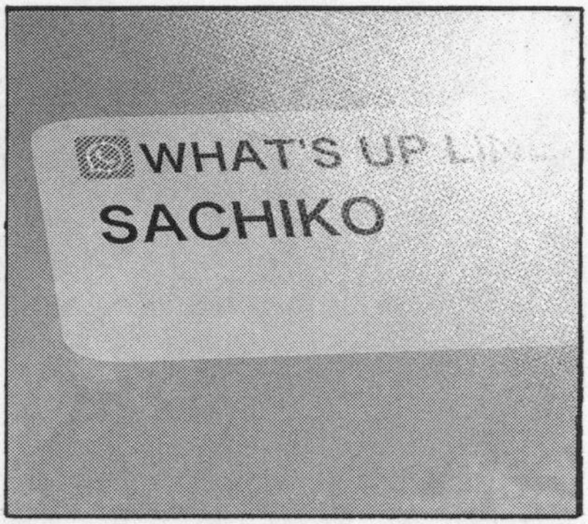
WHAT'S UP LINE
SACHIKO

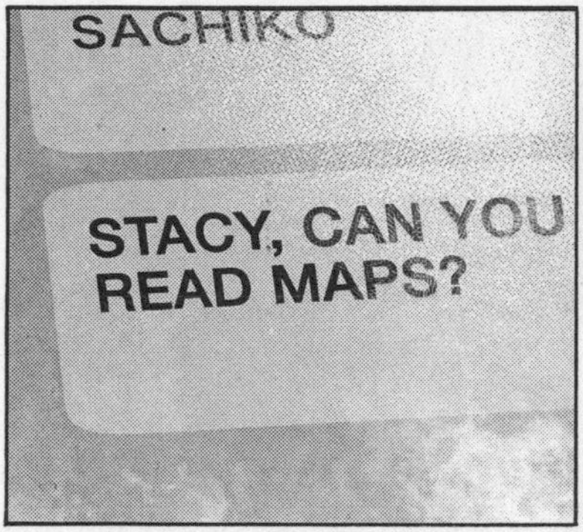
SACHIKO
STACY, CAN YOU READ MAPS?

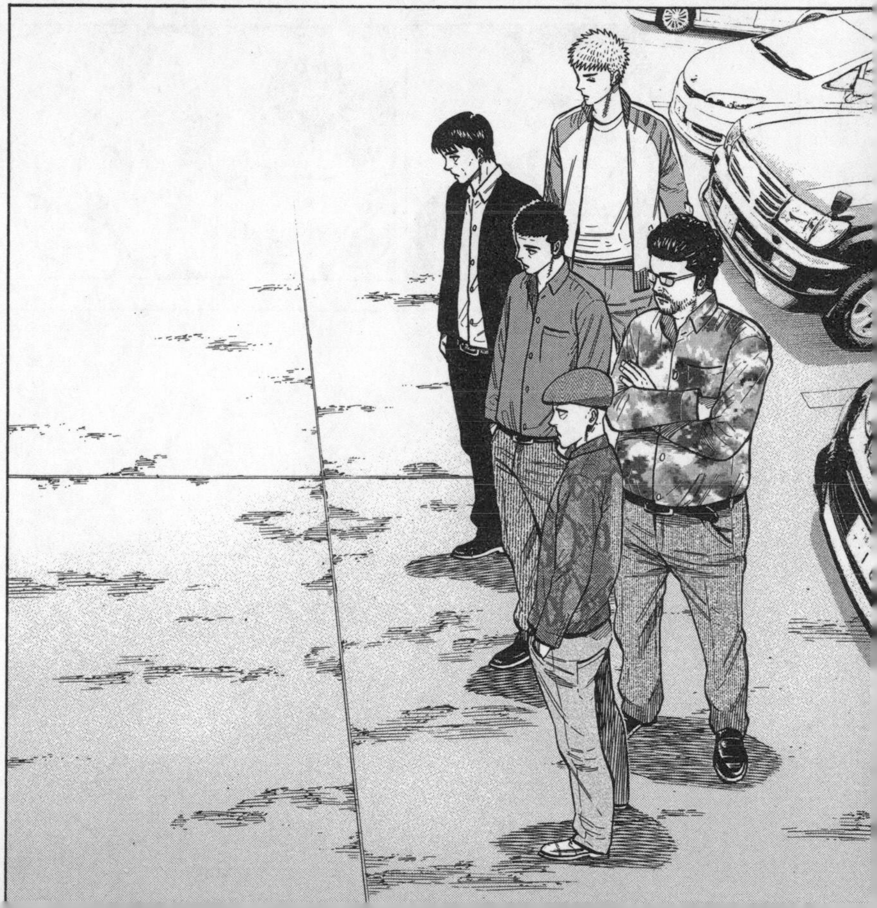

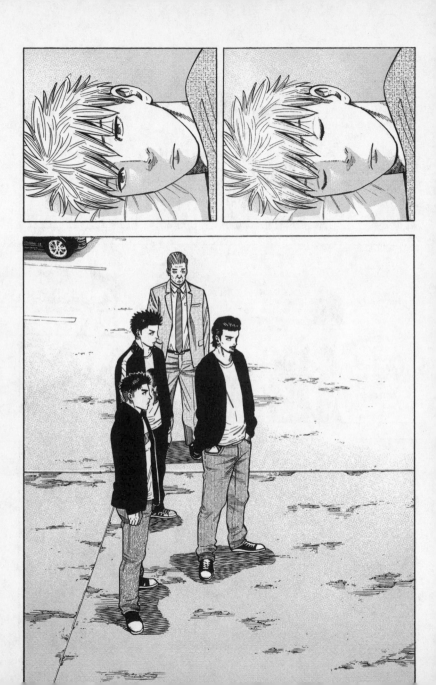

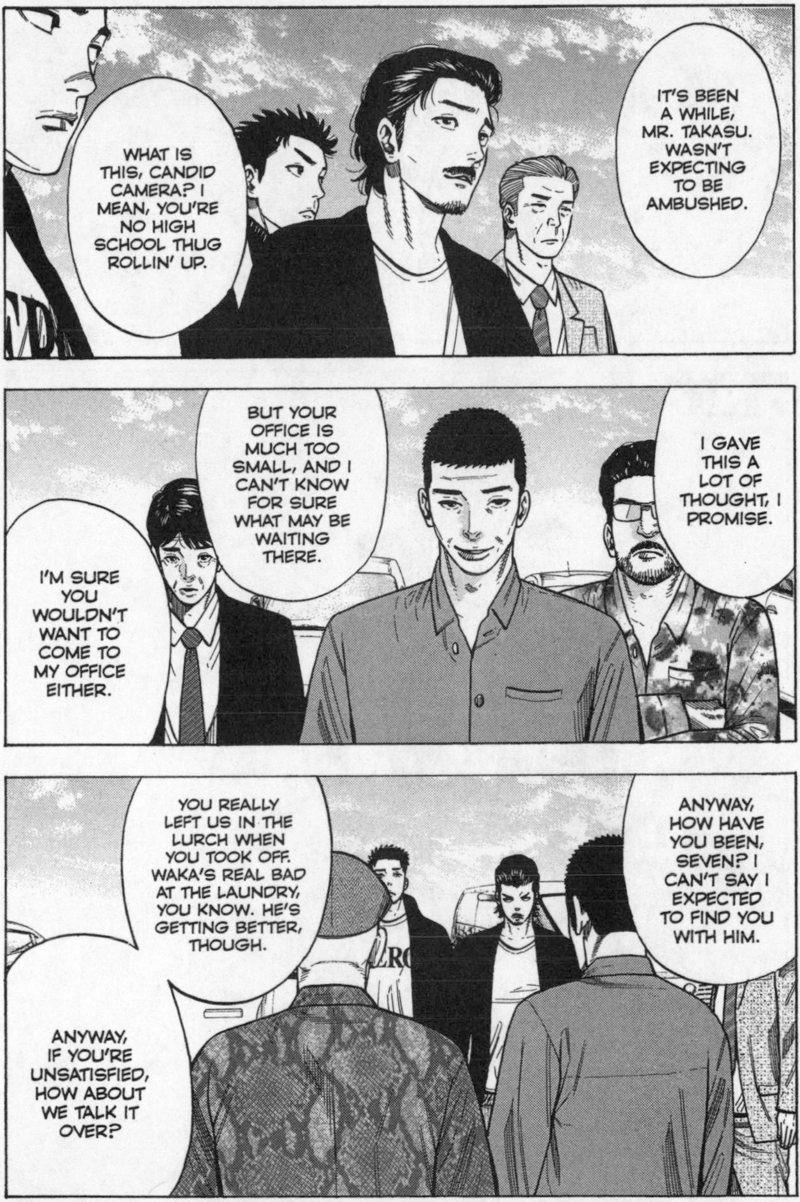
IT'S BEEN A WHILE, MR. TAKASU. WASN'T EXPECTING TO BE AMBUSHED.
WHAT IS THIS, CANDID CAMERA? I MEAN, YOU'RE NO HIGH SCHOOL THUG ROLLIN' UP.
I GAVE THIS A LOT OF THOUGHT, I PROMISE.
BUT YOUR OFFICE IS MUCH TOO SMALL, AND I CAN'T KNOW FOR SURE WHAT MAY BE WAITING THERE.
I'M SURE YOU WOULDN'T WANT TO COME TO MY OFFICE EITHER.
ANYWAY, HOW HAVE YOU BEEN, SEVEN? I CAN'T SAY I EXPECTED TO FIND YOU WITH HIM.
YOU REALLY LEFT US IN THE LURCH WHEN YOU TOOK OFF. WAKA'S REAL BAD AT THE LAUNDRY, YOU KNOW. HE'S GETTING BETTER, THOUGH.
ANYWAY, IF YOU'RE UNSATISFIED, HOW ABOUT WE TALK IT OVER?

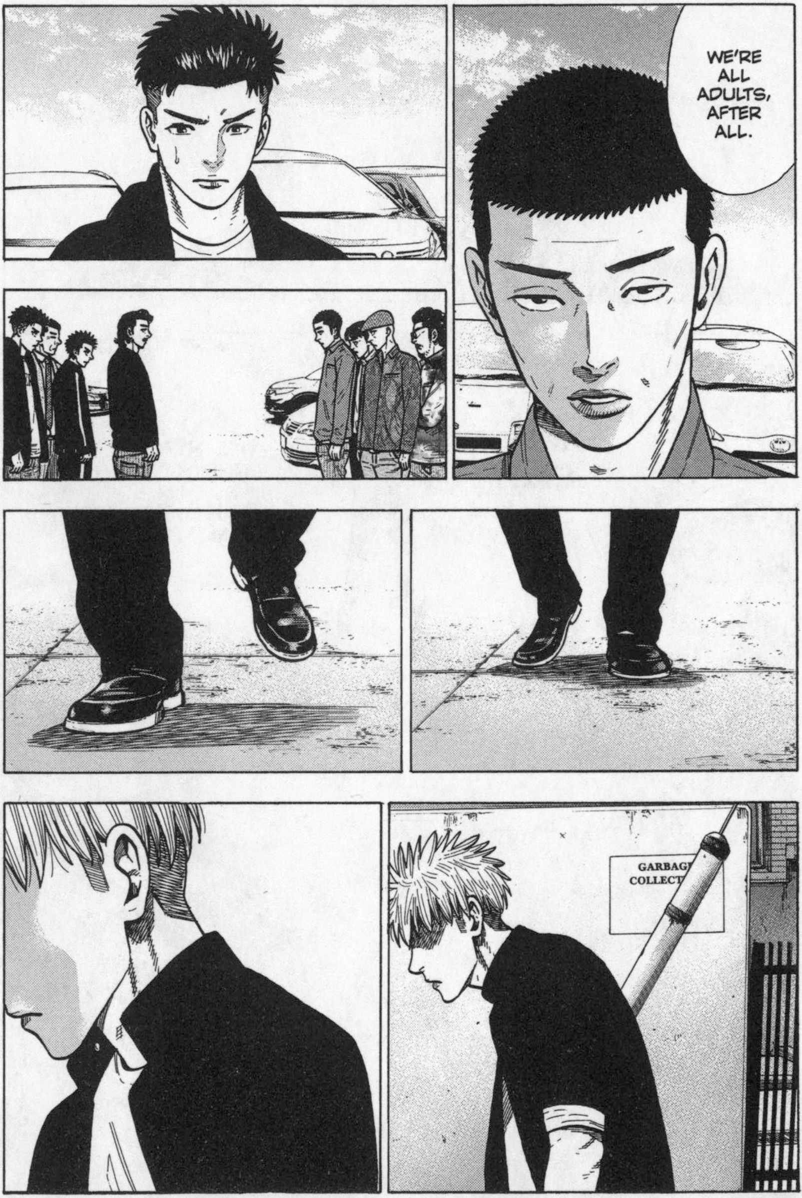
WE'RE ALL ADULTS, AFTER ALL.

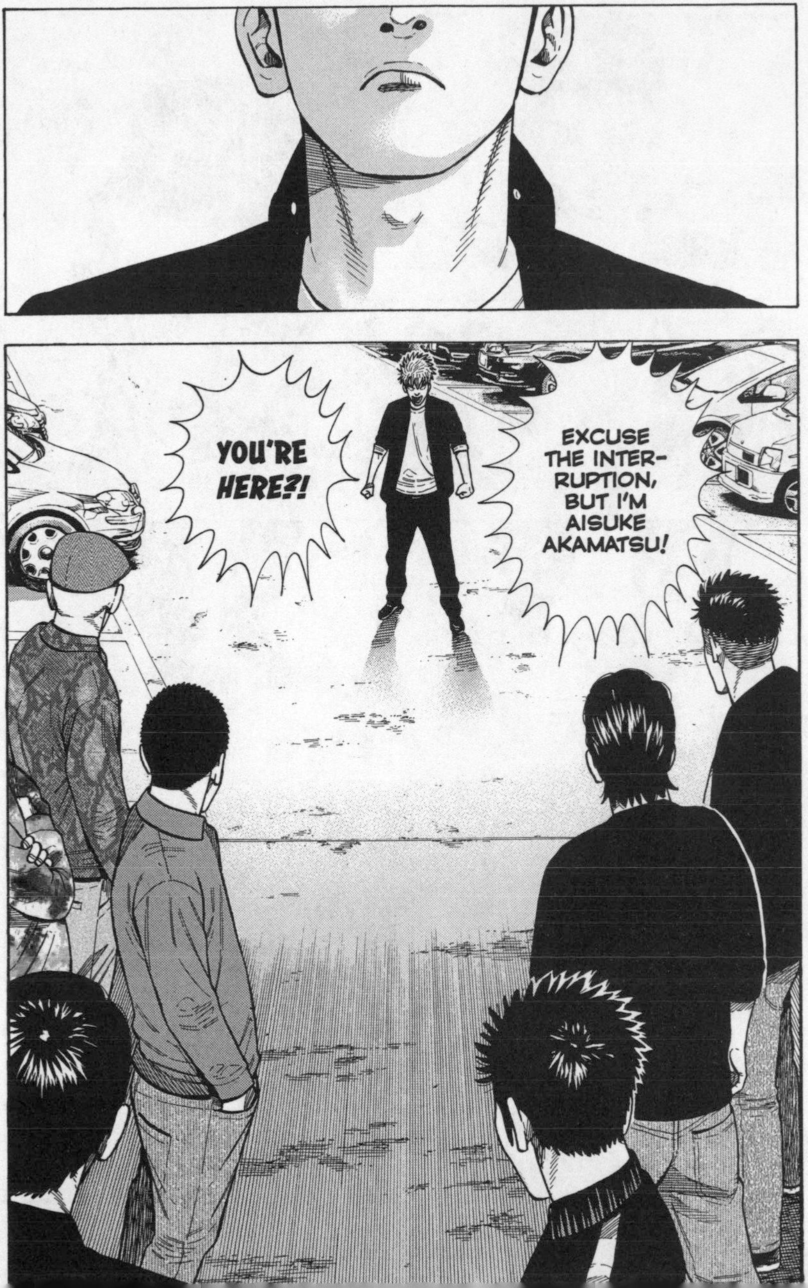
EXCUSE THE INTER-RUPTION, BUT I'M AISUKE AKAMATSU!
YOU'RE HERE?!

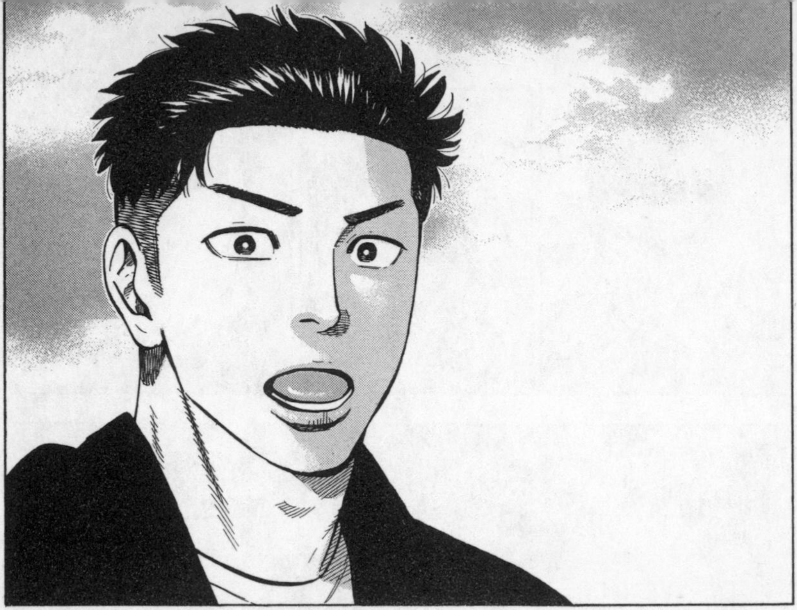
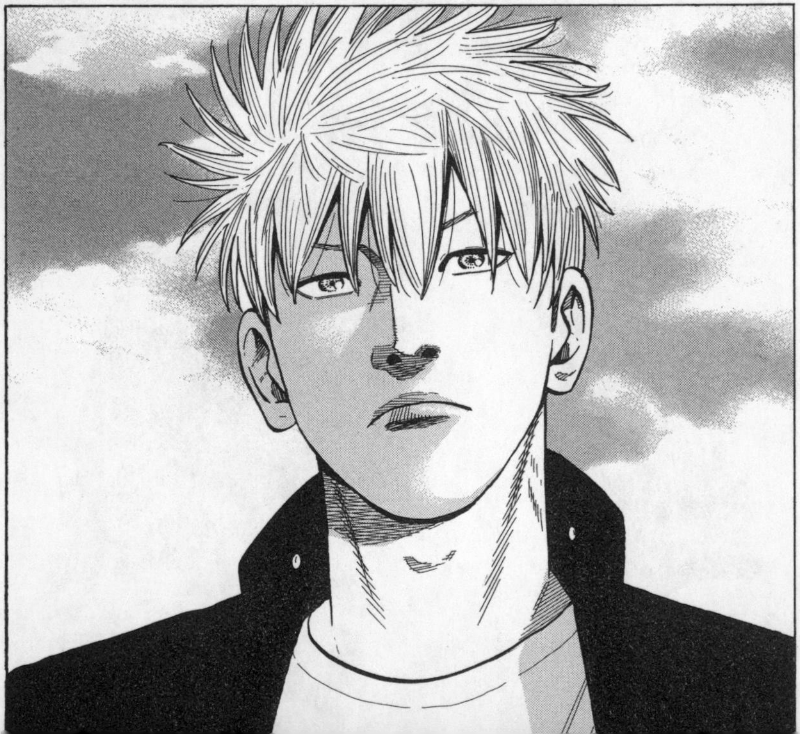

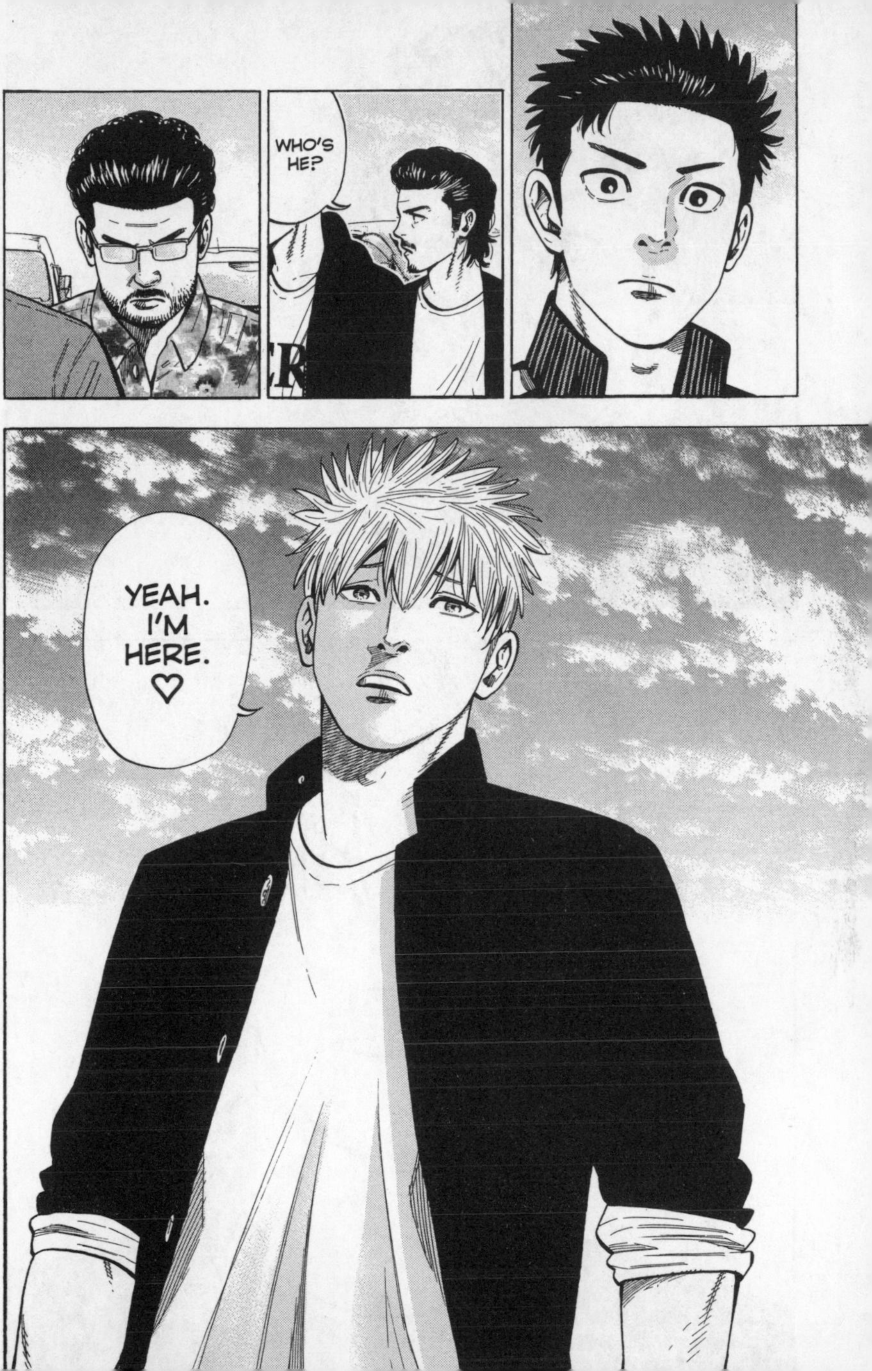
WHO'S HE?
YEAH. I'M HERE. ♡

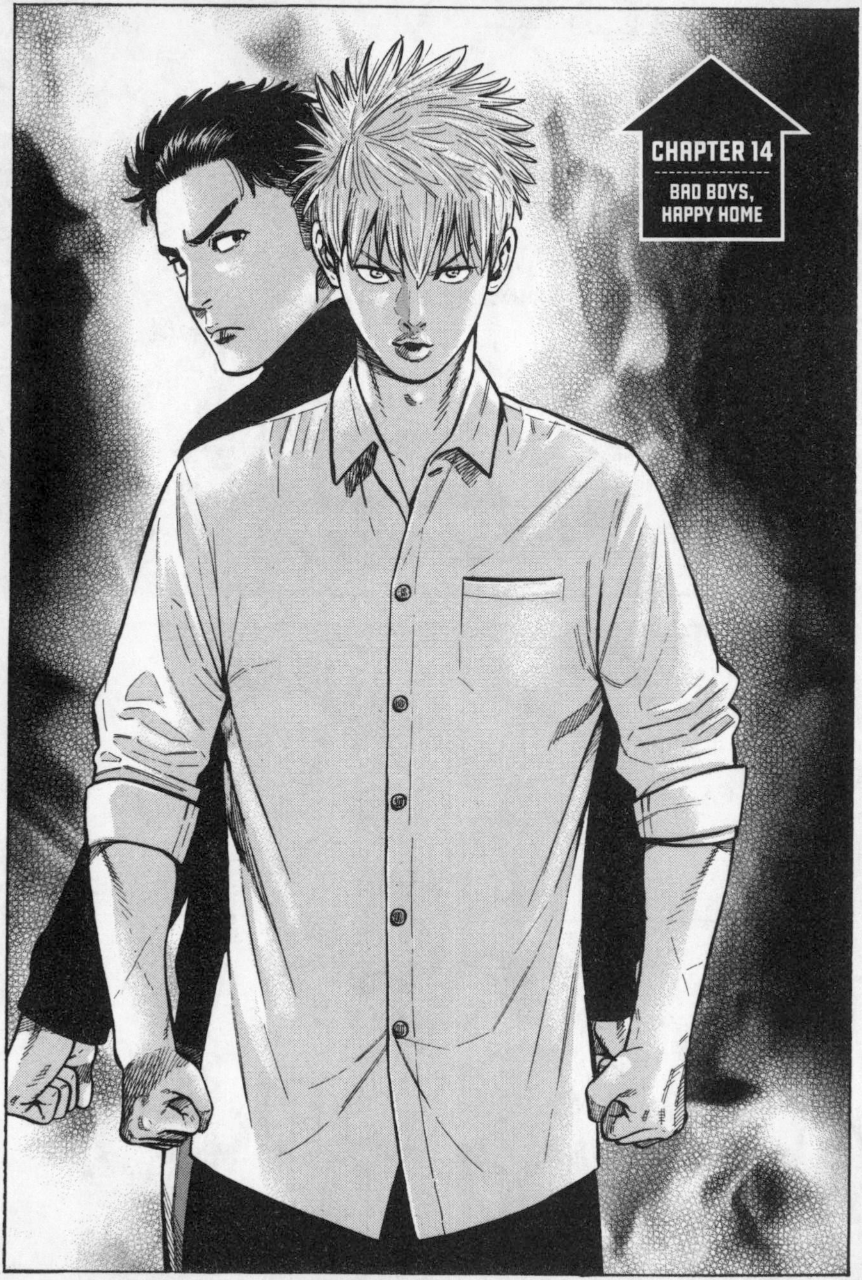
CHAPTER 14
BAD BOYS, HAPPY HOME

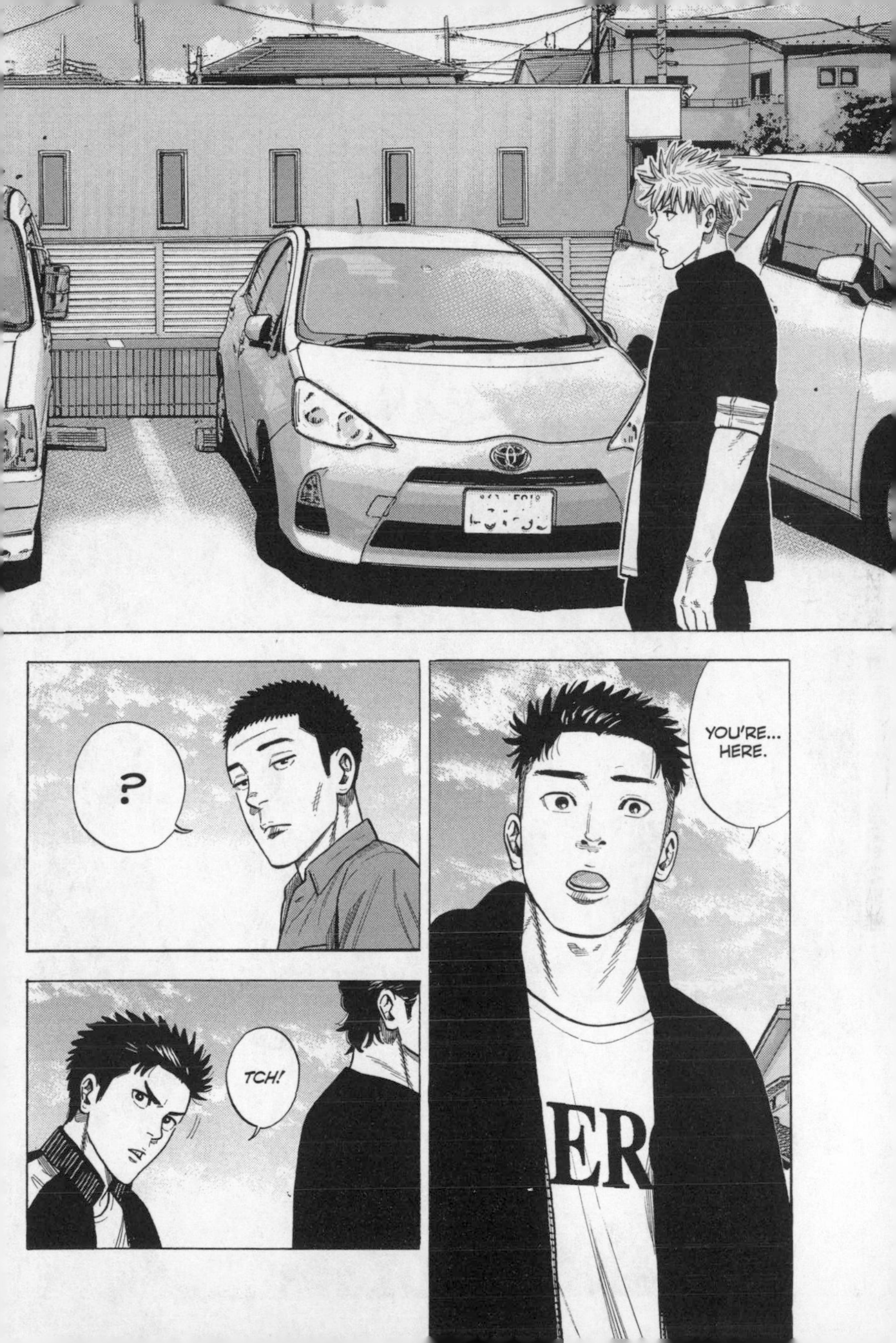
YOU'RE... HERE.
?
TCH!

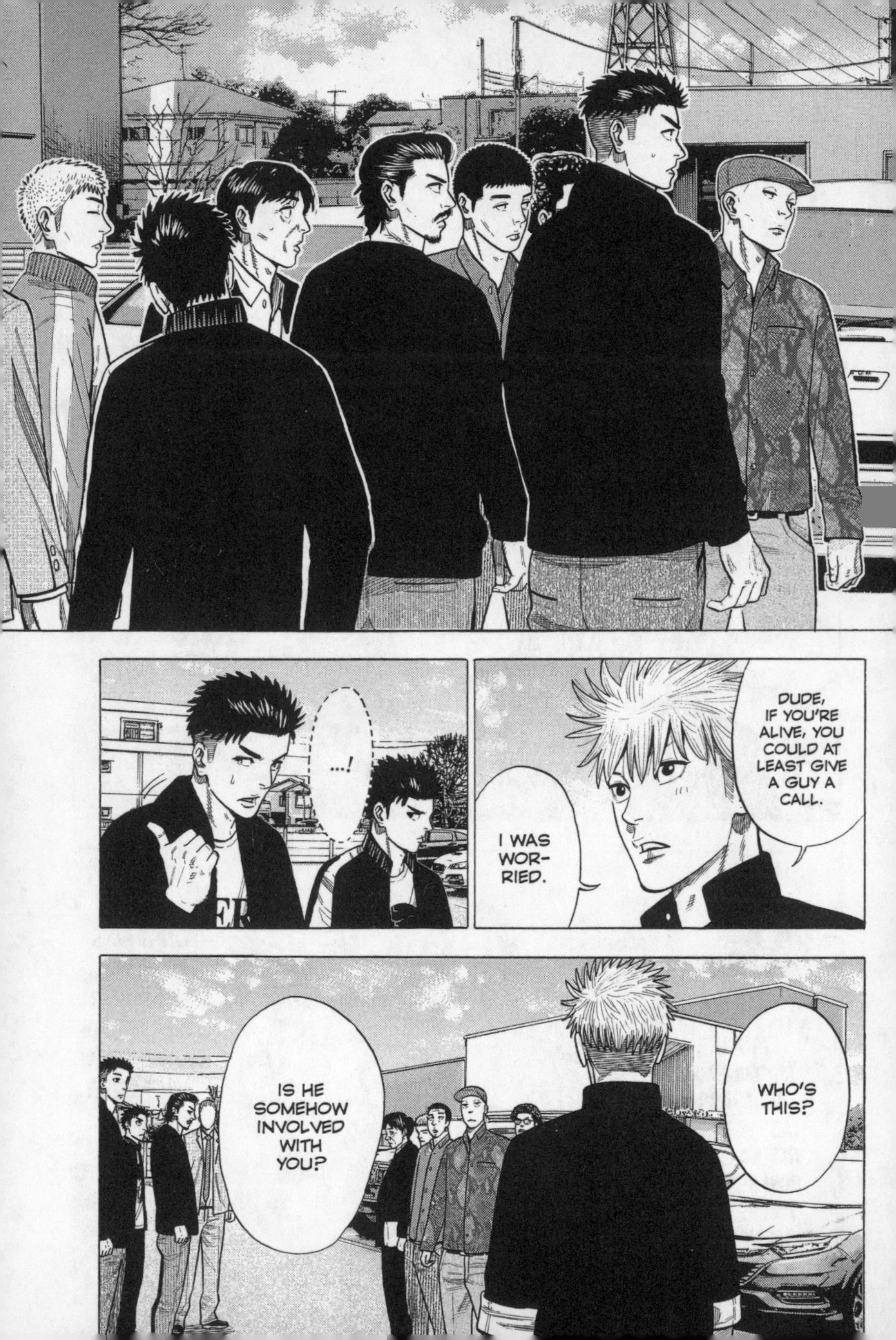
DUDE, IF YOU'RE ALIVE, YOU COULD AT LEAST GIVE A GUY A CALL.
I WAS WOR-RIED.
...!
WHO'S THIS?
IS HE SOMEHOW INVOLVED WITH YOU?

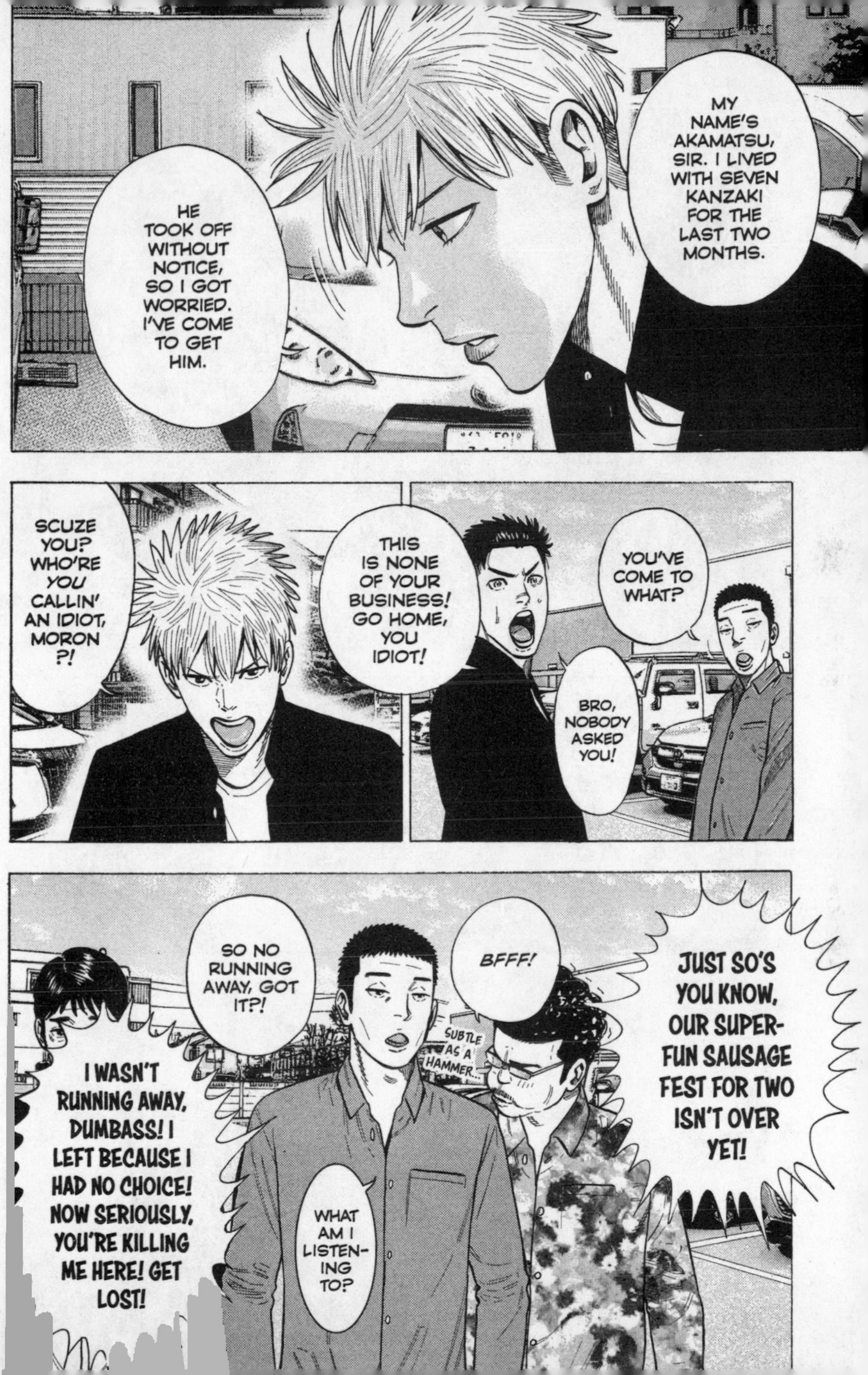
MY NAME'S AKAMATSU, SIR. I LIVED WITH SEVEN KANZAKI FOR THE LAST TWO MONTHS.
HE TOOK OFF WITHOUT NOTICE, SO I GOT WORRIED. I'VE COME TO GET HIM.
YOU'VE COME TO WHAT?
THIS IS NONE OF YOUR BUSINESS! GO HOME, YOU IDIOT!
BRO, NOBODY ASKED YOU!
SCUZE YOU? WHO'RE *YOU* CALLIN' AN IDIOT, MORON ?!
JUST SO'S YOU KNOW, OUR SUPER-FUN SAUSAGE FEST FOR TWO ISN'T OVER YET!
BFFF!
SUBTLE AS A HAMMER...
SO NO RUNNING AWAY, GOT IT?!
I WASN'T RUNNING AWAY, DUMBASS! I LEFT BECAUSE I HAD NO CHOICE! NOW SERIOUSLY, YOU'RE KILLING ME HERE! GET LOST!
WHAT AM I LISTEN-ING TO?

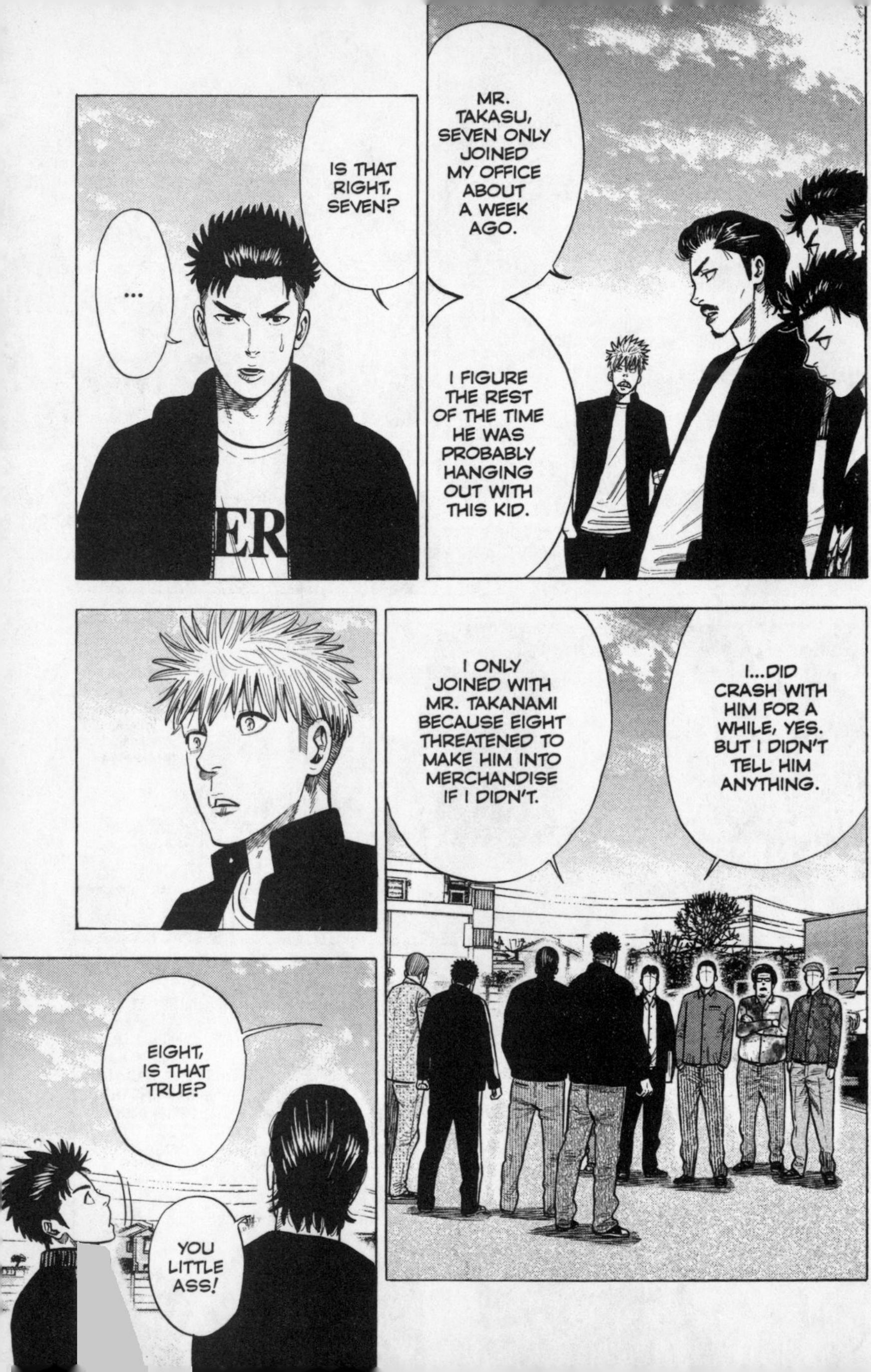
MR. TAKASU, SEVEN ONLY JOINED MY OFFICE ABOUT A WEEK AGO.
I FIGURE THE REST OF THE TIME HE WAS PROBABLY HANGING OUT WITH THIS KID.
IS THAT RIGHT, SEVEN?
...
I...DID CRASH WITH HIM FOR A WHILE, YES. BUT I DIDN'T TELL HIM ANYTHING.
I ONLY JOINED WITH MR. TAKANAMI BECAUSE EIGHT THREATENED TO MAKE HIM INTO MERCHANDISE IF I DIDN'T.
EIGHT, IS THAT TRUE?
YOU LITTLE ASS!

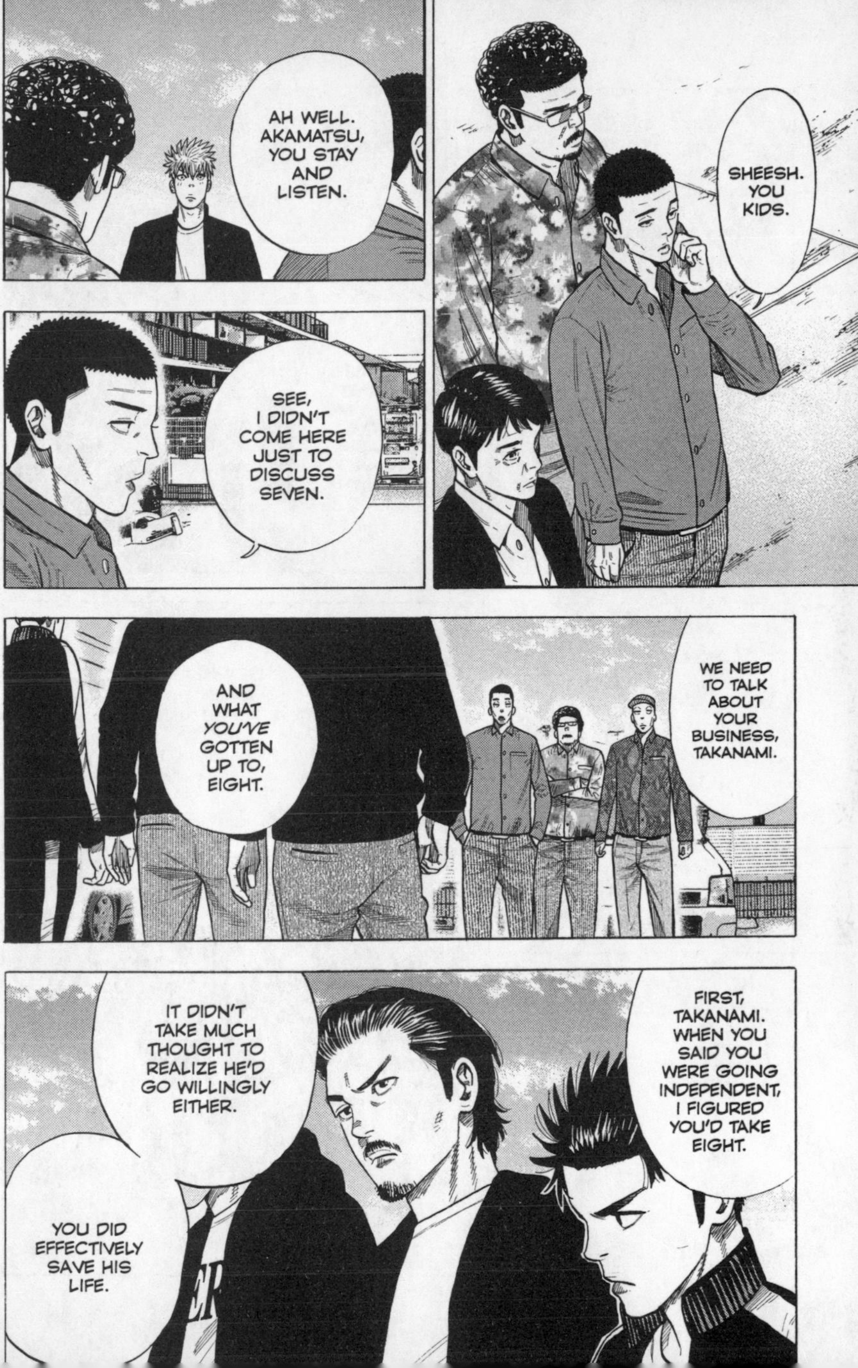
SHEESH. YOU KIDS.
AH WELL. AKAMATSU, YOU STAY AND LISTEN.
SEE, I DIDN'T COME HERE JUST TO DISCUSS SEVEN.
WE NEED TO TALK ABOUT YOUR BUSINESS, TAKANAMI.
AND WHAT *YOU'VE* GOTTEN UP TO, EIGHT.
FIRST, TAKANAMI. WHEN YOU SAID YOU WERE GOING INDEPENDENT, I FIGURED YOU'D TAKE EIGHT.
IT DIDN'T TAKE MUCH THOUGHT TO REALIZE HE'D GO WILLINGLY EITHER.
YOU DID EFFECTIVELY SAVE HIS LIFE.

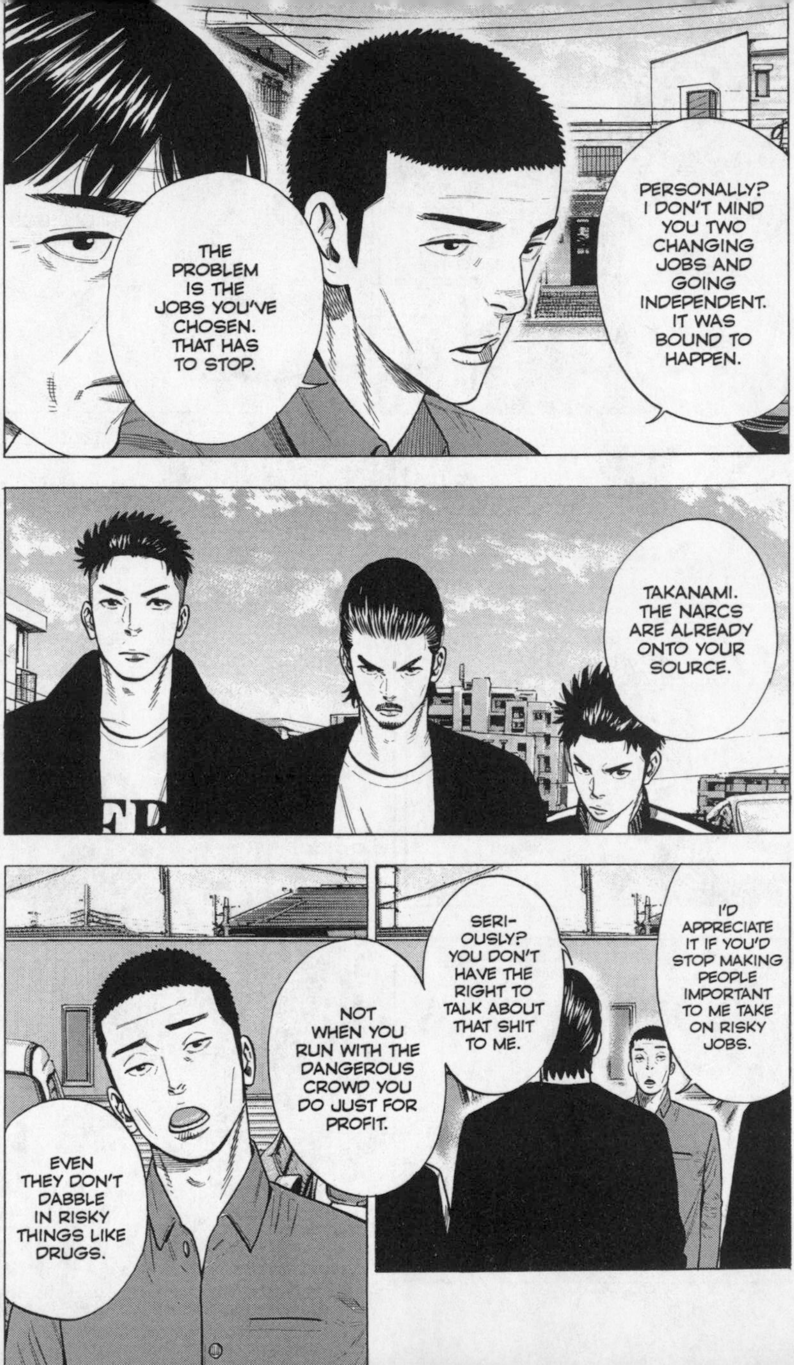
PERSONALLY? I DON'T MIND YOU TWO CHANGING JOBS AND GOING INDEPENDENT. IT WAS BOUND TO HAPPEN.
THE PROBLEM IS THE JOBS YOU'VE CHOSEN. THAT HAS TO STOP.
TAKANAMI. THE NARCS ARE ALREADY ONTO YOUR SOURCE.
I'D APPRECIATE IT IF YOU'D STOP MAKING PEOPLE IMPORTANT TO ME TAKE ON RISKY JOBS.
SERI-OUSLY? YOU DON'T HAVE THE RIGHT TO TALK ABOUT THAT SHIT TO ME.
NOT WHEN YOU RUN WITH THE DANGEROUS CROWD YOU DO JUST FOR PROFIT.
EVEN THEY DON'T DABBLE IN RISKY THINGS LIKE DRUGS.

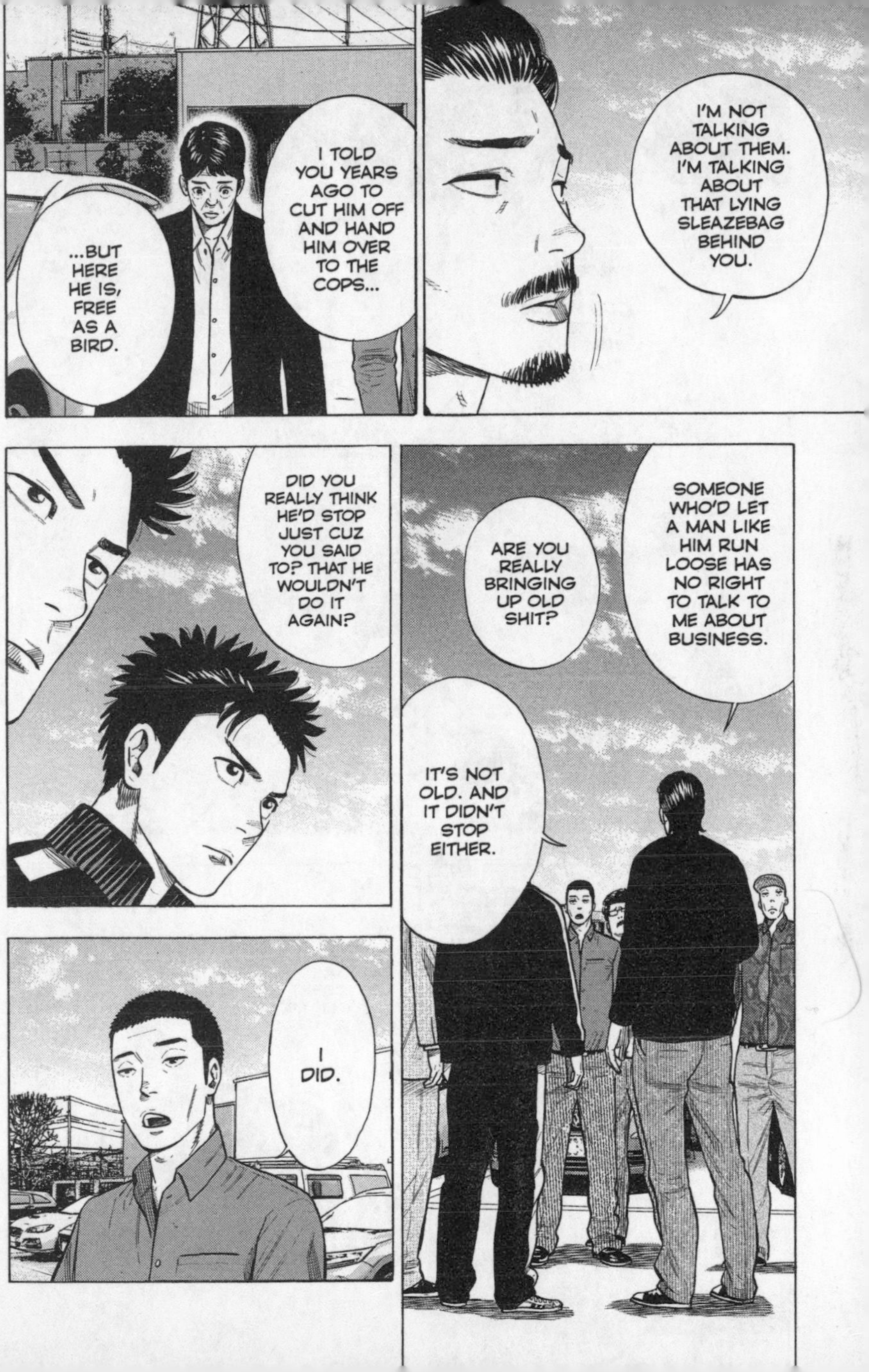
I'M NOT TALKING ABOUT THEM. I'M TALKING ABOUT THAT LYING SLEAZEBAG BEHIND YOU.
I TOLD YOU YEARS AGO TO CUT HIM OFF AND HAND HIM OVER TO THE COPS...
...BUT HERE HE IS, FREE AS A BIRD.
SOMEONE WHO'D LET A MAN LIKE HIM RUN LOOSE HAS NO RIGHT TO TALK TO ME ABOUT BUSINESS.
ARE YOU REALLY BRINGING UP OLD SHIT?
IT'S NOT OLD. AND IT DIDN'T STOP EITHER.
DID YOU REALLY THINK HE'D STOP JUST CUZ YOU SAID TO? THAT HE WOULDN'T DO IT AGAIN?
I DID.

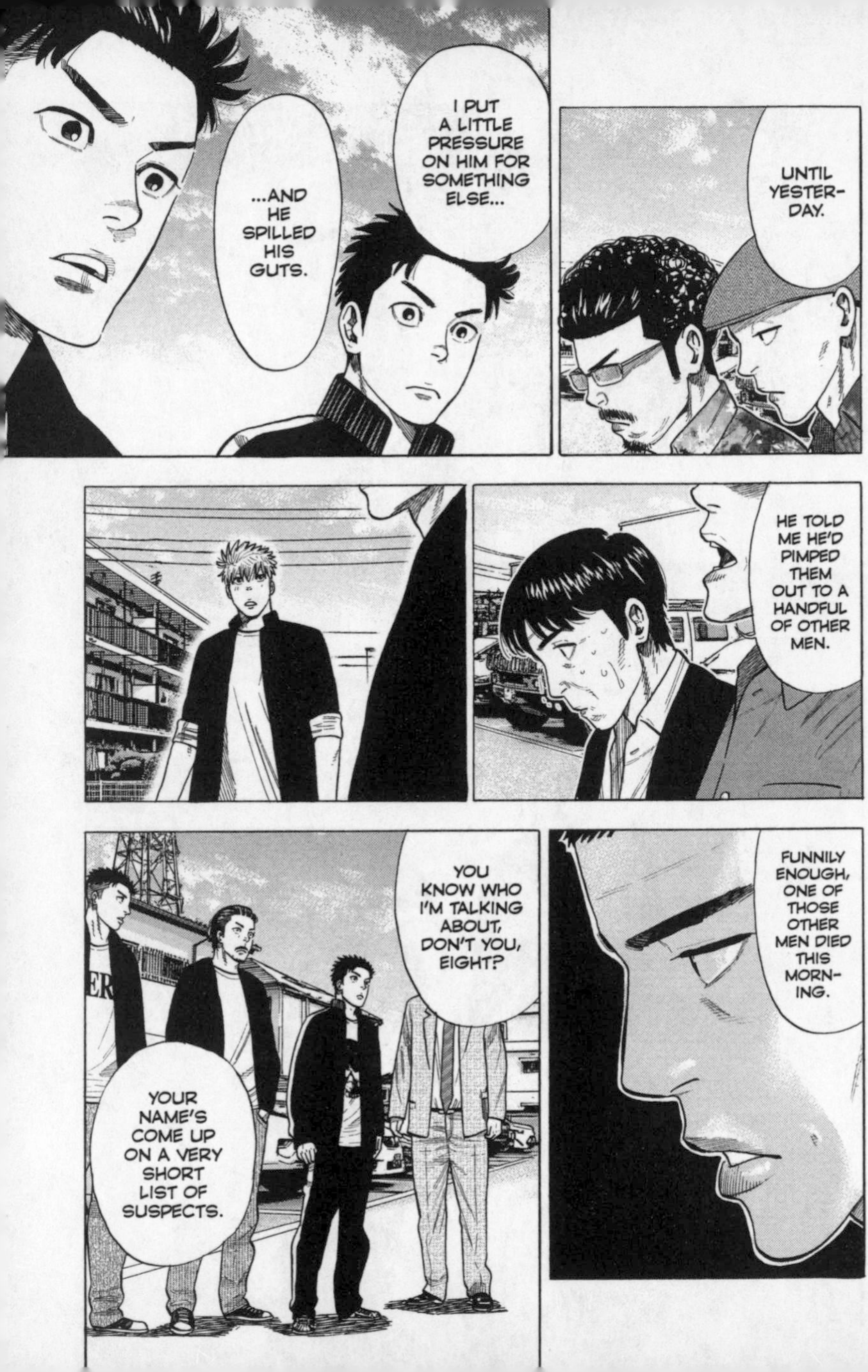
UNTIL YESTER-DAY.
I PUT A LITTLE PRESSURE ON HIM FOR SOMETHING ELSE...
...AND HE SPILLED HIS GUTS.
HE TOLD ME HE'D PIMPED THEM OUT TO A HANDFUL OF OTHER MEN.
FUNNILY ENOUGH, ONE OF THOSE OTHER MEN DIED THIS MORNING.
YOU KNOW WHO I'M TALKING ABOUT, DON'T YOU, EIGHT?
YOUR NAME'S COME UP ON A VERY SHORT LIST OF SUSPECTS.

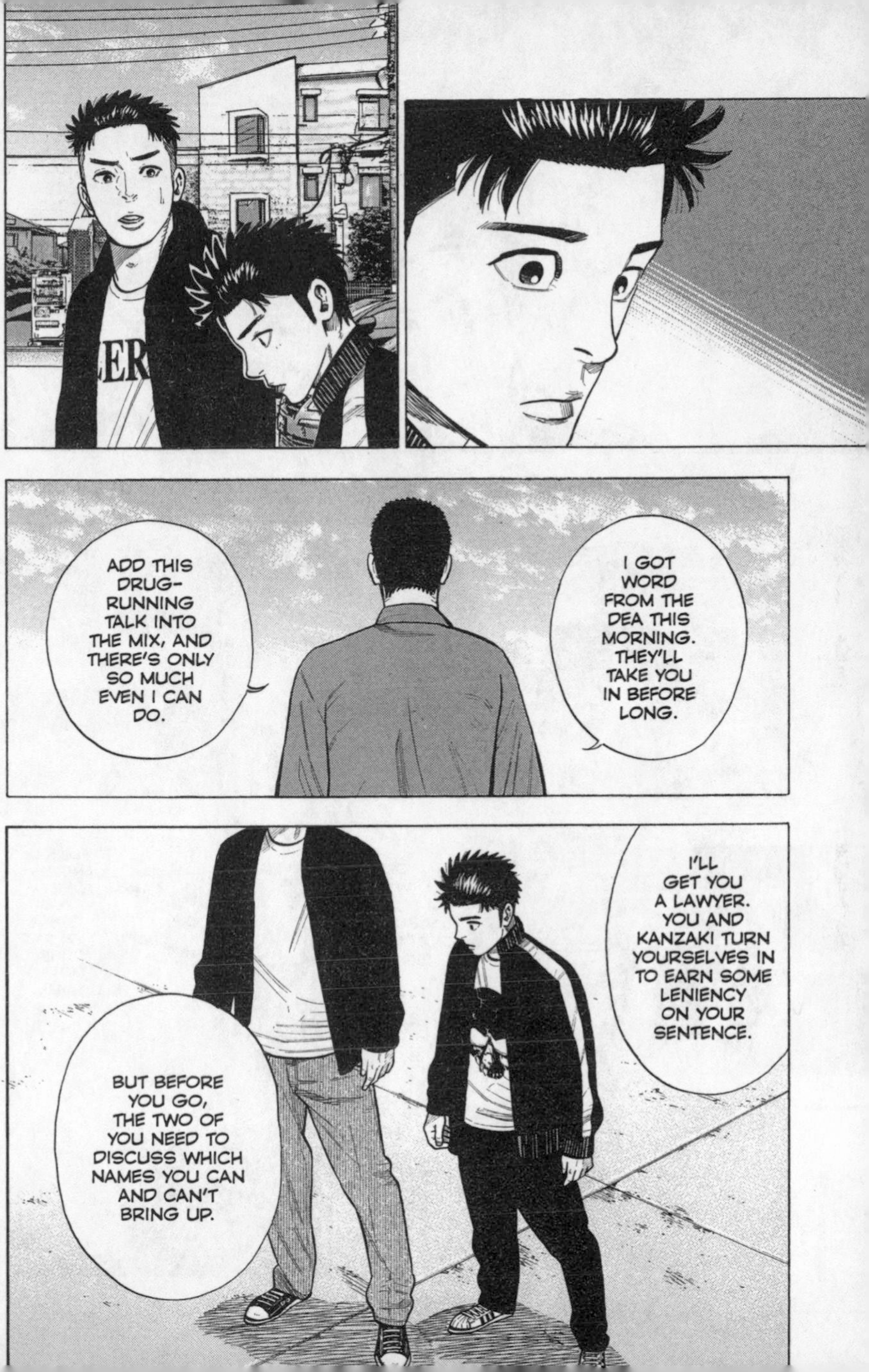
I GOT WORD FROM THE DEA THIS MORNING. THEY'LL TAKE YOU IN BEFORE LONG.
ADD THIS DRUG-RUNNING TALK INTO THE MIX, AND THERE'S ONLY SO MUCH EVEN I CAN DO.
I'LL GET YOU A LAWYER. YOU AND KANZAKI TURN YOURSELVES IN TO EARN SOME LENIENCY ON YOUR SENTENCE.
BUT BEFORE YOU GO, THE TWO OF YOU NEED TO DISCUSS WHICH NAMES YOU CAN AND CAN'T BRING UP.

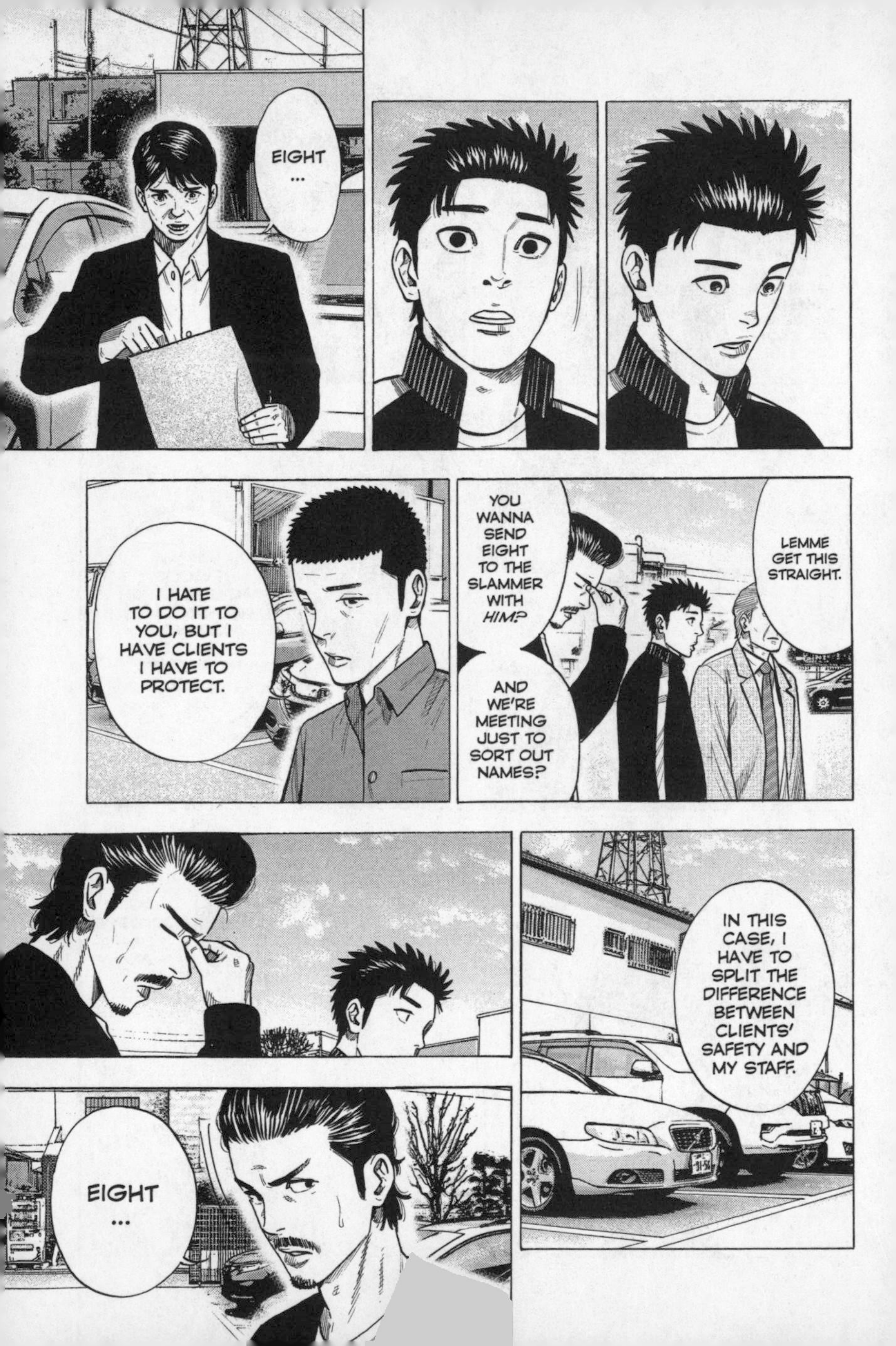
EIGHT ...
LEMME GET THIS STRAIGHT.
YOU WANNA SEND EIGHT TO THE SLAMMER WITH *HIM*?
AND WE'RE MEETING JUST TO SORT OUT NAMES?
I HATE TO DO IT TO YOU, BUT I HAVE CLIENTS I HAVE TO PROTECT.
IN THIS CASE, I HAVE TO SPLIT THE DIFFERENCE BETWEEN CLIENTS' SAFETY AND MY STAFF.
EIGHT ...

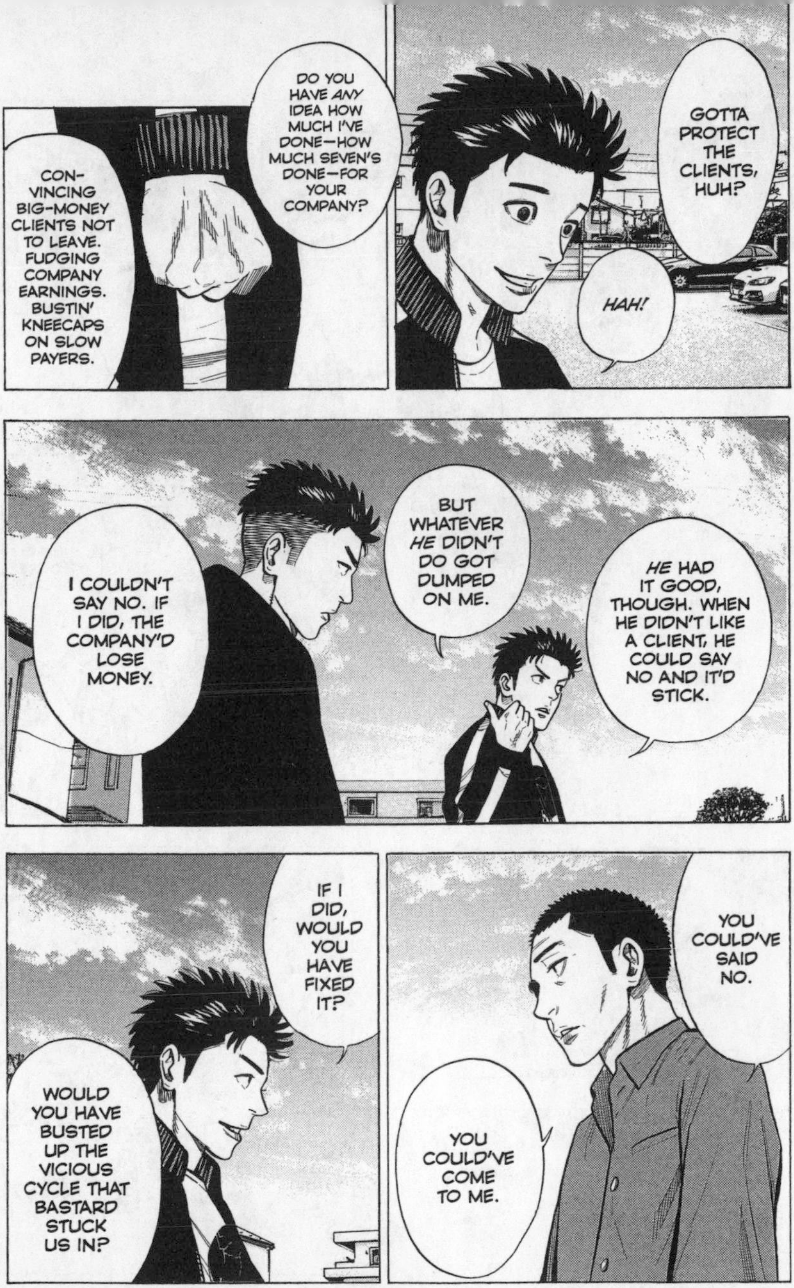
GOTTA PROTECT THE CLIENTS, HUH?
HAH!
DO YOU HAVE *ANY* IDEA HOW MUCH I'VE DONE—HOW MUCH SEVEN'S DONE—FOR YOUR COMPANY?
CON-VINCING BIG-MONEY CLIENTS NOT TO LEAVE. FUDGING COMPANY EARNINGS. BUSTIN' KNEECAPS ON SLOW PAYERS.
HE HAD IT GOOD, THOUGH. WHEN HE DIDN'T LIKE A CLIENT, HE COULD SAY NO AND IT'D STICK.
BUT WHATEVER *HE* DIDN'T DO GOT DUMPED ON ME.
I COULDN'T SAY NO. IF I DID, THE COMPANY'D LOSE MONEY.
YOU COULD'VE SAID NO.
YOU COULD'VE COME TO ME.
IF I DID, WOULD YOU HAVE FIXED IT?
WOULD YOU HAVE BUSTED UP THE VICIOUS CYCLE THAT BASTARD STUCK US IN?

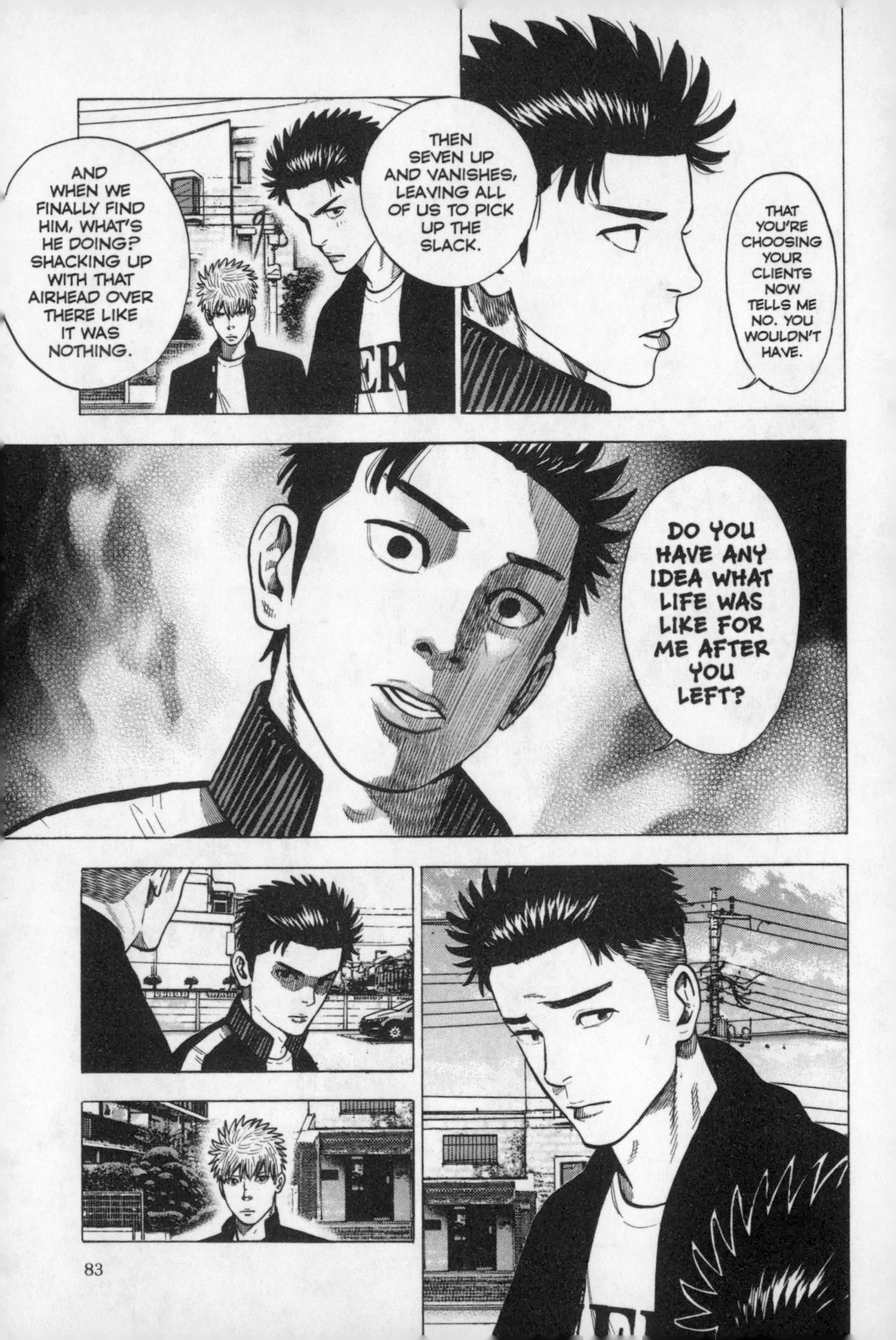
THAT YOU'RE CHOOSING YOUR CLIENTS NOW TELLS ME NO. YOU WOULDN'T HAVE.
THEN SEVEN UP AND VANISHES, LEAVING ALL OF US TO PICK UP THE SLACK.
AND WHEN WE FINALLY FIND HIM, WHAT'S HE DOING? SHACKING UP WITH THAT AIRHEAD OVER THERE LIKE IT WAS NOTHING.
DO YOU HAVE ANY IDEA WHAT LIFE WAS LIKE FOR ME AFTER YOU LEFT?

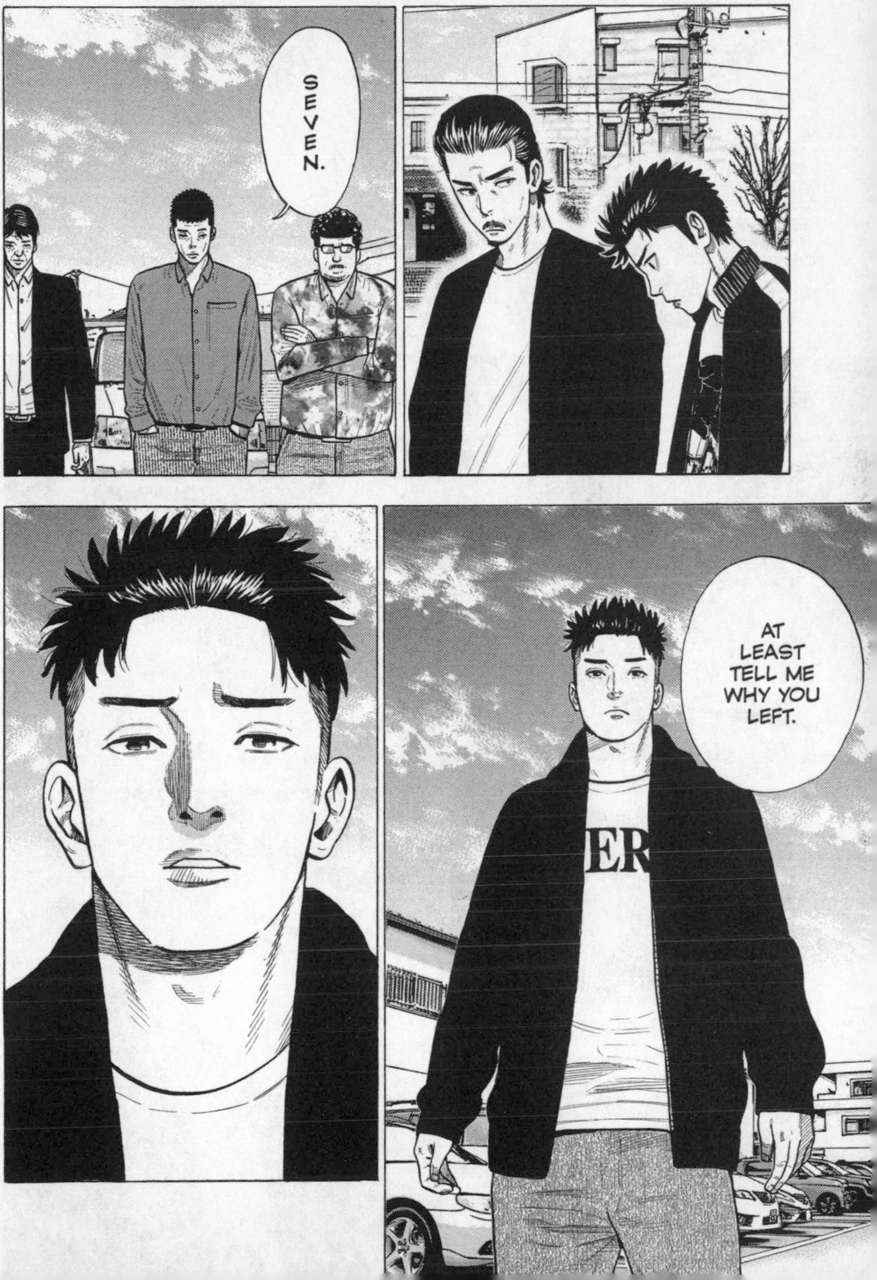
SEVEN.
AT LEAST TELL ME WHY YOU LEFT.

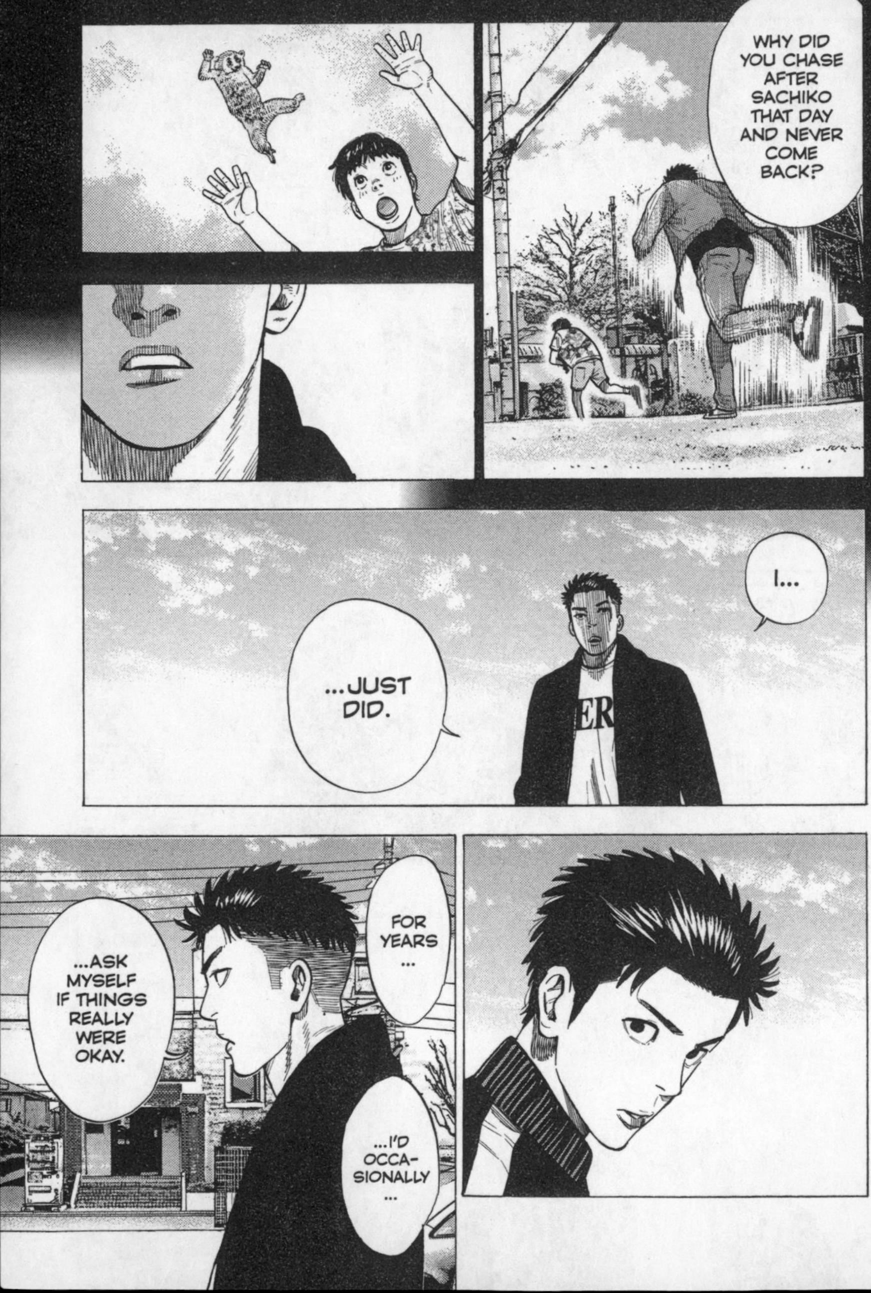
WHY DID YOU CHASE AFTER SACHIKO THAT DAY AND NEVER COME BACK?
I...
...JUST DID.
FOR YEARS...
...I'D OCCASIONALLY...
...ASK MYSELF IF THINGS REALLY WERE OKAY.

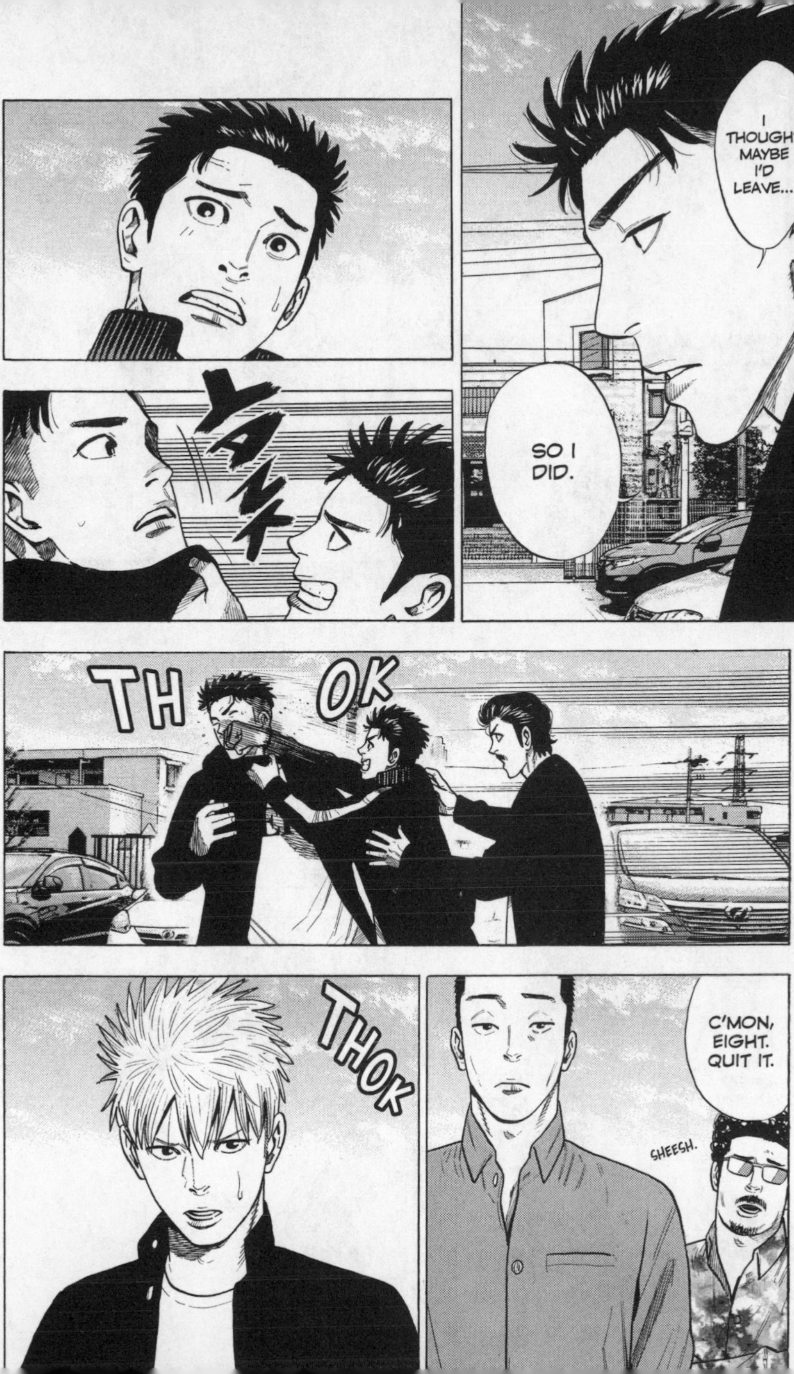
I THOUGHT MAYBE I'D LEAVE...
SO I DID.
YANK
TH OK
C'MON, EIGHT. QUIT IT.
SHEESH.
THOK

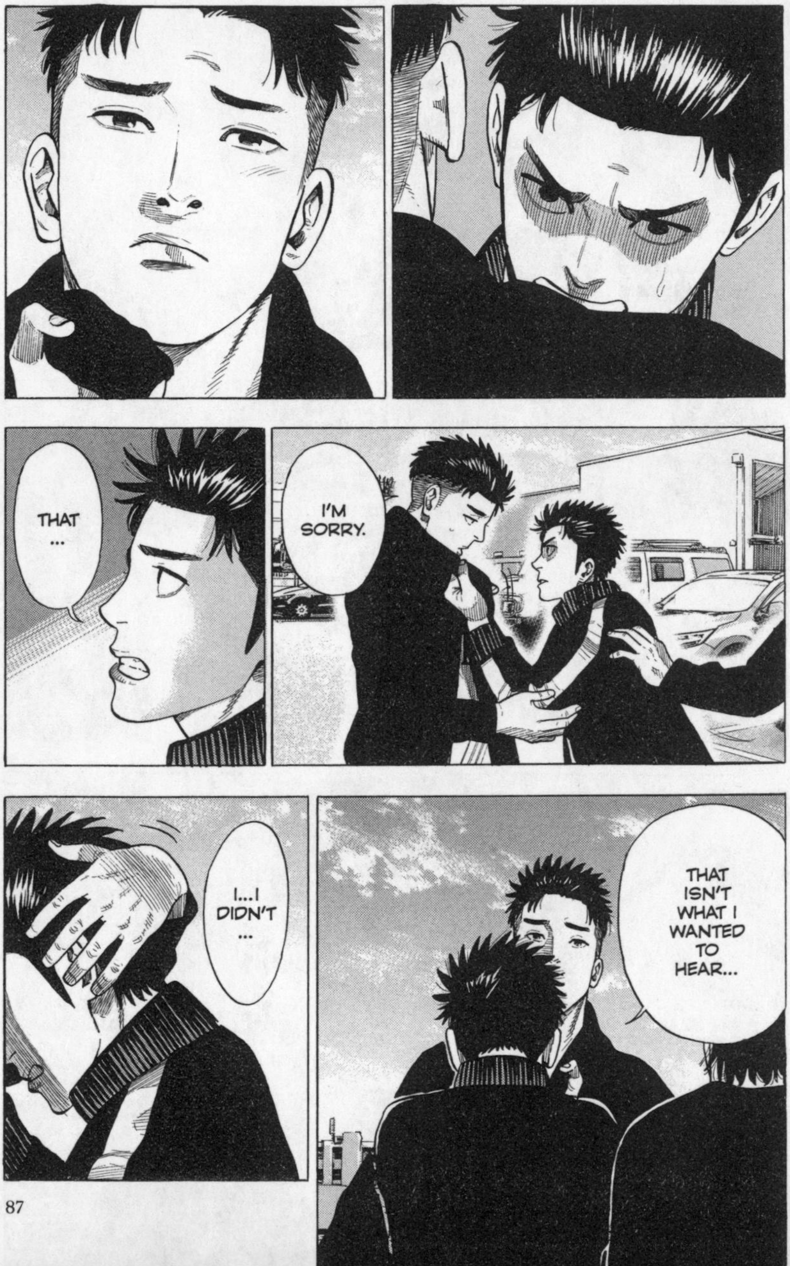
I'M SORRY.
THAT ...
THAT ISN'T WHAT I WANTED TO HEAR...
I...I DIDN'T ...

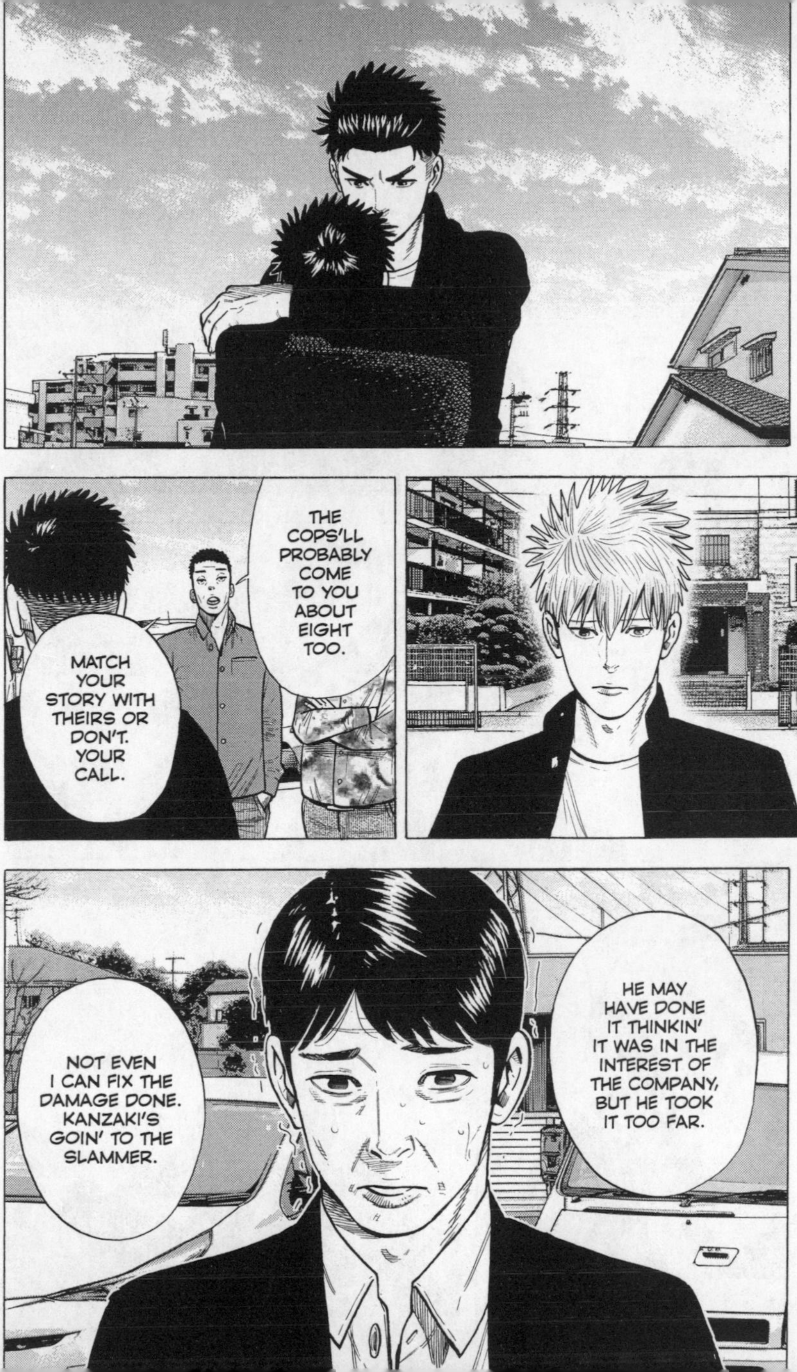
THE COPS'LL PROBABLY COME TO YOU ABOUT EIGHT TOO.
MATCH YOUR STORY WITH THEIRS OR DON'T. YOUR CALL.
HE MAY HAVE DONE IT THINKIN' IT WAS IN THE INTEREST OF THE COMPANY, BUT HE TOOK IT TOO FAR.
NOT EVEN I CAN FIX THE DAMAGE DONE. KANZAKI'S GOIN' TO THE SLAMMER.

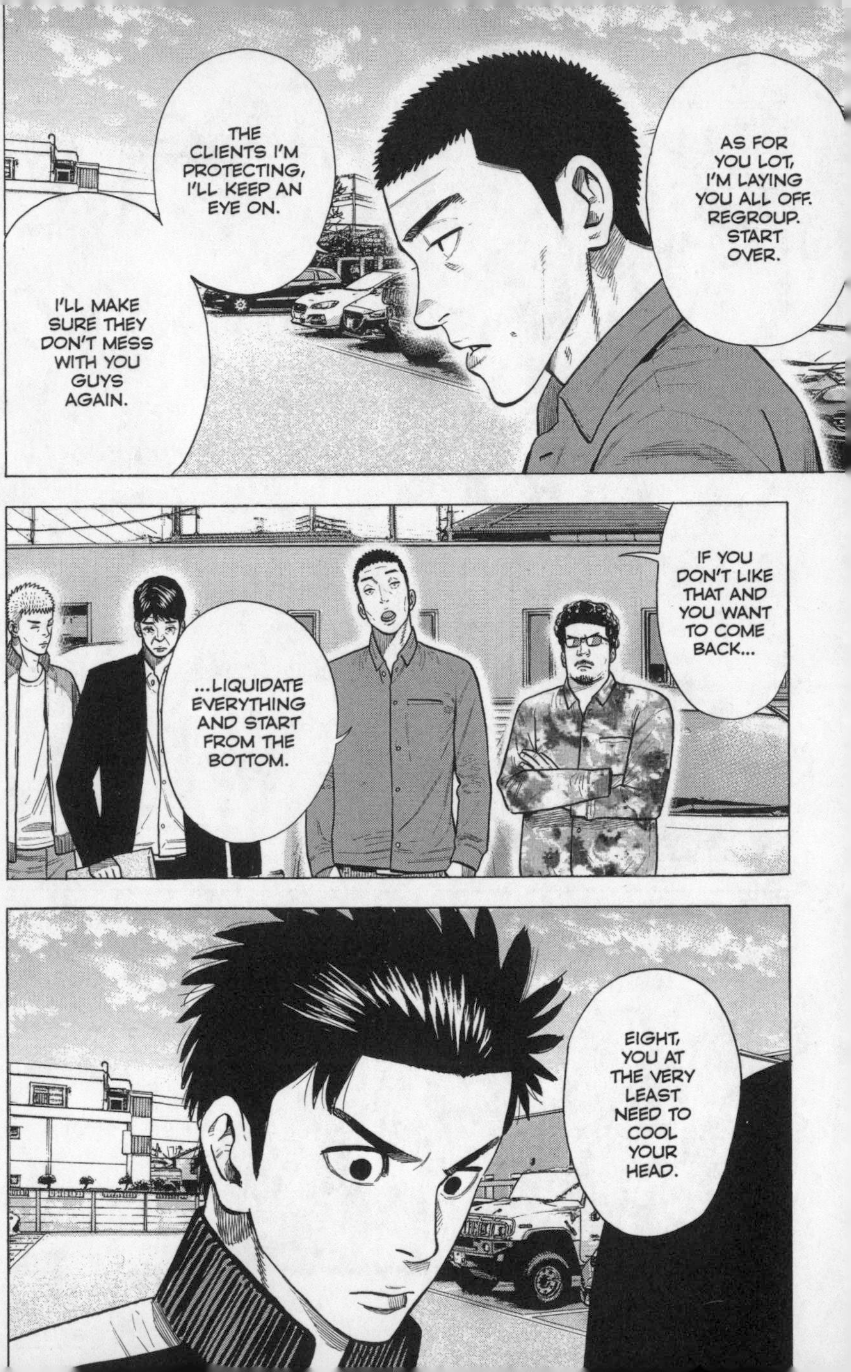
AS FOR YOU LOT, I'M LAYING YOU ALL OFF. REGROUP. START OVER.
THE CLIENTS I'M PROTECTING, I'LL KEEP AN EYE ON.
I'LL MAKE SURE THEY DON'T MESS WITH YOU GUYS AGAIN.
IF YOU DON'T LIKE THAT AND YOU WANT TO COME BACK...
...LIQUIDATE EVERYTHING AND START FROM THE BOTTOM.
EIGHT, YOU AT THE VERY LEAST NEED TO COOL YOUR HEAD.

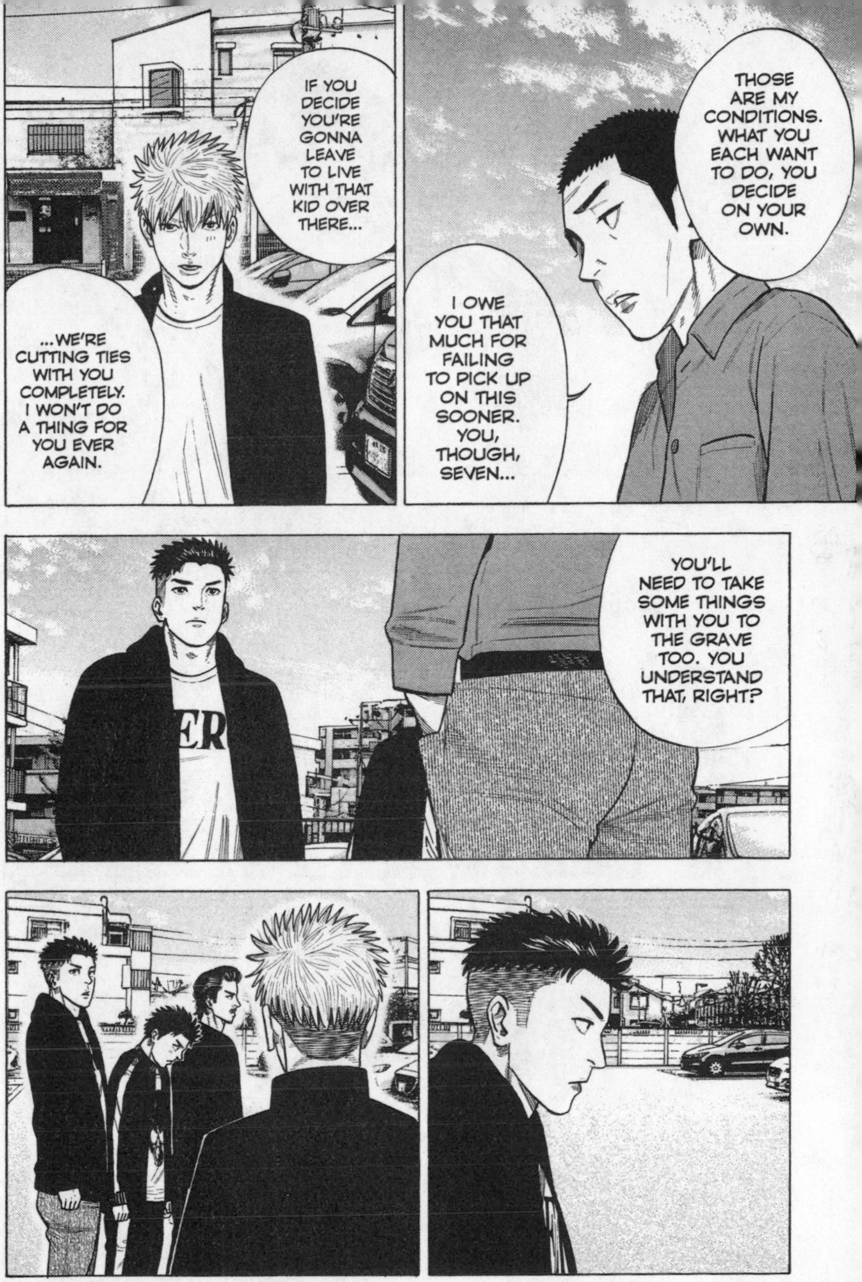
THOSE ARE MY CONDITIONS. WHAT YOU EACH WANT TO DO, YOU DECIDE ON YOUR OWN.
I OWE YOU THAT MUCH FOR FAILING TO PICK UP ON THIS SOONER. YOU, THOUGH, SEVEN...
IF YOU DECIDE YOU'RE GONNA LEAVE TO LIVE WITH THAT KID OVER THERE...
...WE'RE CUTTING TIES WITH YOU COMPLETELY. I WON'T DO A THING FOR YOU EVER AGAIN.
YOU'LL NEED TO TAKE SOME THINGS WITH YOU TO THE GRAVE TOO. YOU UNDERSTAND THAT, RIGHT?

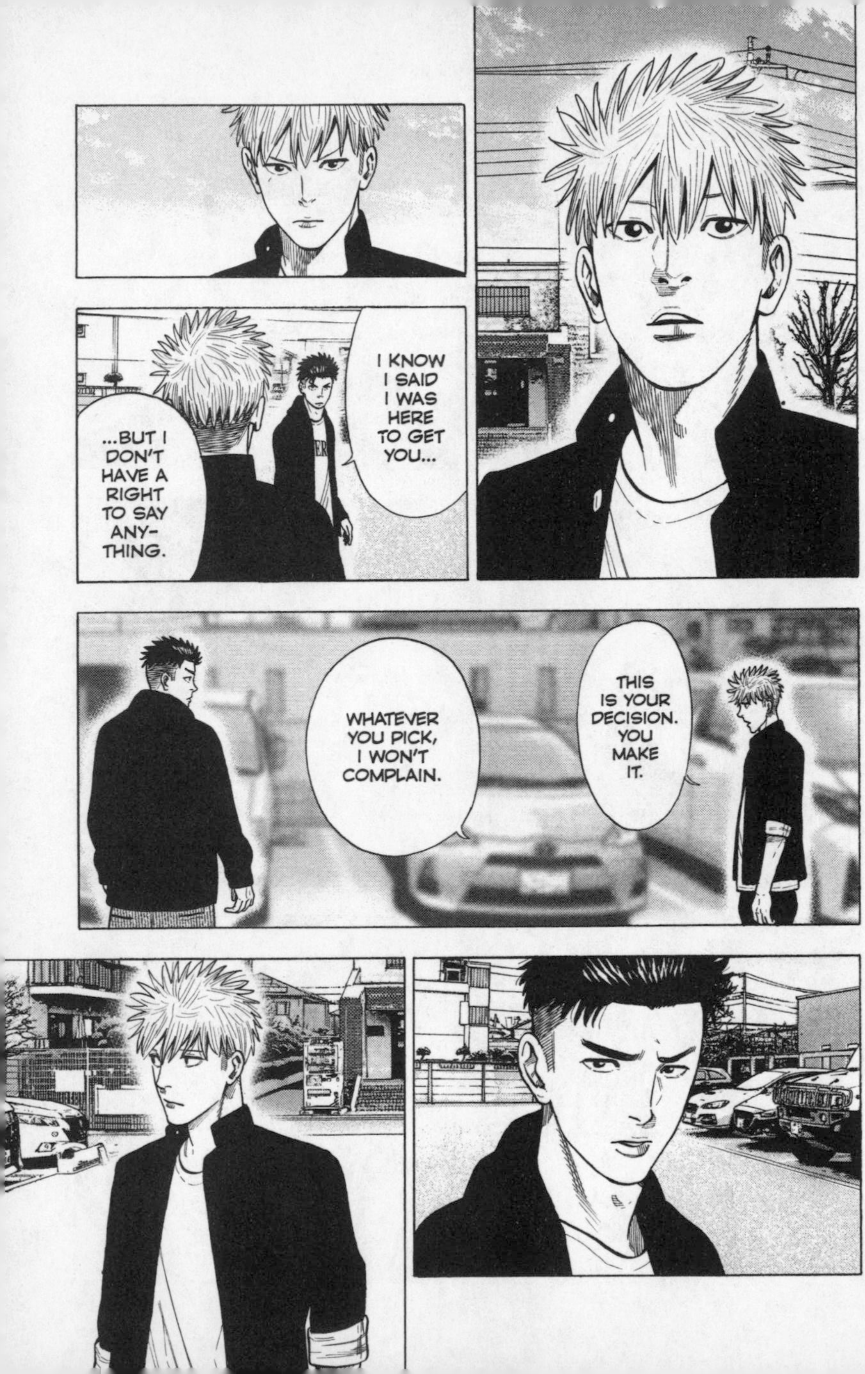
I KNOW I SAID I WAS HERE TO GET YOU...
...BUT I DON'T HAVE A RIGHT TO SAY ANY-THING.
THIS IS YOUR DECISION. YOU MAKE IT.
WHATEVER YOU PICK, I WON'T COMPLAIN.

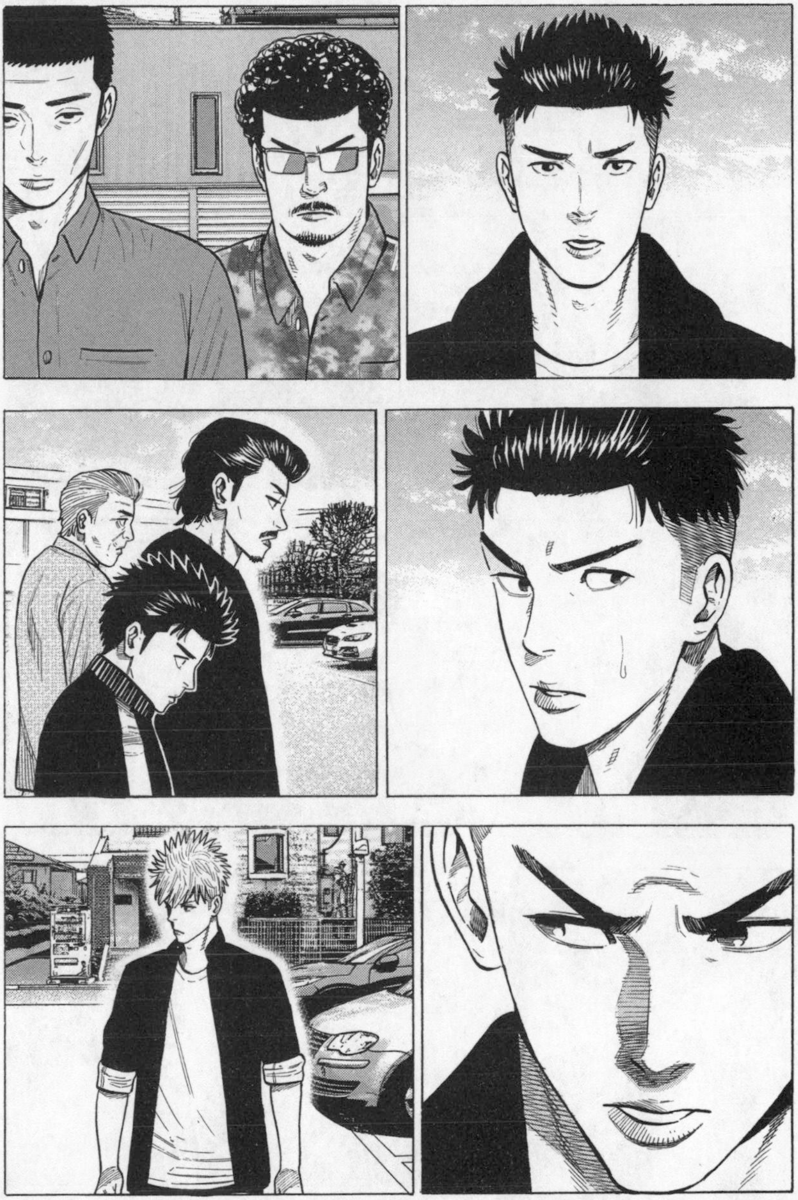

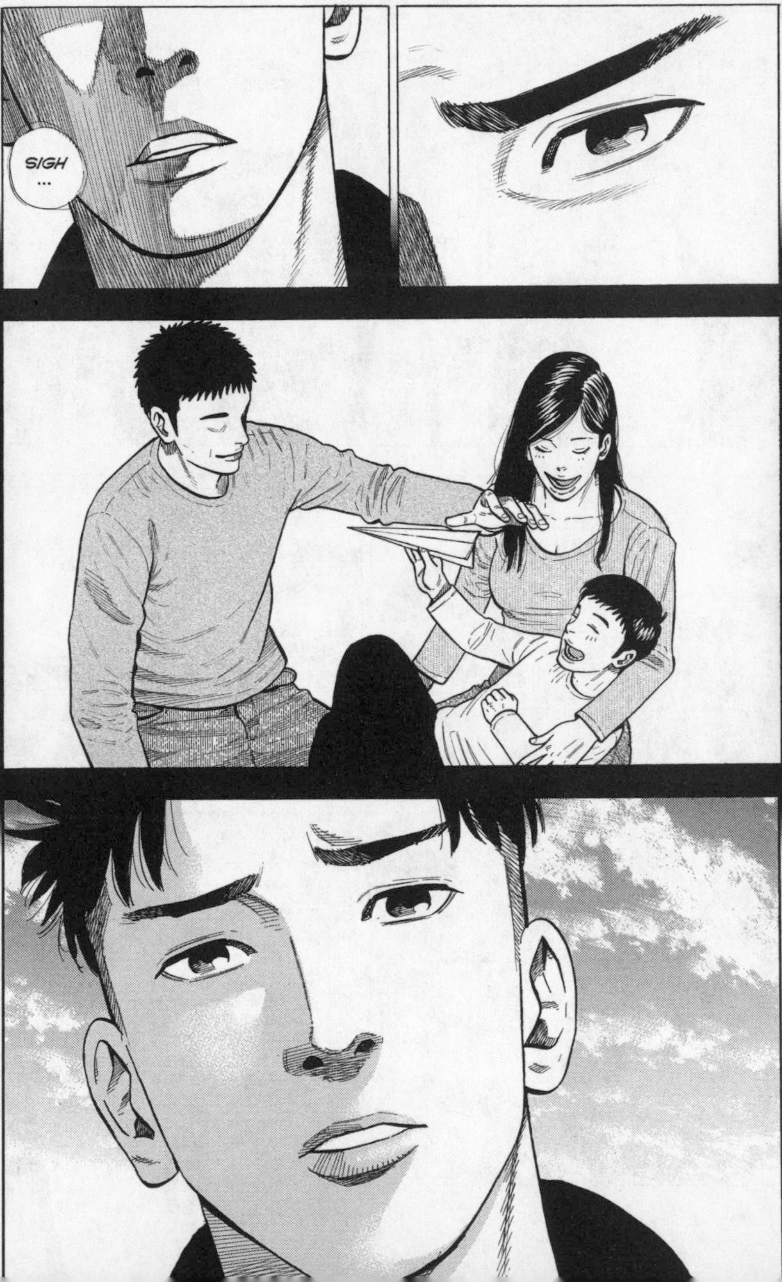
SIGH ...

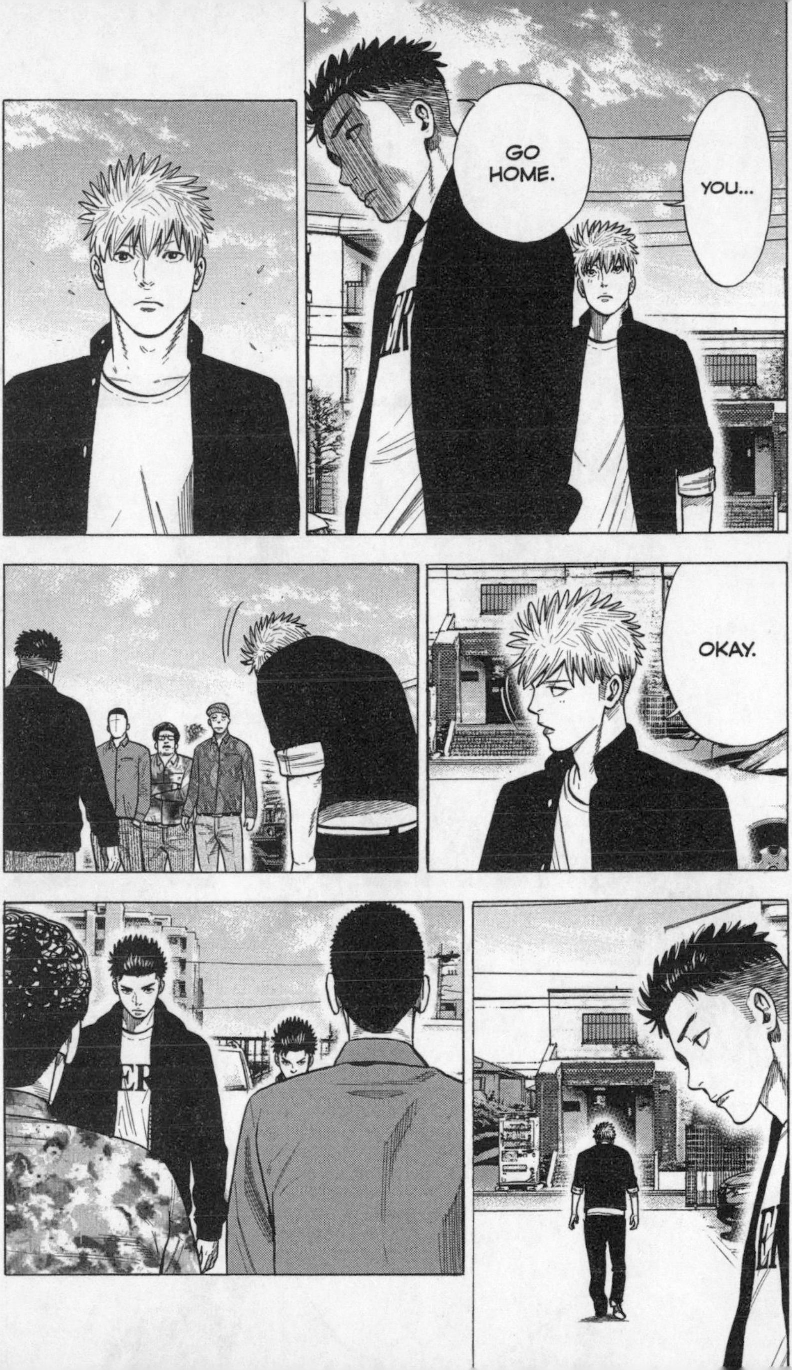
YOU...
GO HOME.
OKAY.

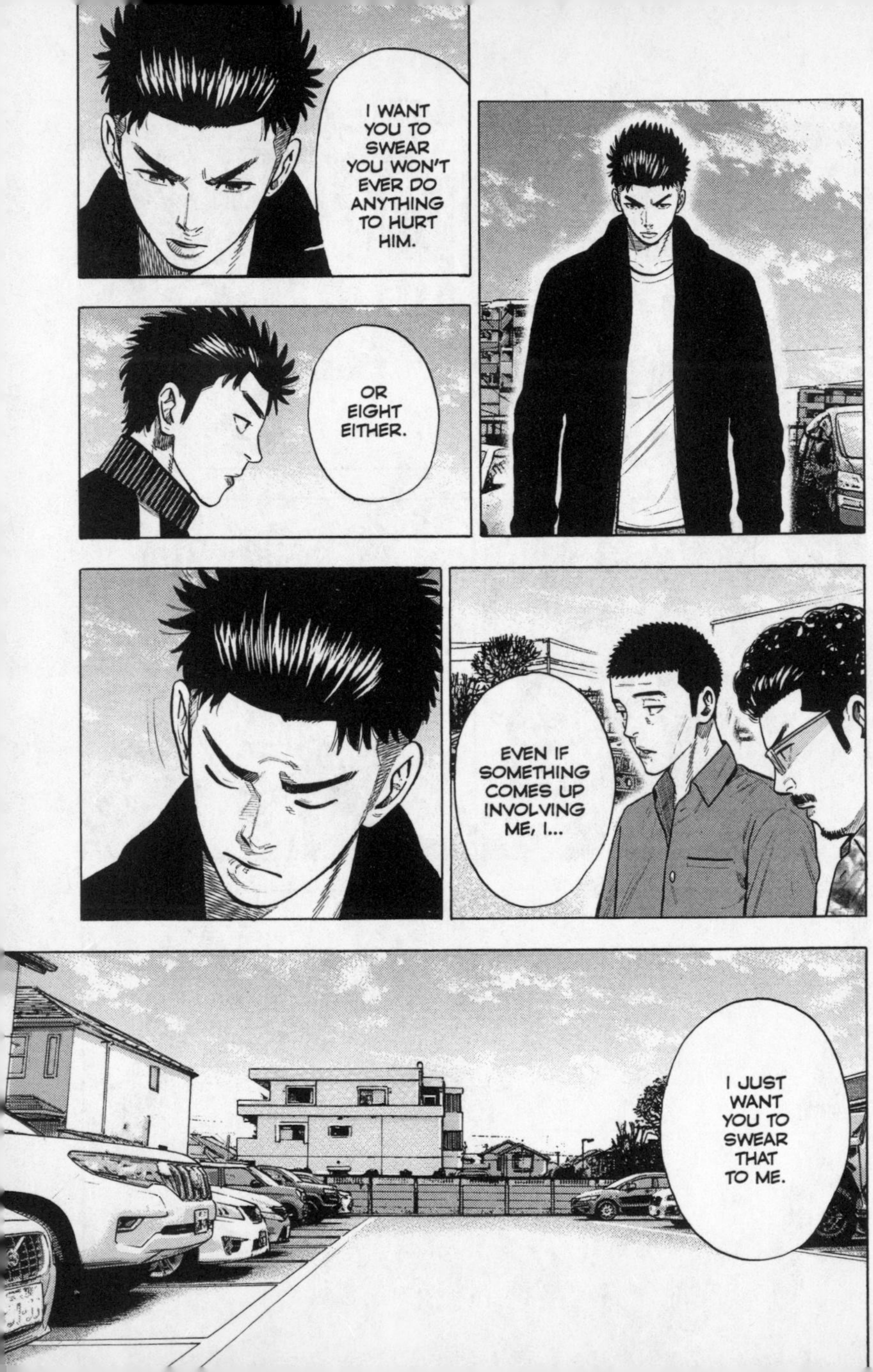
I WANT YOU TO SWEAR YOU WON'T EVER DO ANYTHING TO HURT HIM.
OR EIGHT EITHER.
EVEN IF SOMETHING COMES UP INVOLVING ME, I...
I JUST WANT YOU TO SWEAR THAT TO ME.

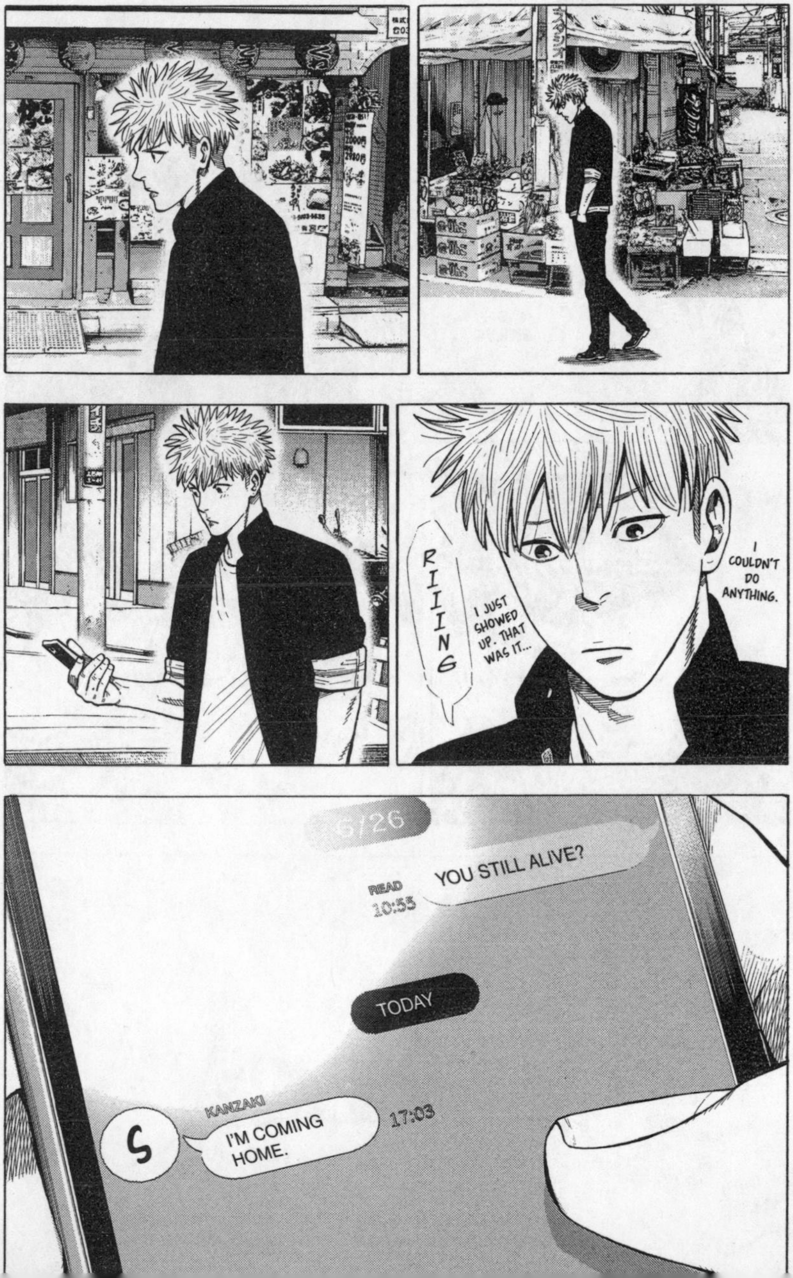
I COULDN'T DO ANYTHING.
I JUST SHOWED UP. THAT WAS IT...
RIIING
6/26
YOU STILL ALIVE?
READ 10:55
TODAY
KANZAKI
I'M COMING HOME.
17:03

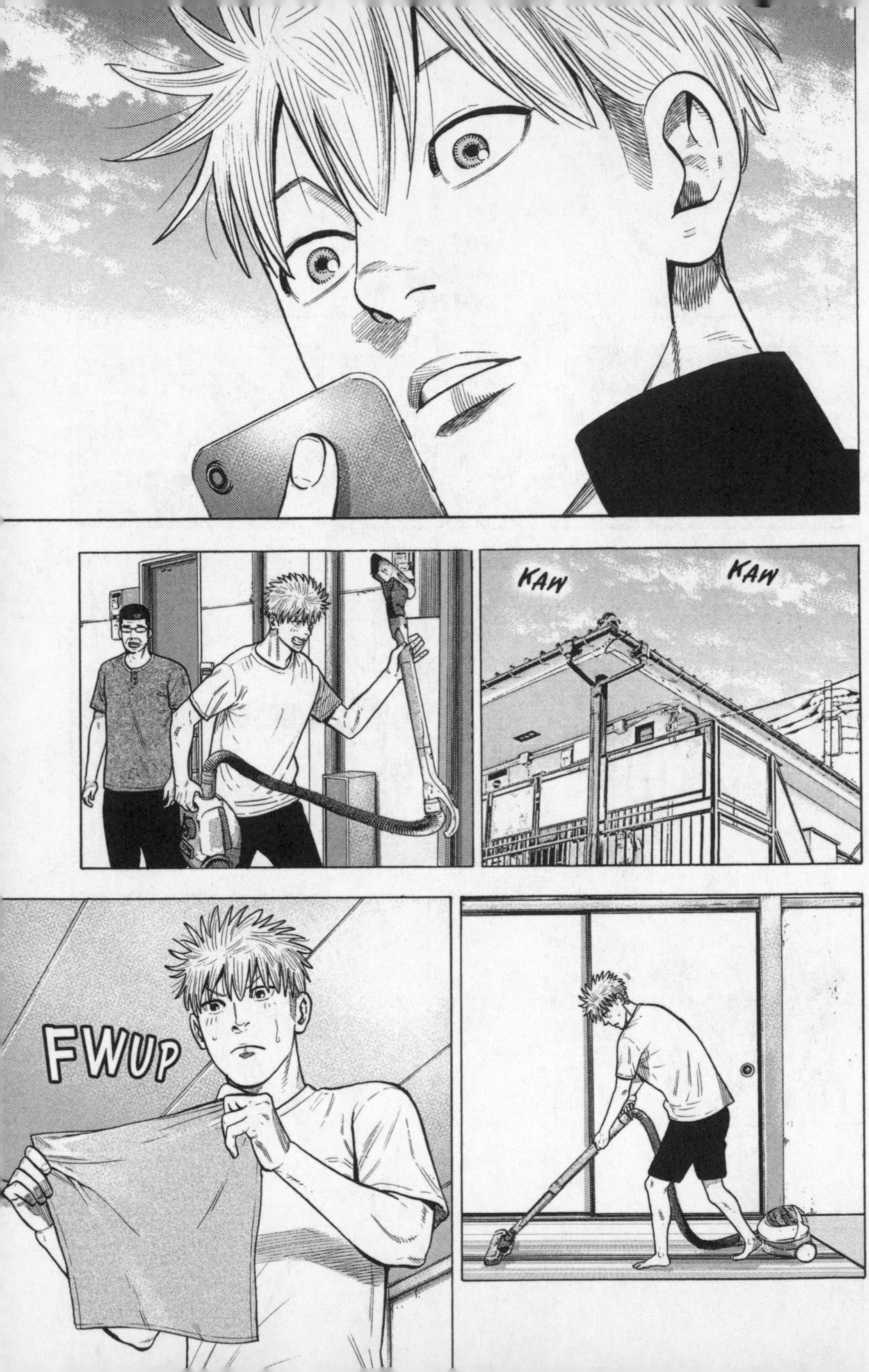
KAW
KAW
FWUP

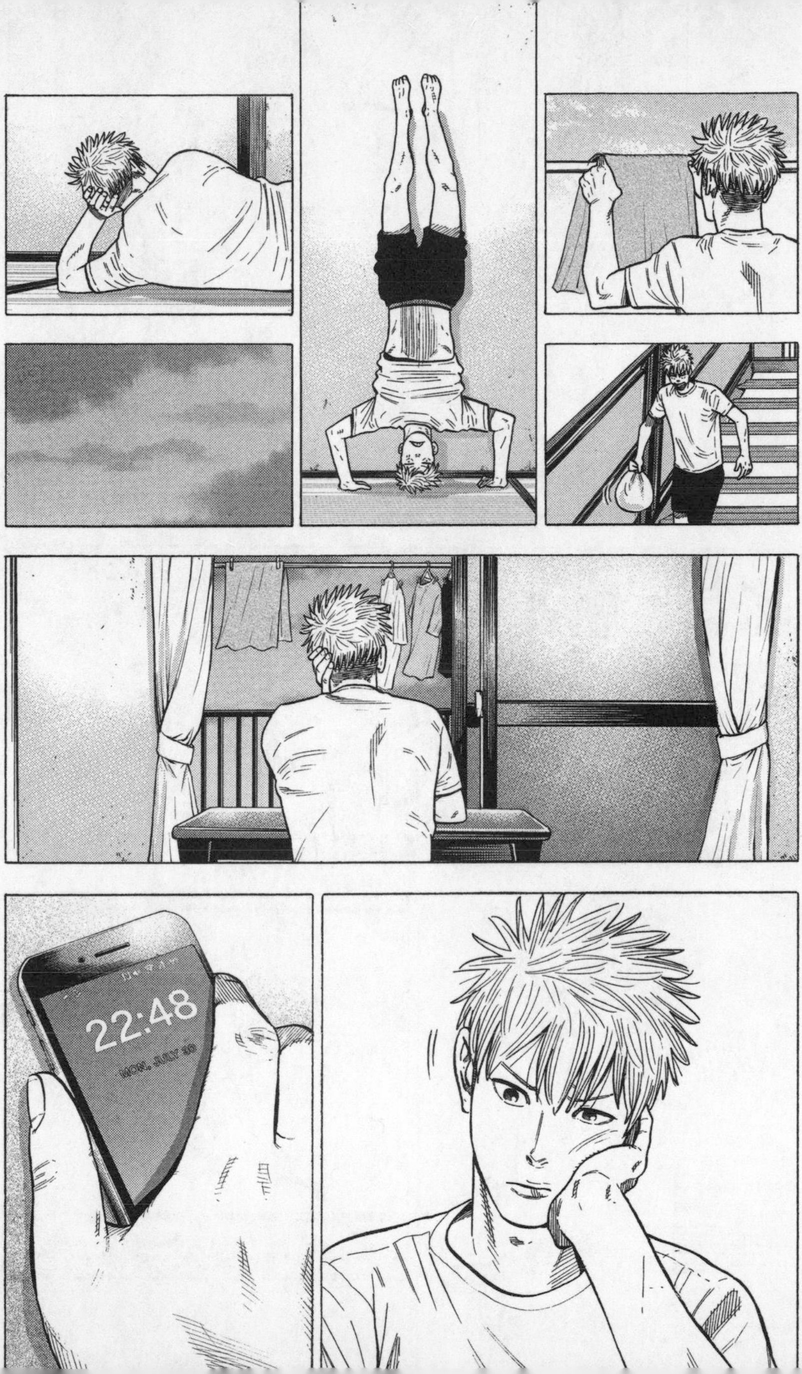
22:48
MON, JULY 30

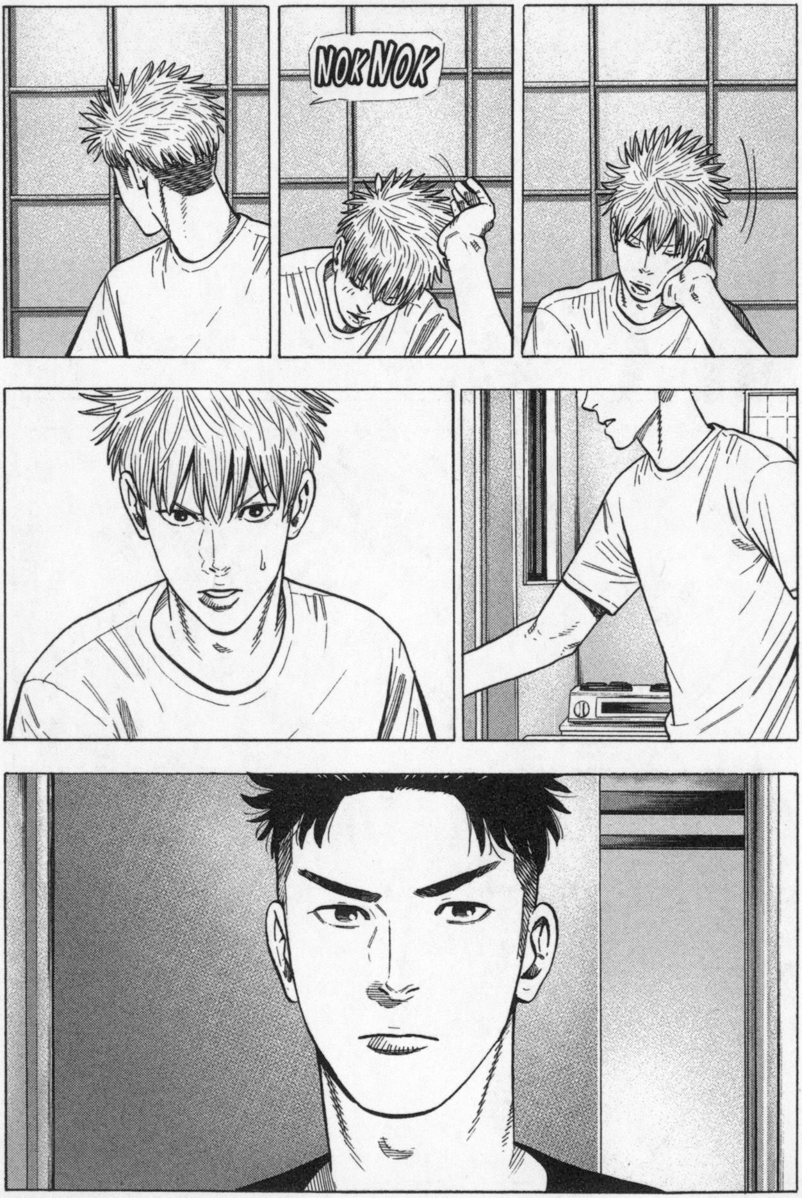
NOK NOK

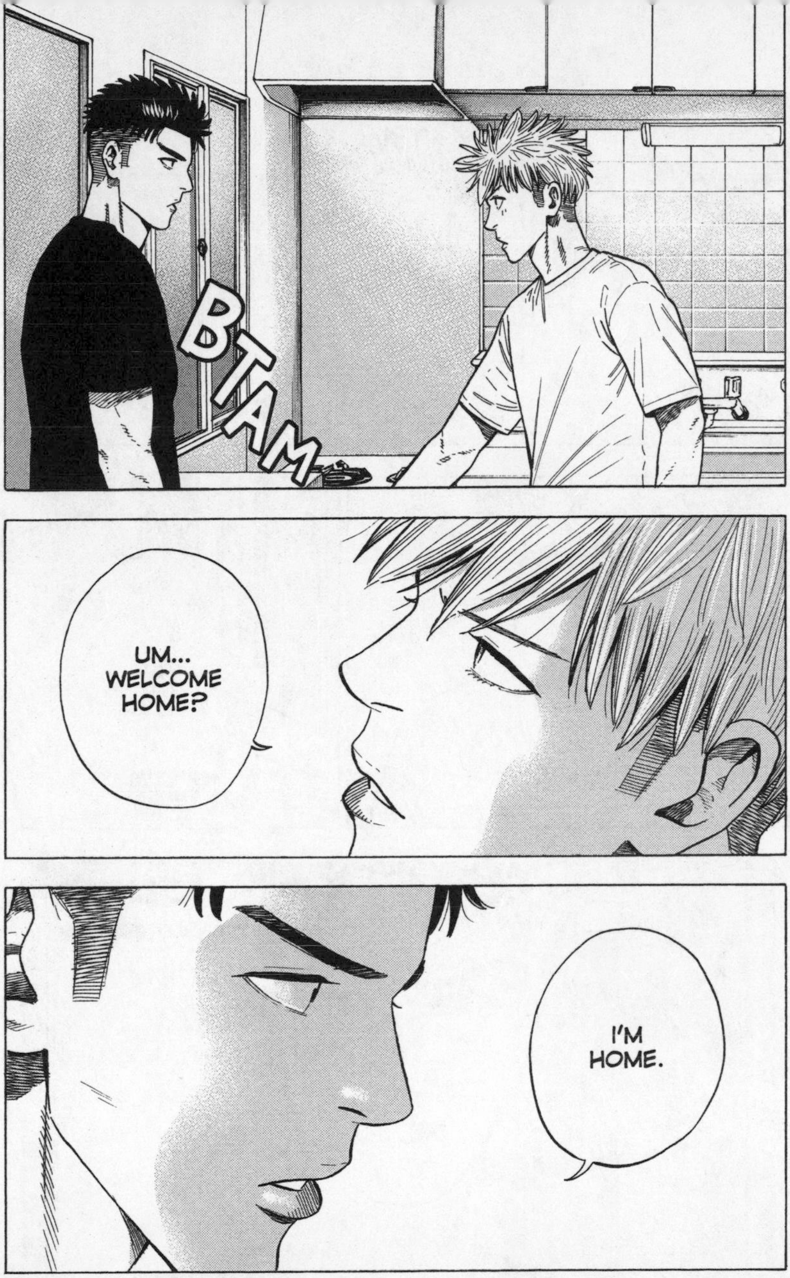
BTAM
UM... WELCOME HOME?
I'M HOME.

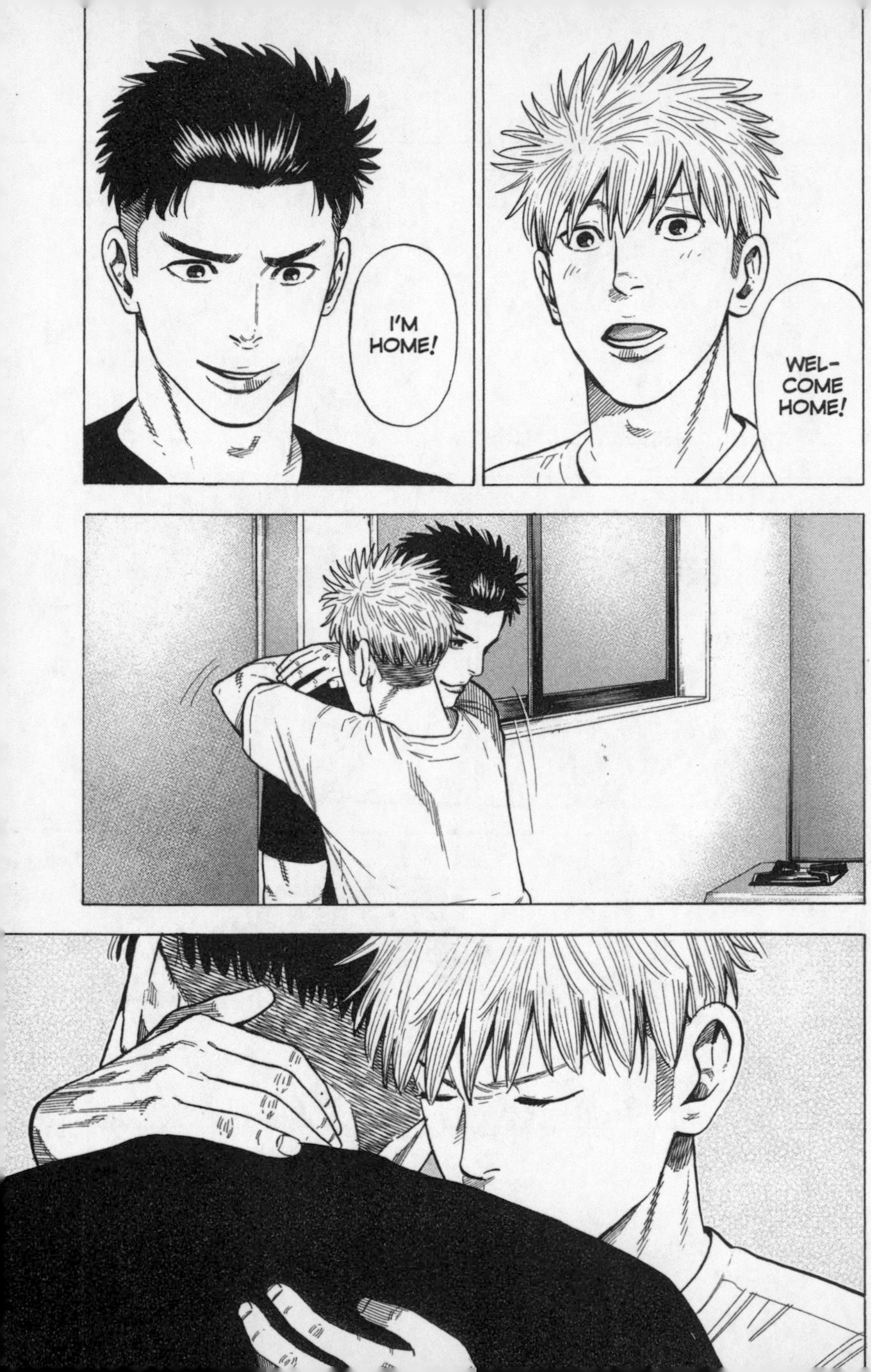
WEL-COME HOME!
I'M HOME!

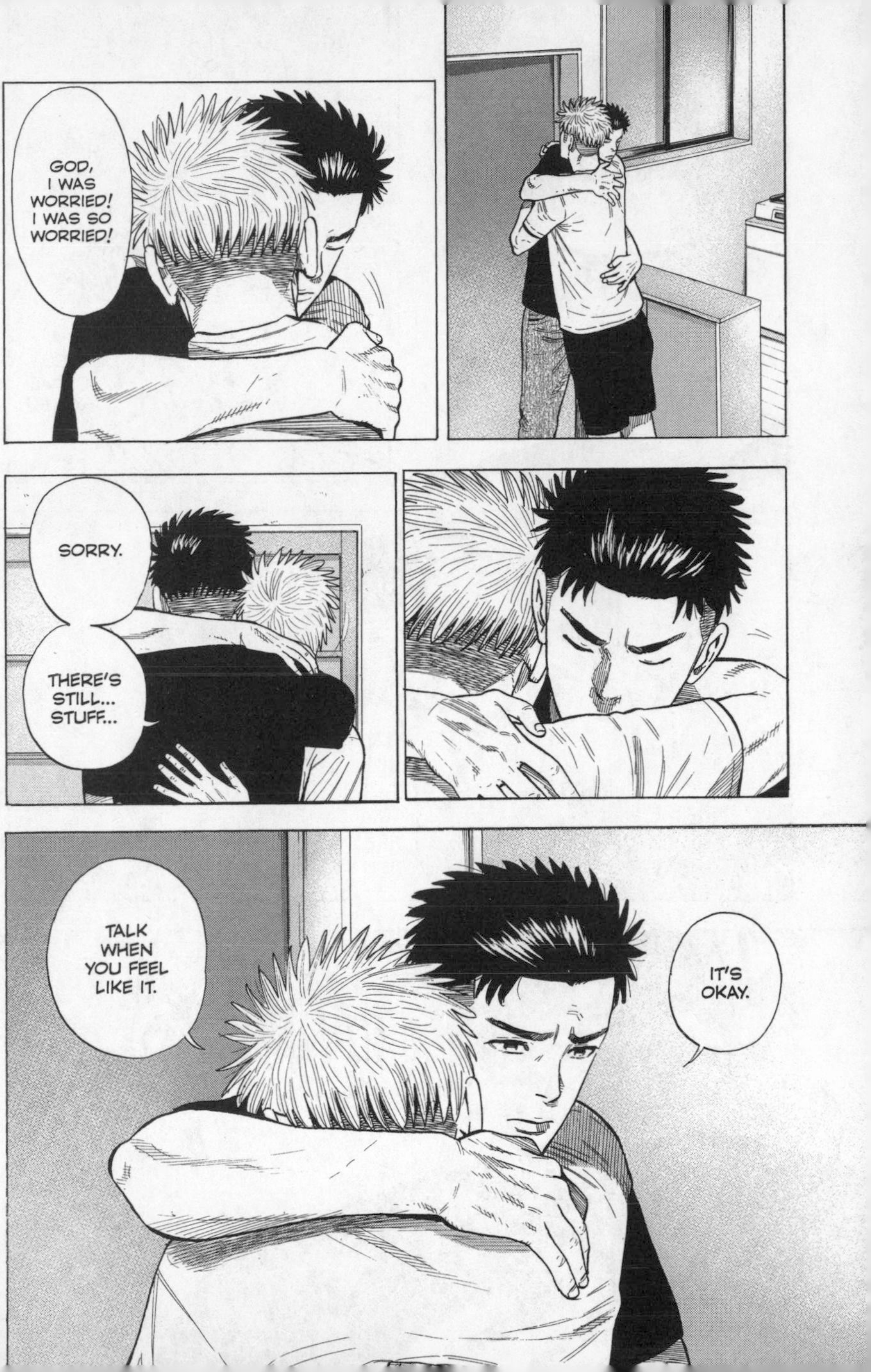
GOD, I WAS WORRIED! I WAS SO WORRIED!
SORRY.
THERE'S STILL... STUFF...
IT'S OKAY.
TALK WHEN YOU FEEL LIKE IT.

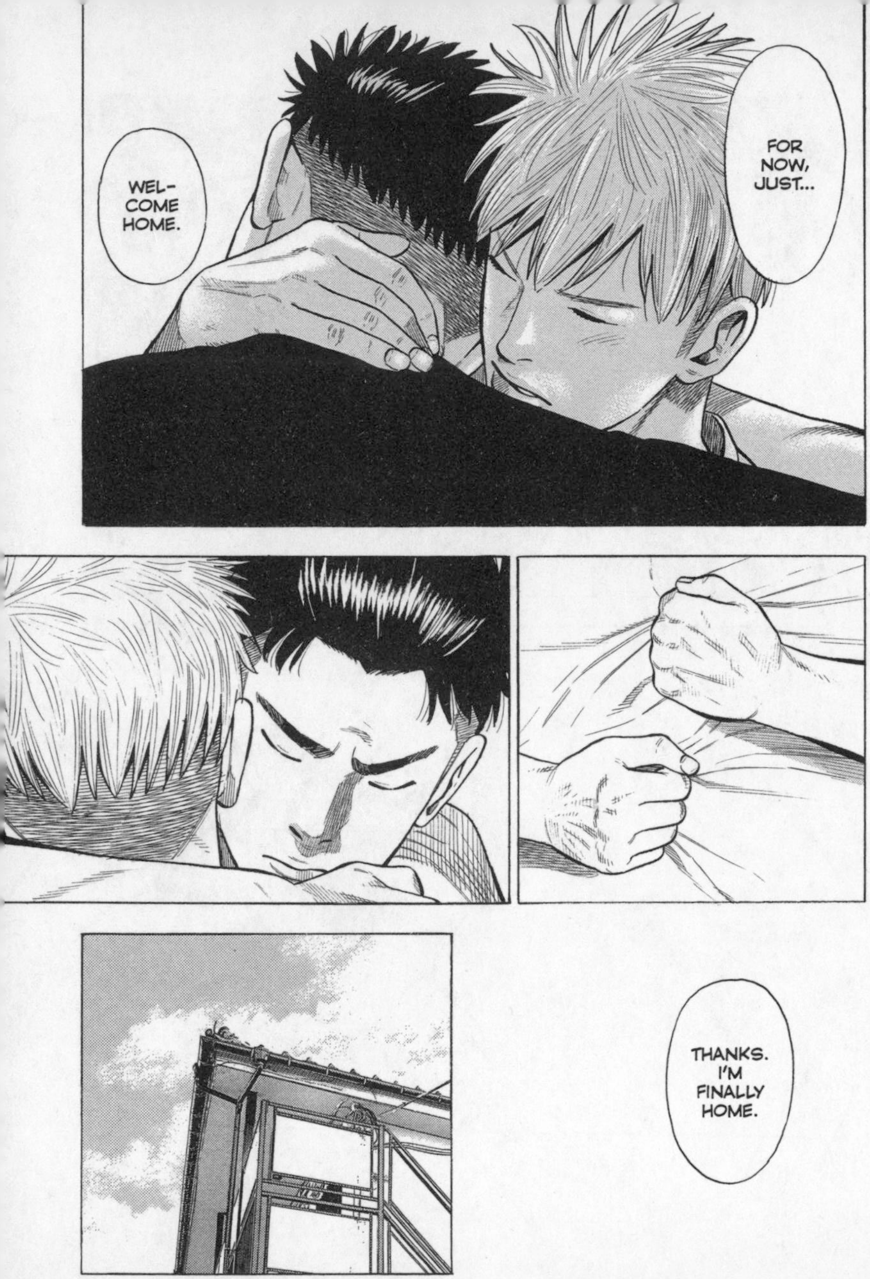
FOR NOW, JUST...
WEL-COME HOME.
THANKS. I'M FINALLY HOME.

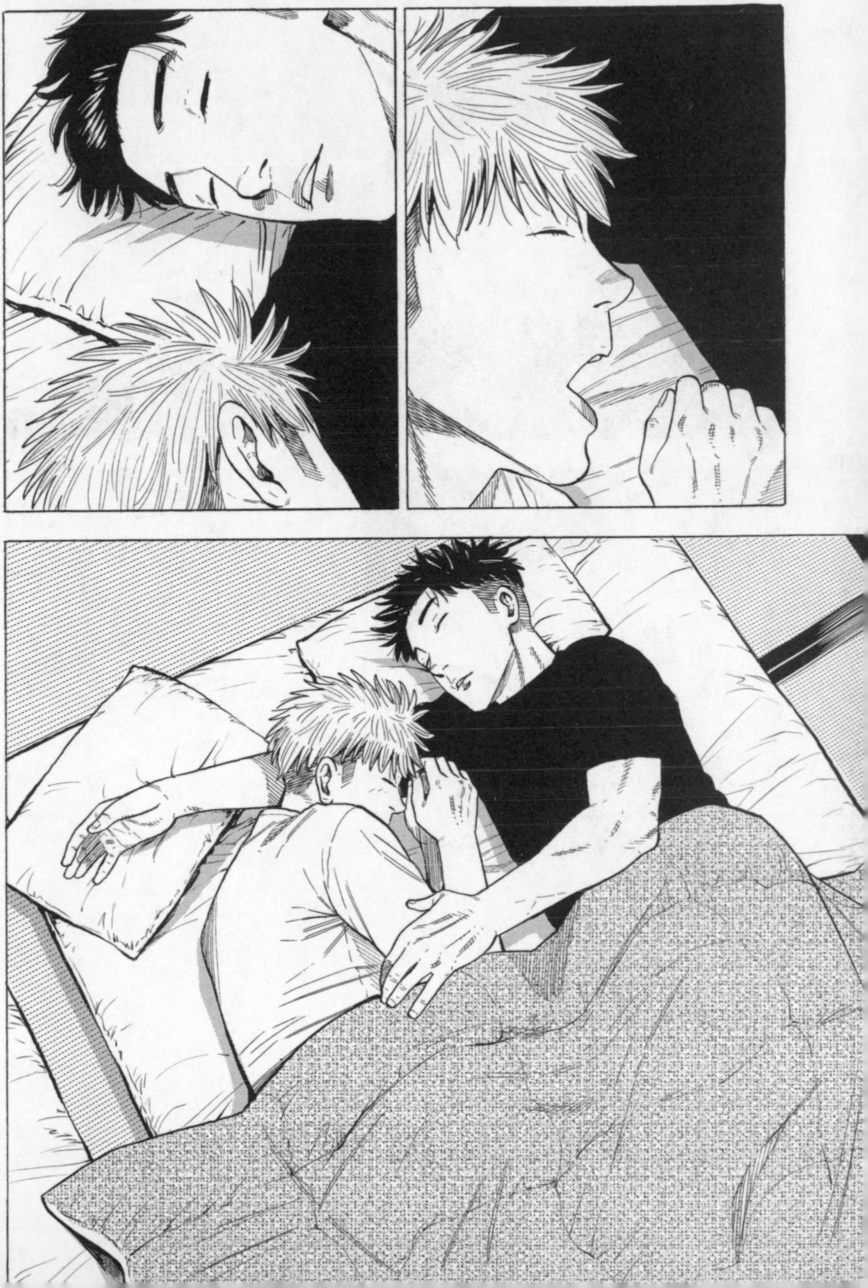

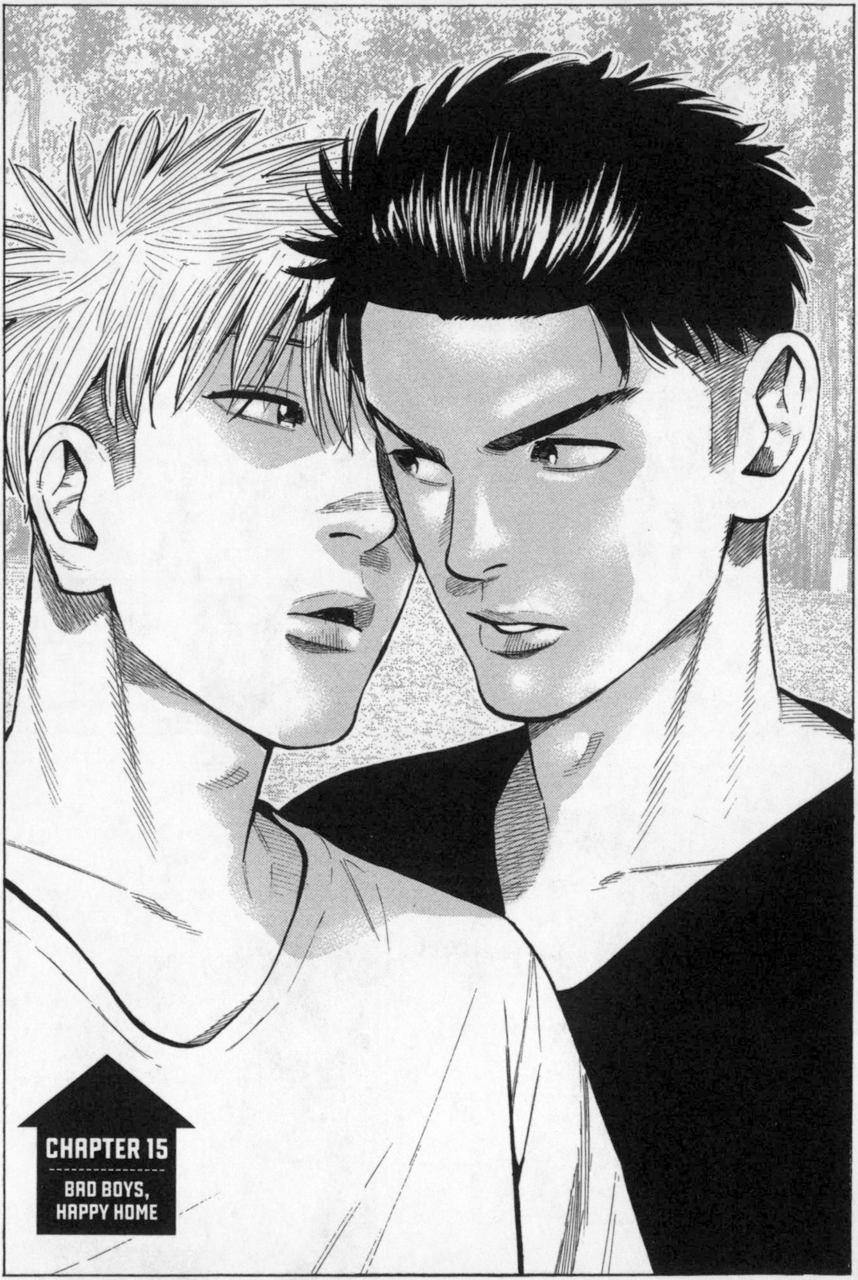
CHAPTER 15
BAD BOYS, HAPPY HOME

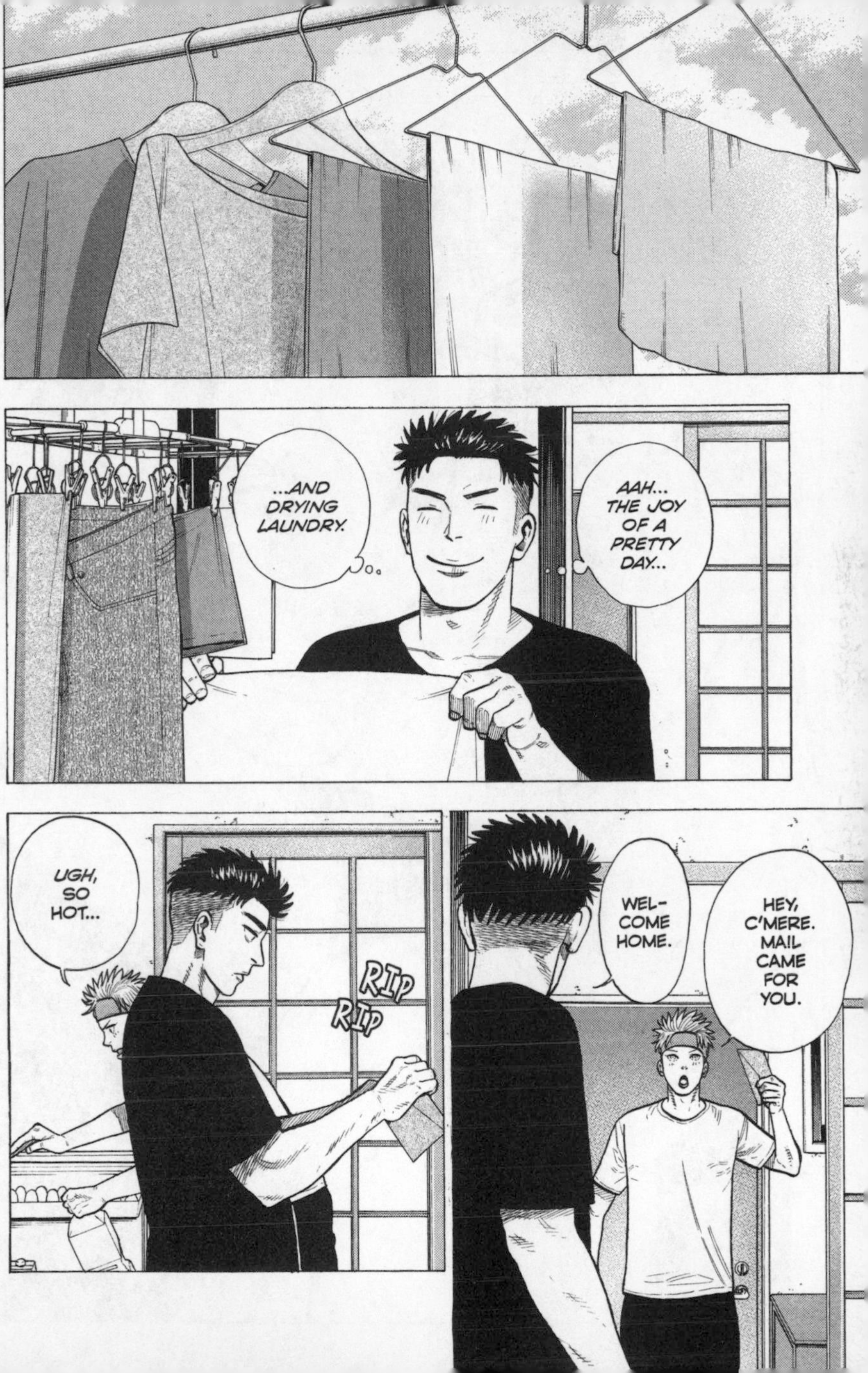
AAH... THE JOY OF A PRETTY DAY...
...AND DRYING LAUNDRY.
HEY, C'MERE. MAIL CAME FOR YOU.
WEL-COME HOME.
UGH, SO HOT...
RIP RIP

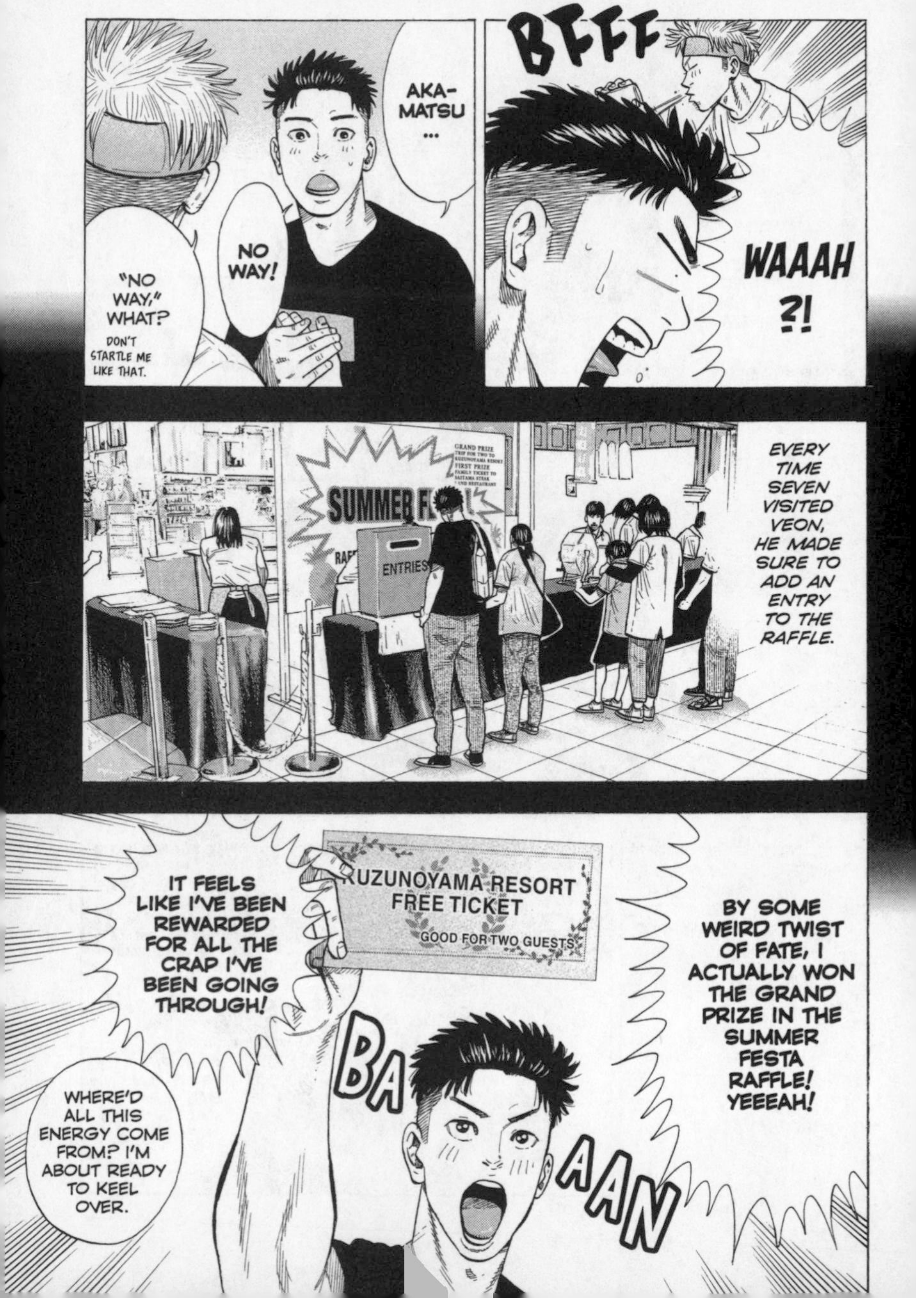
BFFF
WAAAH ?!
AKA-MATSU ...
NO WAY!
"NO WAY," WHAT?
DON'T STARTLE ME LIKE THAT.
EVERY TIME SEVEN VISITED VEON, HE MADE SURE TO ADD AN ENTRY TO THE RAFFLE.
SUMMER F
ENTRIES
BY SOME WEIRD TWIST OF FATE, I ACTUALLY WON THE GRAND PRIZE IN THE SUMMER FESTA RAFFLE! YEEEAH!
KUZUNOYAMA RESORT FREE TICKET
GOOD FOR TWO GUESTS
IT FEELS LIKE I'VE BEEN REWARDED FOR ALL THE CRAP I'VE BEEN GOING THROUGH!
BA AAN
WHERE'D ALL THIS ENERGY COME FROM? I'M ABOUT READY TO KEEL OVER.

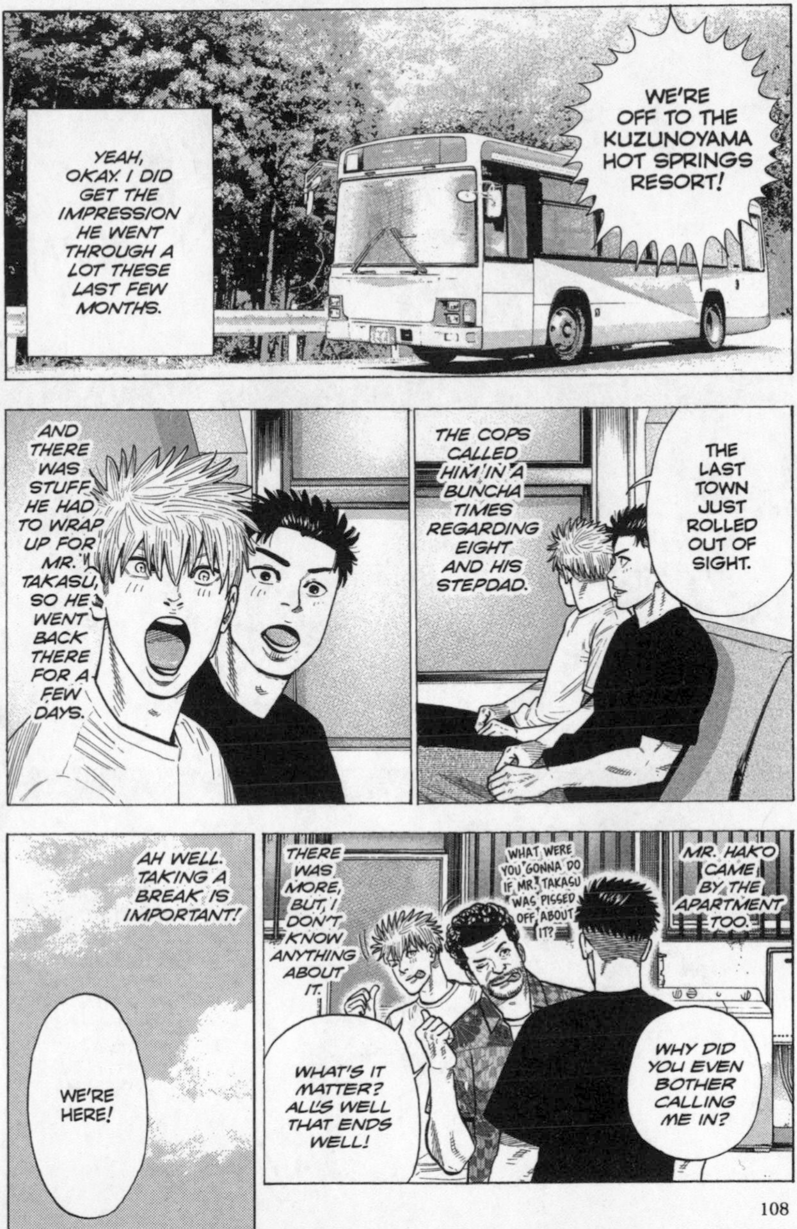
WE'RE OFF TO THE KUZUNOYAMA HOT SPRINGS RESORT!
YEAH, OKAY. I DID GET THE IMPRESSION HE WENT THROUGH A LOT THESE LAST FEW MONTHS.
THE LAST TOWN JUST ROLLED OUT OF SIGHT.
THE COPS CALLED HIM IN A BUNCHA TIMES REGARDING EIGHT AND HIS STEPDAD.
AND THERE WAS STUFF HE HAD TO WRAP UP FOR MR. TAKASU, SO HE WENT BACK THERE FOR A FEW DAYS.
MR. HAKO CAME BY THE APARTMENT TOO.
WHAT WERE YOU GONNA DO IF MR. TAKASU WAS PISSED OFF ABOUT IT?
THERE WAS MORE, BUT I DON'T KNOW ANYTHING ABOUT IT.
WHY DID YOU EVEN BOTHER CALLING ME IN?
WHAT'S IT MATTER? ALL'S WELL THAT ENDS WELL!
AH WELL. TAKING A BREAK IS IMPORTANT!
WE'RE HERE!

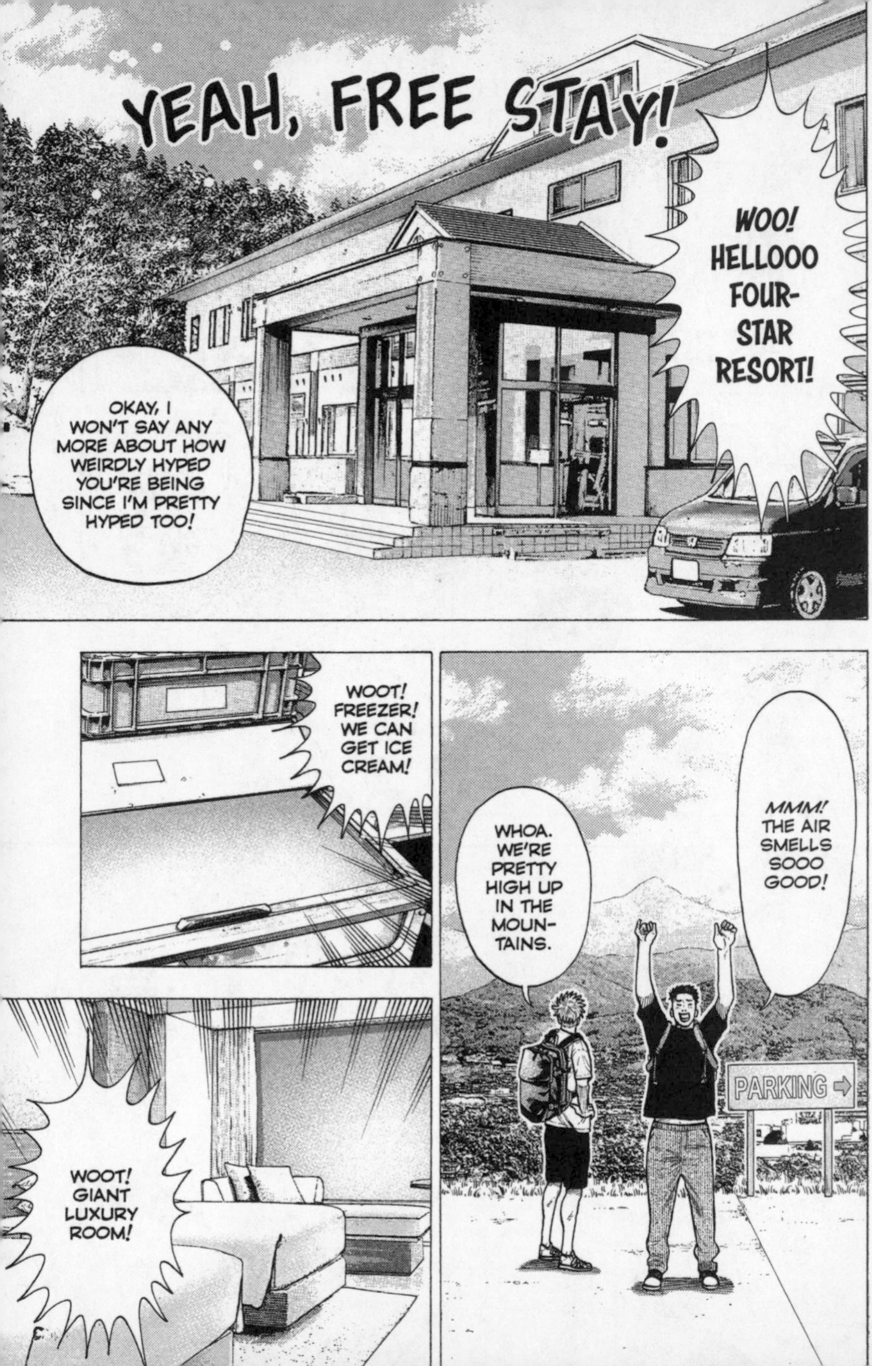
YEAH, FREE STAY!
WOO! HELLOOO FOUR-STAR RESORT!
OKAY, I WON'T SAY ANY MORE ABOUT HOW WEIRDLY HYPED YOU'RE BEING SINCE I'M PRETTY HYPED TOO!
MMM! THE AIR SMELLS SOOO GOOD!
WHOA. WE'RE PRETTY HIGH UP IN THE MOUN-TAINS.
PARKING
WOOT! FREEZER! WE CAN GET ICE CREAM!
WOOT! GIANT LUXURY ROOM!

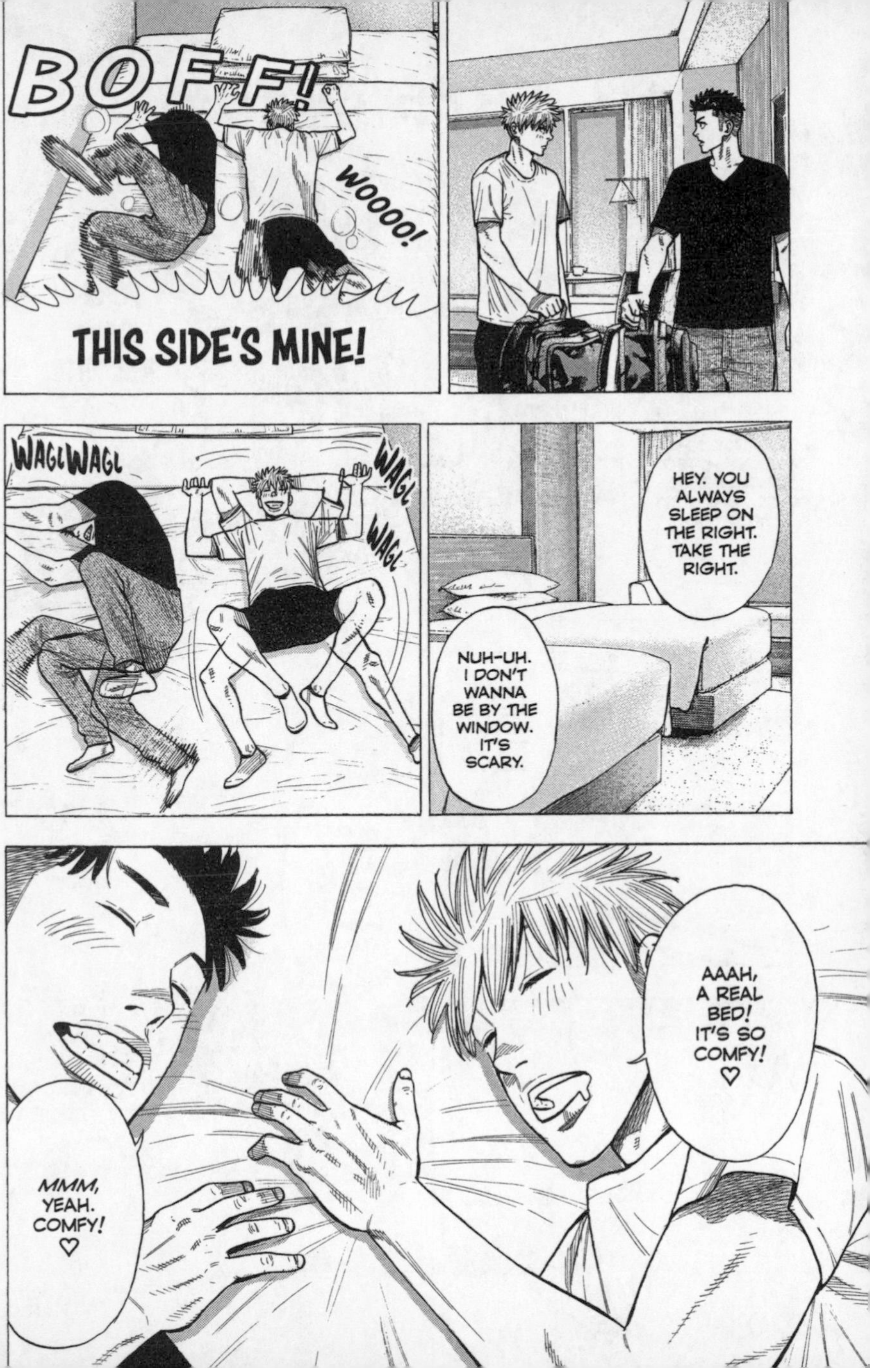
BOFF!
WOOOO!
THIS SIDE'S MINE!
HEY. YOU ALWAYS SLEEP ON THE RIGHT. TAKE THE RIGHT.
NUH-UH. I DON'T WANNA BE BY THE WINDOW. IT'S SCARY.
WAGLWAGL
WAGL WAGL
AAAH, A REAL BED! IT'S SO COMFY! ♡
MMM, YEAH. COMFY! ♡

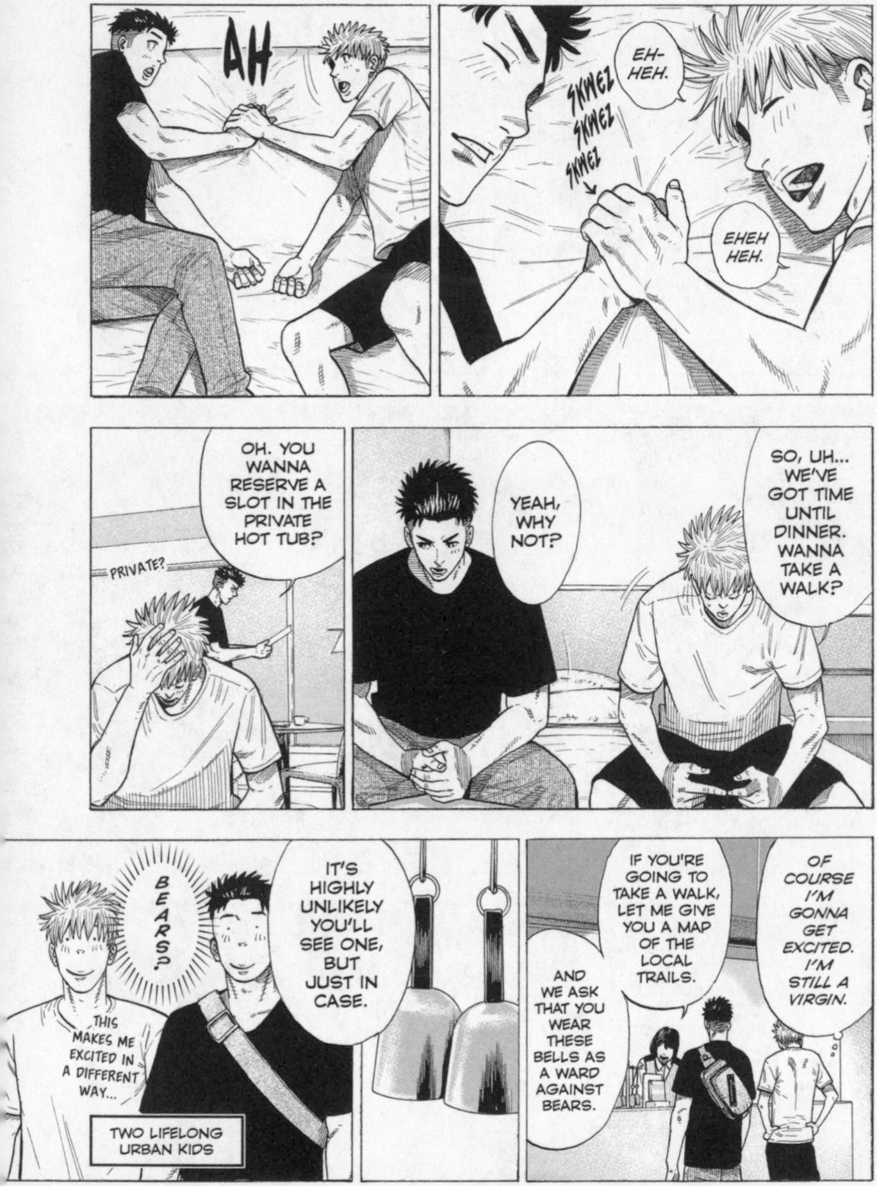
EH-HEH.
SKWEZ SKWEZ SKWEZ
EHEH HEH.
AH
SO, UH... WE'VE GOT TIME UNTIL DINNER. WANNA TAKE A WALK?
YEAH, WHY NOT?
OH. YOU WANNA RESERVE A SLOT IN THE PRIVATE HOT TUB?
PRIVATE?
OF COURSE I'M GONNA GET EXCITED. I'M STILL A VIRGIN.
IF YOU'RE GOING TO TAKE A WALK, LET ME GIVE YOU A MAP OF THE LOCAL TRAILS.
AND WE ASK THAT YOU WEAR THESE BELLS AS A WARD AGAINST BEARS.
IT'S HIGHLY UNLIKELY YOU'LL SEE ONE, BUT JUST IN CASE.
BEARS?
THIS MAKES ME EXCITED IN A DIFFERENT WAY...
TWO LIFELONG URBAN KIDS

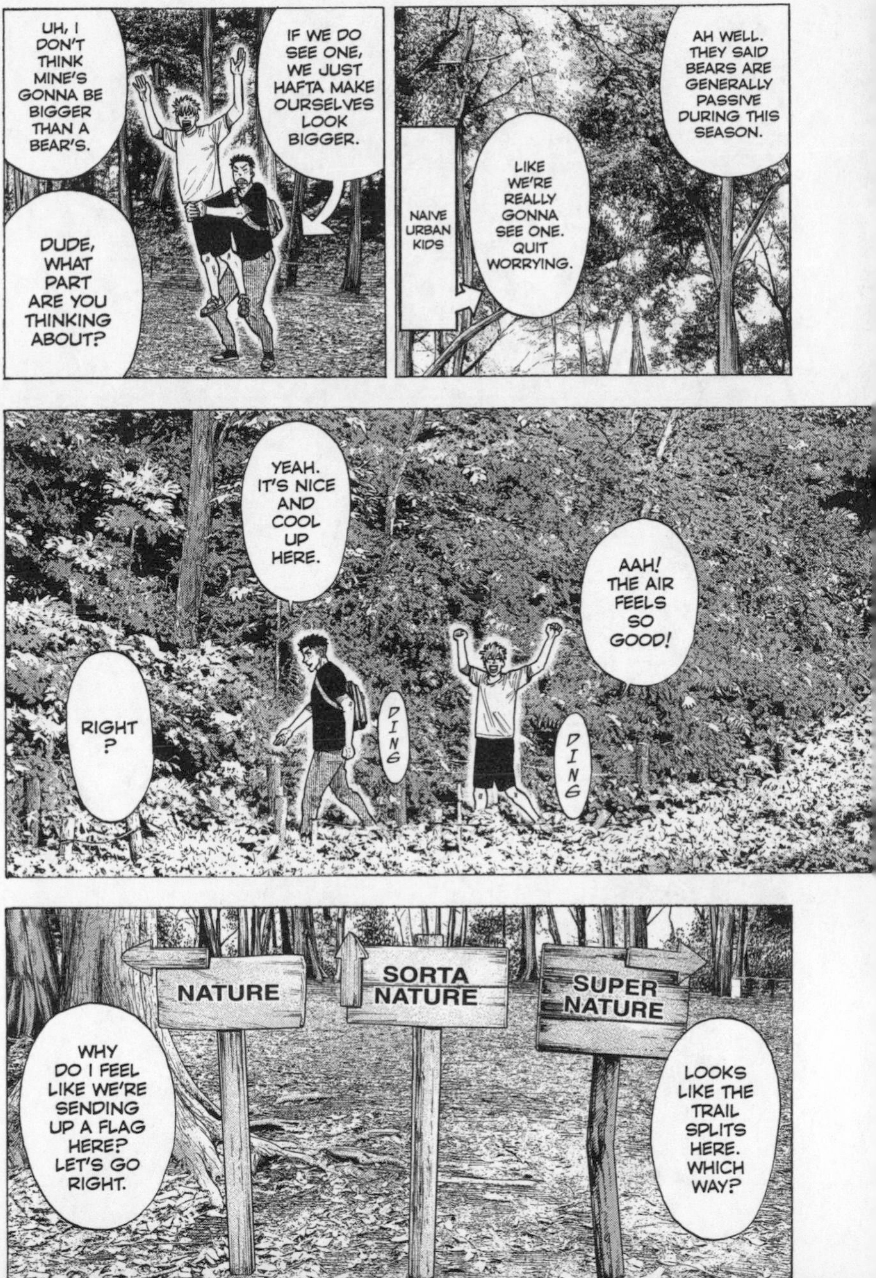
AH WELL. THEY SAID BEARS ARE GENERALLY PASSIVE DURING THIS SEASON.
LIKE WE'RE REALLY GONNA SEE ONE. QUIT WORRYING.
NAIVE URBAN KIDS
IF WE DO SEE ONE, WE JUST HAFTA MAKE OURSELVES LOOK BIGGER.
UH, I DON'T THINK MINE'S GONNA BE BIGGER THAN A BEAR'S.
DUDE, WHAT PART ARE YOU THINKING ABOUT?
AAH! THE AIR FEELS SO GOOD!
DING
YEAH. IT'S NICE AND COOL UP HERE.
DING
RIGHT?
LOOKS LIKE THE TRAIL SPLITS HERE. WHICH WAY?
SUPER NATURE
SORTA NATURE
NATURE
WHY DO I FEEL LIKE WE'RE SENDING UP A FLAG HERE? LET'S GO RIGHT.

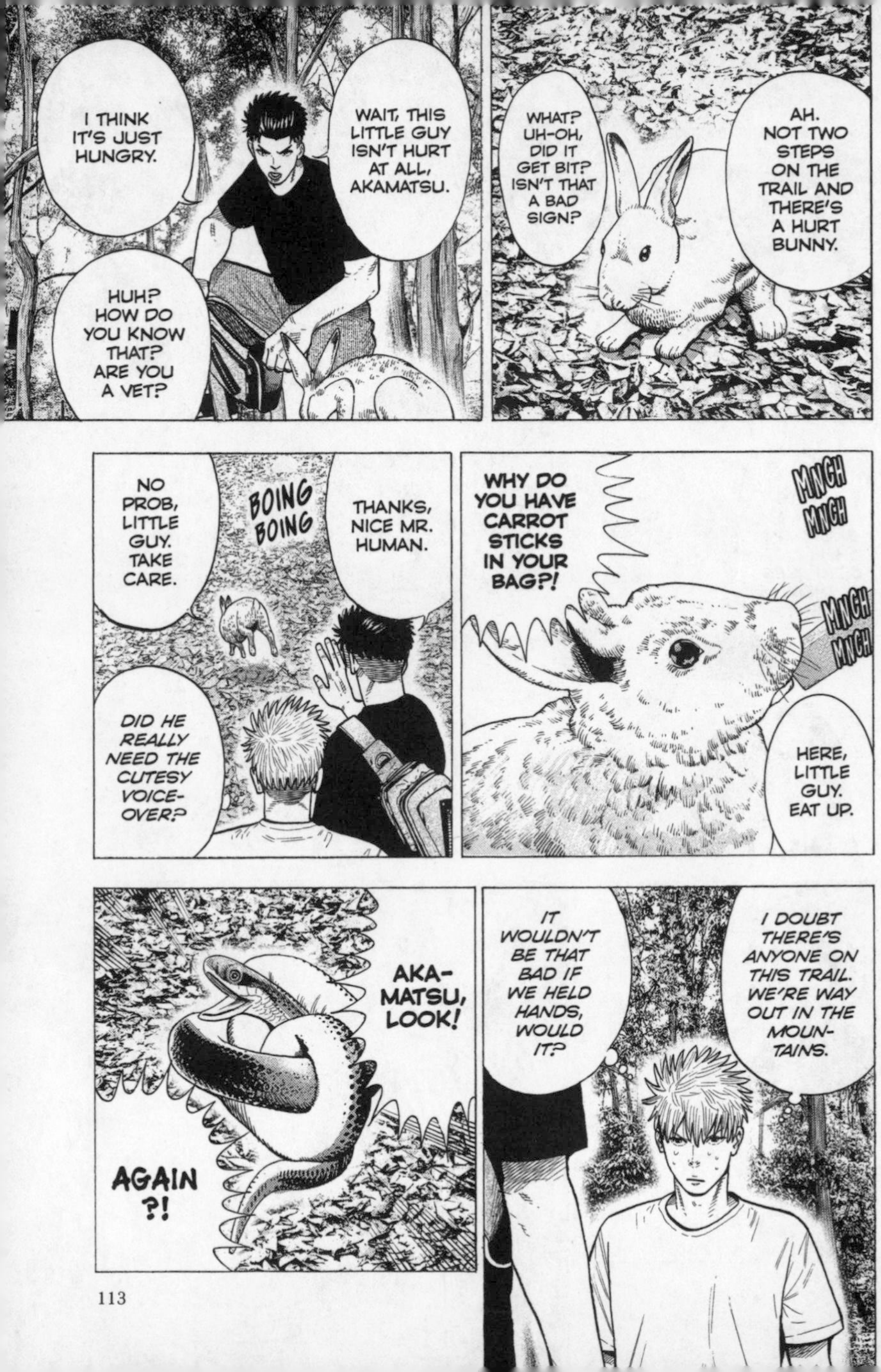
AH. NOT TWO STEPS ON THE TRAIL AND THERE'S A HURT BUNNY.
WHAT? UH-OH, DID IT GET BIT? ISN'T THAT A BAD SIGN?
WAIT, THIS LITTLE GUY ISN'T HURT AT ALL, AKAMATSU.
I THINK IT'S JUST HUNGRY.
HUH? HOW DO YOU KNOW THAT? ARE YOU A VET?
MNGH MNGH
WHY DO YOU HAVE CARROT STICKS IN YOUR BAG?!
MNGH MNGH
HERE, LITTLE GUY. EAT UP.
THANKS, NICE MR. HUMAN.
BOING BOING
NO PROB, LITTLE GUY. TAKE CARE.
DID HE REALLY NEED THE CUTESY VOICE-OVER?
I DOUBT THERE'S ANYONE ON THIS TRAIL. WE'RE WAY OUT IN THE MOUN-TAINS.
IT WOULDN'T BE THAT BAD IF WE HELD HANDS, WOULD IT?
AKA-MATSU, LOOK!
AGAIN ?!

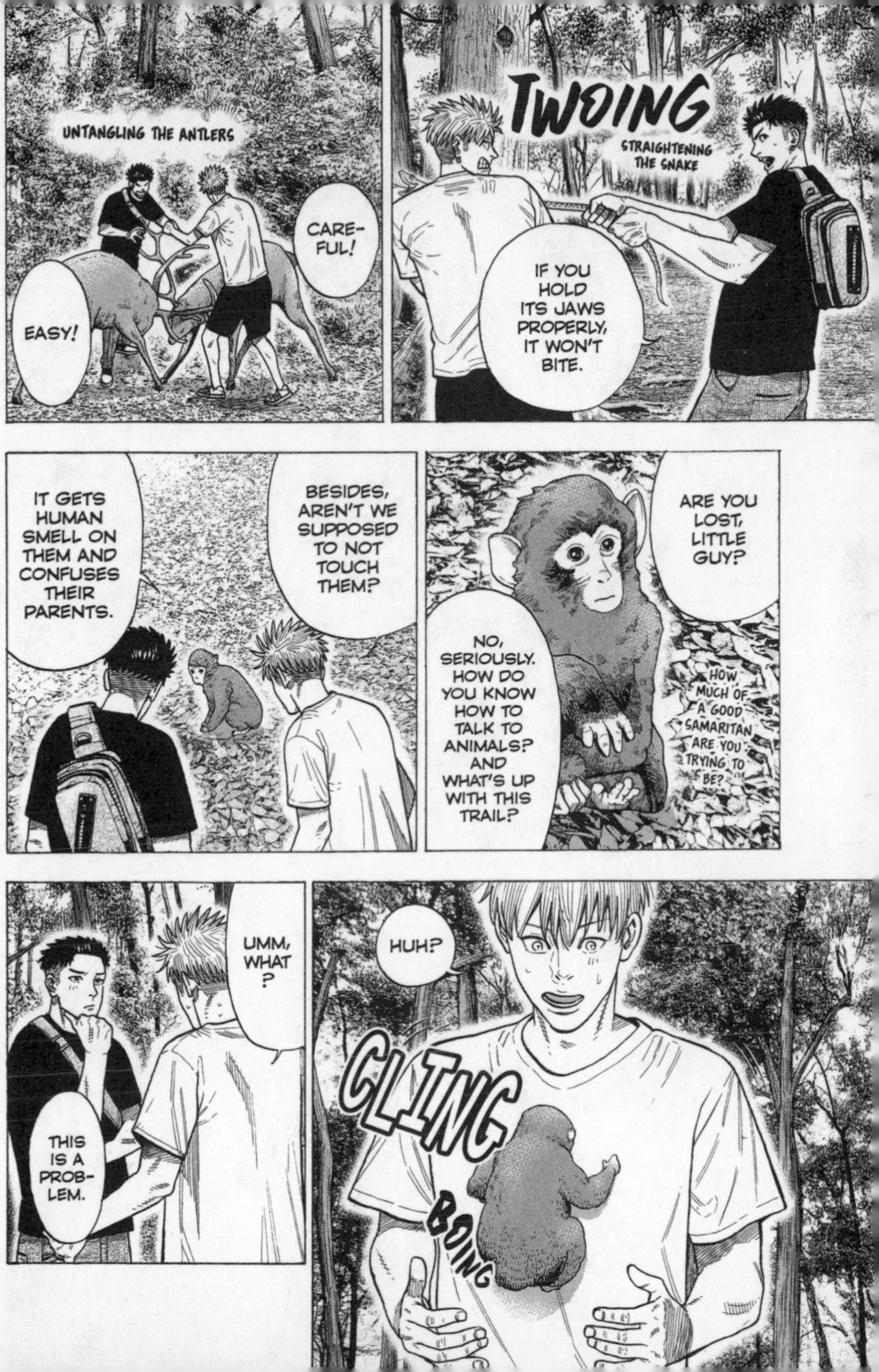
TWOING
STRAIGHTENING THE SNAKE
IF YOU HOLD ITS JAWS PROPERLY, IT WON'T BITE.
UNTANGLING THE ANTLERS
CAREFUL!
EASY!
ARE YOU LOST, LITTLE GUY?
HOW MUCH OF A GOOD SAMARITAN ARE YOU TRYING TO BE?
NO, SERIOUSLY. HOW DO YOU KNOW HOW TO TALK TO ANIMALS? AND WHAT'S UP WITH THIS TRAIL?
BESIDES, AREN'T WE SUPPOSED TO NOT TOUCH THEM?
IT GETS HUMAN SMELL ON THEM AND CONFUSES THEIR PARENTS.
HUH?
CLING
BOING
UMM, WHAT?
THIS IS A PROBLEM.

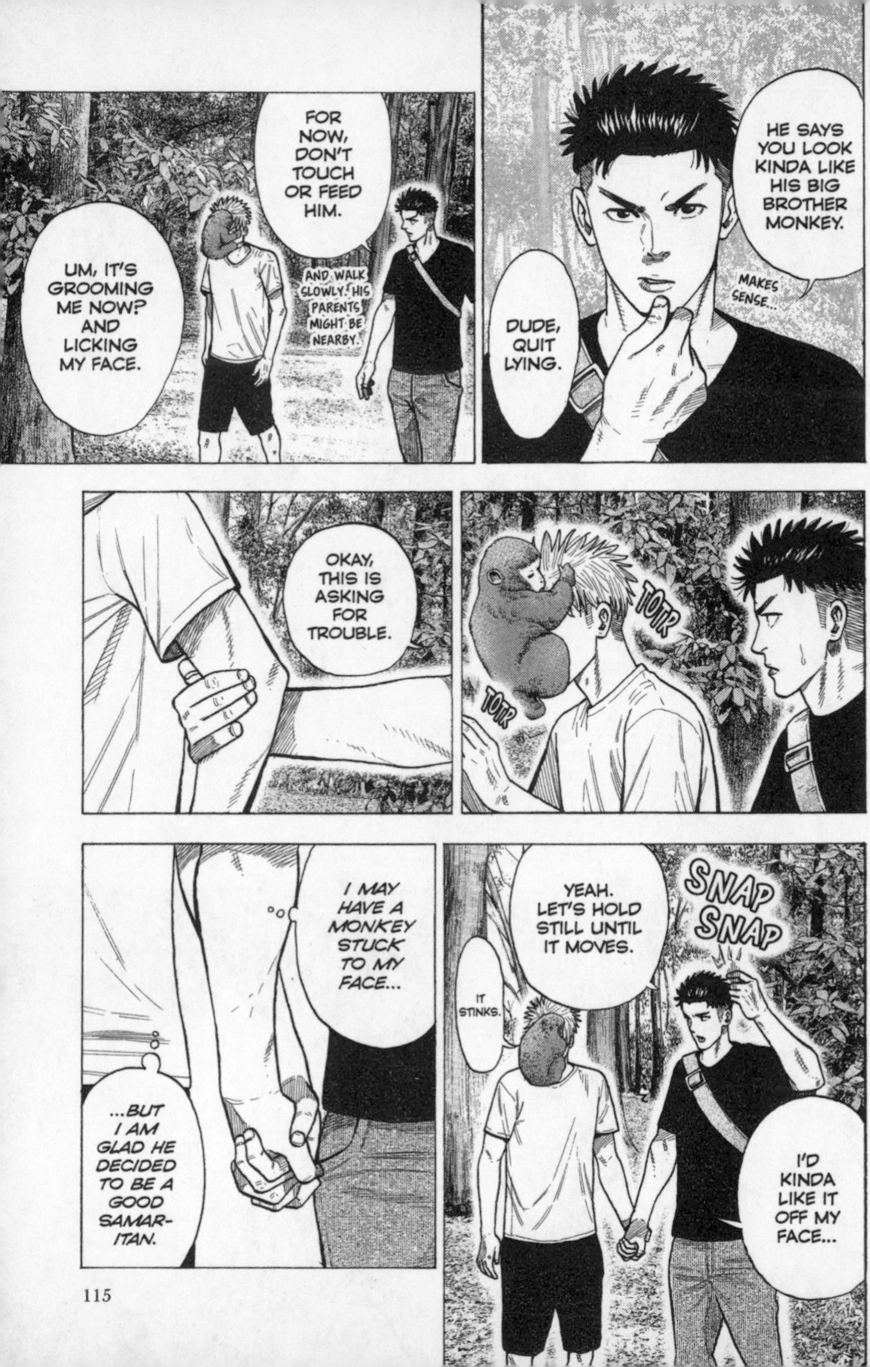
HE SAYS YOU LOOK KINDA LIKE HIS BIG BROTHER MONKEY.
MAKES SENSE...
DUDE, QUIT LYING.
FOR NOW, DON'T TOUCH OR FEED HIM.
AND WALK SLOWLY. HIS PARENTS MIGHT BE NEARBY.
UM, IT'S GROOMING ME NOW? AND LICKING MY FACE.
TOTR
TOTR
OKAY, THIS IS ASKING FOR TROUBLE.
SNAP SNAP
YEAH. LET'S HOLD STILL UNTIL IT MOVES.
IT STINKS.
I'D KINDA LIKE IT OFF MY FACE...
I MAY HAVE A MONKEY STUCK TO MY FACE...
...BUT I AM GLAD HE DECIDED TO BE A GOOD SAMAR-ITAN.

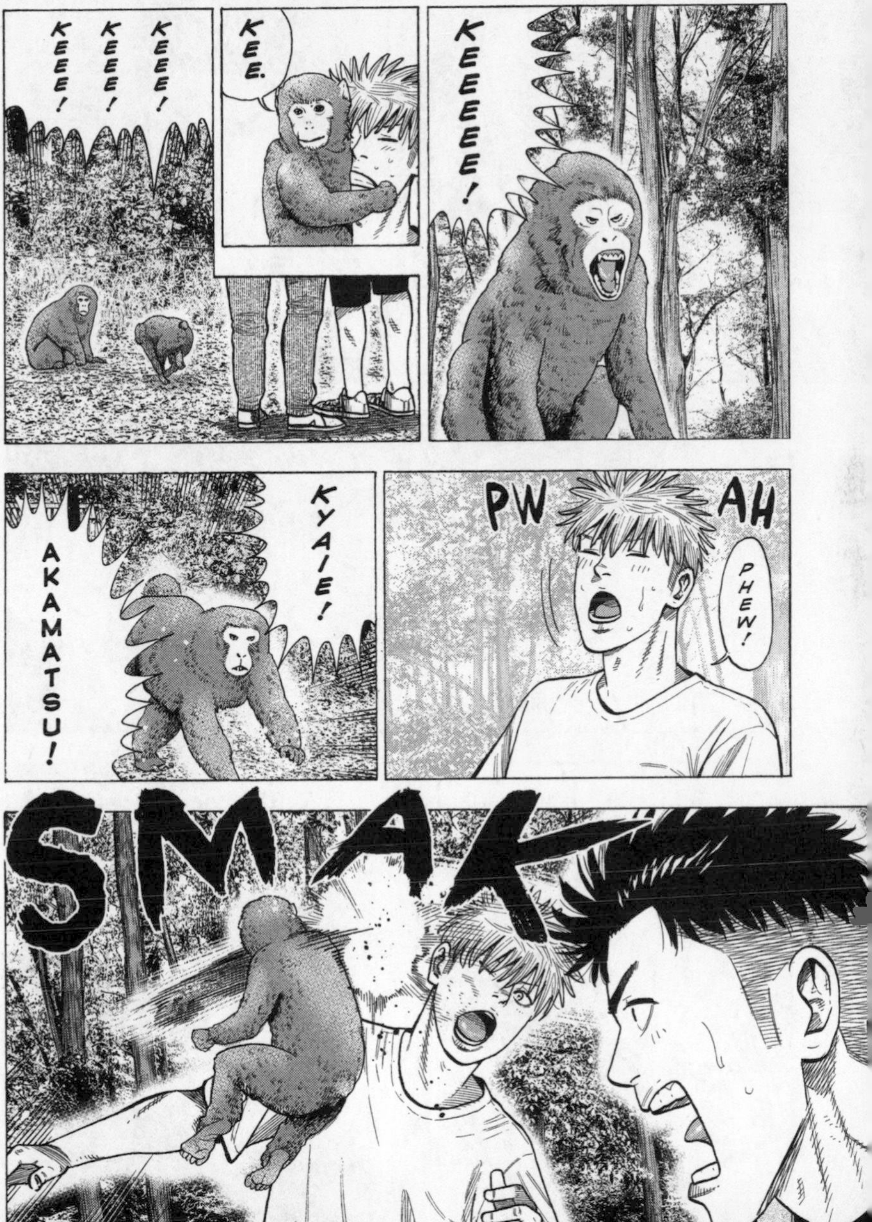
KEEEEEE!
KEE.
KEEE! KEEE! KEEE!
PW AH
PHEW!
KYAIE!
AKAMATSU!
SMAK

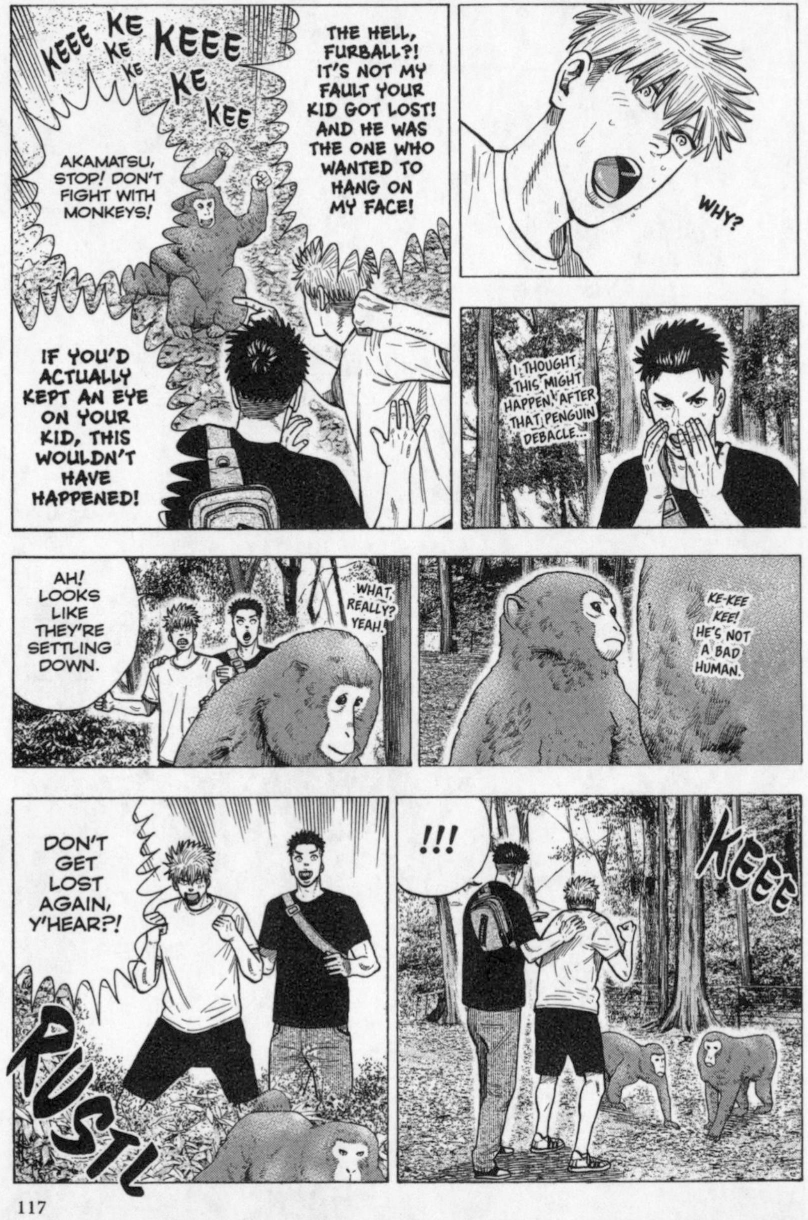
WHY?
I THOUGHT THIS MIGHT HAPPEN, AFTER THAT PENGUIN DEBACLE...
KEEE KE KE KE KEEEE KE KEE
THE HELL, FURBALL?! IT'S NOT MY FAULT YOUR KID GOT LOST! AND HE WAS THE ONE WHO WANTED TO HANG ON MY FACE!
AKAMATSU, STOP! DON'T FIGHT WITH MONKEYS!
IF YOU'D ACTUALLY KEPT AN EYE ON YOUR KID, THIS WOULDN'T HAVE HAPPENED!
KE-KEE KEE! HE'S NOT A BAD HUMAN.
WHAT, REALLY? YEAH!
AH! LOOKS LIKE THEY'RE SETTLING DOWN.
!!!
KEEE
DON'T GET LOST AGAIN, Y'HEAR?!
RUSTL

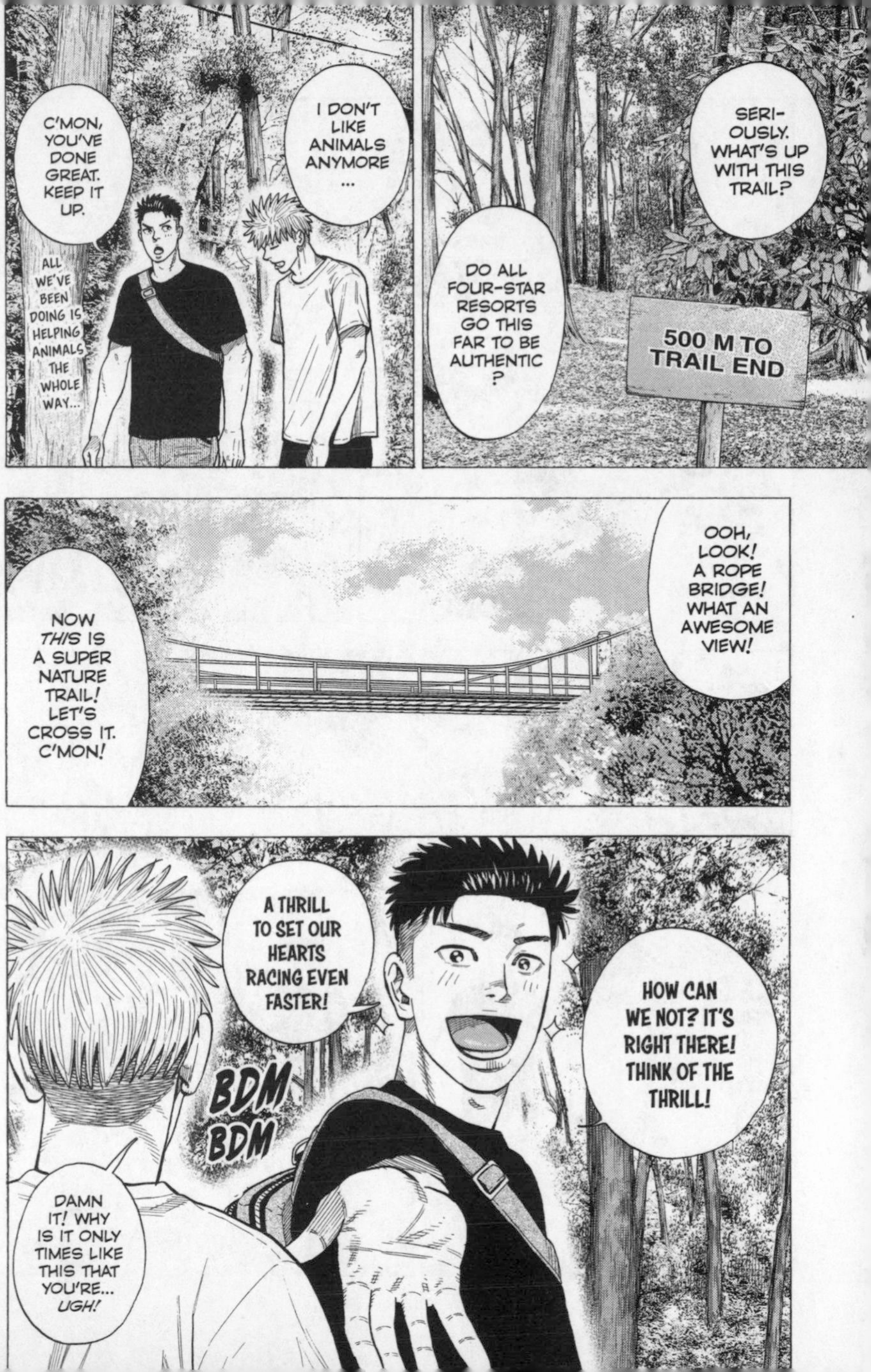
SERIOUSLY. WHAT'S UP WITH THIS TRAIL?
DO ALL FOUR-STAR RESORTS GO THIS FAR TO BE AUTHENTIC?
500 M TO TRAIL END
I DON'T LIKE ANIMALS ANYMORE...
C'MON, YOU'VE DONE GREAT. KEEP IT UP.
ALL WE'VE BEEN DOING IS HELPING ANIMALS THE WHOLE WAY...
OOH, LOOK! A ROPE BRIDGE! WHAT AN AWESOME VIEW!
NOW *THIS* IS A SUPER NATURE TRAIL! LET'S CROSS IT. C'MON!
HOW CAN WE NOT? IT'S RIGHT THERE! THINK OF THE THRILL!
A THRILL TO SET OUR HEARTS RACING EVEN FASTER!
BDM BDM
DAMN IT! WHY IS IT ONLY TIMES LIKE THIS THAT YOU'RE... *UGH!*

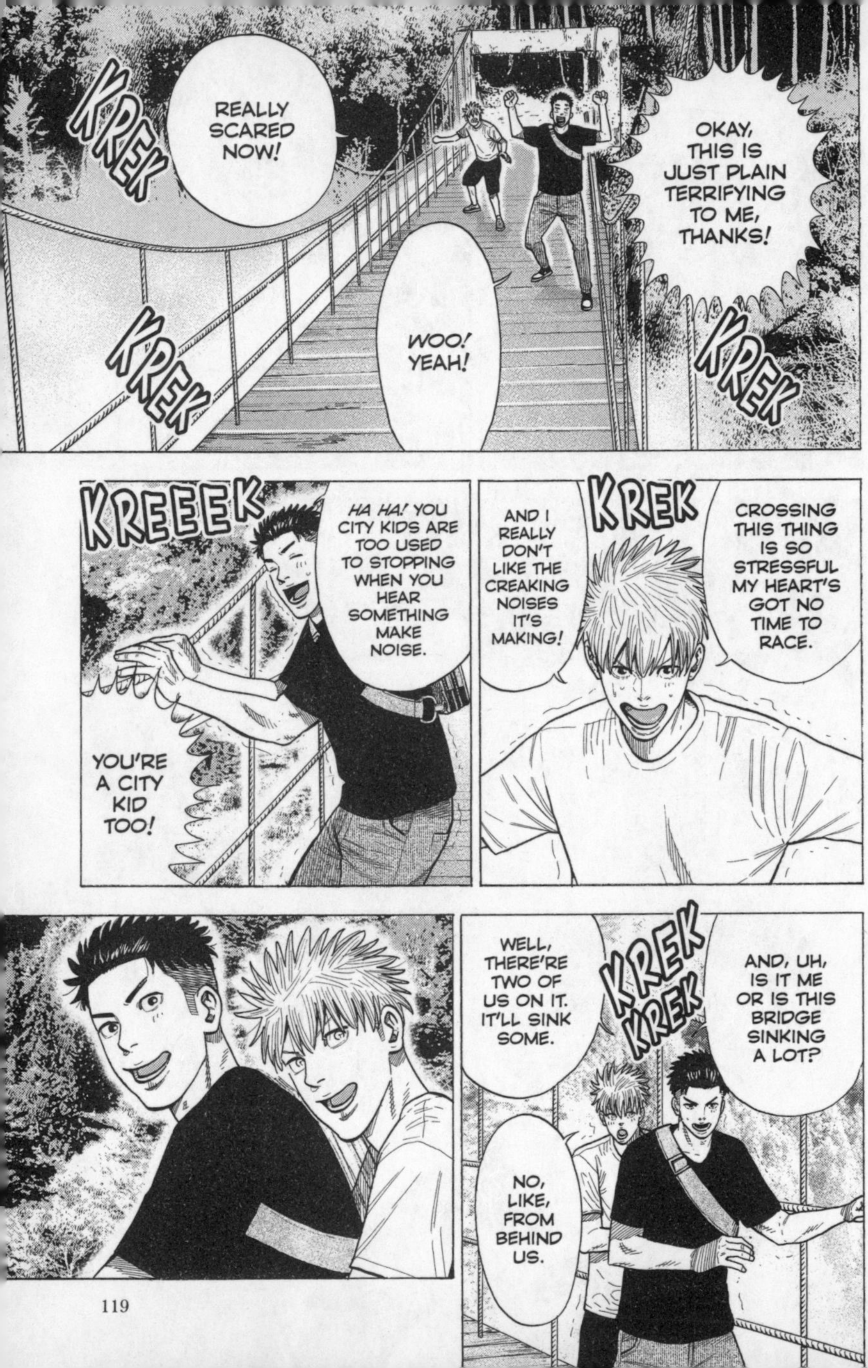
OKAY, THIS IS JUST PLAIN TERRIFYING TO ME, THANKS!
REALLY SCARED NOW!
KREK
WOO! YEAH!
KREK
KREK
KREK
CROSSING THIS THING IS SO STRESSFUL MY HEART'S GOT NO TIME TO RACE.
AND I REALLY DON'T LIKE THE CREAKING NOISES IT'S MAKING!
KREEEK
HA HA! YOU CITY KIDS ARE TOO USED TO STOPPING WHEN YOU HEAR SOMETHING MAKE NOISE.
YOU'RE A CITY KID TOO!
AND, UH, IS IT ME OR IS THIS BRIDGE SINKING A LOT?
KREK
KREK
WELL, THERE'RE TWO OF US ON IT. IT'LL SINK SOME.
NO, LIKE, FROM BEHIND US.

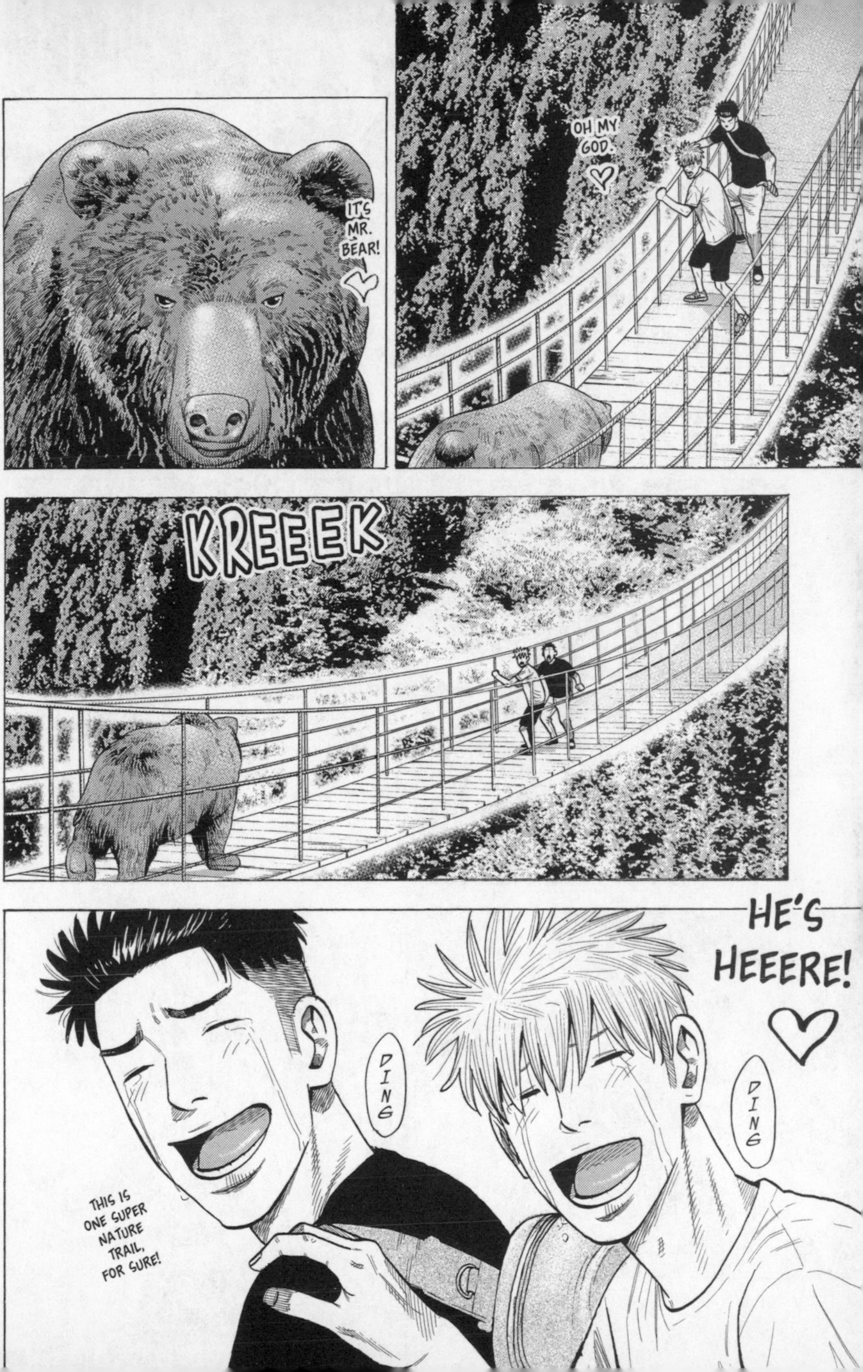
OH MY GOD. ♡
IT'S MR. BEAR! ♡
KREEEK
HE'S HEEERE! ♡
DING
DING
THIS IS ONE SUPER NATURE TRAIL, FOR SURE!

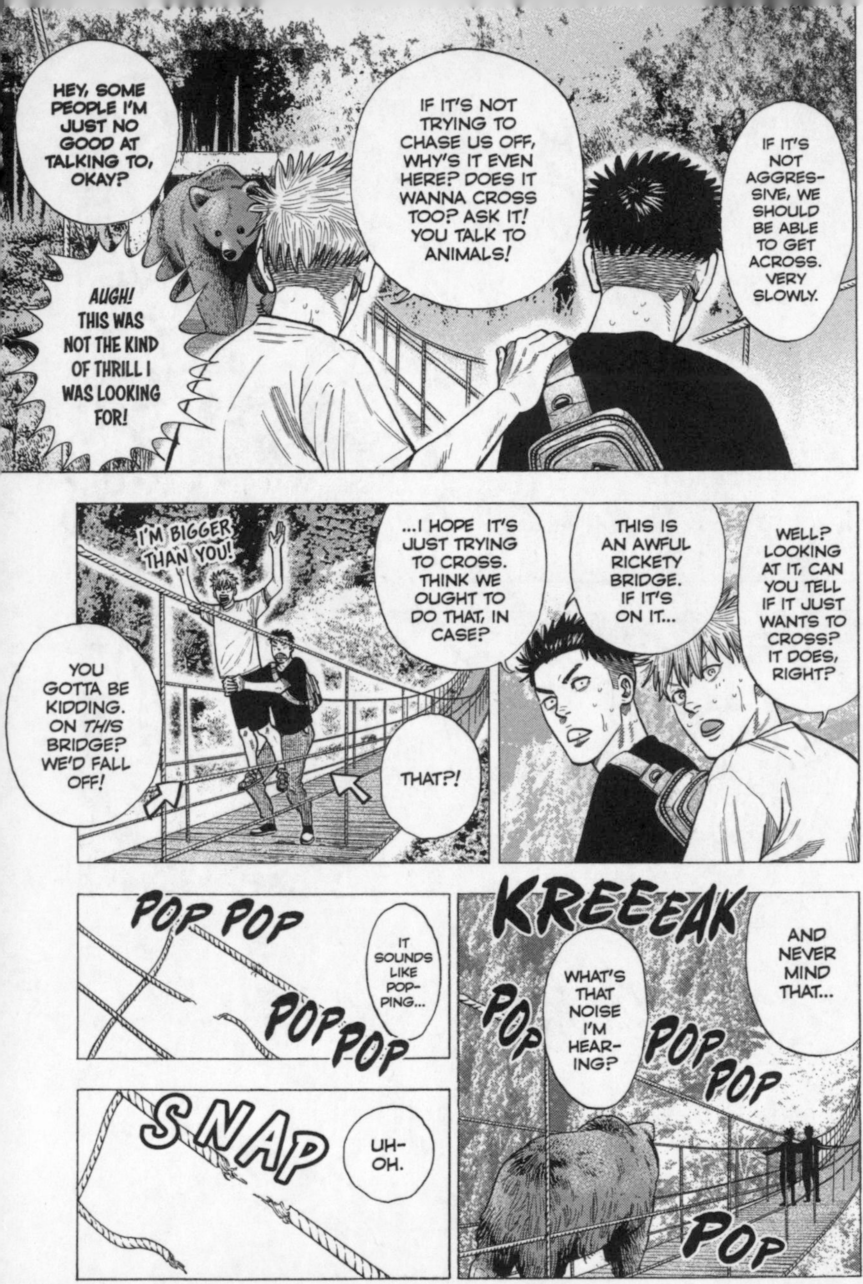
IF IT'S NOT AGGRES-SIVE, WE SHOULD BE ABLE TO GET ACROSS. VERY SLOWLY.
IF IT'S NOT TRYING TO CHASE US OFF, WHY'S IT EVEN HERE? DOES IT WANNA CROSS TOO? ASK IT! YOU TALK TO ANIMALS!
HEY, SOME PEOPLE I'M JUST NO GOOD AT TALKING TO, OKAY?
AUGH! THIS WAS NOT THE KIND OF THRILL I WAS LOOKING FOR!
WELL? LOOKING AT IT, CAN YOU TELL IF IT JUST WANTS TO CROSS? IT DOES, RIGHT?
THIS IS AN AWFUL RICKETY BRIDGE. IF IT'S ON IT...
...I HOPE IT'S JUST TRYING TO CROSS. THINK WE OUGHT TO DO THAT, IN CASE?
I'M BIGGER THAN YOU!
THAT?!
YOU GOTTA BE KIDDING. ON *THIS* BRIDGE? WE'D FALL OFF!
KREEEAK
AND NEVER MIND THAT...
WHAT'S THAT NOISE I'M HEAR-ING?
POP
POP POP POP
POP
POP POP
IT SOUNDS LIKE POP-PING...
POP POP
SNAP
UH-OH.

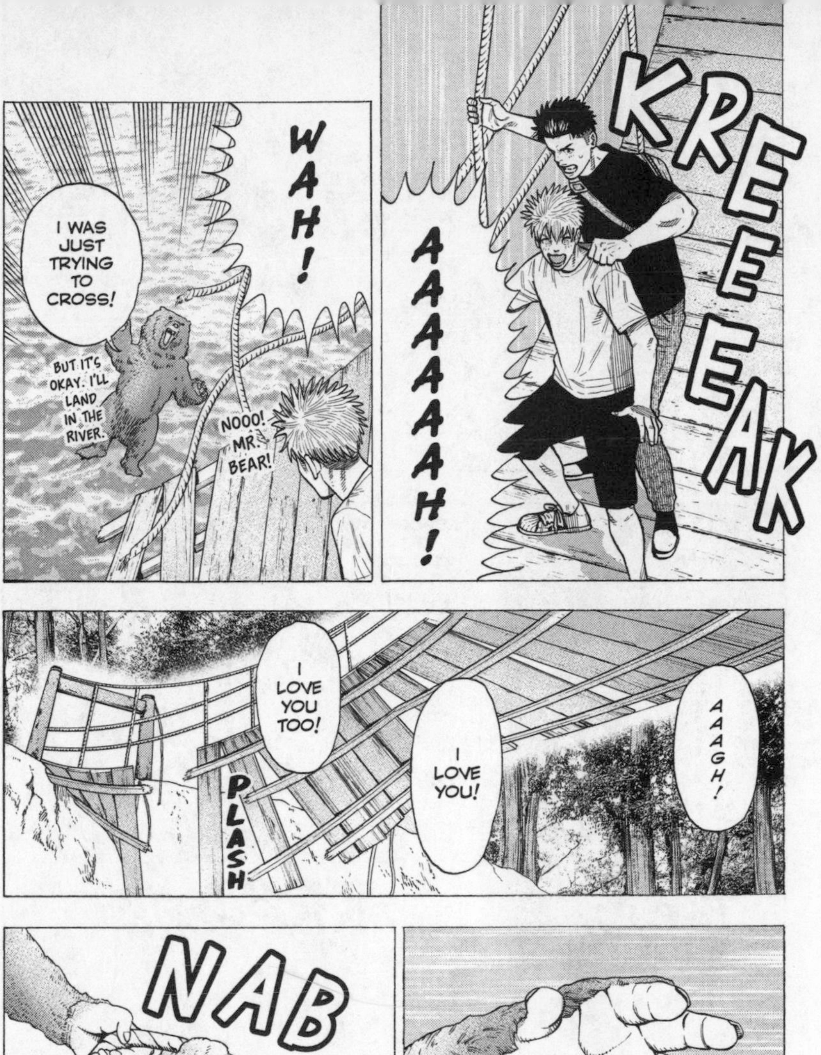
KREEEEAK
AAAAAAAH!
WAH!
I WAS JUST TRYING TO CROSS!
BUT IT'S OKAY. I'LL LAND IN THE RIVER.
NOOO! MR. BEAR!
AAAGH!
I LOVE YOU!
I LOVE YOU TOO!
PLASH
NAB

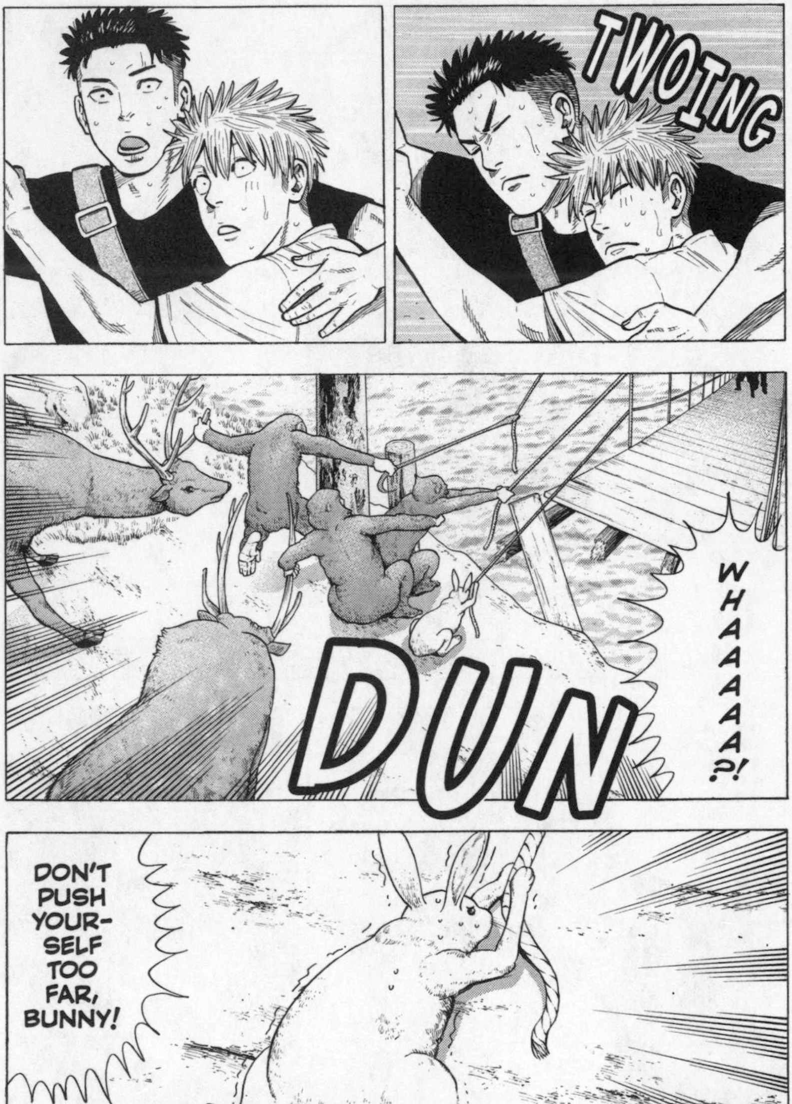
TWOING
WHAAAAAA?!
DUN
DON'T PUSH YOUR-SELF TOO FAR, BUNNY!

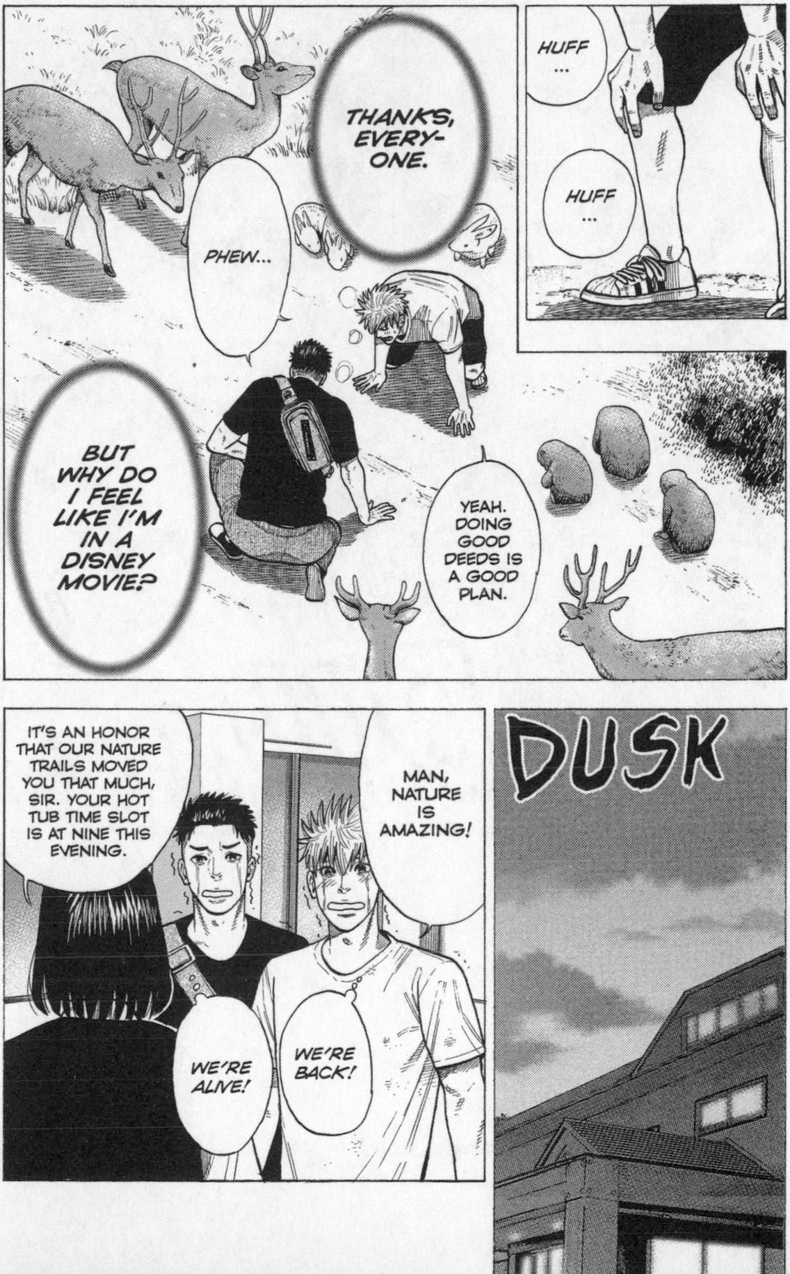
HUFF ...
HUFF ...
THANKS, EVERYONE.
PHEW...
YEAH. DOING GOOD DEEDS IS A GOOD PLAN.
BUT WHY DO I FEEL LIKE I'M IN A DISNEY MOVIE?
DUSK
MAN, NATURE IS AMAZING!
IT'S AN HONOR THAT OUR NATURE TRAILS MOVED YOU THAT MUCH, SIR. YOUR HOT TUB TIME SLOT IS AT NINE THIS EVENING.
WE'RE BACK!
WE'RE ALIVE!

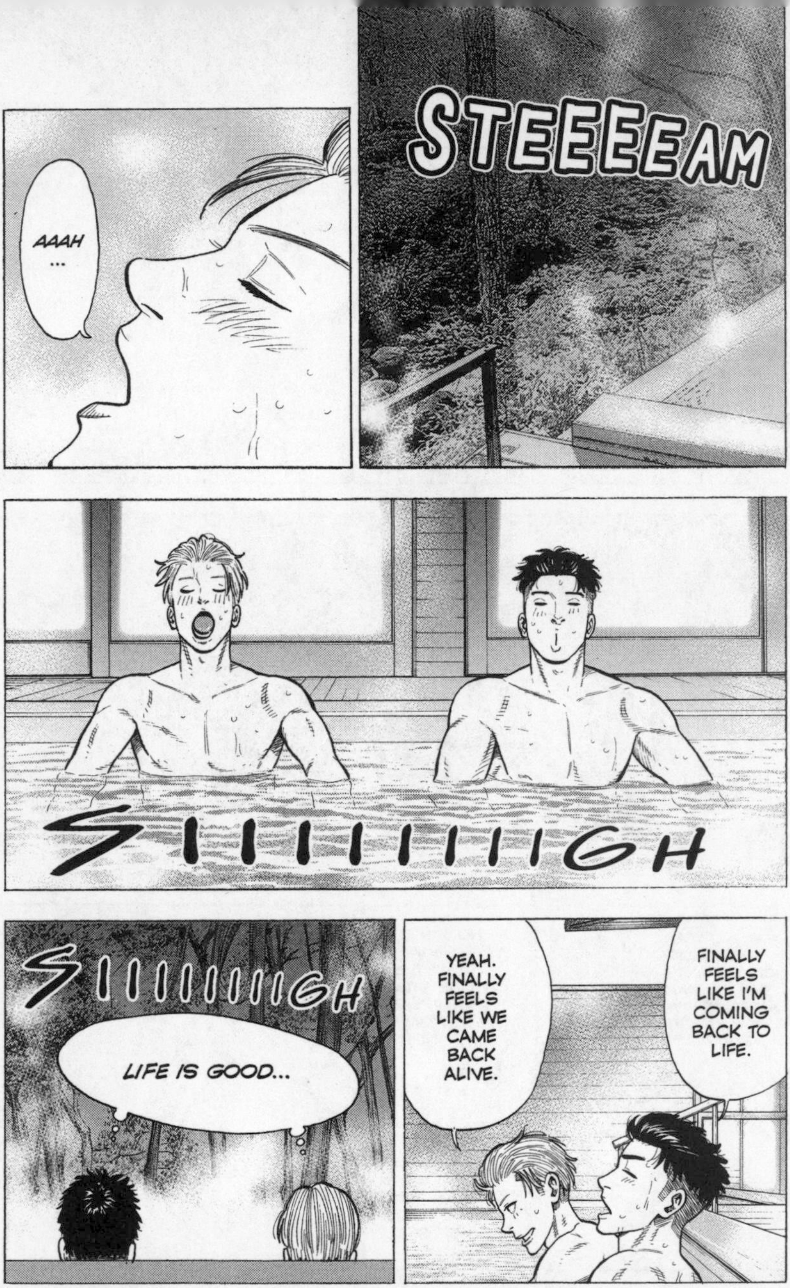
STEEEEEAM
AAAH...
SIIIIIIIGH
FINALLY FEELS LIKE I'M COMING BACK TO LIFE.
YEAH. FINALLY FEELS LIKE WE CAME BACK ALIVE.
SIIIIIIIIIGH
LIFE IS GOOD...

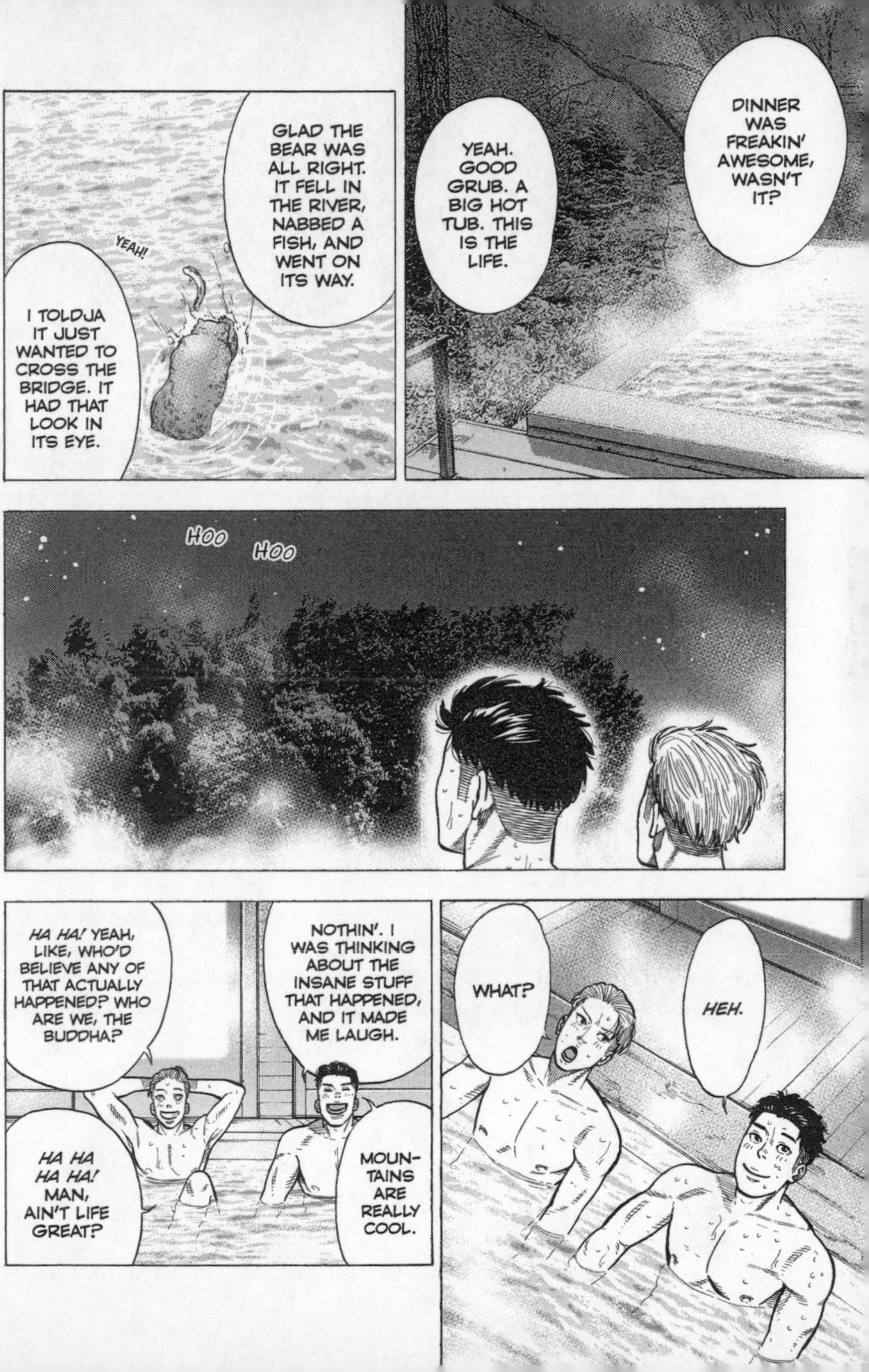
DINNER WAS FREAKIN' AWESOME, WASN'T IT?
YEAH. GOOD GRUB. A BIG HOT TUB. THIS IS THE LIFE.
GLAD THE BEAR WAS ALL RIGHT. IT FELL IN THE RIVER, NABBED A FISH, AND WENT ON ITS WAY.
YEAH!
I TOLDJA IT JUST WANTED TO CROSS THE BRIDGE. IT HAD THAT LOOK IN ITS EYE.
HOO
HOO
HEH.
WHAT?
NOTHIN'. I WAS THINKING ABOUT THE INSANE STUFF THAT HAPPENED, AND IT MADE ME LAUGH.
HA HA! YEAH, LIKE, WHO'D BELIEVE ANY OF THAT ACTUALLY HAPPENED? WHO ARE WE, THE BUDDHA?
MOUN-TAINS ARE REALLY COOL.
HA HA HA HA! MAN, AIN'T LIFE GREAT?

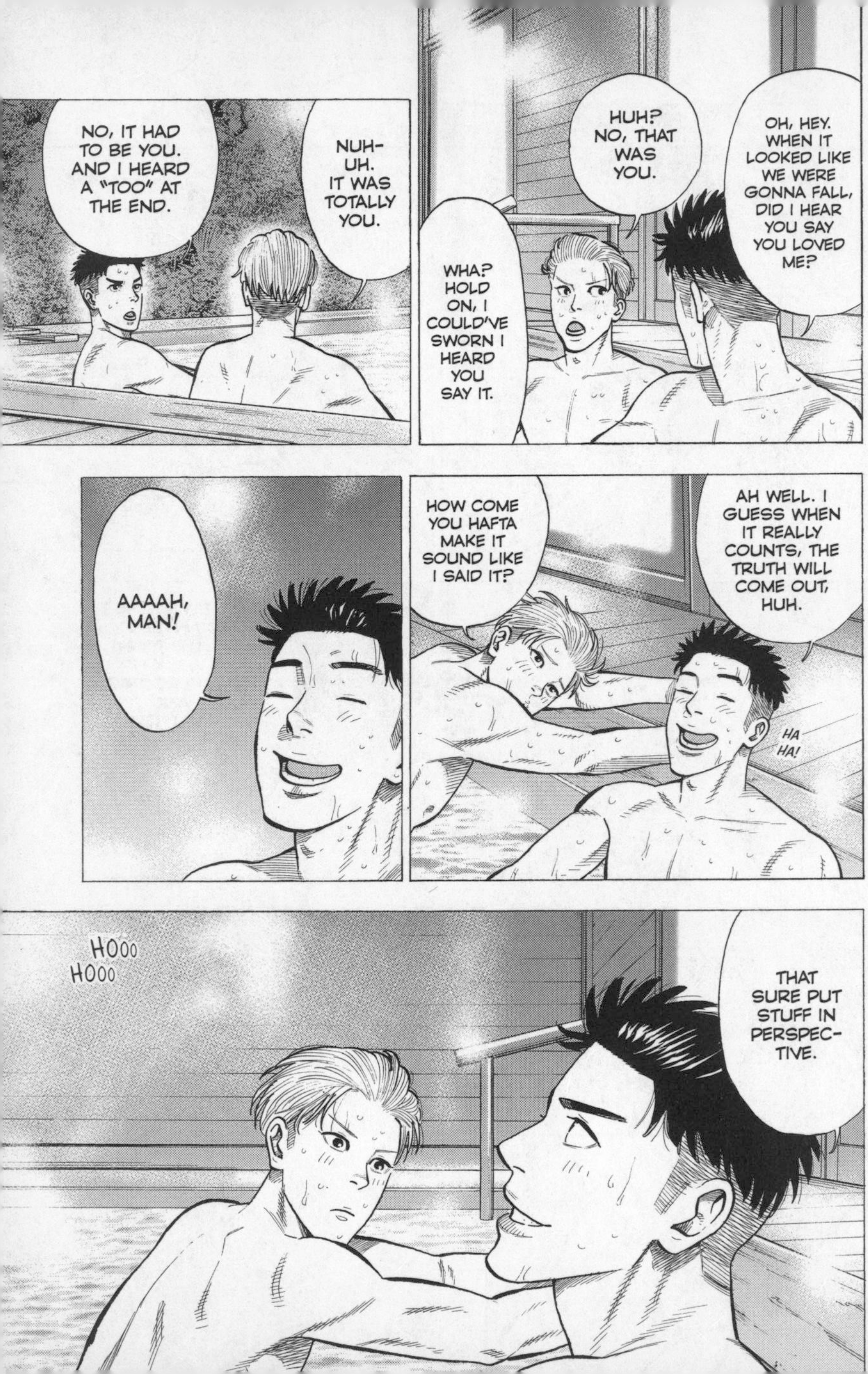
OH, HEY. WHEN IT LOOKED LIKE WE WERE GONNA FALL, DID I HEAR YOU SAY YOU LOVED ME?
HUH? NO, THAT WAS YOU.
WHA? HOLD ON, I COULD'VE SWORN I HEARD YOU SAY IT.
NUH-UH. IT WAS TOTALLY YOU.
NO, IT HAD TO BE YOU. AND I HEARD A "TOO" AT THE END.
AH WELL. I GUESS WHEN IT REALLY COUNTS, THE TRUTH WILL COME OUT, HUH.
HOW COME YOU HAFTA MAKE IT SOUND LIKE I SAID IT?
HA HA!
AAAAH, MAN!
THAT SURE PUT STUFF IN PERSPEC-TIVE.
HOOO HOOO

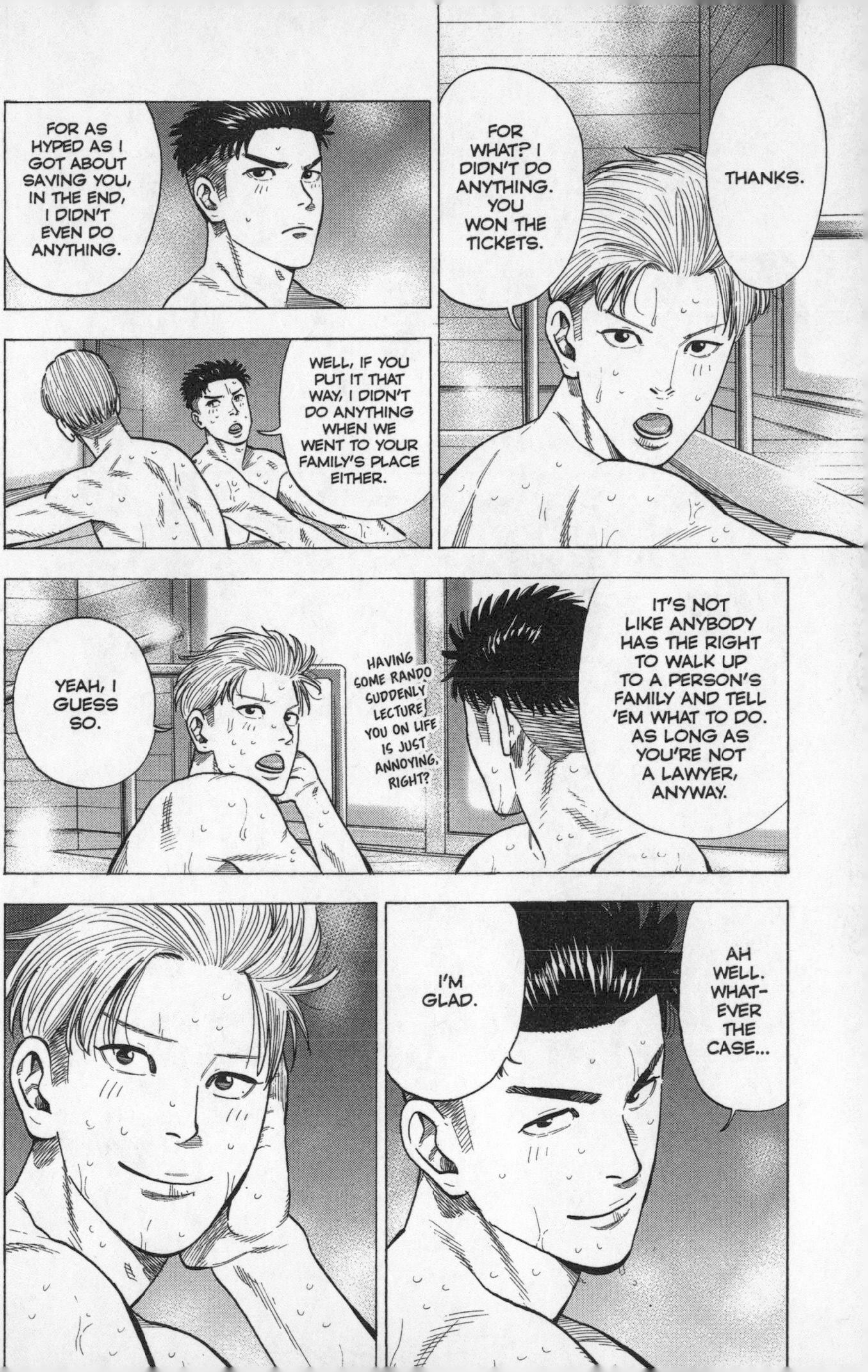
THANKS.
FOR WHAT? I DIDN'T DO ANYTHING. YOU WON THE TICKETS.
FOR AS HYPED AS I GOT ABOUT SAVING YOU, IN THE END, I DIDN'T EVEN DO ANYTHING.
WELL, IF YOU PUT IT THAT WAY, I DIDN'T DO ANYTHING WHEN WE WENT TO YOUR FAMILY'S PLACE EITHER.
IT'S NOT LIKE ANYBODY HAS THE RIGHT TO WALK UP TO A PERSON'S FAMILY AND TELL 'EM WHAT TO DO. AS LONG AS YOU'RE NOT A LAWYER, ANYWAY.
HAVING SOME RANDO SUDDENLY LECTURE YOU ON LIFE IS JUST ANNOYING, RIGHT?
YEAH, I GUESS SO.
AH WELL. WHATEVER THE CASE...
I'M GLAD.

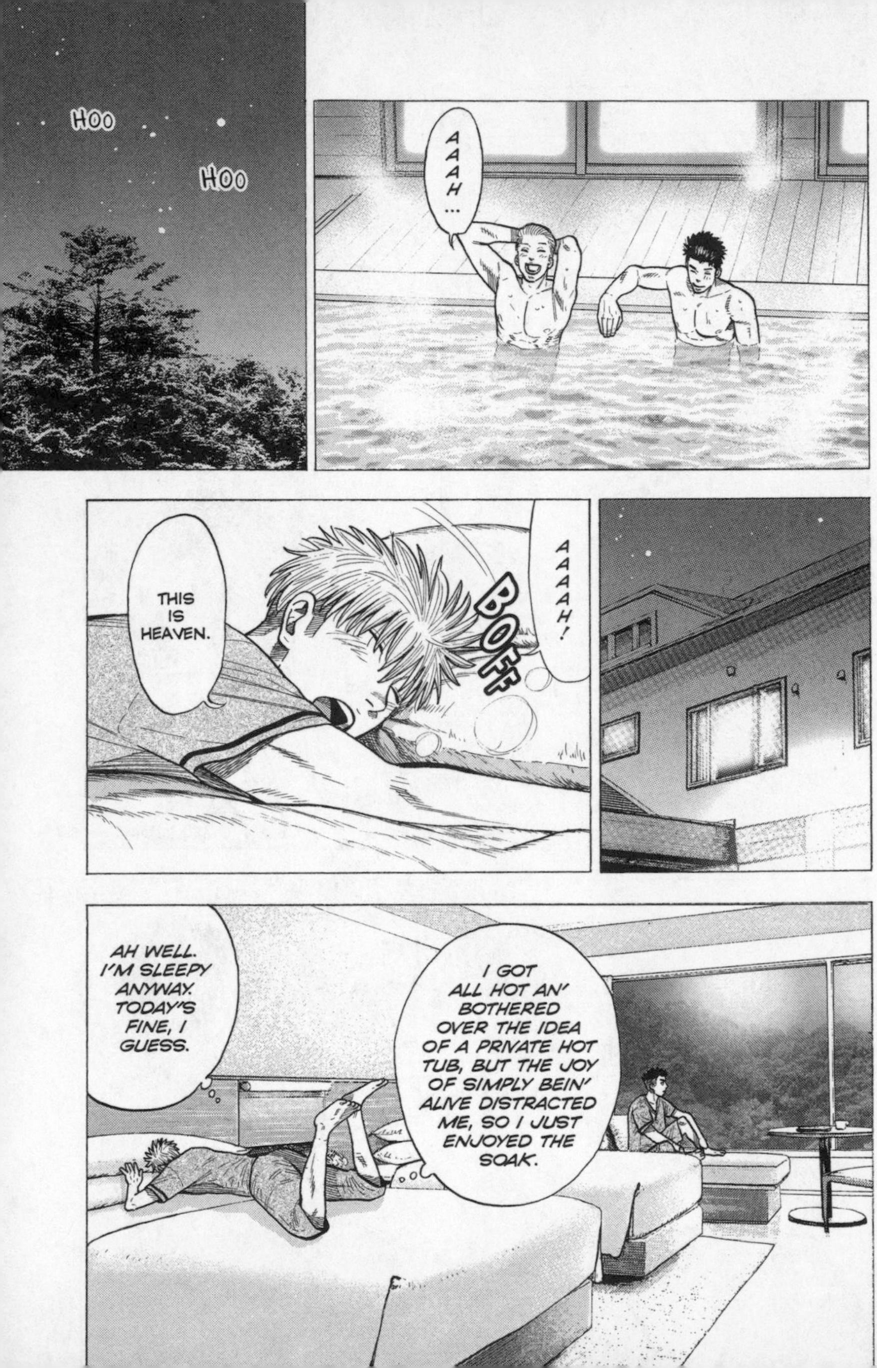
AAAH...
HOO
HOO
AAAAAH!
BOFF
THIS IS HEAVEN.
I GOT ALL HOT AN' BOTHERED OVER THE IDEA OF A PRIVATE HOT TUB, BUT THE JOY OF SIMPLY BEIN' ALIVE DISTRACTED ME, SO I JUST ENJOYED THE SOAK.
AH WELL. I'M SLEEPY ANYWAY. TODAY'S FINE, I GUESS.

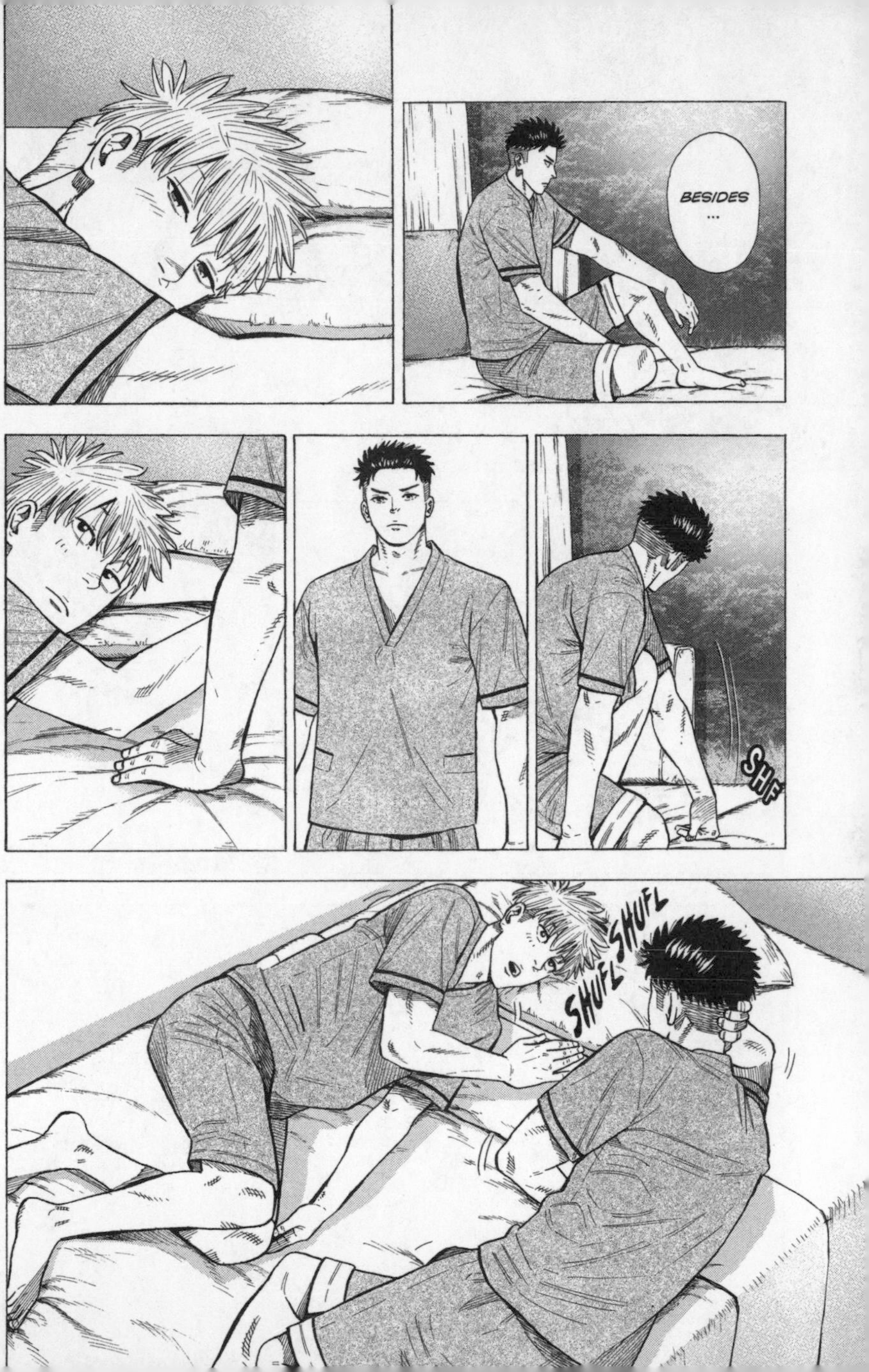
BESIDES ...
SHF
SHUFL SHUFL

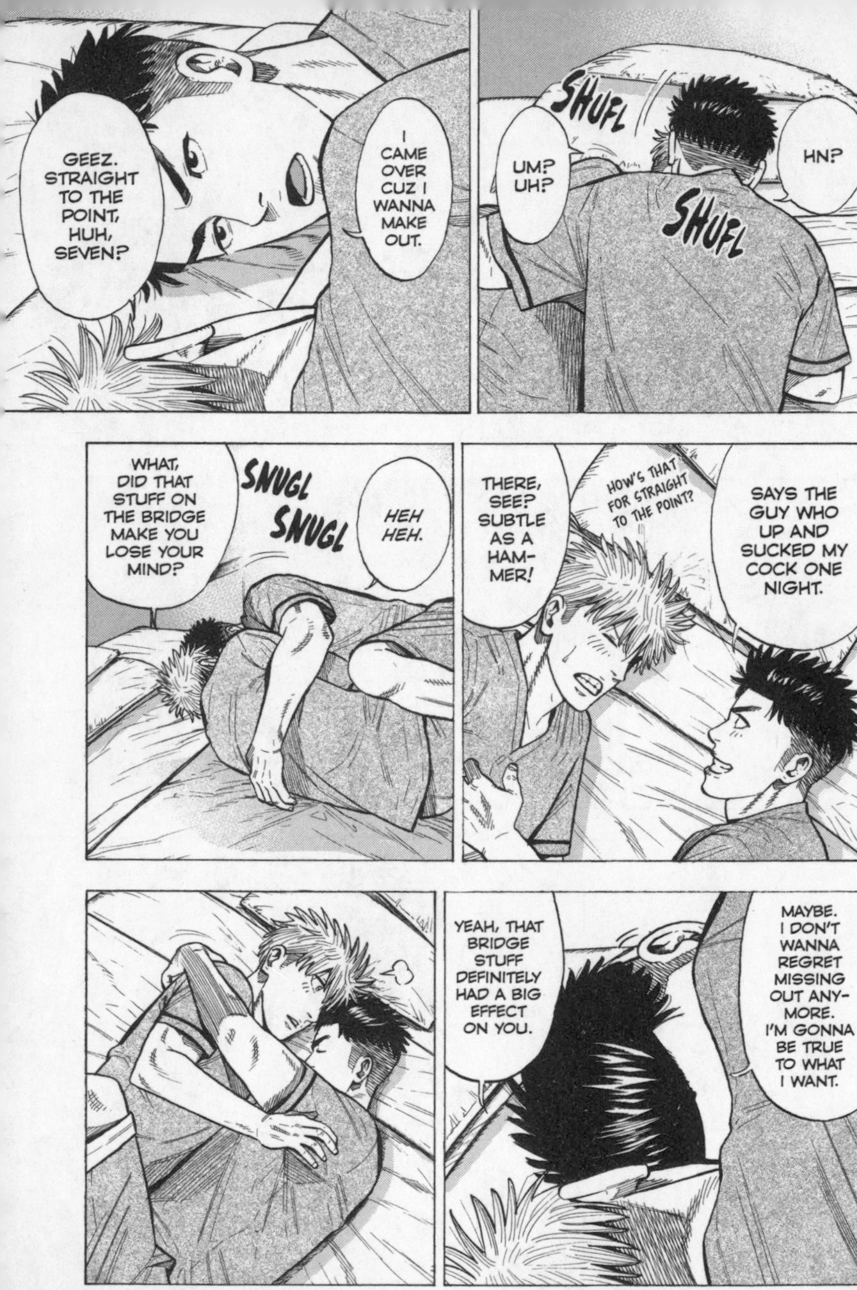
HN?
SHUFL
UM? UH?
SHUFL
I CAME OVER CUZ I WANNA MAKE OUT.
GEEZ. STRAIGHT TO THE POINT, HUH, SEVEN?
SAYS THE GUY WHO UP AND SUCKED MY COCK ONE NIGHT.
HOW'S THAT FOR STRAIGHT TO THE POINT?
THERE, SEE? SUBTLE AS A HAM-MER!
HEH HEH.
SNUGL SNUGL
WHAT, DID THAT STUFF ON THE BRIDGE MAKE YOU LOSE YOUR MIND?
MAYBE. I DON'T WANNA REGRET MISSING OUT ANY-MORE. I'M GONNA BE TRUE TO WHAT I WANT.
YEAH, THAT BRIDGE STUFF DEFINITELY HAD A BIG EFFECT ON YOU.

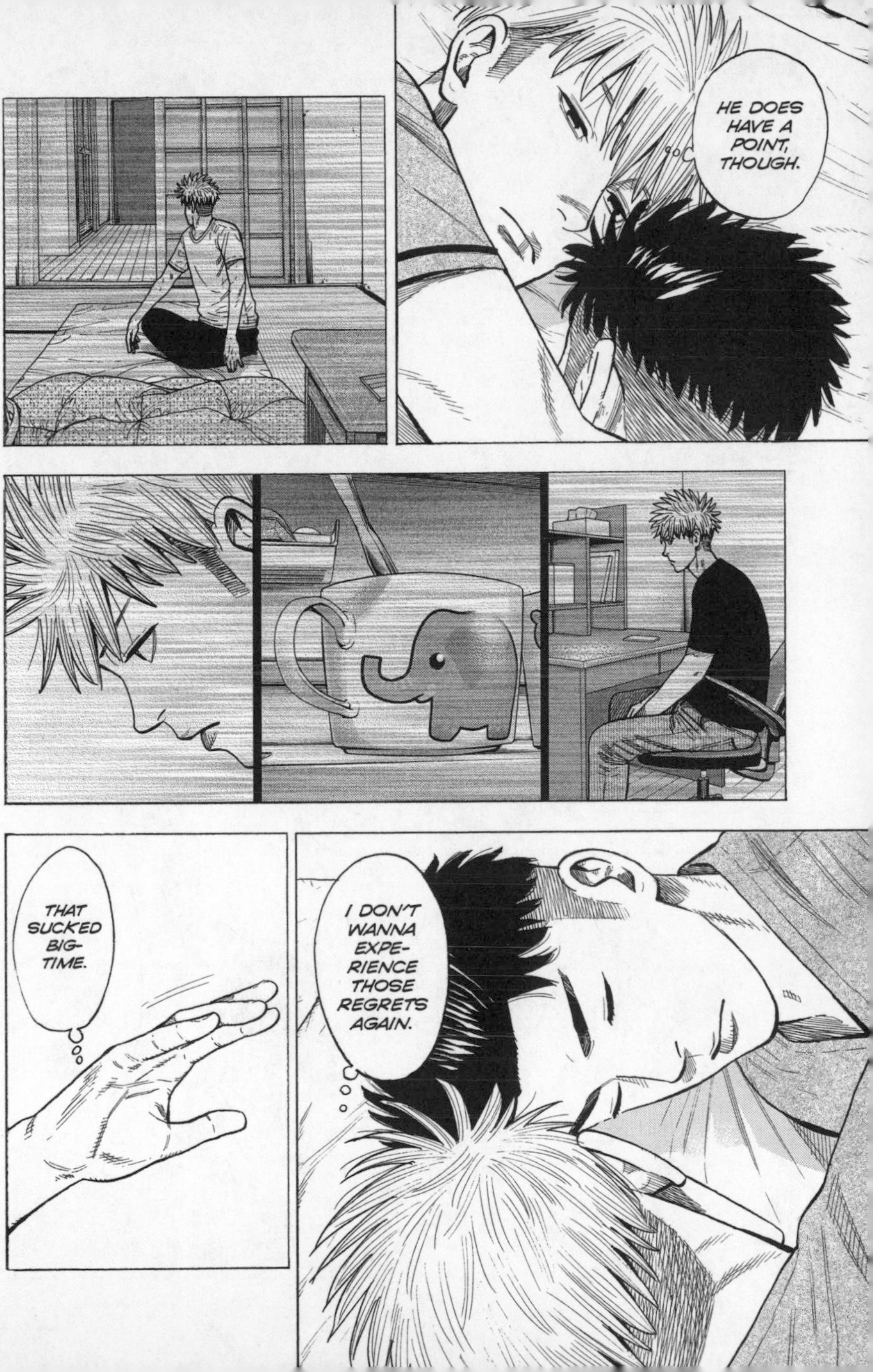
HE DOES HAVE A POINT, THOUGH.
I DON'T WANNA EXPERIENCE THOSE REGRETS AGAIN.
THAT SUCKED BIG-TIME.

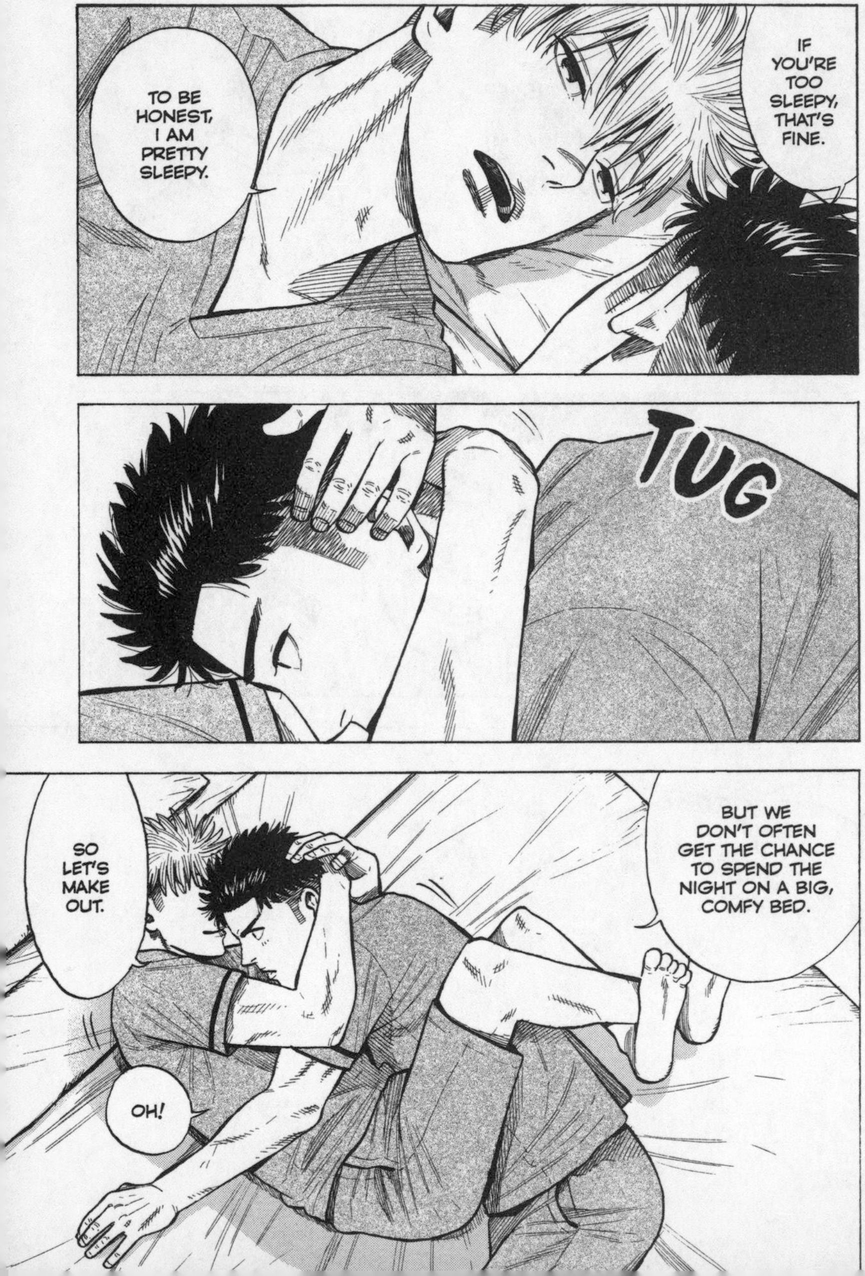
IF YOU'RE TOO SLEEPY, THAT'S FINE.
TO BE HONEST, I AM PRETTY SLEEPY.
TUG
BUT WE DON'T OFTEN GET THE CHANCE TO SPEND THE NIGHT ON A BIG, COMFY BED.
SO LET'S MAKE OUT.
OH!

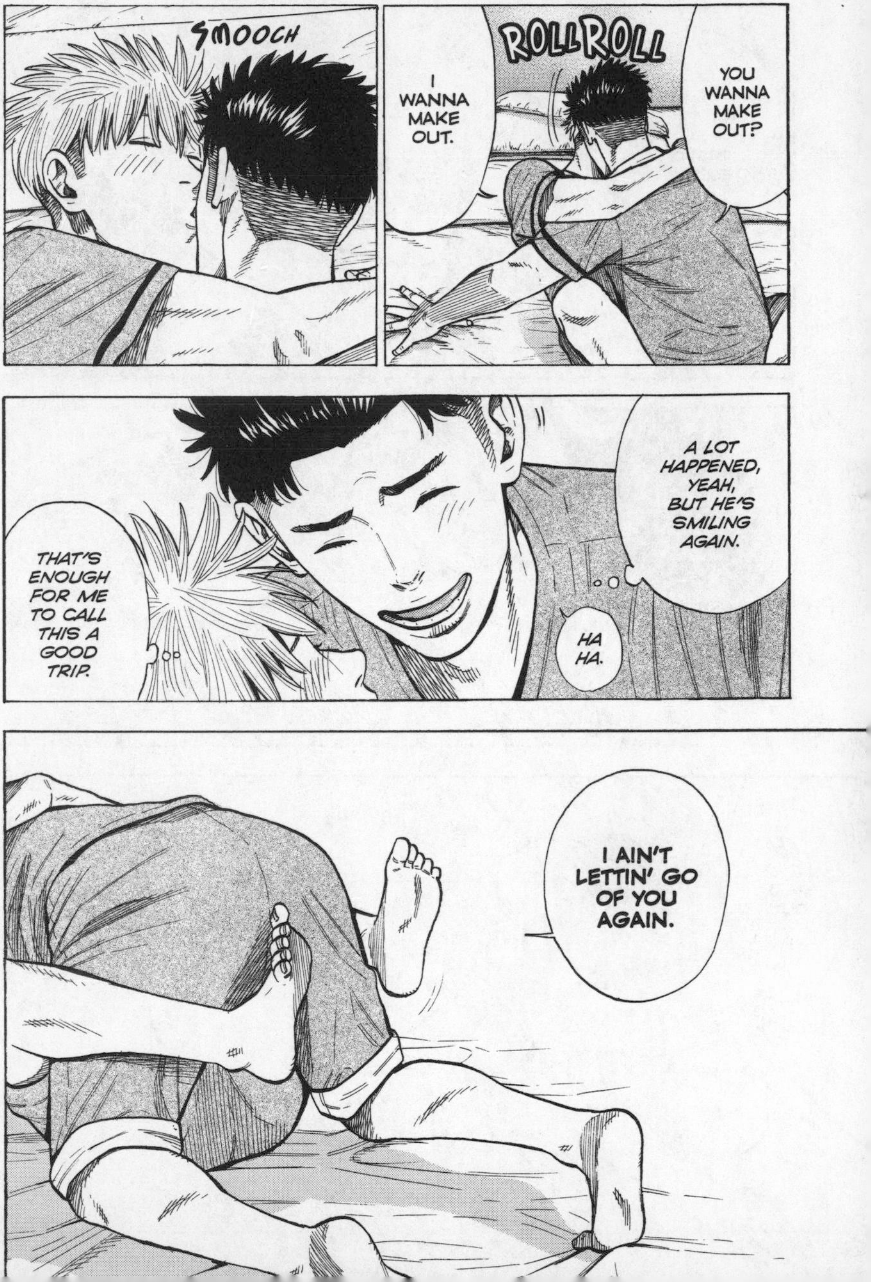
YOU WANNA MAKE OUT?
ROLLROLL
I WANNA MAKE OUT.
SMOOCH
A LOT HAPPENED, YEAH, BUT HE'S SMILING AGAIN.
HA HA.
THAT'S ENOUGH FOR ME TO CALL THIS A GOOD TRIP.
I AIN'T LETTIN' GO OF YOU AGAIN.

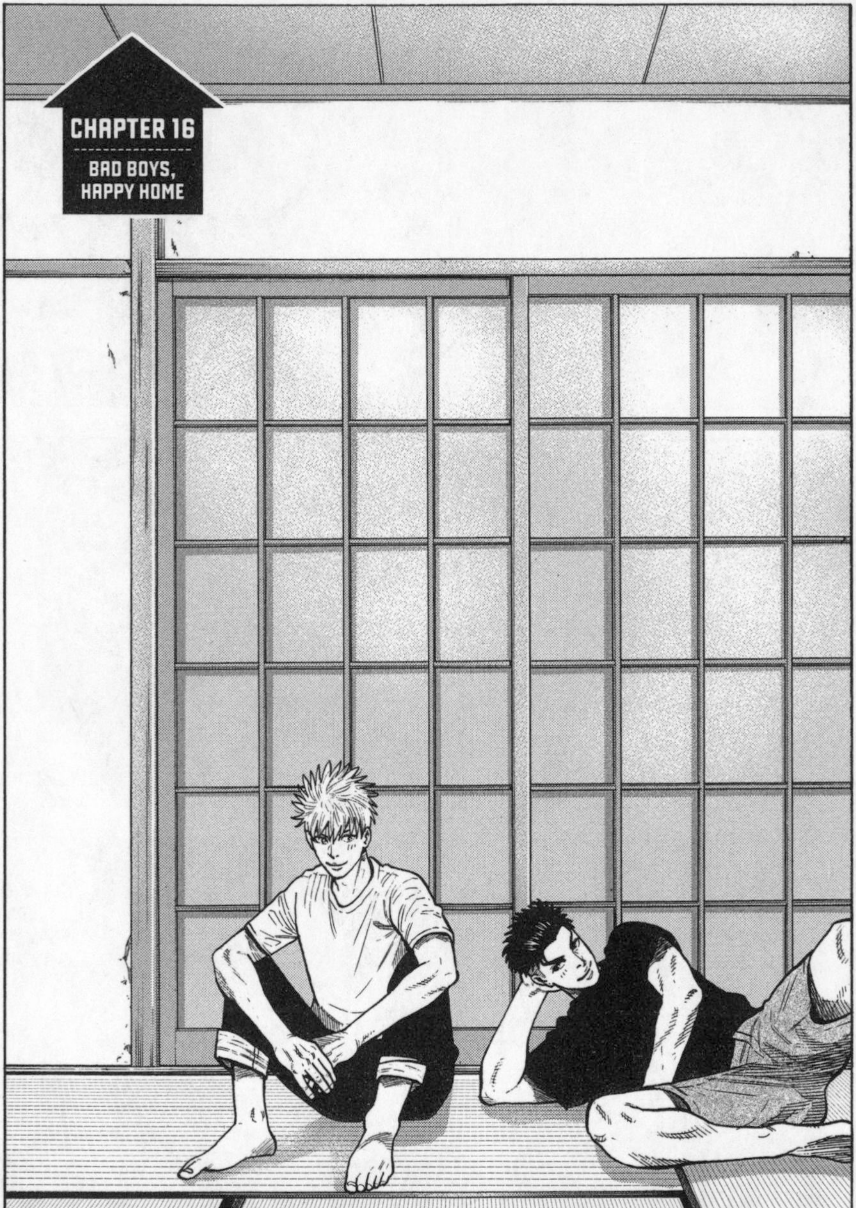
CHAPTER 16
BAD BOYS, HAPPY HOME

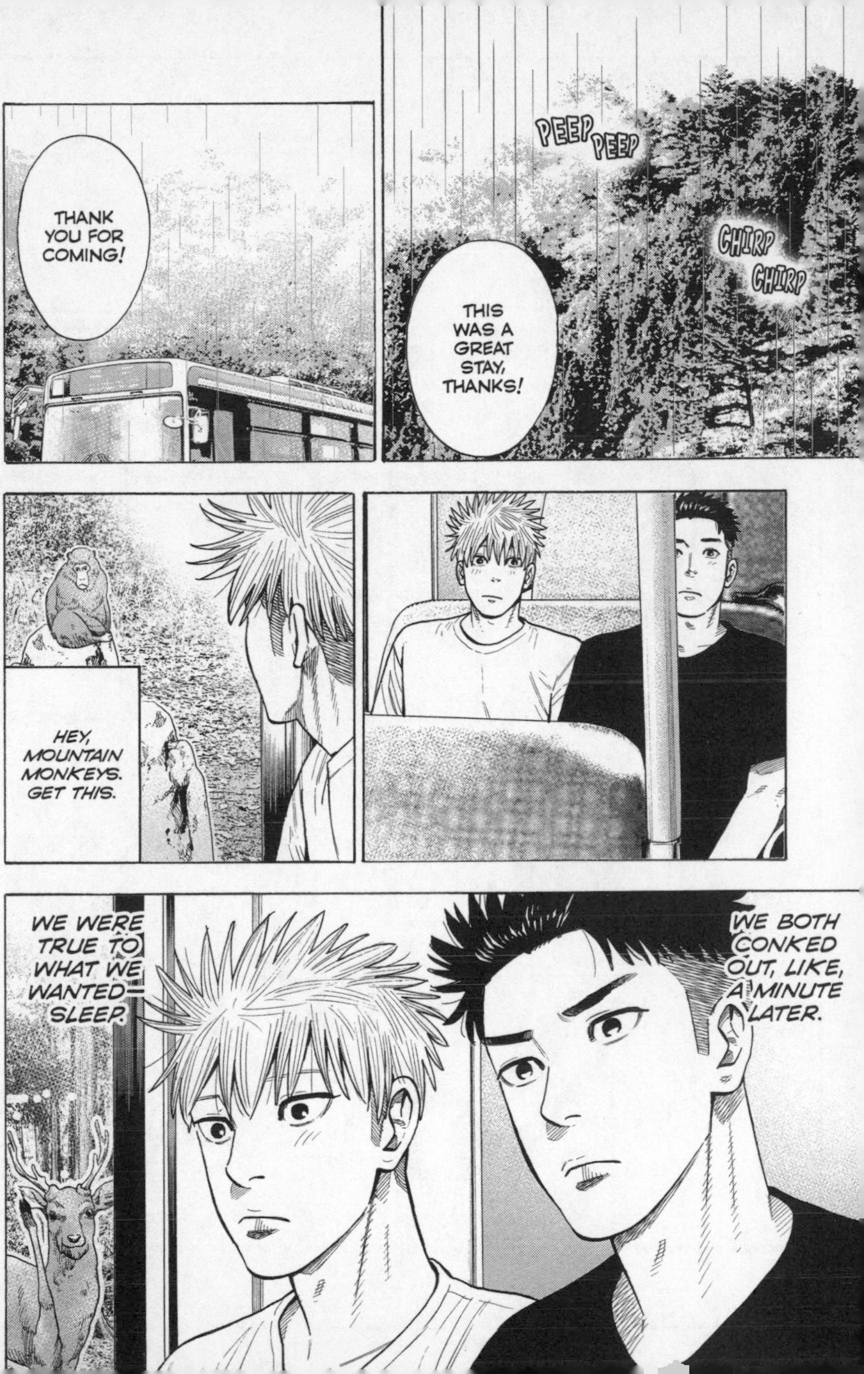
PEEP PEEP
CHIRP CHIRP
THIS WAS A GREAT STAY, THANKS!
THANK YOU FOR COMING!
HEY, MOUNTAIN MONKEYS. GET THIS.
WE WERE TRUE TO WHAT WE WANTED—SLEEP.
WE BOTH CONKED OUT, LIKE, A MINUTE LATER.

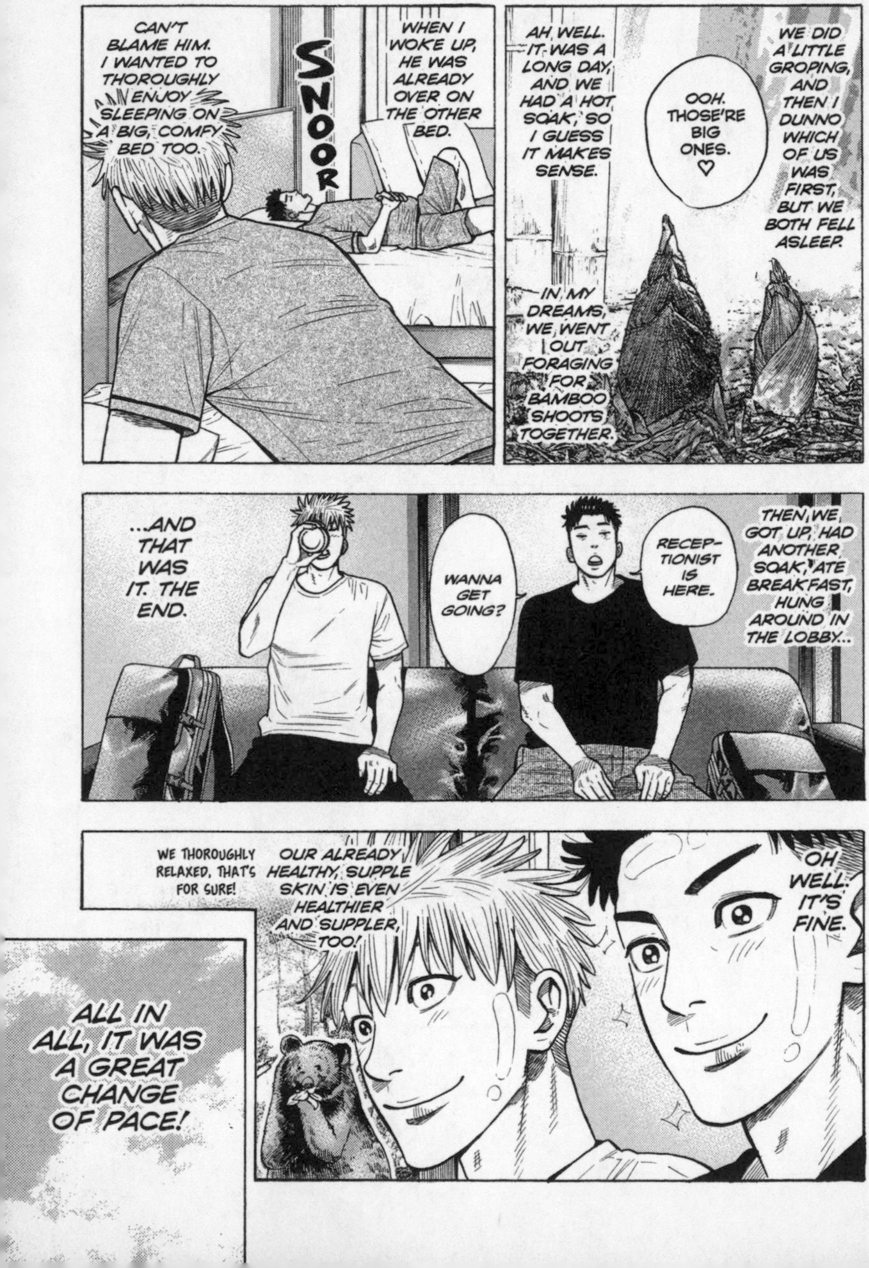
WE DID A LITTLE GROPING, AND THEN I DUNNO WHICH OF US WAS FIRST, BUT WE BOTH FELL ASLEEP.
OOH. THOSE'RE BIG ONES. ♡
AH WELL. IT WAS A LONG DAY, AND WE HAD A HOT SOAK, SO I GUESS IT MAKES SENSE.
IN MY DREAMS, WE WENT OUT FORAGING FOR BAMBOO SHOOTS TOGETHER.
WHEN I WOKE UP, HE WAS ALREADY OVER ON THE OTHER BED.
SNOOR
CAN'T BLAME HIM. I WANTED TO THOROUGHLY ENJOY SLEEPING ON A BIG, COMFY BED TOO.
THEN WE GOT UP, HAD ANOTHER SOAK, ATE BREAKFAST, HUNG AROUND IN THE LOBBY...
RECEPTIONIST IS HERE.
WANNA GET GOING?
...AND THAT WAS IT. THE END.
OH WELL. IT'S FINE.
OUR ALREADY HEALTHY, SUPPLE SKIN IS EVEN HEALTHIER AND SUPPLER, TOO!
WE THOROUGHLY RELAXED, THAT'S FOR SURE!
ALL IN ALL, IT WAS A GREAT CHANGE OF PACE!

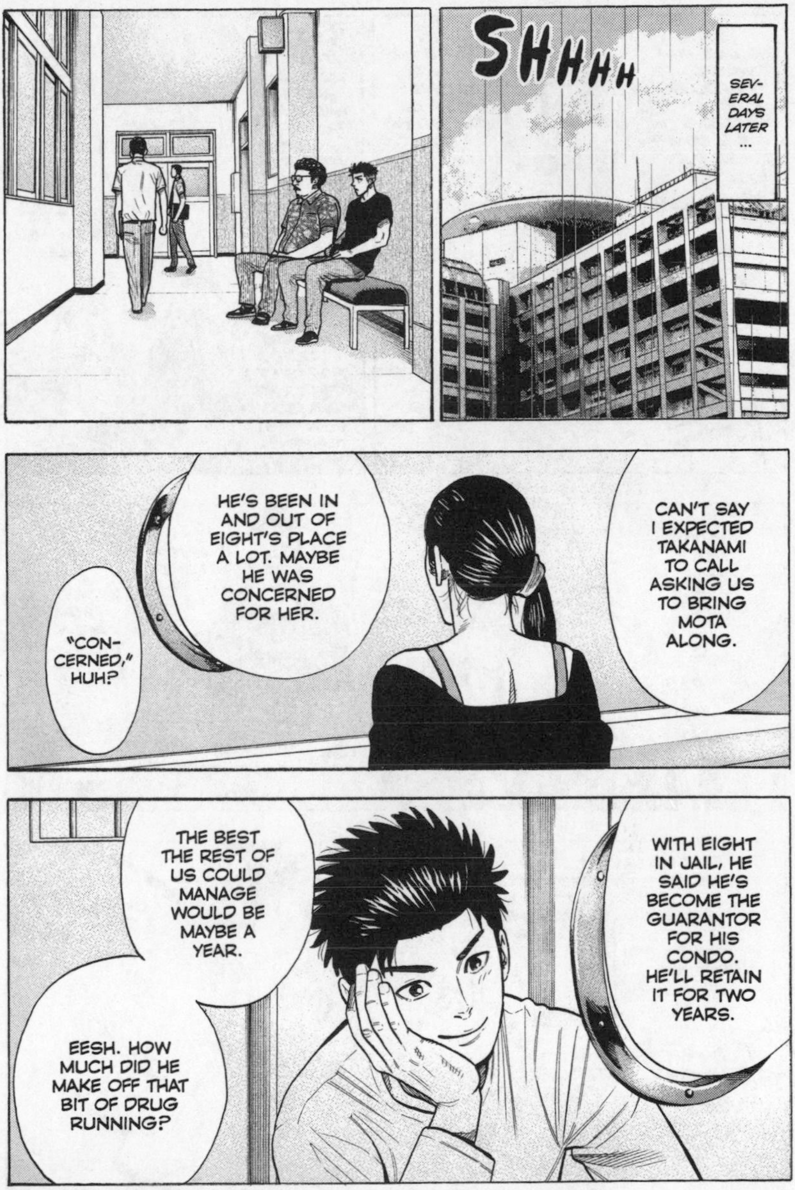
SHHHH
SEV-ERAL DAYS LATER ...
CAN'T SAY I EXPECTED TAKANAMI TO CALL ASKING US TO BRING MOTA ALONG.
HE'S BEEN IN AND OUT OF EIGHT'S PLACE A LOT. MAYBE HE WAS CONCERNED FOR HER.
"CON-CERNED," HUH?
WITH EIGHT IN JAIL, HE SAID HE'S BECOME THE GUARANTOR FOR HIS CONDO. HE'LL RETAIN IT FOR TWO YEARS.
THE BEST THE REST OF US COULD MANAGE WOULD BE MAYBE A YEAR.
EESH. HOW MUCH DID HE MAKE OFF THAT BIT OF DRUG RUNNING?

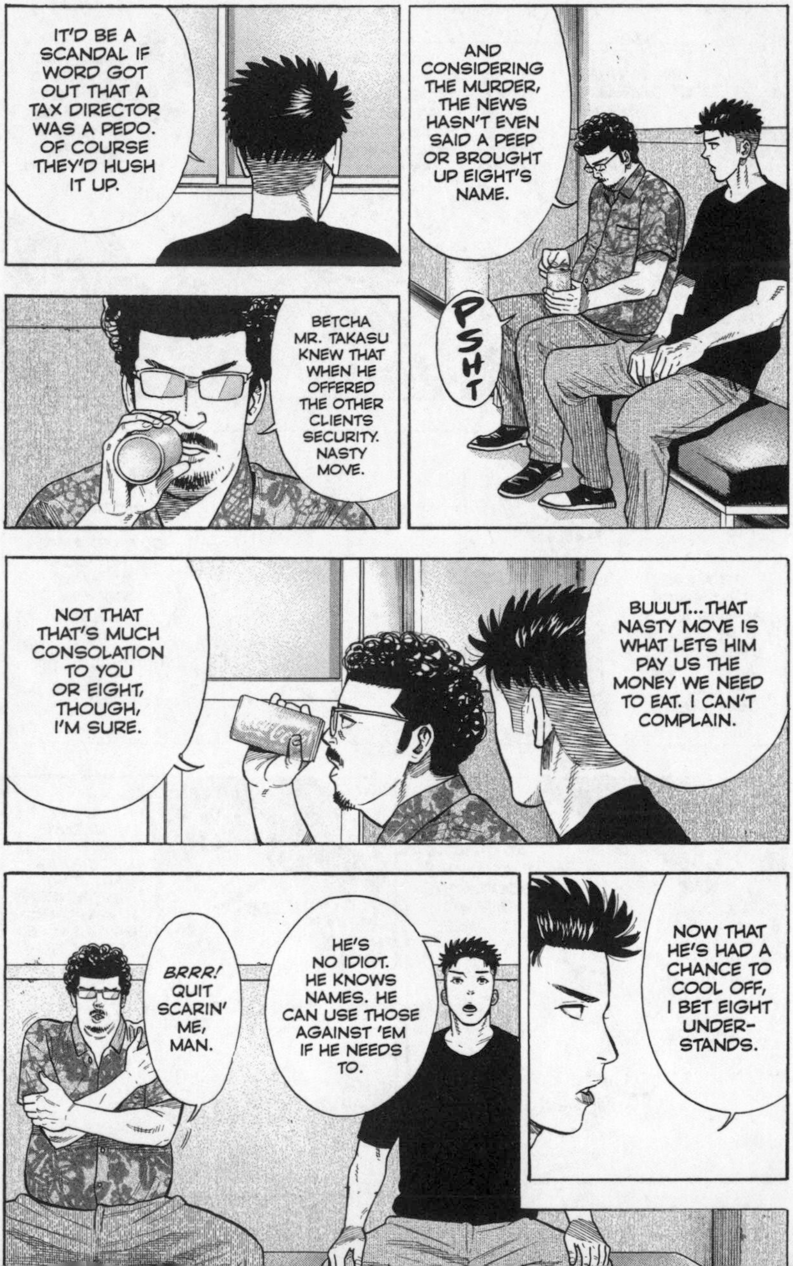
AND CONSIDERING THE MURDER, THE NEWS HASN'T EVEN SAID A PEEP OR BROUGHT UP EIGHT'S NAME.
PSHT
IT'D BE A SCANDAL IF WORD GOT OUT THAT A TAX DIRECTOR WAS A PEDO. OF COURSE THEY'D HUSH IT UP.
BETCHA MR. TAKASU KNEW THAT WHEN HE OFFERED THE OTHER CLIENTS SECURITY. NASTY MOVE.
BUUUT...THAT NASTY MOVE IS WHAT LETS HIM PAY US THE MONEY WE NEED TO EAT. I CAN'T COMPLAIN.
NOT THAT THAT'S MUCH CONSOLATION TO YOU OR EIGHT, THOUGH, I'M SURE.
NOW THAT HE'S HAD A CHANCE TO COOL OFF, I BET EIGHT UNDER-STANDS.
HE'S NO IDIOT. HE KNOWS NAMES. HE CAN USE THOSE AGAINST 'EM IF HE NEEDS TO.
BRRR! QUIT SCARIN' ME, MAN.

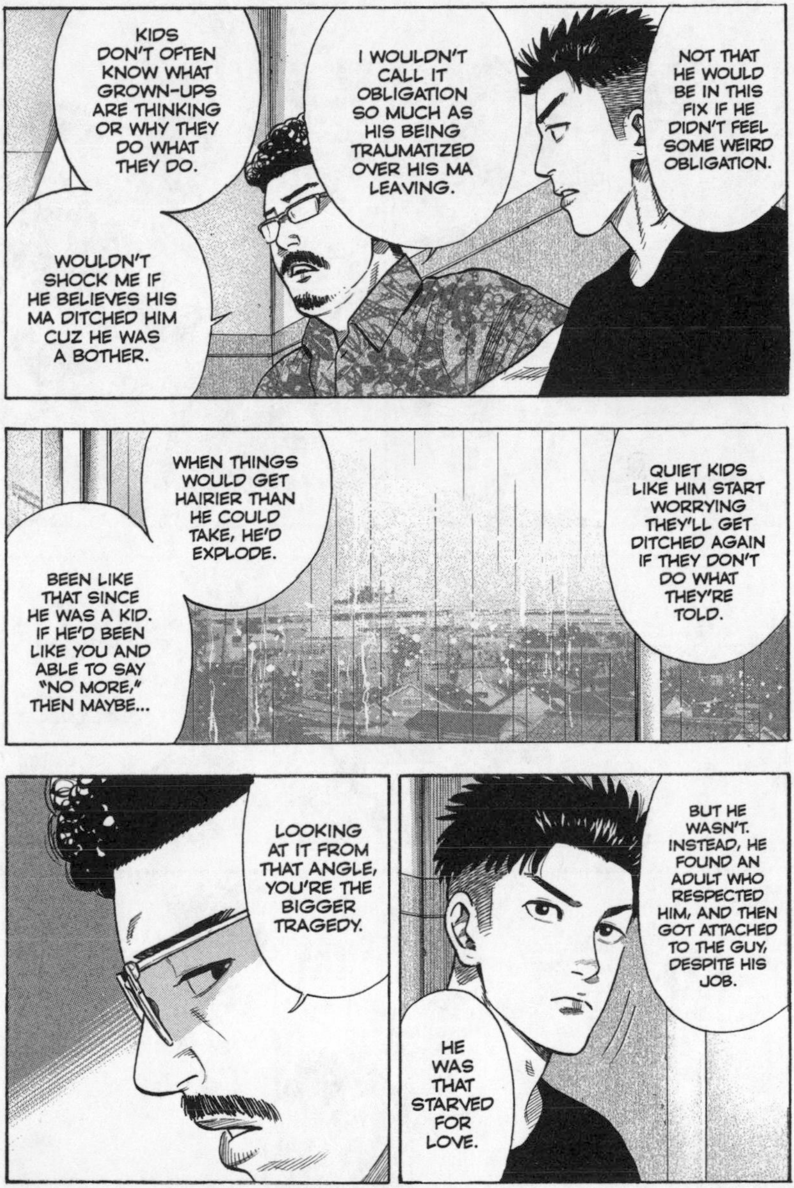
NOT THAT HE WOULD BE IN THIS FIX IF HE DIDN'T FEEL SOME WEIRD OBLIGATION.
I WOULDN'T CALL IT OBLIGATION SO MUCH AS HIS BEING TRAUMATIZED OVER HIS MA LEAVING.
KIDS DON'T OFTEN KNOW WHAT GROWN-UPS ARE THINKING OR WHY THEY DO WHAT THEY DO.
WOULDN'T SHOCK ME IF HE BELIEVES HIS MA DITCHED HIM CUZ HE WAS A BOTHER.
QUIET KIDS LIKE HIM START WORRYING THEY'LL GET DITCHED AGAIN IF THEY DON'T DO WHAT THEY'RE TOLD.
WHEN THINGS WOULD GET HAIRIER THAN HE COULD TAKE, HE'D EXPLODE.
BEEN LIKE THAT SINCE HE WAS A KID. IF HE'D BEEN LIKE YOU AND ABLE TO SAY "NO MORE," THEN MAYBE...
BUT HE WASN'T. INSTEAD, HE FOUND AN ADULT WHO RESPECTED HIM, AND THEN GOT ATTACHED TO THE GUY, DESPITE HIS JOB.
HE WAS THAT STARVED FOR LOVE.
LOOKING AT IT FROM THAT ANGLE, YOU'RE THE BIGGER TRAGEDY.

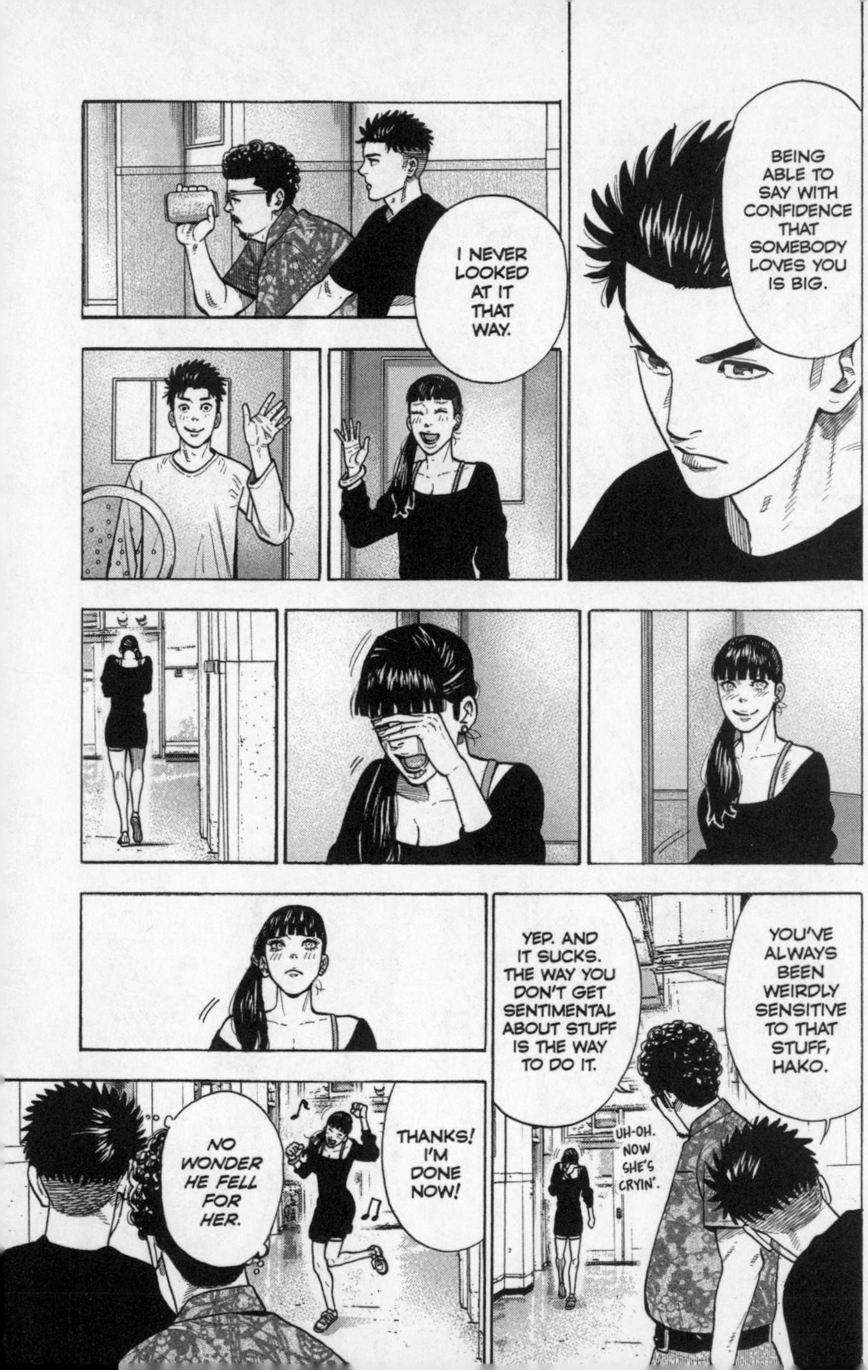
BEING ABLE TO SAY WITH CONFIDENCE THAT SOMEBODY LOVES YOU IS BIG.
I NEVER LOOKED AT IT THAT WAY.
YOU'VE ALWAYS BEEN WEIRDLY SENSITIVE TO THAT STUFF, HAKO.
YEP. AND IT SUCKS. THE WAY YOU DON'T GET SENTIMENTAL ABOUT STUFF IS THE WAY TO DO IT.
UH-OH. NOW SHE'S CRYIN'.
THANKS! I'M DONE NOW!
NO WONDER HE FELL FOR HER.

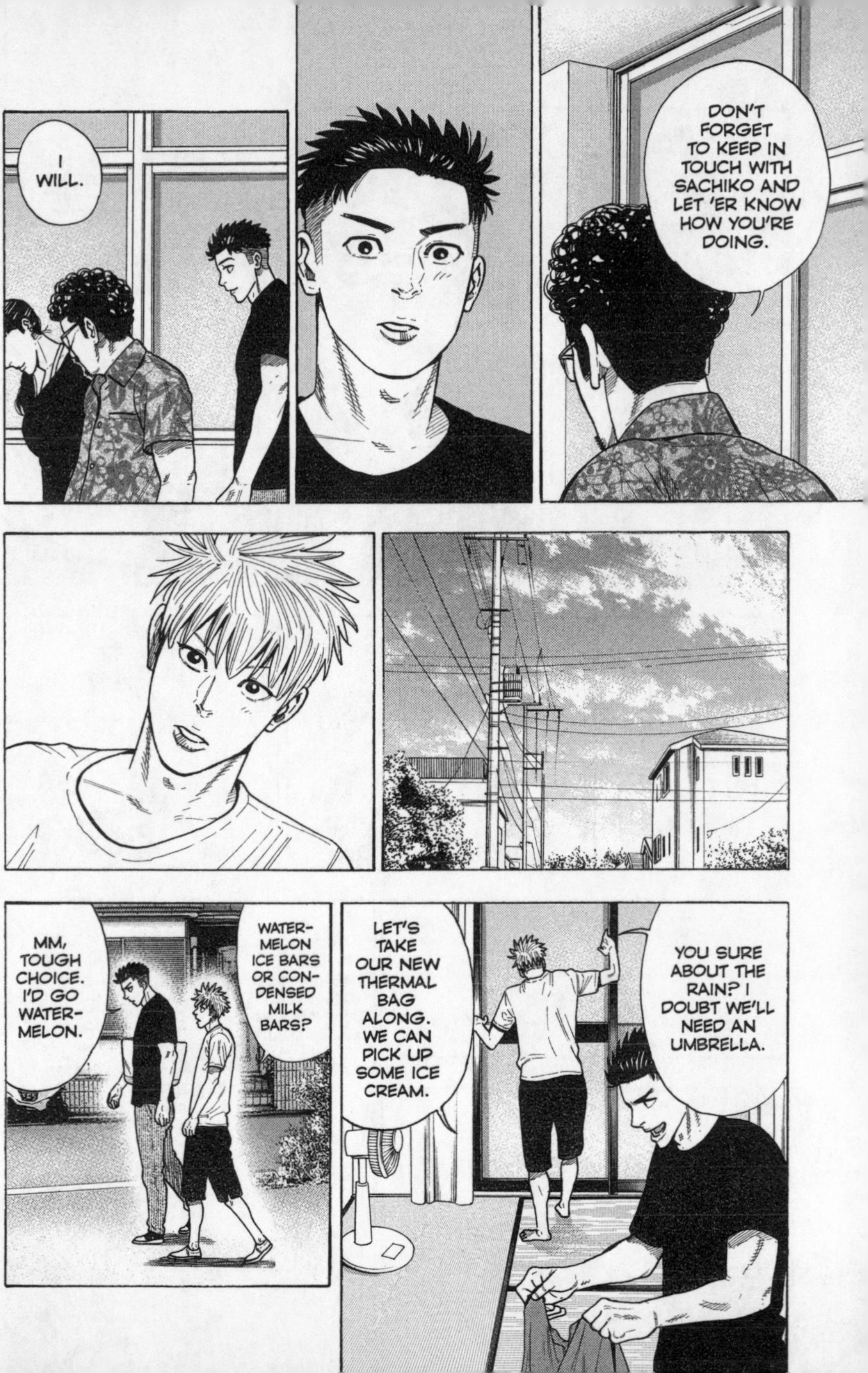
DON'T FORGET TO KEEP IN TOUCH WITH SACHIKO AND LET 'ER KNOW HOW YOU'RE DOING.
I WILL.
YOU SURE ABOUT THE RAIN? I DOUBT WE'LL NEED AN UMBRELLA.
LET'S TAKE OUR NEW THERMAL BAG ALONG. WE CAN PICK UP SOME ICE CREAM.
WATER-MELON ICE BARS OR CON-DENSED MILK BARS?
MM, TOUGH CHOICE. I'D GO WATER-MELON.

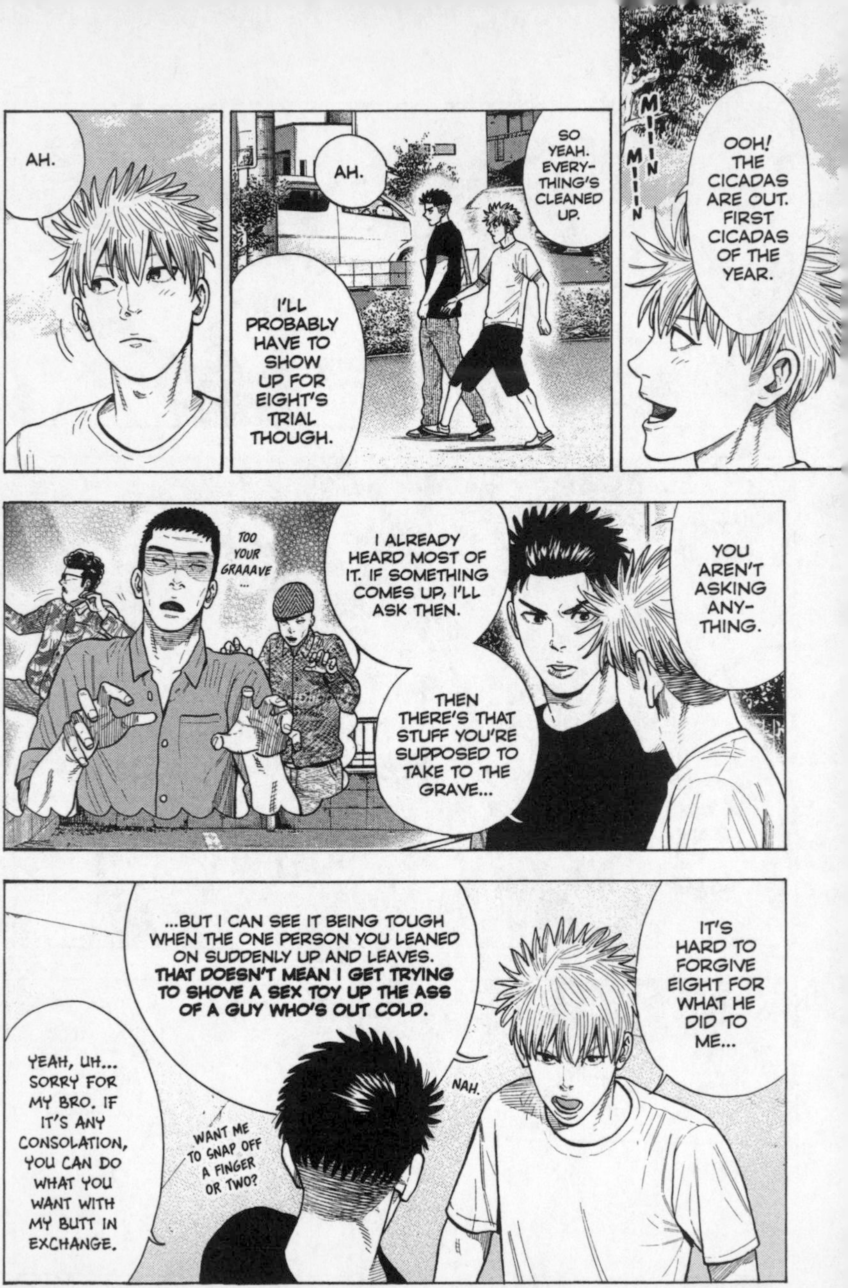

MI-I-IN
MI-I-IN
OOH! THE CICADAS ARE OUT. FIRST CICADAS OF THE YEAR.
SO YEAH. EVERYTHING'S CLEANED UP.
AH.
I'LL PROBABLY HAVE TO SHOW UP FOR EIGHT'S TRIAL THOUGH.
AH.
YOU AREN'T ASKING ANYTHING.
I ALREADY HEARD MOST OF IT. IF SOMETHING COMES UP, I'LL ASK THEN.
THEN THERE'S THAT STUFF YOU'RE SUPPOSED TO TAKE TO THE GRAVE...
TOO YOUR GRAAAVE ...
IT'S HARD TO FORGIVE EIGHT FOR WHAT HE DID TO ME...
...BUT I CAN SEE IT BEING TOUGH WHEN THE ONE PERSON YOU LEANED ON SUDDENLY UP AND LEAVES. THAT DOESN'T MEAN I GET TRYING TO SHOVE A SEX TOY UP THE ASS OF A GUY WHO'S OUT COLD.
NAH.
WANT ME TO SNAP OFF A FINGER OR TWO?
YEAH, UH... SORRY FOR MY BRO. IF IT'S ANY CONSOLATION, YOU CAN DO WHAT YOU WANT WITH MY BUTT IN EXCHANGE.

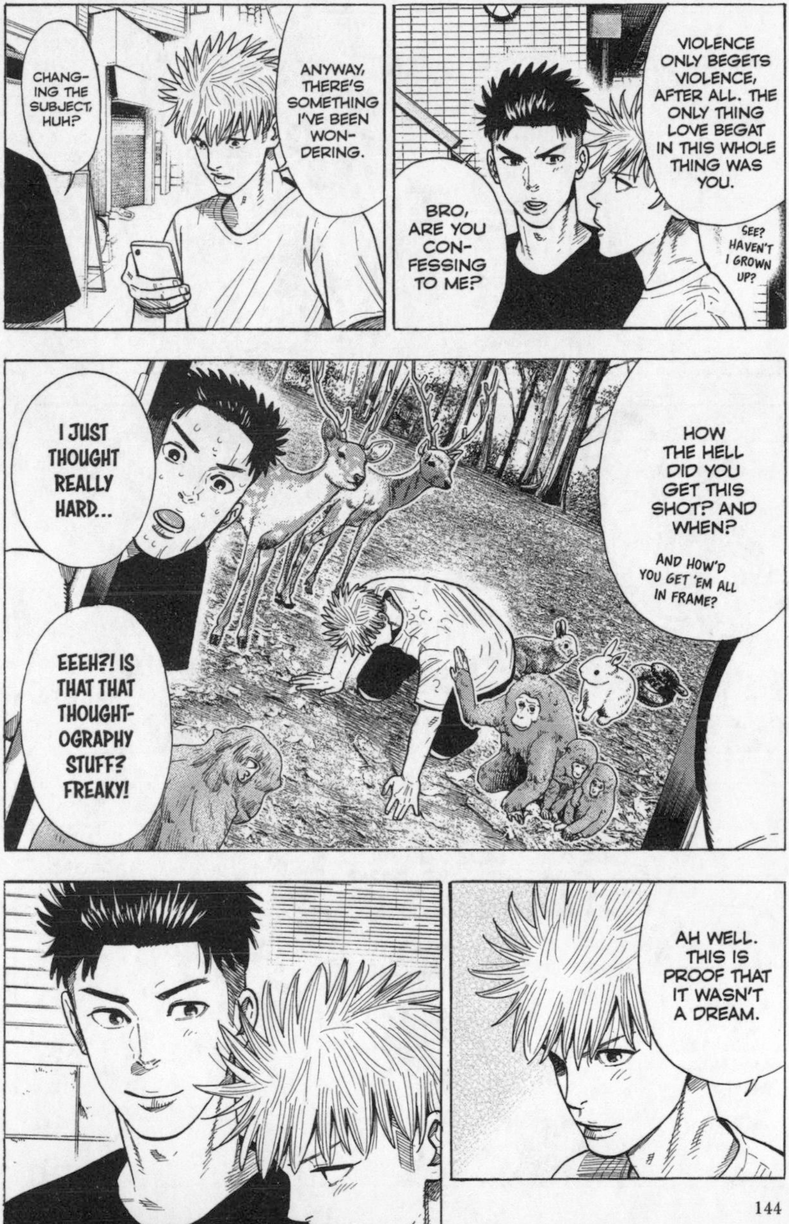
VIOLENCE ONLY BEGETS VIOLENCE, AFTER ALL. THE ONLY THING LOVE BEGAT IN THIS WHOLE THING WAS YOU.
SEE? HAVEN'T I GROWN UP?
BRO, ARE YOU CON-FESSING TO ME?
ANYWAY, THERE'S SOMETHING I'VE BEEN WON-DERING.
CHANG-ING THE SUBJECT, HUH?
HOW THE HELL DID YOU GET THIS SHOT? AND WHEN?
AND HOW'D YOU GET 'EM ALL IN FRAME?
I JUST THOUGHT REALLY HARD...
EEEH?! IS THAT THAT THOUGHT-OGRAPHY STUFF? FREAKY!
AH WELL. THIS IS PROOF THAT IT WASN'T A DREAM.

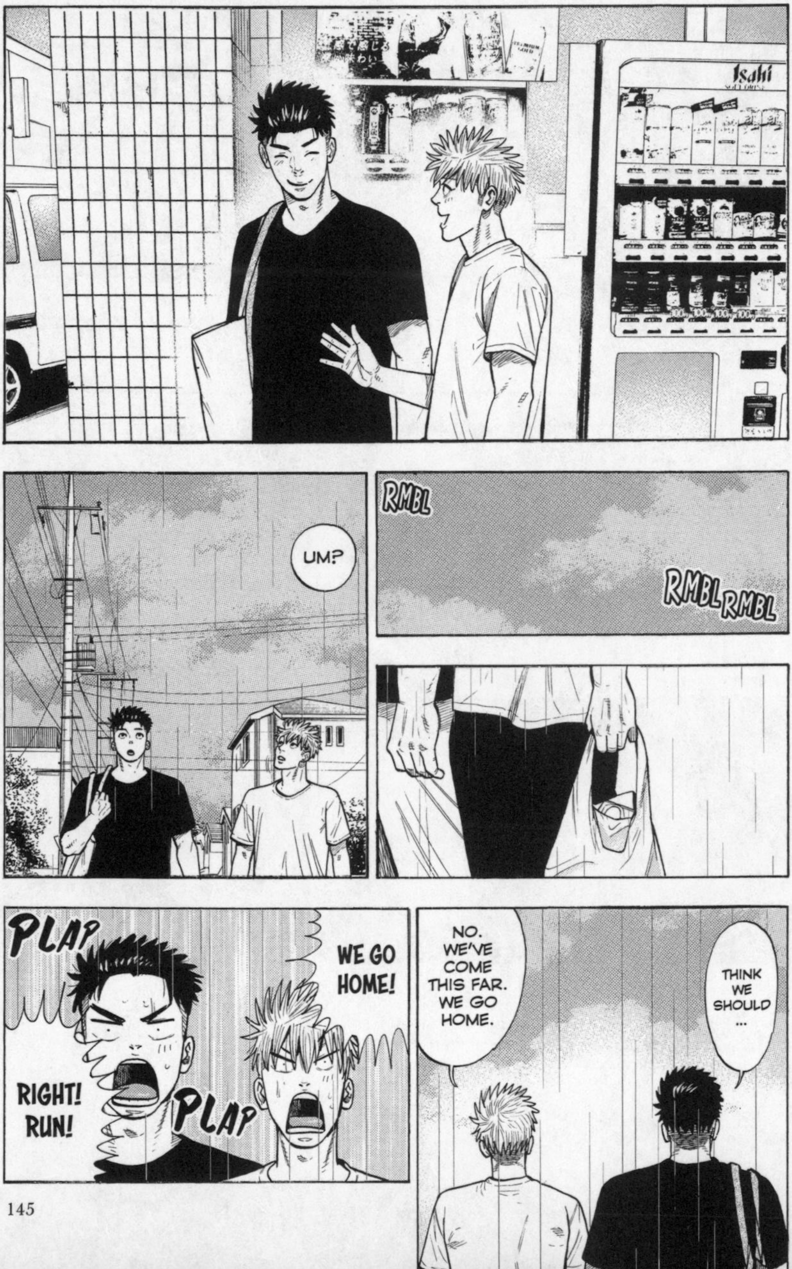
RMBL
RMBL RMBL
UM?
THINK WE SHOULD ...
NO. WE'VE COME THIS FAR. WE GO HOME.
WE GO HOME!
PLAP
RIGHT! RUN!
PLAP

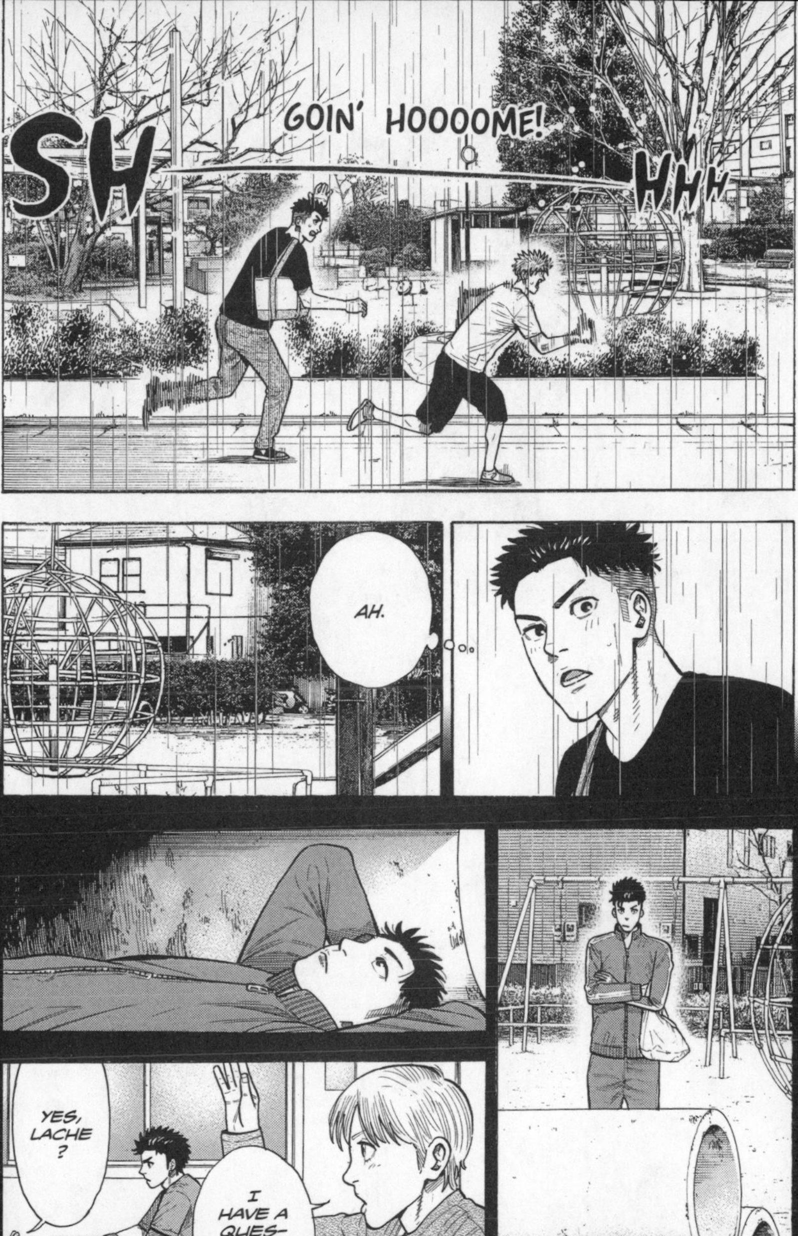
SH
GOIN' HOOOOME!
HHH
AH.
I HAVE A QUES-TION.
YES, LACHE?

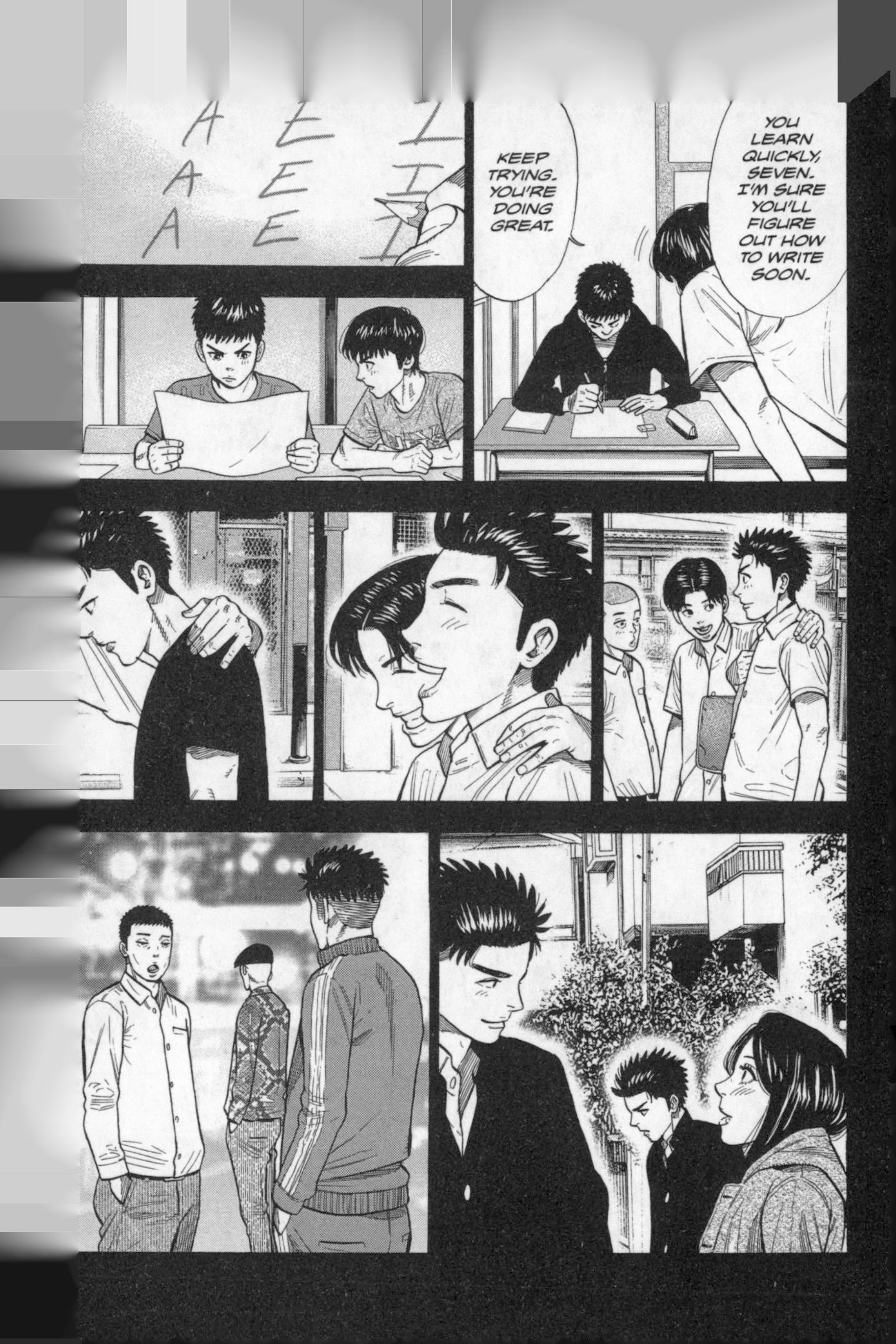
YOU LEARN QUICKLY, SEVEN. I'M SURE YOU'LL FIGURE OUT HOW TO WRITE SOON.
KEEP TRYING. YOU'RE DOING GREAT.
A E I
A E I
A E I

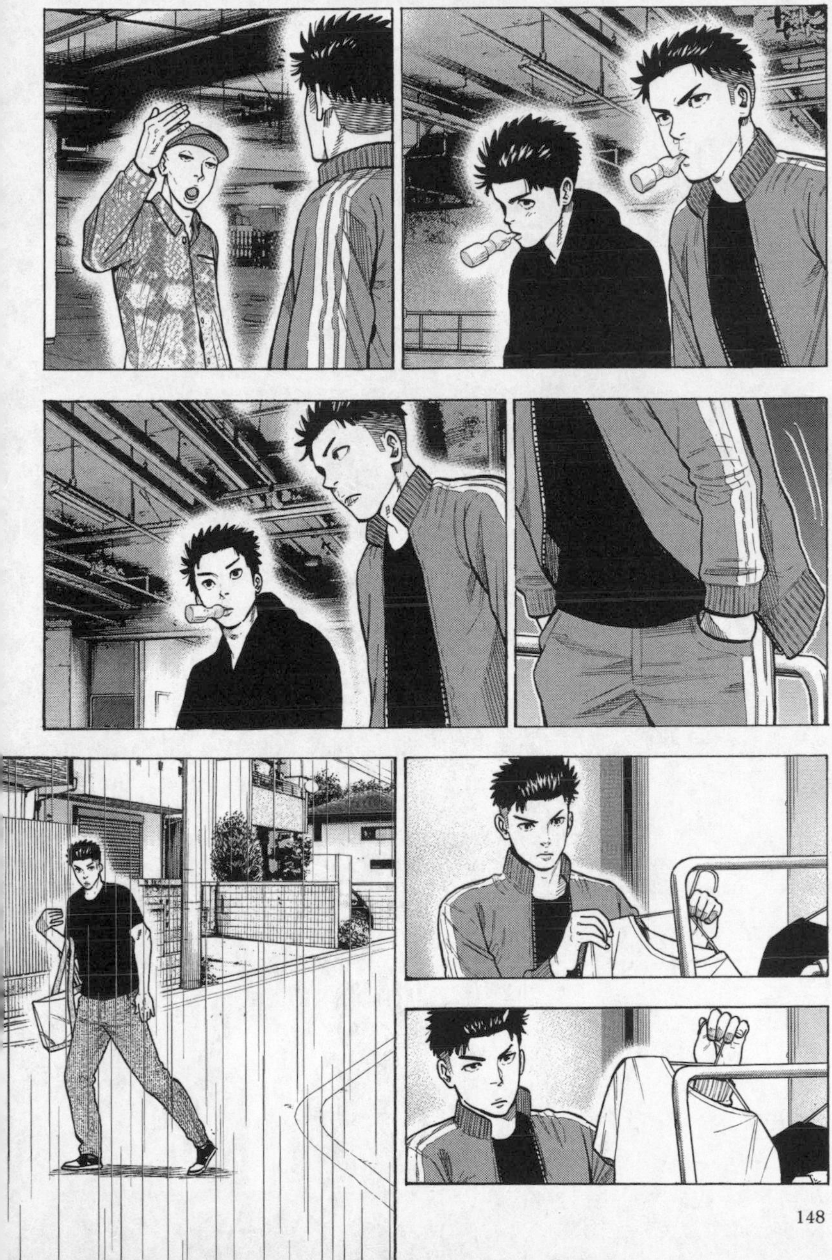

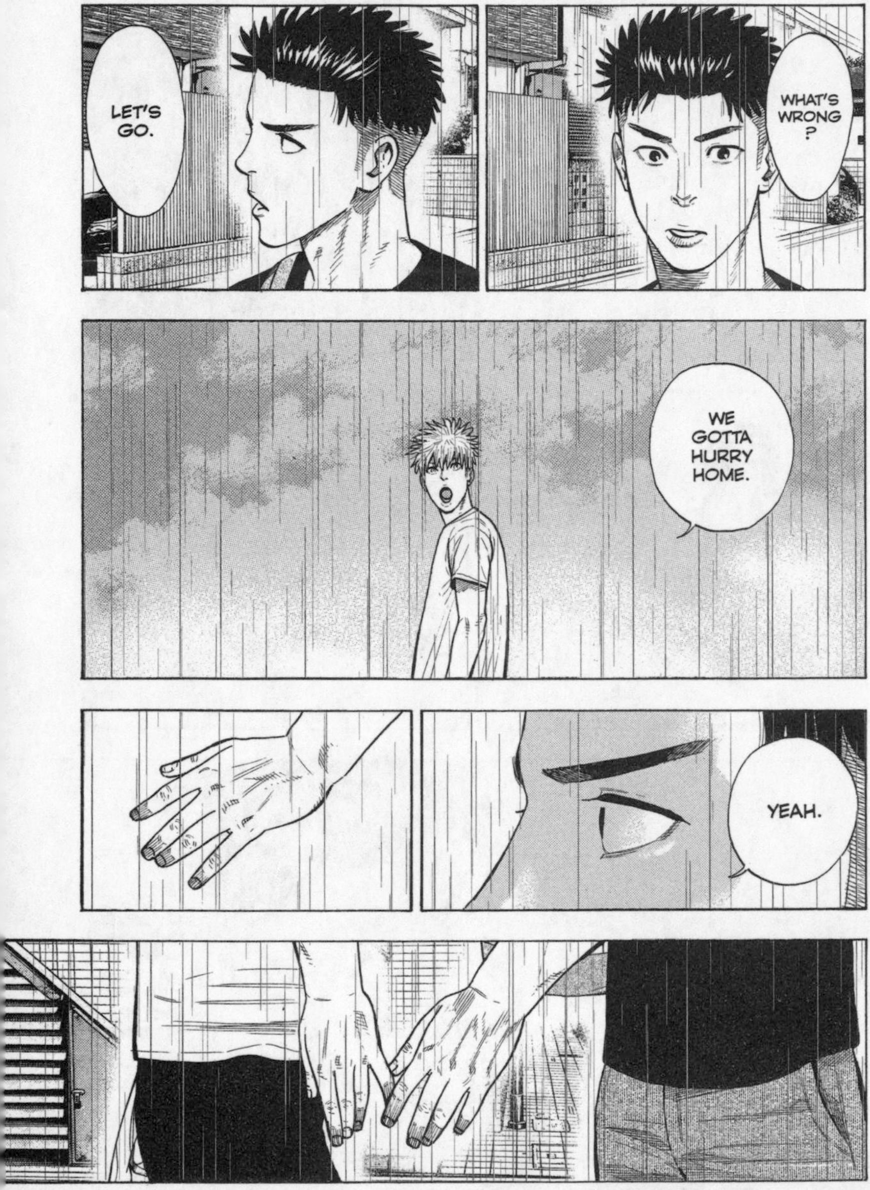
WHAT'S WRONG ?
LET'S GO.
WE GOTTA HURRY HOME.
YEAH.

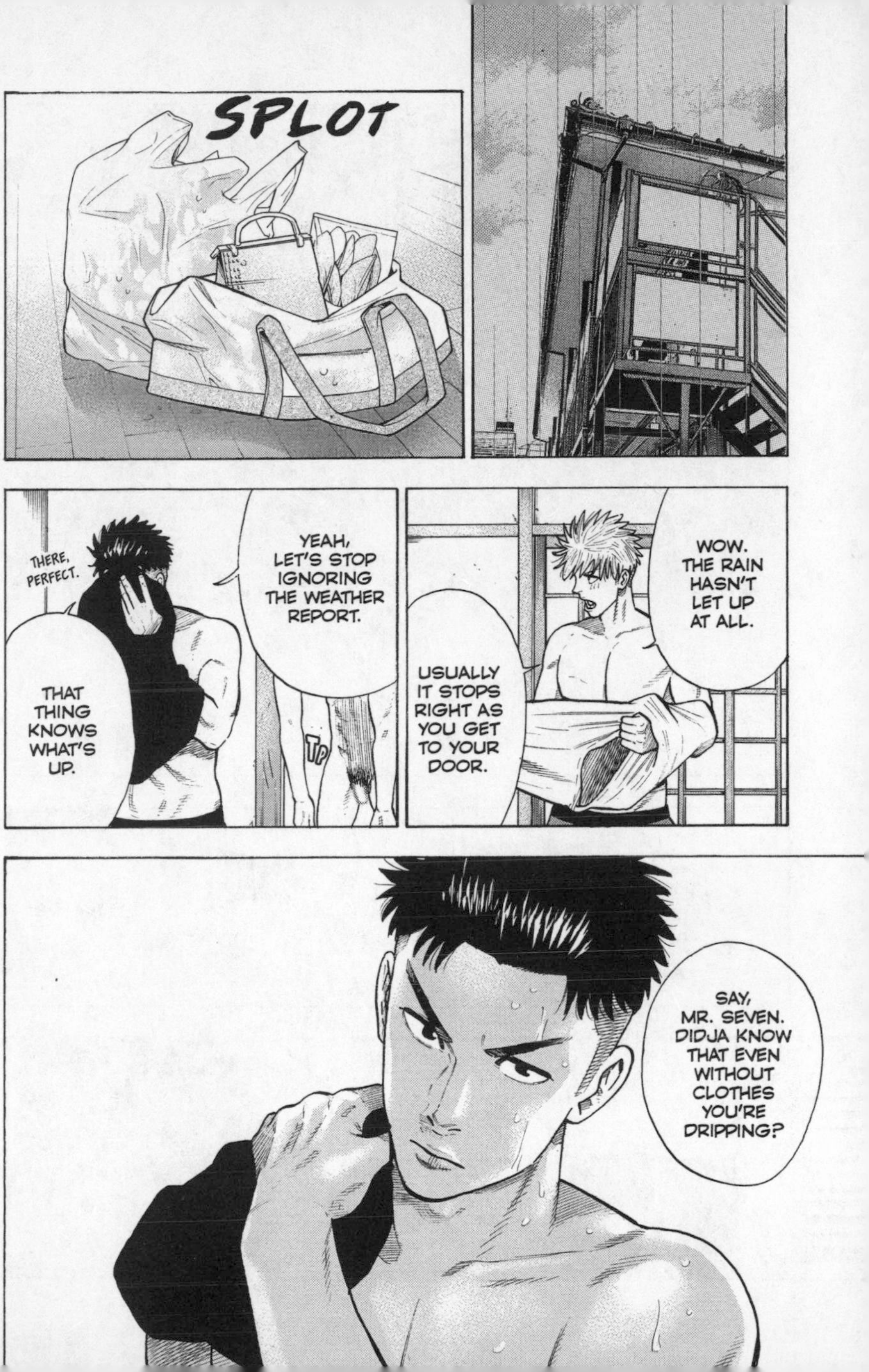
SPLOT
WOW. THE RAIN HASN'T LET UP AT ALL.
USUALLY IT STOPS RIGHT AS YOU GET TO YOUR DOOR.
YEAH, LET'S STOP IGNORING THE WEATHER REPORT.
TP
THERE, PERFECT.
THAT THING KNOWS WHAT'S UP.
SAY, MR. SEVEN. DIDJA KNOW THAT EVEN WITHOUT CLOTHES YOU'RE DRIPPING?

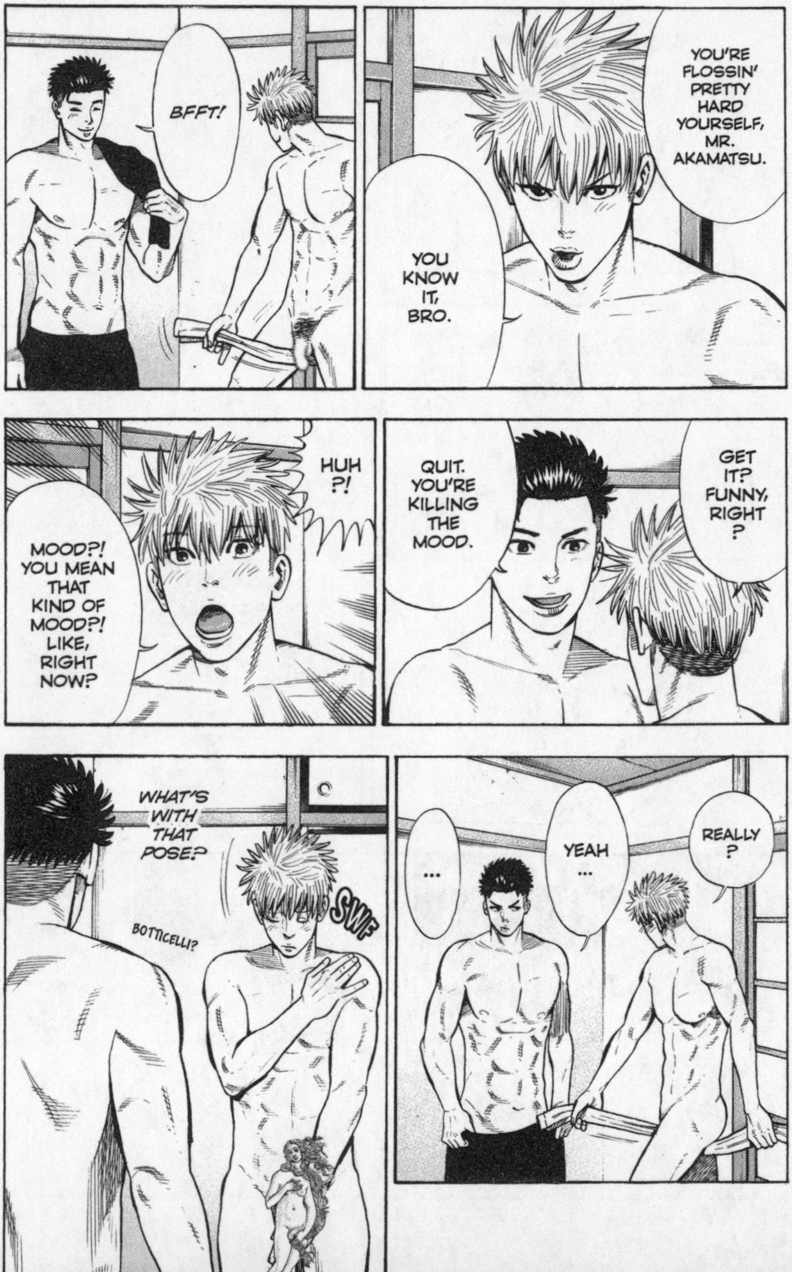
YOU'RE FLOSSIN' PRETTY HARD YOURSELF, MR. AKAMATSU.
YOU KNOW IT, BRO.
BFFT!
GET IT? FUNNY, RIGHT?
QUIT. YOU'RE KILLING THE MOOD.
HUH?!
MOOD?! YOU MEAN THAT KIND OF MOOD?! LIKE, RIGHT NOW?
REALLY?
YEAH...
...
WHAT'S WITH THAT POSE?
SWF
BOTTICELLI?

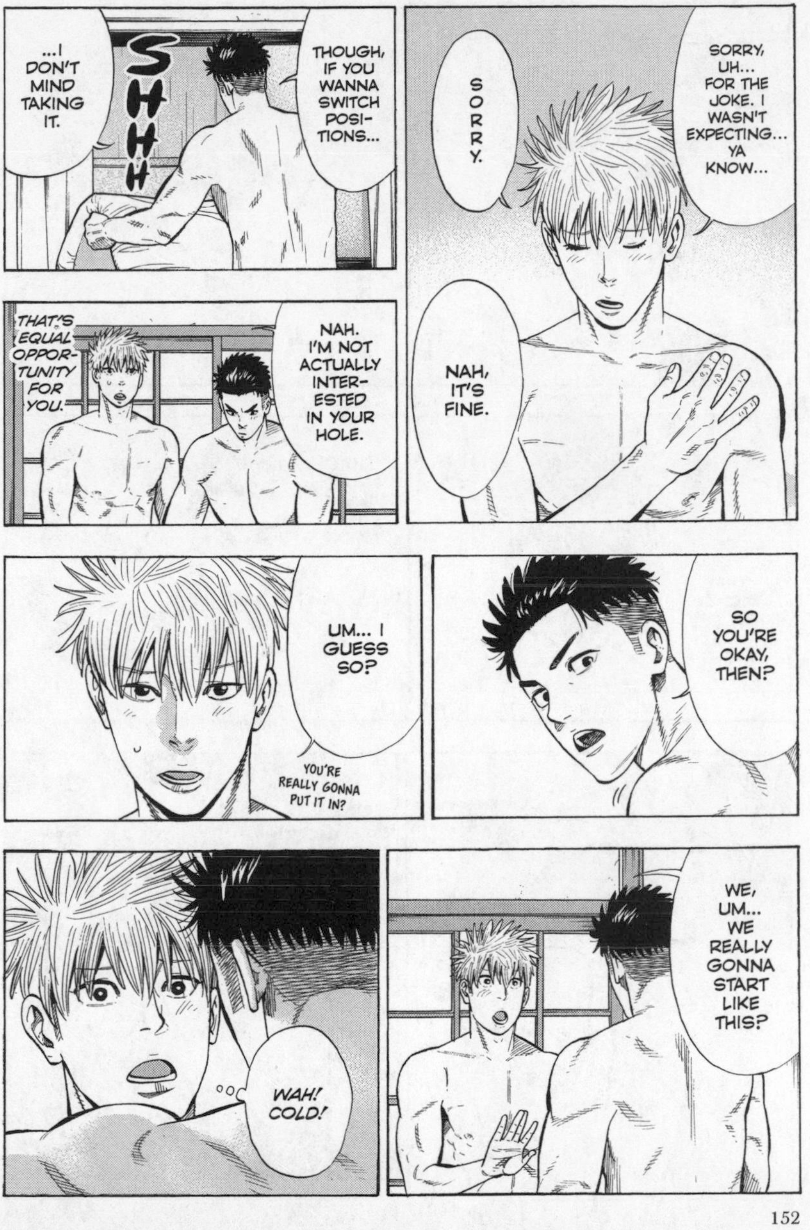
SORRY, UH... FOR THE JOKE. I WASN'T EXPECTING... YA KNOW...
SORRY.
NAH, IT'S FINE.
THOUGH, IF YOU WANNA SWITCH POSITIONS...
SHHHH
...I DON'T MIND TAKING IT.
NAH. I'M NOT ACTUALLY INTERESTED IN YOUR HOLE.
THAT'S EQUAL OPPORTUNITY FOR YOU.
SO YOU'RE OKAY, THEN?
UM... I GUESS SO?
YOU'RE REALLY GONNA PUT IT IN?
WE, UM... WE REALLY GONNA START LIKE THIS?
WAH! COLD!

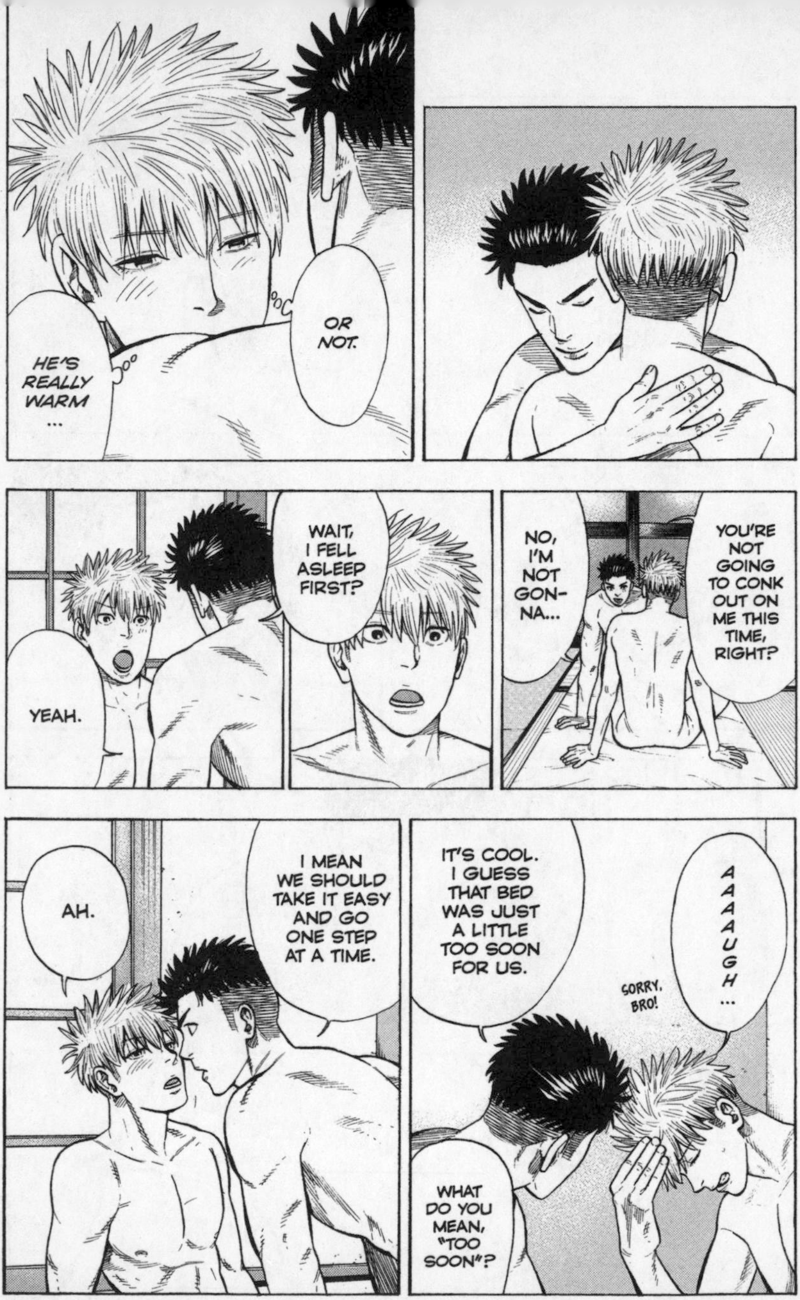
OR NOT.
HE'S REALLY WARM ...
YOU'RE NOT GOING TO CONK OUT ON ME THIS TIME, RIGHT?
NO, I'M NOT GON-NA...
WAIT, I FELL ASLEEP FIRST?
YEAH.
AAAAUGH ...
IT'S COOL. I GUESS THAT BED WAS JUST A LITTLE TOO SOON FOR US.
SORRY, BRO!
WHAT DO YOU MEAN, "TOO SOON"?
I MEAN WE SHOULD TAKE IT EASY AND GO ONE STEP AT A TIME.
AH.

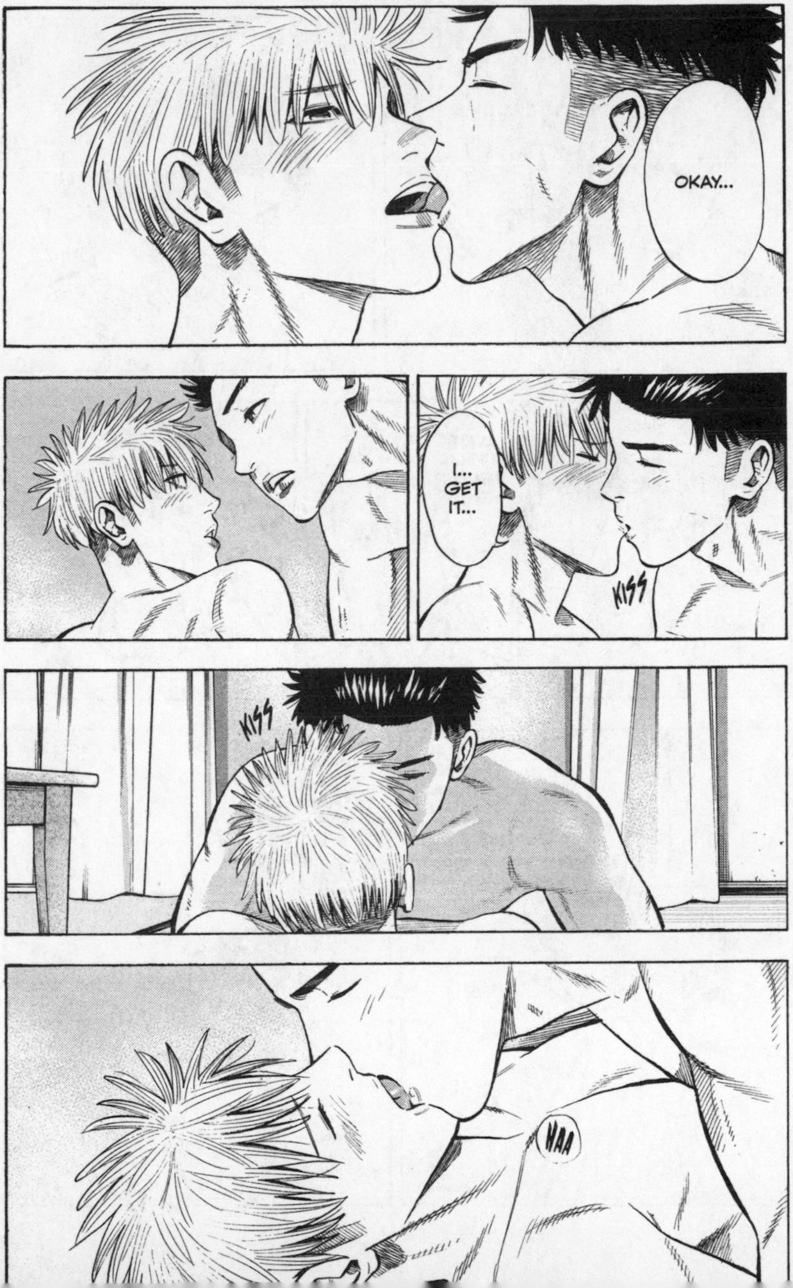
OKAY...
I... GET IT...
KISS
KISS
HAA

KISS
KISS
SWF
COME TO THINK OF IT...
BATHTUB ASIDE...
KISS
YEAH, FUNNILY ENOUGH.
THIS IS THE FIRST WE'VE DONE IT BUCK NAKED.
KISS
HAA

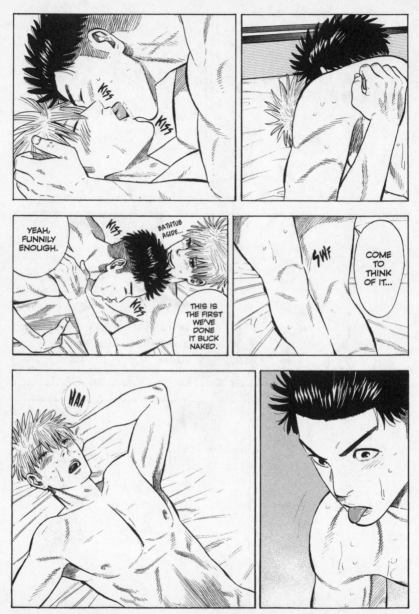

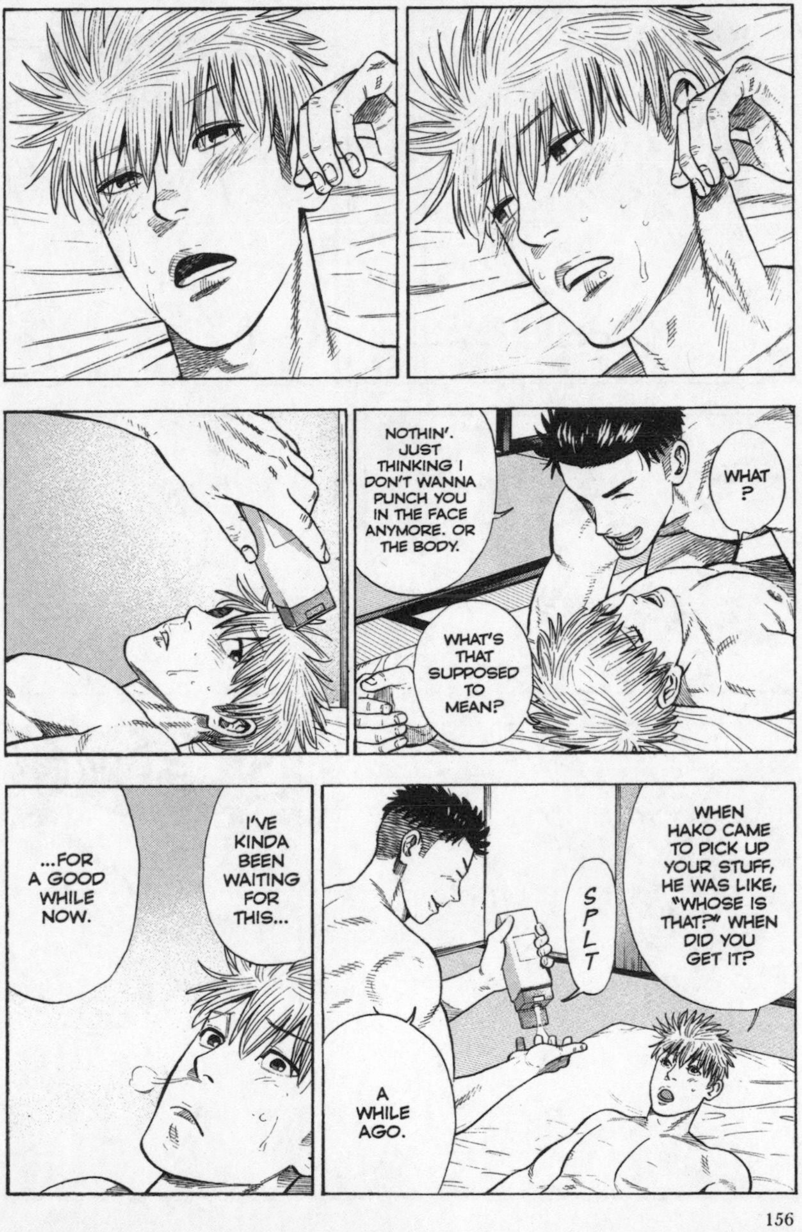
WHAT?
NOTHIN'. JUST THINKING I DON'T WANNA PUNCH YOU IN THE FACE ANYMORE. OR THE BODY.
WHAT'S THAT SUPPOSED TO MEAN?
WHEN HAKO CAME TO PICK UP YOUR STUFF, HE WAS LIKE, "WHOSE IS THAT?" WHEN DID YOU GET IT?
SPLT
A WHILE AGO.
I'VE KINDA BEEN WAITING FOR THIS...
...FOR A GOOD WHILE NOW.

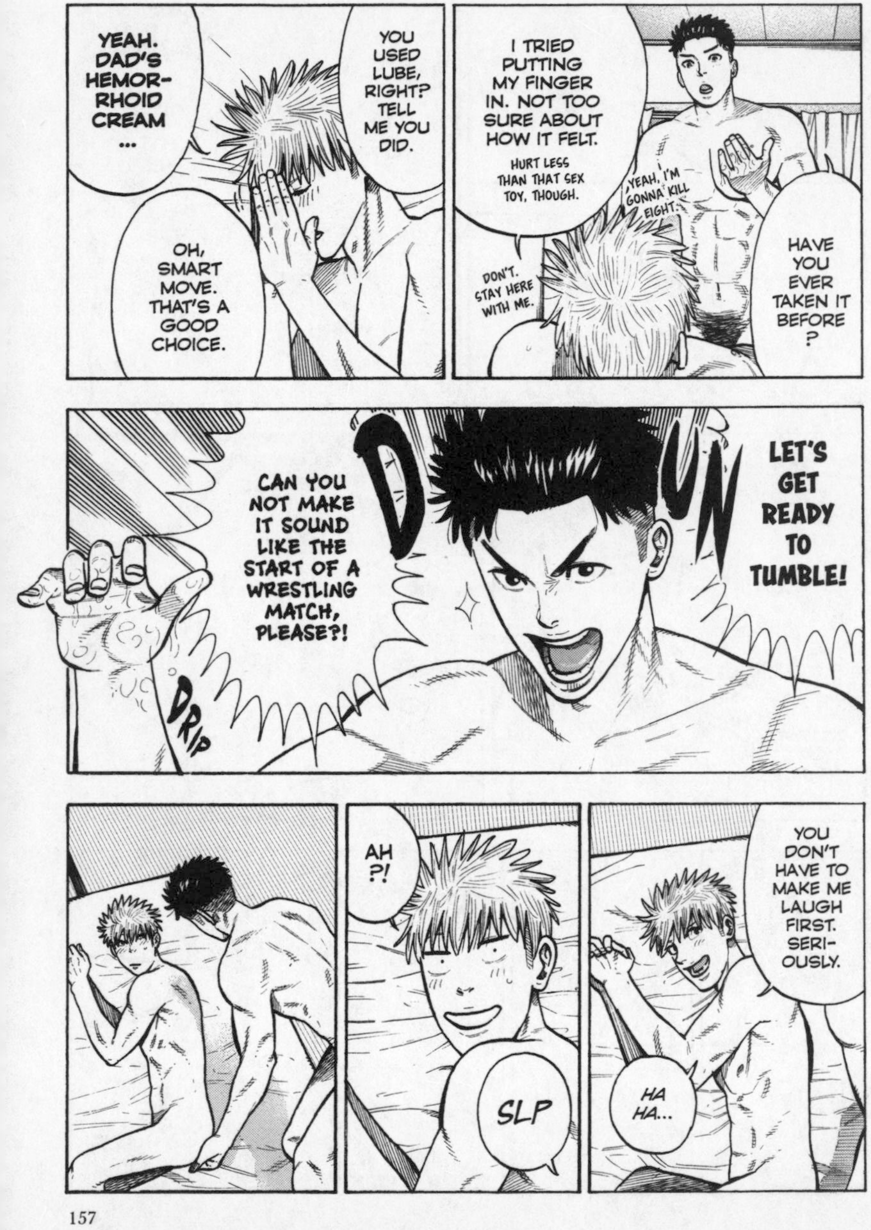
HAVE YOU EVER TAKEN IT BEFORE?
I TRIED PUTTING MY FINGER IN. NOT TOO SURE ABOUT HOW IT FELT.
HURT LESS THAN THAT SEX TOY, THOUGH.
YEAH, I'M GONNA KILL EIGHT.
DON'T. STAY HERE WITH ME.
YOU USED LUBE, RIGHT? TELL ME YOU DID.
YEAH. DAD'S HEMOR-RHOID CREAM...
OH, SMART MOVE. THAT'S A GOOD CHOICE.
LET'S GET READY TO TUMBLE!
DUN
CAN YOU NOT MAKE IT SOUND LIKE THE START OF A WRESTLING MATCH, PLEASE?!
DRIP
YOU DON'T HAVE TO MAKE ME LAUGH FIRST. SERI-OUSLY.
HA HA...
AH?!
SLP

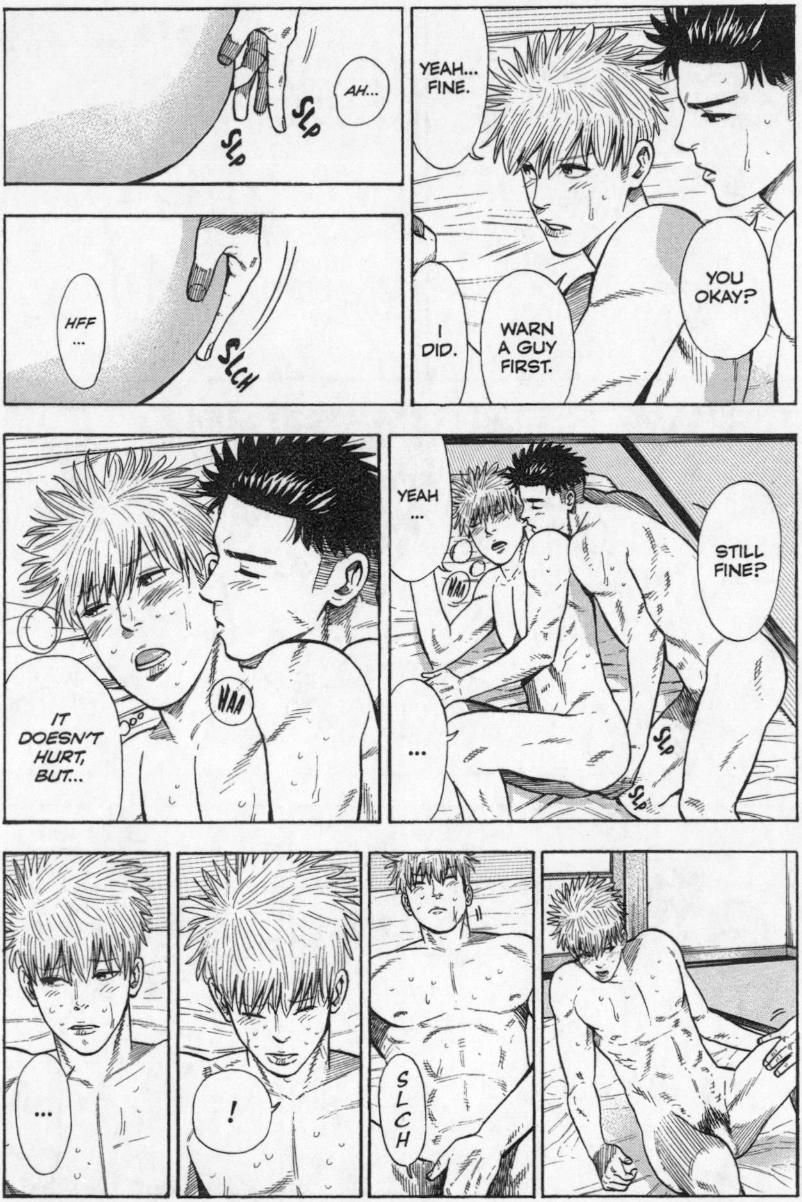
YOU OKAY?
YEAH... FINE.
WARN A GUY FIRST.
I DID.
AH...
SLP
SLP
HFF ...
SLCH
STILL FINE?
YEAH ...
WAA
SLP
SLP
...
WAA
IT DOESN'T HURT, BUT...
SLCH
!
...

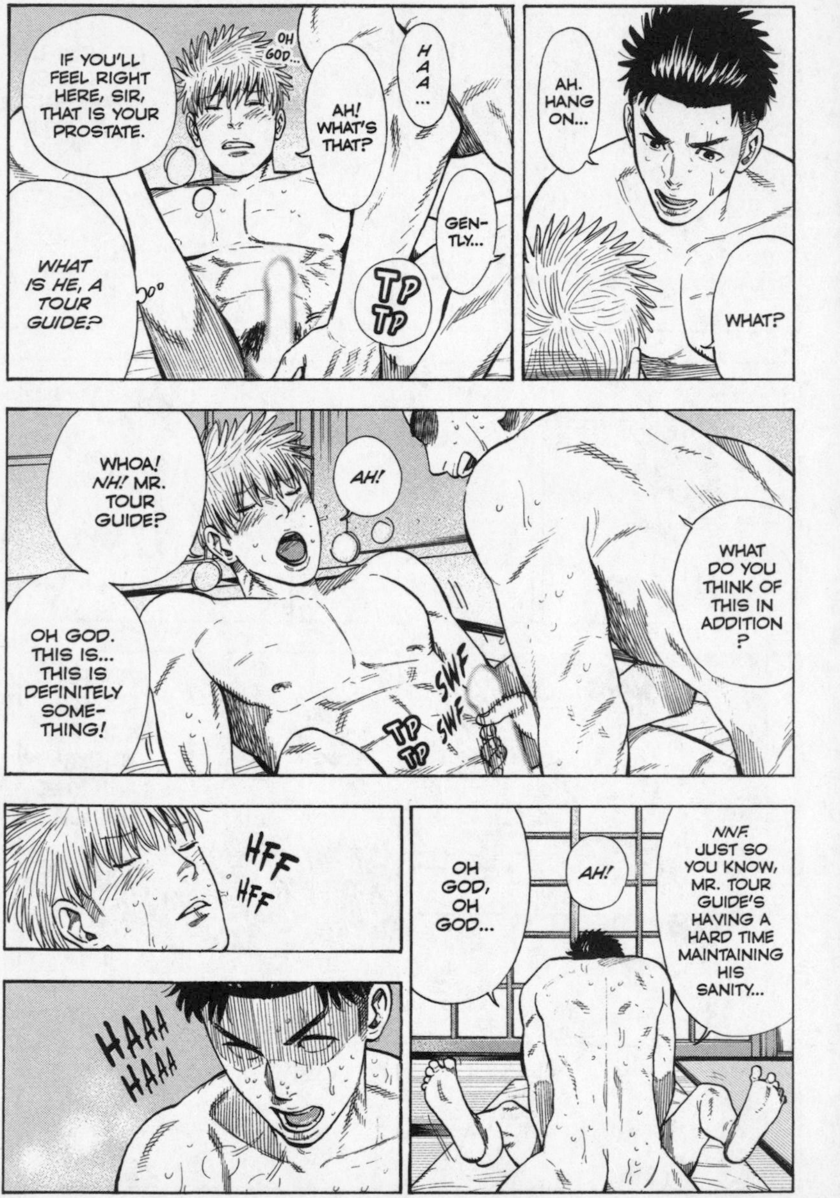
AH. HANG ON...
WHAT?
HAAA...
OH GOD...
AH! WHAT'S THAT?
IF YOU'LL FEEL RIGHT HERE, SIR, THAT IS YOUR PROSTATE.
GENTLY...
TP TP
WHAT IS HE, A TOUR GUIDE?
WHAT DO YOU THINK OF THIS IN ADDITION?
AH!
WHOA! NH! MR. TOUR GUIDE?
SWF SWF
TP TP
OH GOD. THIS IS... THIS IS DEFINITELY SOMETHING!
NNF. JUST SO YOU KNOW, MR. TOUR GUIDE'S HAVING A HARD TIME MAINTAINING HIS SANITY...
AH!
OH GOD, OH GOD...
HFF HFF
HAAA HAAA

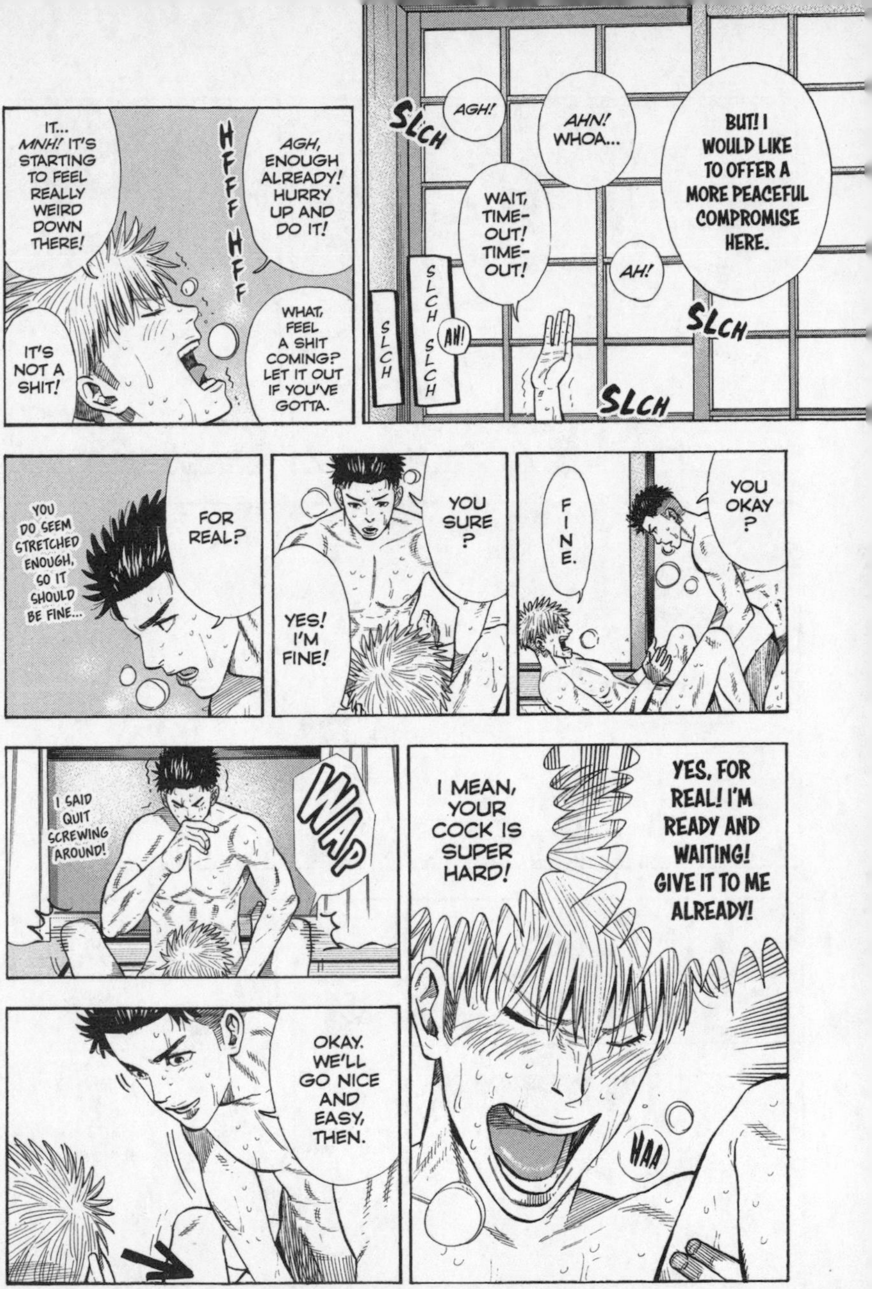

BUT! I WOULD LIKE TO OFFER A MORE PEACEFUL COMPROMISE HERE.
AHN! WHOA...
AGH!
SLCH
WAIT, TIME-OUT! TIME-OUT!
AH!
SLCH
AH!
SLCH SLCH
SLCH
SLCH
AGH, ENOUGH ALREADY! HURRY UP AND DO IT!
HFFF HFFF
IT... MNH! IT'S STARTING TO FEEL REALLY WEIRD DOWN THERE!
WHAT, FEEL A SHIT COMING? LET IT OUT IF YOU'VE GOTTA.
IT'S NOT A SHIT!
YOU OKAY?
FINE.
YOU SURE?
YES! I'M FINE!
FOR REAL?
YOU DO SEEM STRETCHED ENOUGH, SO IT SHOULD BE FINE...
YES, FOR REAL! I'M READY AND WAITING! GIVE IT TO ME ALREADY!
I MEAN, YOUR COCK IS SUPER HARD!
HAA
WAP
I SAID QUIT SCREWING AROUND!
OKAY. WE'LL GO NICE AND EASY, THEN.

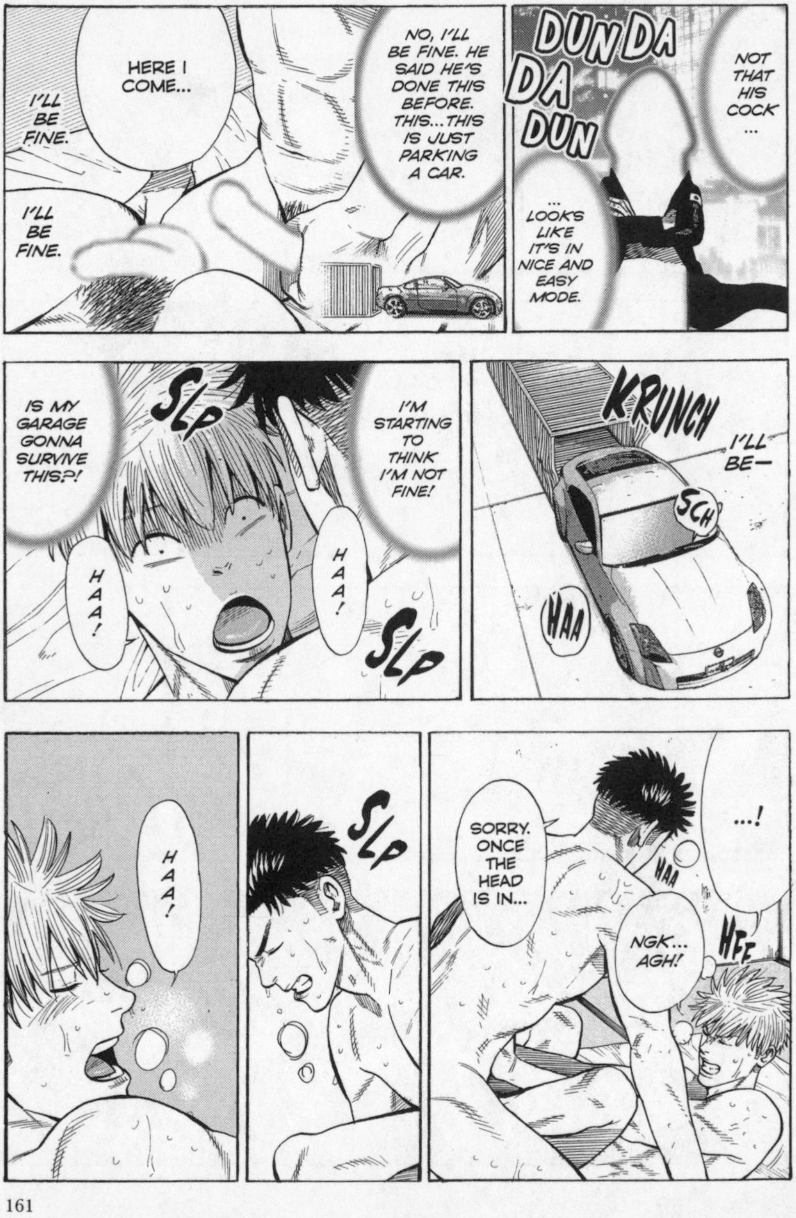

NOT THAT HIS COCK ...
DUN DA DA DUN
... LOOKS LIKE IT'S IN NICE AND EASY MODE.
NO, I'LL BE FINE. HE SAID HE'S DONE THIS BEFORE. THIS...THIS IS JUST PARKING A CAR.
HERE I COME...
I'LL BE FINE.
I'LL BE FINE.
KRUNCH
I'LL BE—
SCH
HAA
I'M STARTING TO THINK I'M NOT FINE!
SLP
IS MY GARAGE GONNA SURVIVE THIS?!
HAA!
HAA!
SLP
...!
SORRY. ONCE THE HEAD IS IN...
HAA
HFF
NGK... AGH!
SLP
HAA!

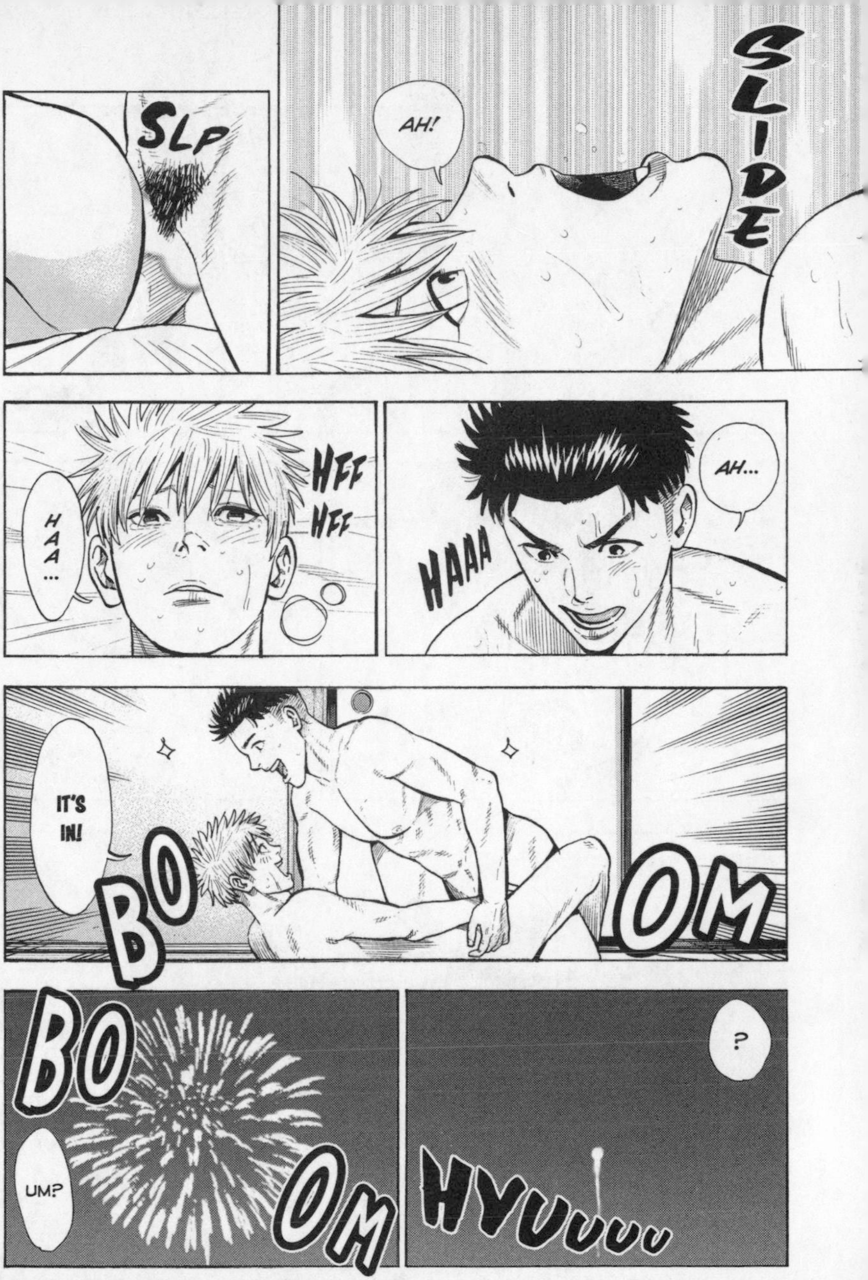
SLIDE
AH!
SLP
AH...
HAAA
HFF HFF
HAA...
IT'S IN!
BOOM
?
HYUUUUU
BOOM
UM?

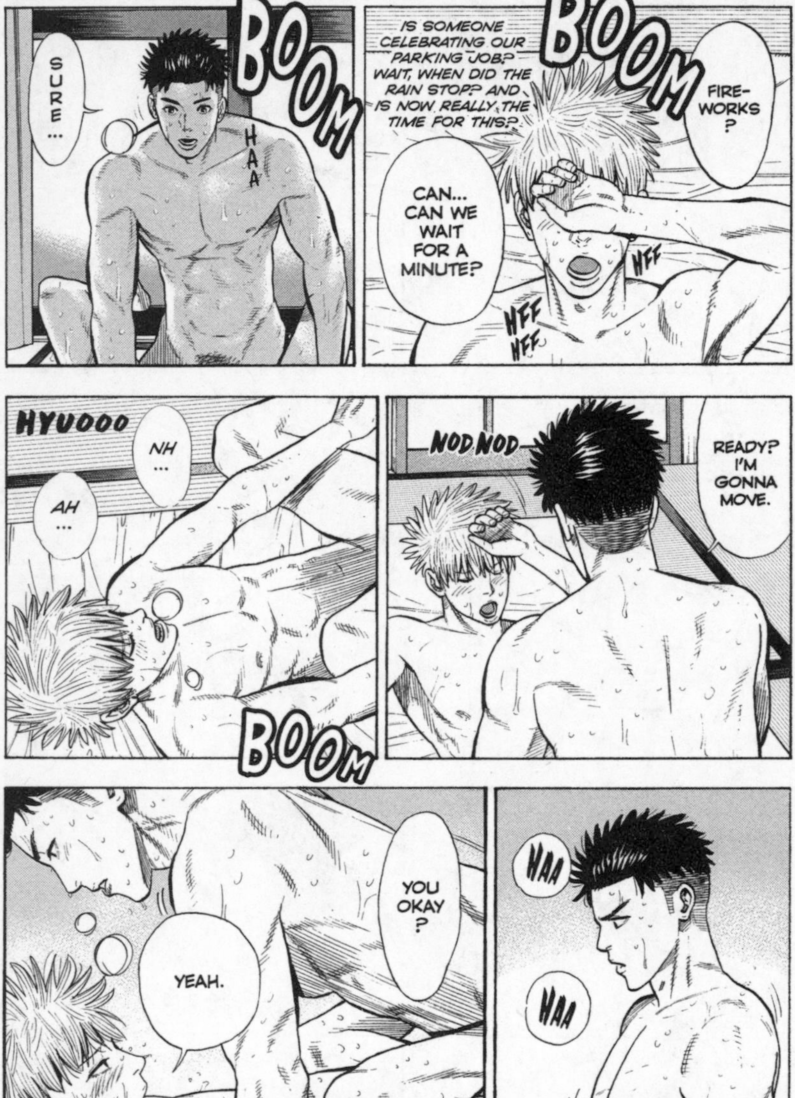
BOOM
FIRE-WORKS?
IS SOMEONE CELEBRATING OUR PARKING JOB? WAIT, WHEN DID THE RAIN STOP? AND IS NOW REALLY THE TIME FOR THIS?
CAN... CAN WE WAIT FOR A MINUTE?
HFF
HFF HFF
BOOM
SURE...
HAA
READY? I'M GONNA MOVE.
NOD NOD
HYUOOO
NH...
AH...
BOOM
HAA
HAA
YOU OKAY?
YEAH.

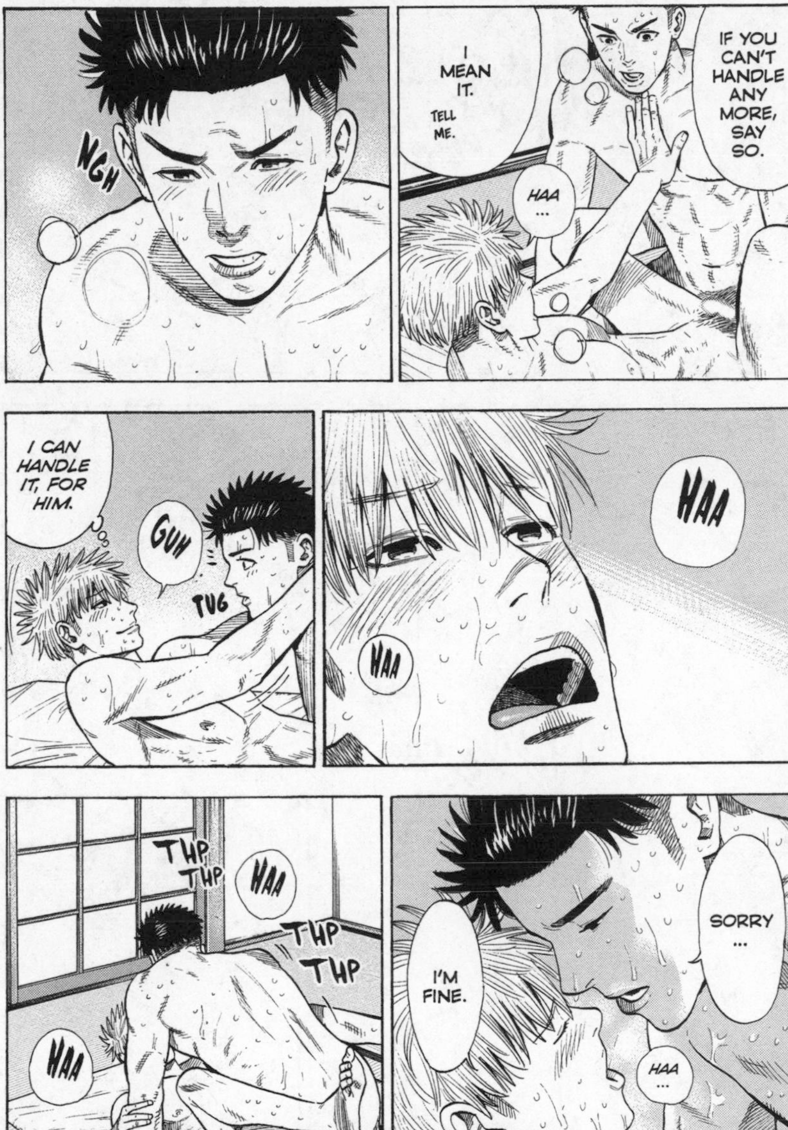

IF YOU CAN'T HANDLE ANY MORE, SAY SO.
I MEAN IT.
TELL ME.
HAA ...
NGH
HAA
HAA
I CAN HANDLE IT, FOR HIM.
GUH
TUG
SORRY ...
I'M FINE.
HAA ...
THP THP
HAA
THP THP
HAA

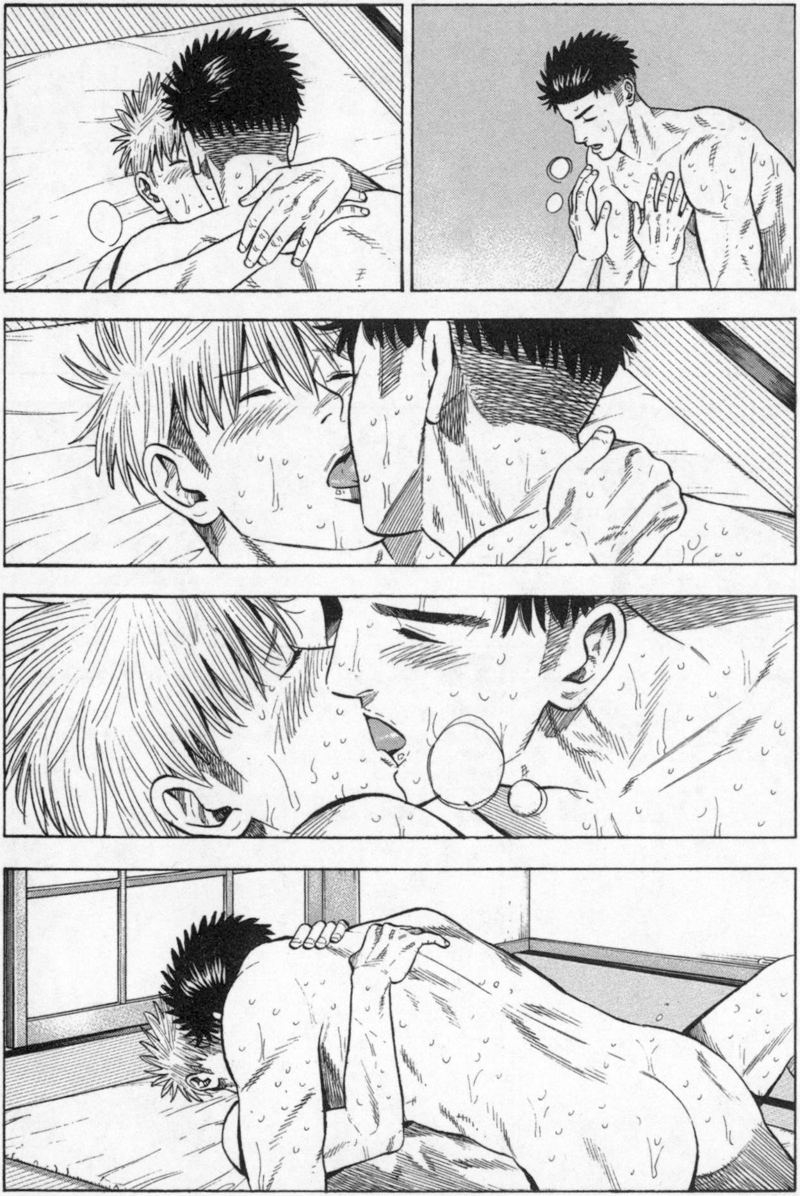

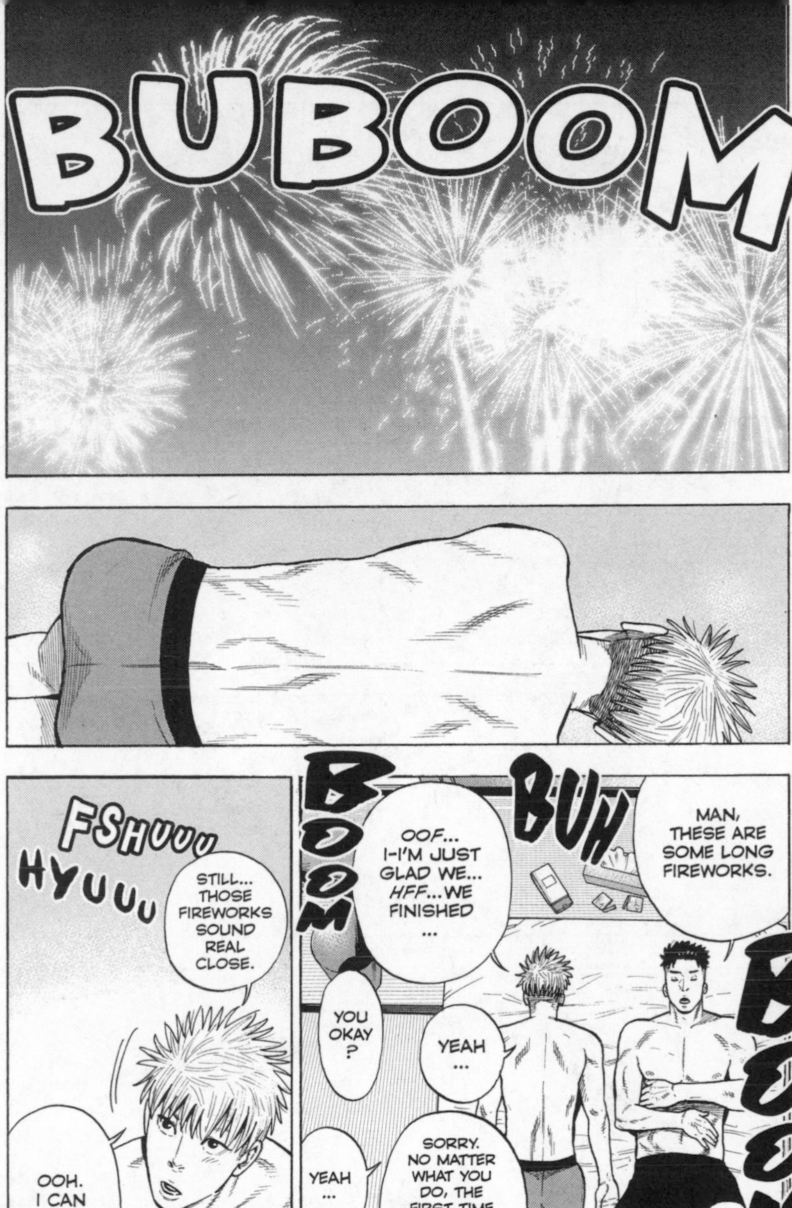
BUBOOM
MAN, THESE ARE SOME LONG FIREWORKS.
BUH
BOOOM
OOF... I-I'M JUST GLAD WE... *HFF*...WE FINISHED ...
BOOM
YOU OKAY ?
YEAH ...
SORRY. NO MATTER WHAT YOU DO, THE FIRST TIME IS ALWAYS... YEAH. YOU'LL GET USED TO IT...
YEAH ...
FSHUUU
HYUUU
STILL... THOSE FIREWORKS SOUND REAL CLOSE.
OOH. I CAN SEE 'EM.

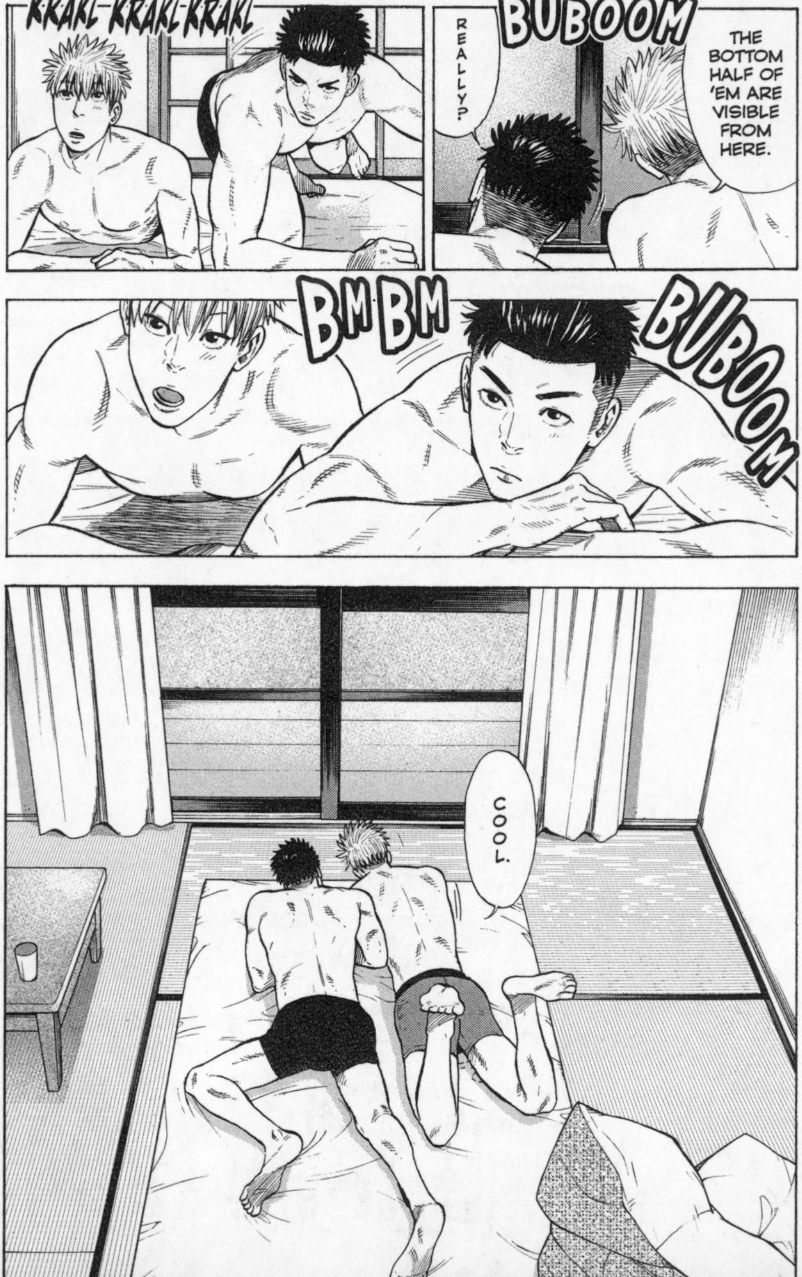
THE BOTTOM HALF OF 'EM ARE VISIBLE FROM HERE.
BUBOOM
REALLY?
KRAKL-KRAKL-KRAKL
BUBOOM
BMBM
COOL.

BAD BOYS
HAPPY HOME

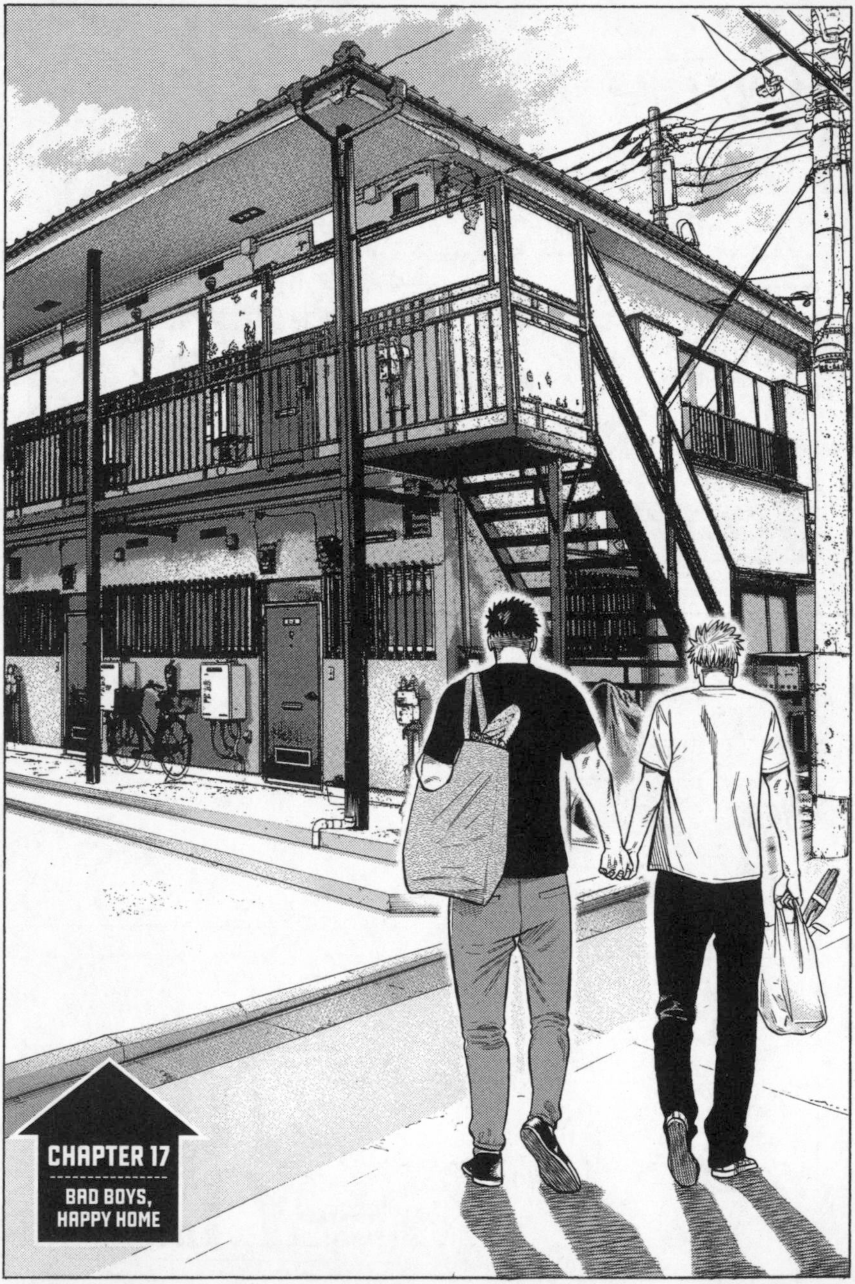
CHAPTER 17
BAD BOYS, HAPPY HOME

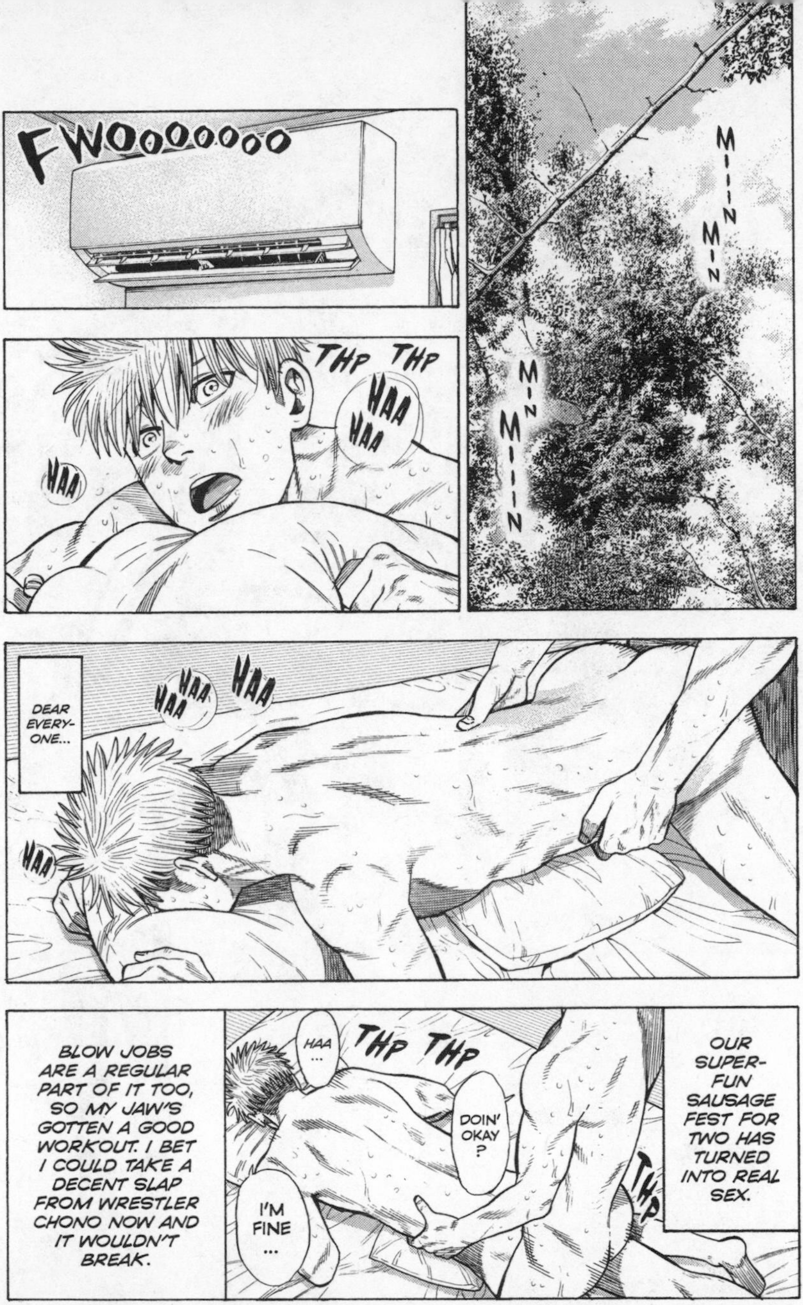
MIIN MIN
MIN MIIIN
FWOOOOOOO
THP THP
HAA HAA
HAA
HAA
HAA HAA
DEAR EVERY-ONE...
HAA
OUR SUPER-FUN SAUSAGE FEST FOR TWO HAS TURNED INTO REAL SEX.
THP THP
HAA ...
DOIN' OKAY ?
THP
I'M FINE ...
BLOW JOBS ARE A REGULAR PART OF IT TOO, SO MY JAW'S GOTTEN A GOOD WORKOUT. I BET I COULD TAKE A DECENT SLAP FROM WRESTLER CHONO NOW AND IT WOULDN'T BREAK.

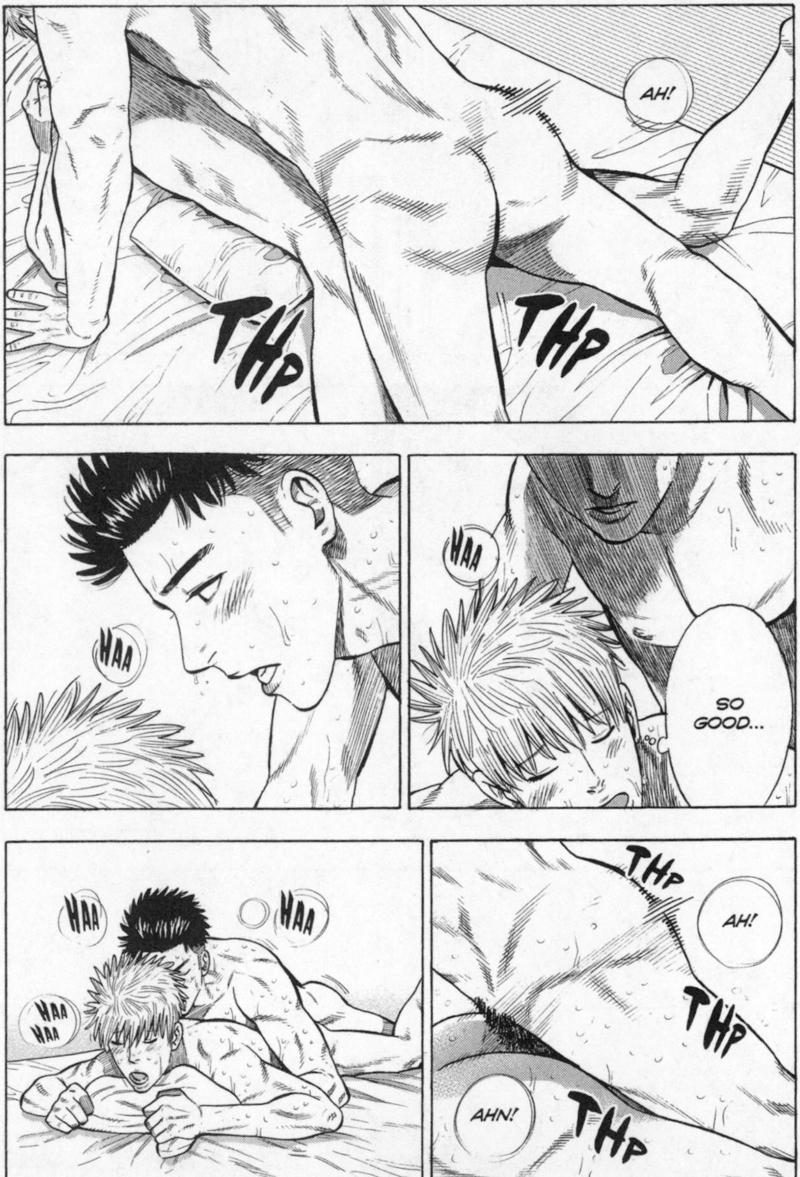
AH!
THP
THP
HAA
SO GOOD...
HAA
THP
AH!
THP
AHN!
THP
HAA
HAA
HAA HAA

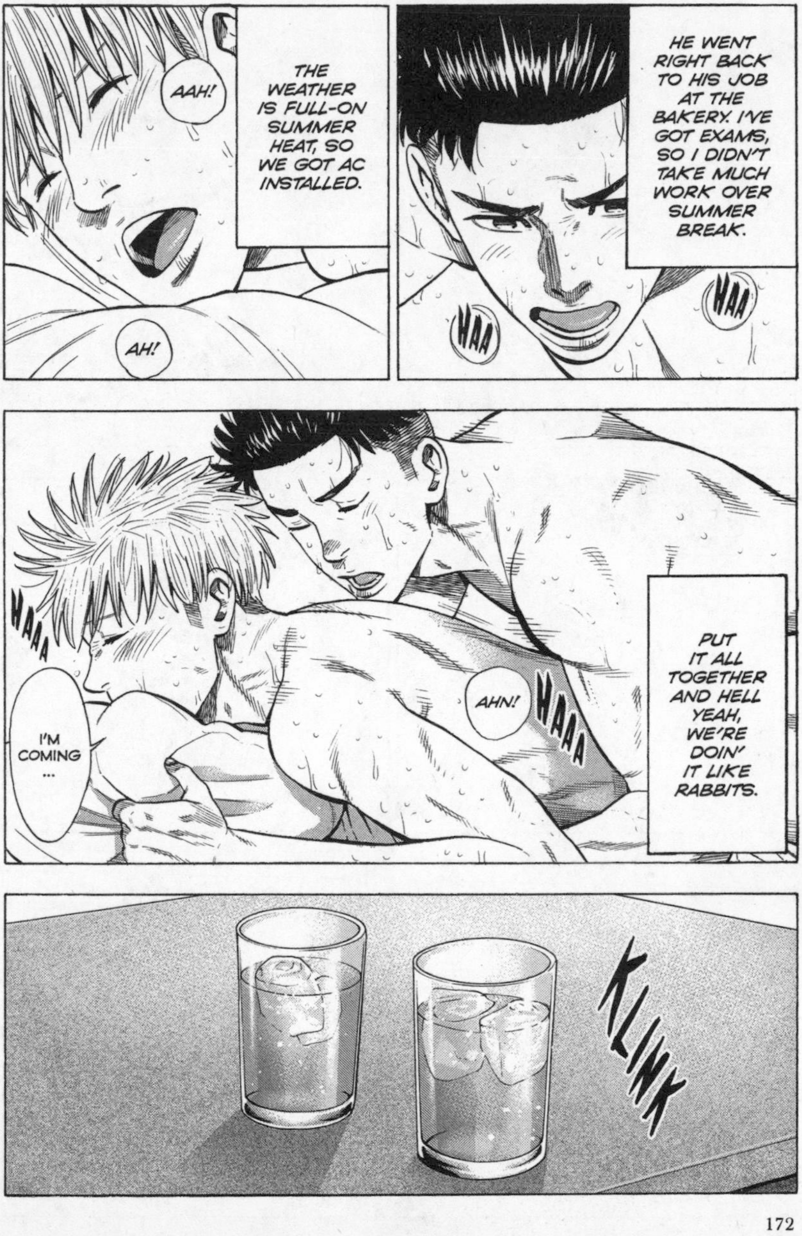
HE WENT RIGHT BACK TO HIS JOB AT THE BAKERY. I'VE GOT EXAMS, SO I DIDN'T TAKE MUCH WORK OVER SUMMER BREAK.
HAA
HAA
THE WEATHER IS FULL-ON SUMMER HEAT, SO WE GOT AC INSTALLED.
AAH!
AH!
PUT IT ALL TOGETHER AND HELL YEAH, WE'RE DOIN' IT LIKE RABBITS.
HAAA
AHN!
HAAA
I'M COMING ...
KLINK

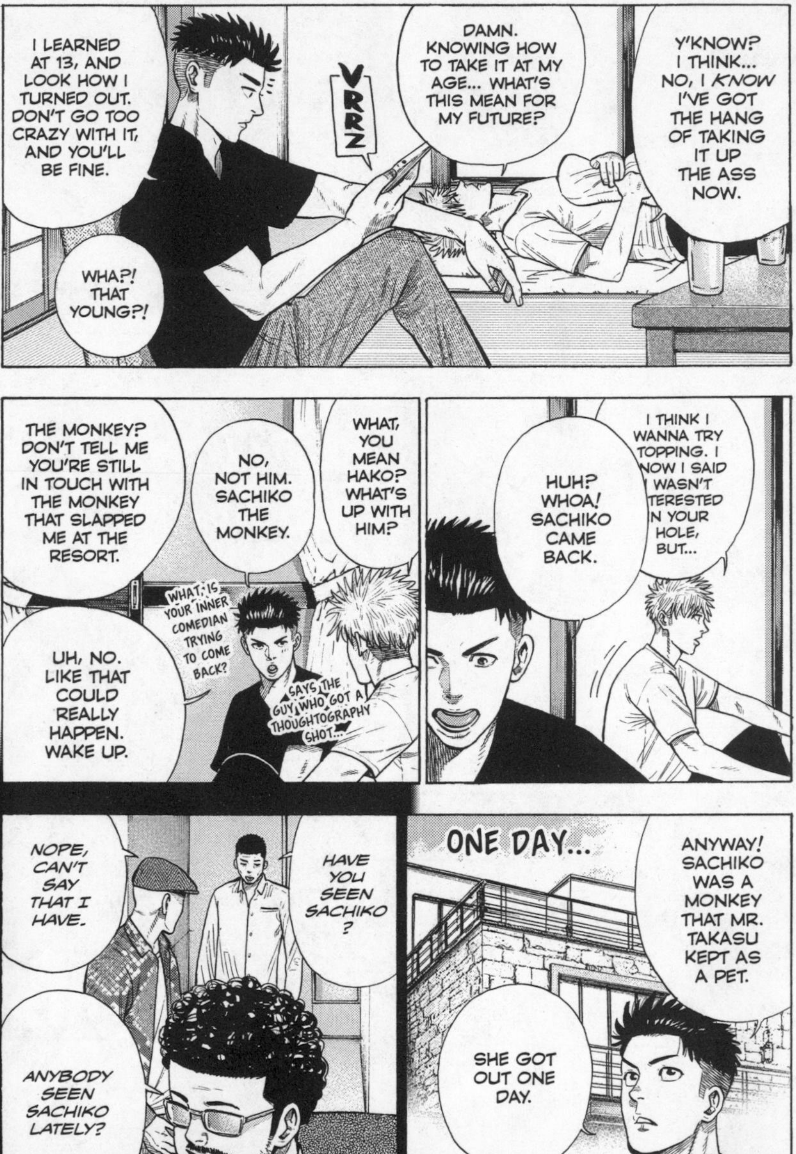
Y'KNOW? I THINK... NO, I *KNOW* I'VE GOT THE HANG OF TAKING IT UP THE ASS NOW.
DAMN. KNOWING HOW TO TAKE IT AT MY AGE... WHAT'S THIS MEAN FOR MY FUTURE?
VRRZ
I LEARNED AT 13, AND LOOK HOW I TURNED OUT. DON'T GO TOO CRAZY WITH IT, AND YOU'LL BE FINE.
WHA?! THAT YOUNG?!
I THINK I WANNA TRY TOPPING. I NOW I SAID I WASN'T TERESTED IN YOUR HOLE, BUT...
HUH? WHOA! SACHIKO CAME BACK.
WHAT, YOU MEAN HAKO? WHAT'S UP WITH HIM?
NO, NOT HIM. SACHIKO THE MONKEY.
THE MONKEY? DON'T TELL ME YOU'RE STILL IN TOUCH WITH THE MONKEY THAT SLAPPED ME AT THE RESORT.
WHAT, IS YOUR INNER COMEDIAN TRYING TO COME BACK?
SAYS THE GUY WHO GOT A THOUGHTOGRAPHY SHOT...
UH, NO. LIKE THAT COULD REALLY HAPPEN. WAKE UP.
ONE DAY...
ANYWAY! SACHIKO WAS A MONKEY THAT MR. TAKASU KEPT AS A PET.
SHE GOT OUT ONE DAY.
HAVE YOU SEEN SACHIKO?
NOPE, CAN'T SAY THAT I HAVE.
ANYBODY SEEN SACHIKO LATELY?

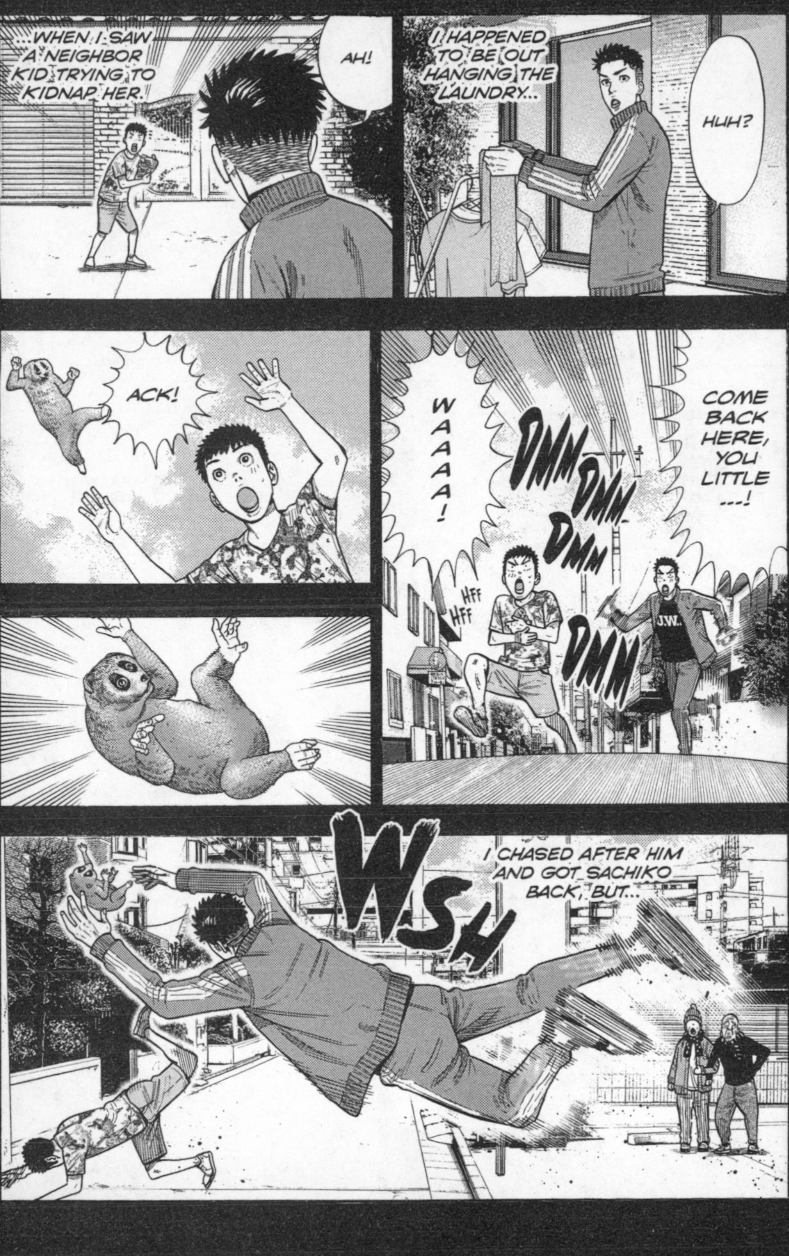
I HAPPENED TO BE OUT HANGING THE LAUNDRY...
HUH?
...WHEN I SAW A NEIGHBOR KID TRYING TO KIDNAP HER.
AH!
COME BACK HERE, YOU LITTLE ---!
DMM DMM DMM
DMM
WAAAAA!
HFF HFF
J.W.
ACK!
I CHASED AFTER HIM AND GOT SACHIKO BACK, BUT...
WSH

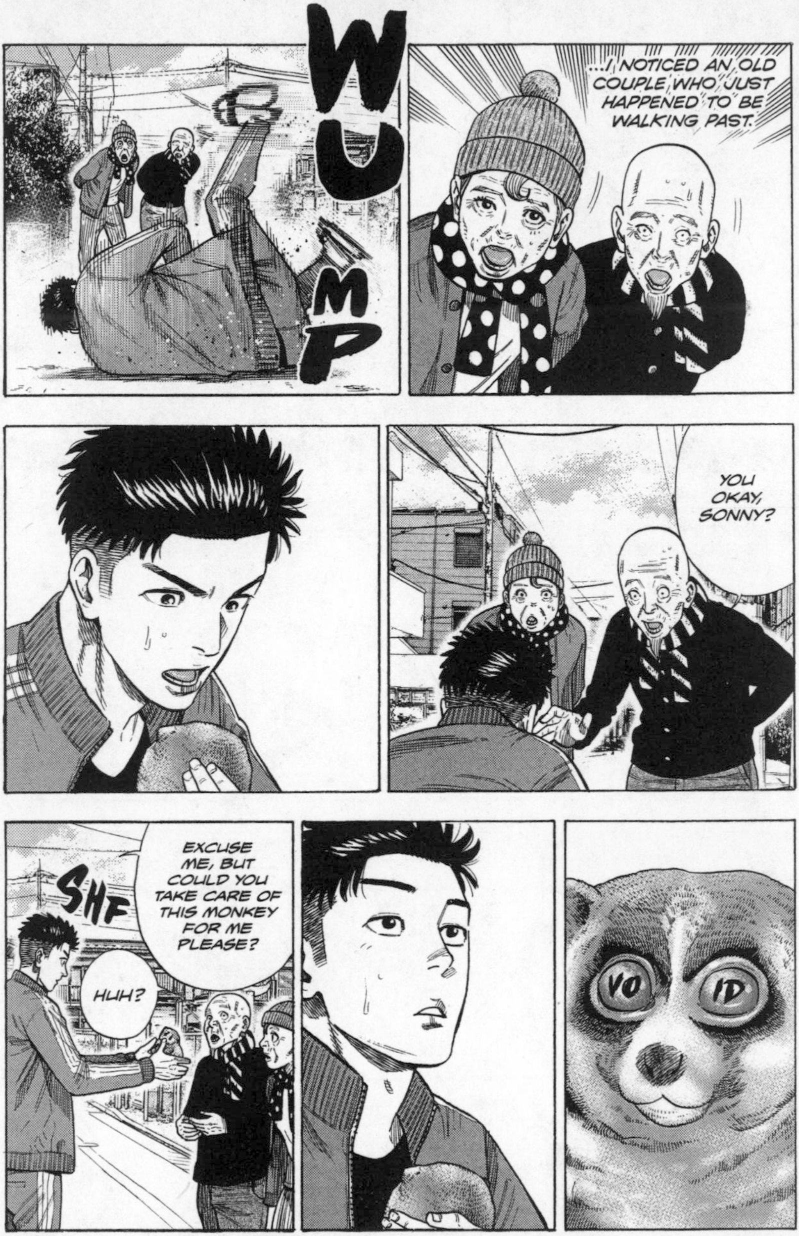
...I NOTICED AN OLD COUPLE WHO JUST HAPPENED TO BE WALKING PAST.
WUMP
YOU OKAY, SONNY?
VO ID
EXCUSE ME, BUT COULD YOU TAKE CARE OF THIS MONKEY FOR ME PLEASE?
SHF
HUH?

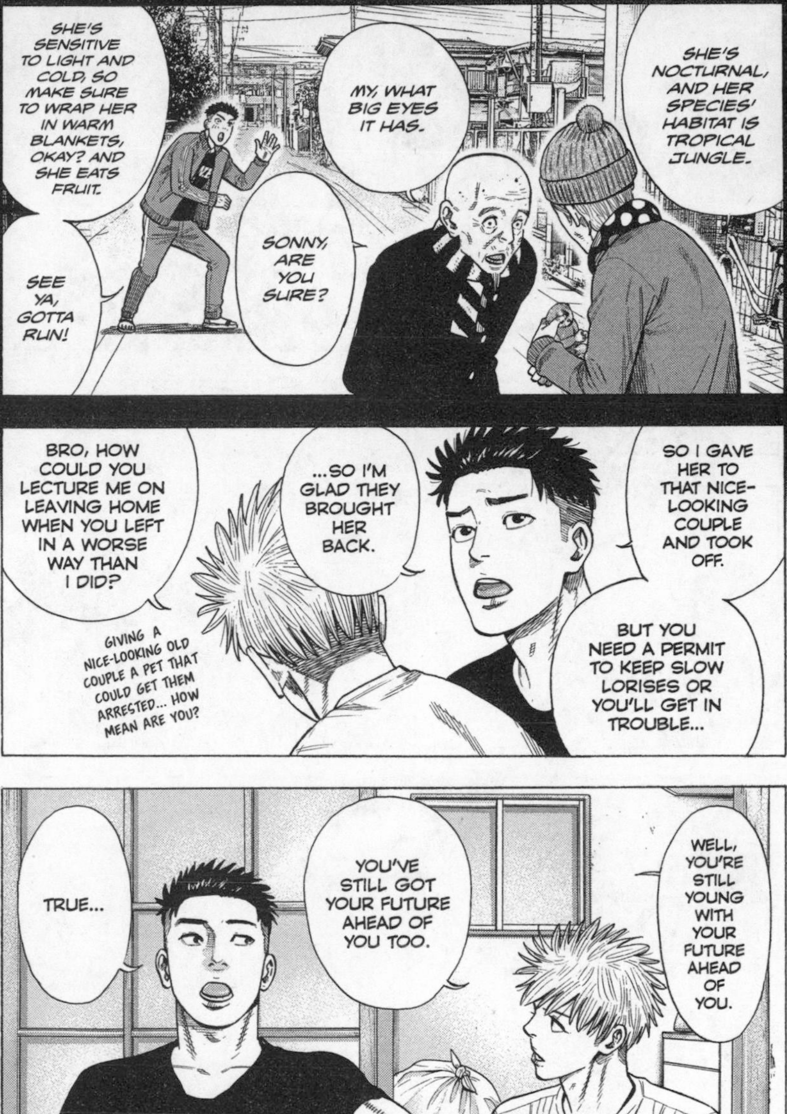
SHE'S NOCTURNAL, AND HER SPECIES' HABITAT IS TROPICAL JUNGLE.
MY, WHAT BIG EYES IT HAS.
SHE'S SENSITIVE TO LIGHT AND COLD, SO MAKE SURE TO WRAP HER IN WARM BLANKETS, OKAY? AND SHE EATS FRUIT.
SONNY, ARE YOU SURE?
SEE YA, GOTTA RUN!
SO I GAVE HER TO THAT NICE-LOOKING COUPLE AND TOOK OFF.
BUT YOU NEED A PERMIT TO KEEP SLOW LORISES OR YOU'LL GET IN TROUBLE...
...SO I'M GLAD THEY BROUGHT HER BACK.
BRO, HOW COULD YOU LECTURE ME ON LEAVING HOME WHEN YOU LEFT IN A WORSE WAY THAN I DID?
GIVING A NICE-LOOKING OLD COUPLE A PET THAT COULD GET THEM ARRESTED... HOW MEAN ARE YOU?
WELL, YOU'RE STILL YOUNG WITH YOUR FUTURE AHEAD OF YOU.
YOU'VE STILL GOT YOUR FUTURE AHEAD OF YOU TOO.
TRUE...

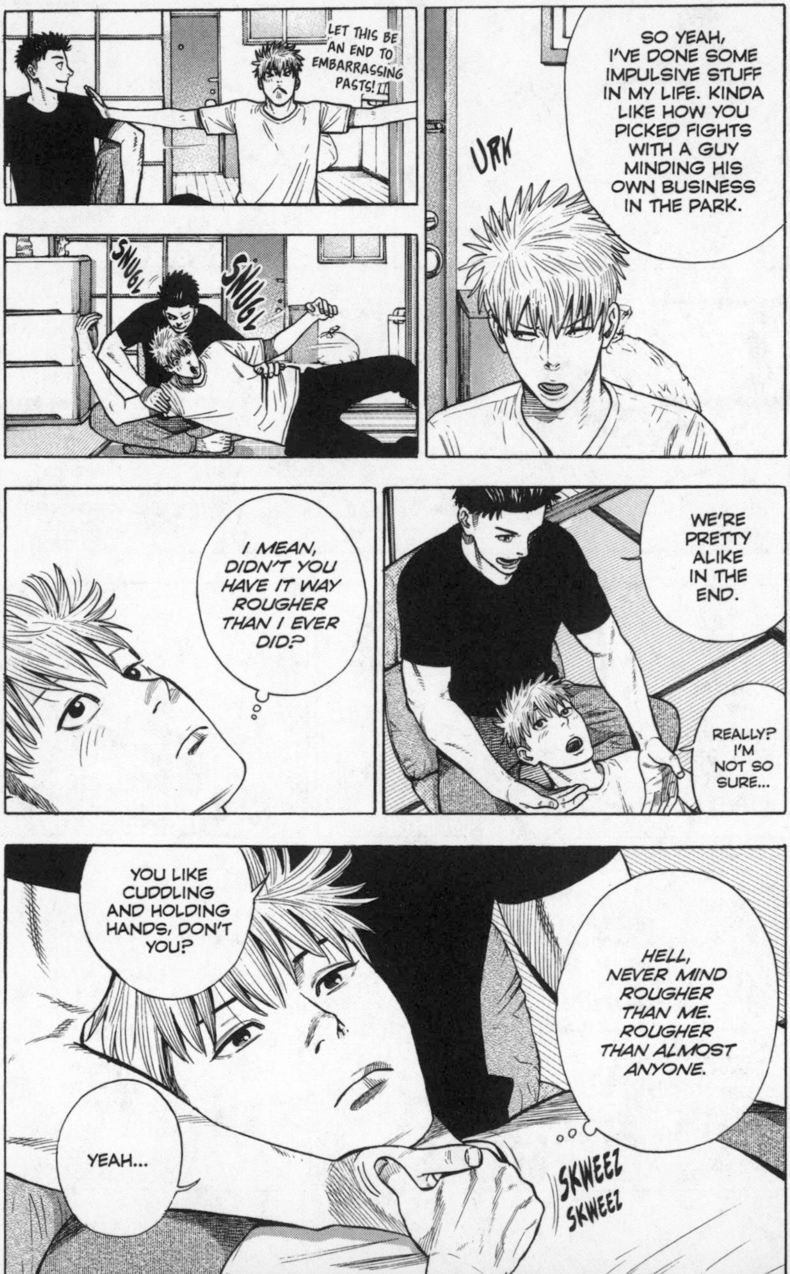
SO YEAH, I'VE DONE SOME IMPULSIVE STUFF IN MY LIFE. KINDA LIKE HOW YOU PICKED FIGHTS WITH A GUY MINDING HIS OWN BUSINESS IN THE PARK.
URK
LET THIS BE AN END TO EMBARRASSING PASTS!
SNUGL
SNUGL
WE'RE PRETTY ALIKE IN THE END.
REALLY? I'M NOT SO SURE...
I MEAN, DIDN'T YOU HAVE IT WAY ROUGHER THAN I EVER DID?
YOU LIKE CUDDLING AND HOLDING HANDS, DON'T YOU?
HELL, NEVER MIND ROUGHER THAN ME. ROUGHER THAN ALMOST ANYONE.
YEAH...
SKWEEZ
SKWEEZ

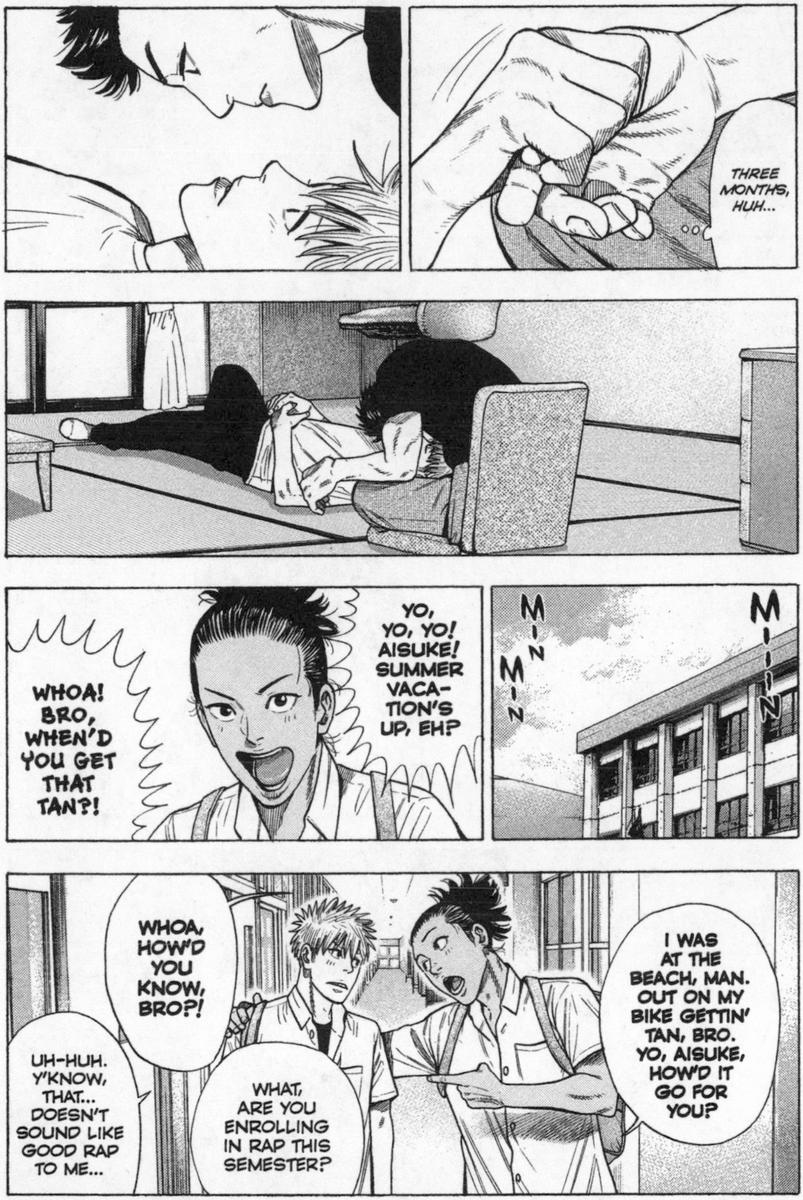
THREE MONTHS, HUH...
MIIIN
MIN
MIN
YO, YO, YO! AISUKE! SUMMER VACATION'S UP, EH?
WHOA! BRO, WHEN'D YOU GET THAT TAN?!
I WAS AT THE BEACH, MAN. OUT ON MY BIKE GETTIN' TAN, BRO. YO, AISUKE, HOW'D IT GO FOR YOU?
WHOA, HOW'D YOU KNOW, BRO?!
WHAT, ARE YOU ENROLLING IN RAP THIS SEMESTER?
UH-HUH. Y'KNOW, THAT... DOESN'T SOUND LIKE GOOD RAP TO ME...

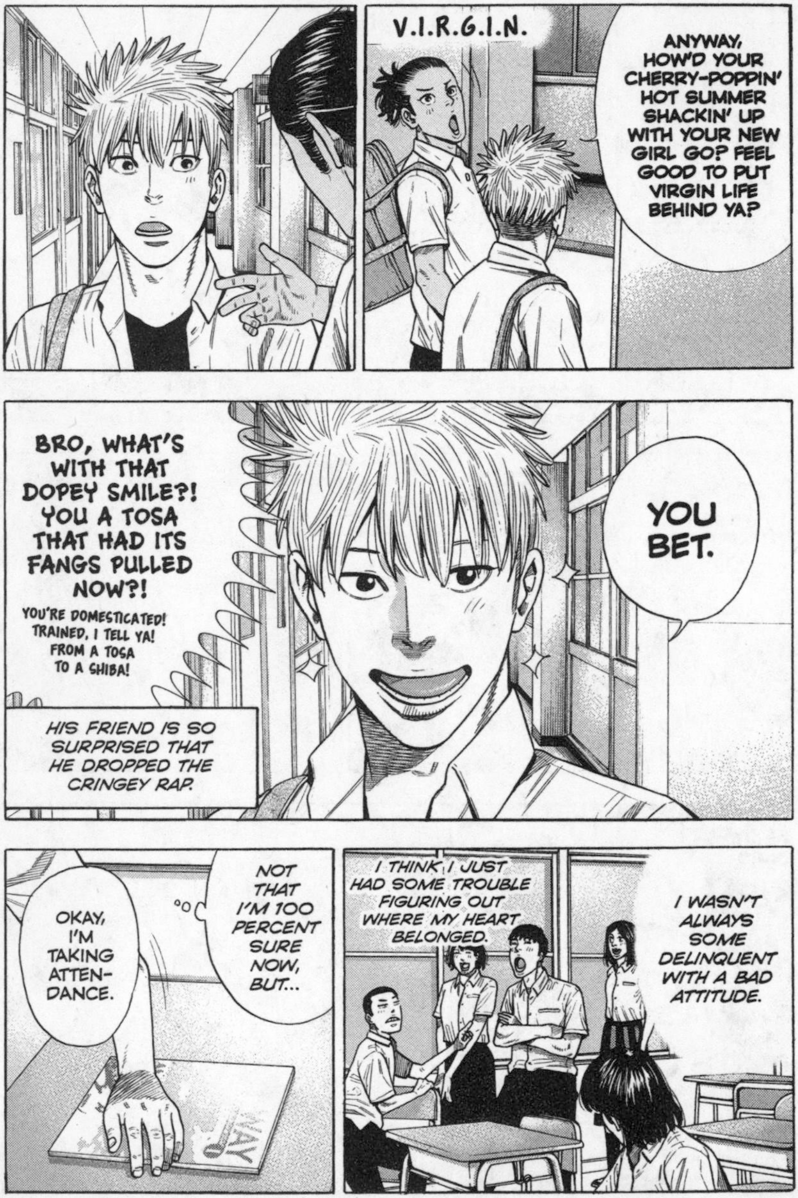
V.I.R.G.I.N.
ANYWAY, HOW'D YOUR CHERRY-POPPIN' HOT SUMMER SHACKIN' UP WITH YOUR NEW GIRL GO? FEEL GOOD TO PUT VIRGIN LIFE BEHIND YA?
YOU BET.
BRO, WHAT'S WITH THAT DOPEY SMILE?! YOU A TOSA THAT HAD ITS FANGS PULLED NOW?!
YOU'RE DOMESTICATED! TRAINED, I TELL YA! FROM A TOSA TO A SHIBA!
HIS FRIEND IS SO SURPRISED THAT HE DROPPED THE CRINGEY RAP.
I WASN'T ALWAYS SOME DELINQUENT WITH A BAD ATTITUDE.
I THINK I JUST HAD SOME TROUBLE FIGURING OUT WHERE MY HEART BELONGED.
NOT THAT I'M 100 PERCENT SURE NOW, BUT...
OKAY, I'M TAKING ATTEN-DANCE.

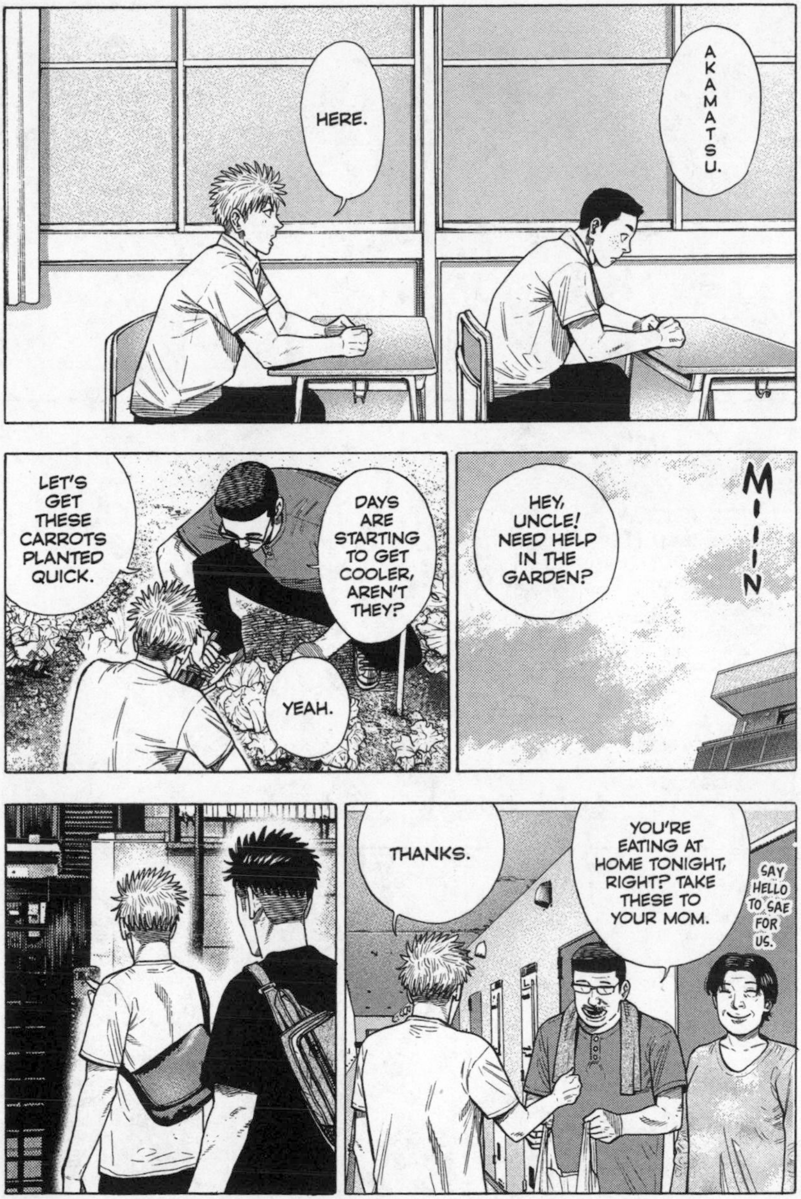
AKAMATSU.
HERE.
MIIIN
HEY, UNCLE! NEED HELP IN THE GARDEN?
DAYS ARE STARTING TO GET COOLER, AREN'T THEY?
LET'S GET THESE CARROTS PLANTED QUICK.
YEAH.
SAY HELLO TO SAE FOR US.
YOU'RE EATING AT HOME TONIGHT, RIGHT? TAKE THESE TO YOUR MOM.
THANKS.

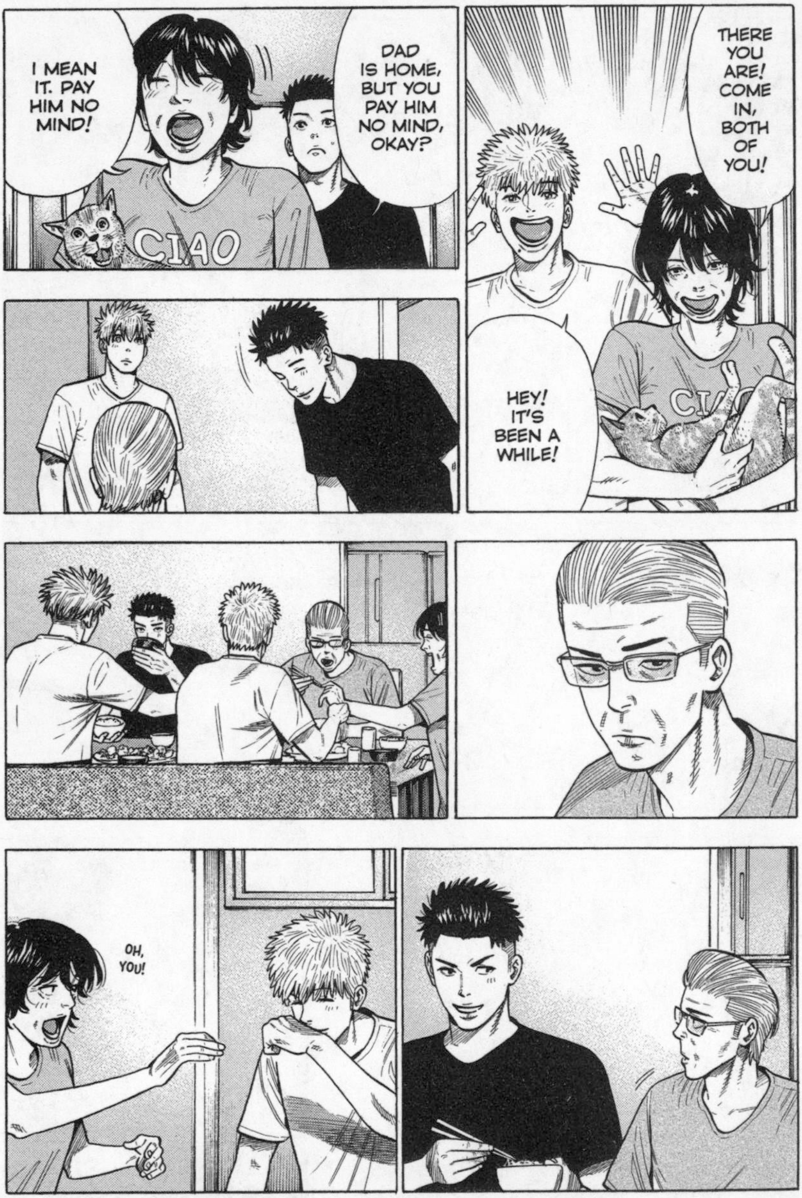
THERE YOU ARE! COME IN, BOTH OF YOU!
HEY! IT'S BEEN A WHILE!
DAD IS HOME, BUT YOU PAY HIM NO MIND, OKAY?
I MEAN IT. PAY HIM NO MIND!
CIAO
OH, YOU!

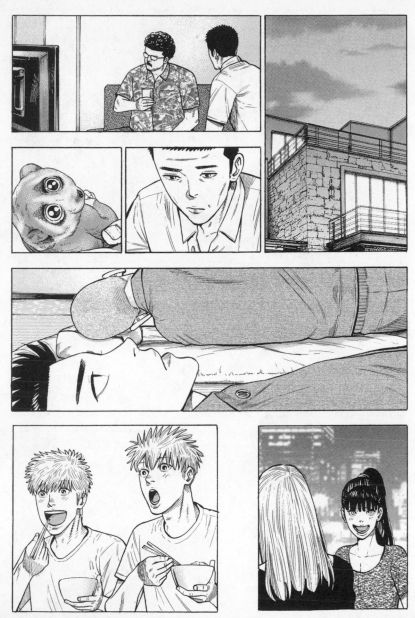

182

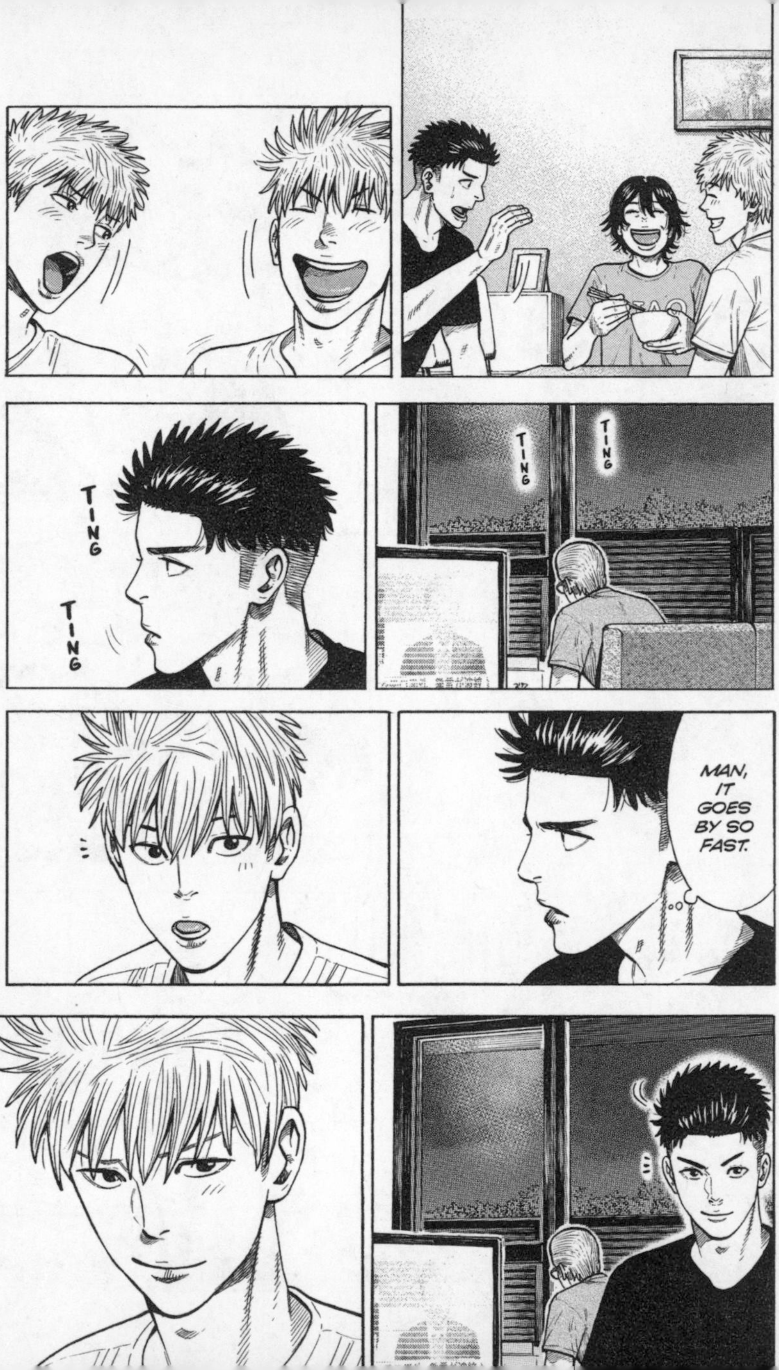
TING
TING
TING
TING
MAN, IT GOES BY SO FAST.

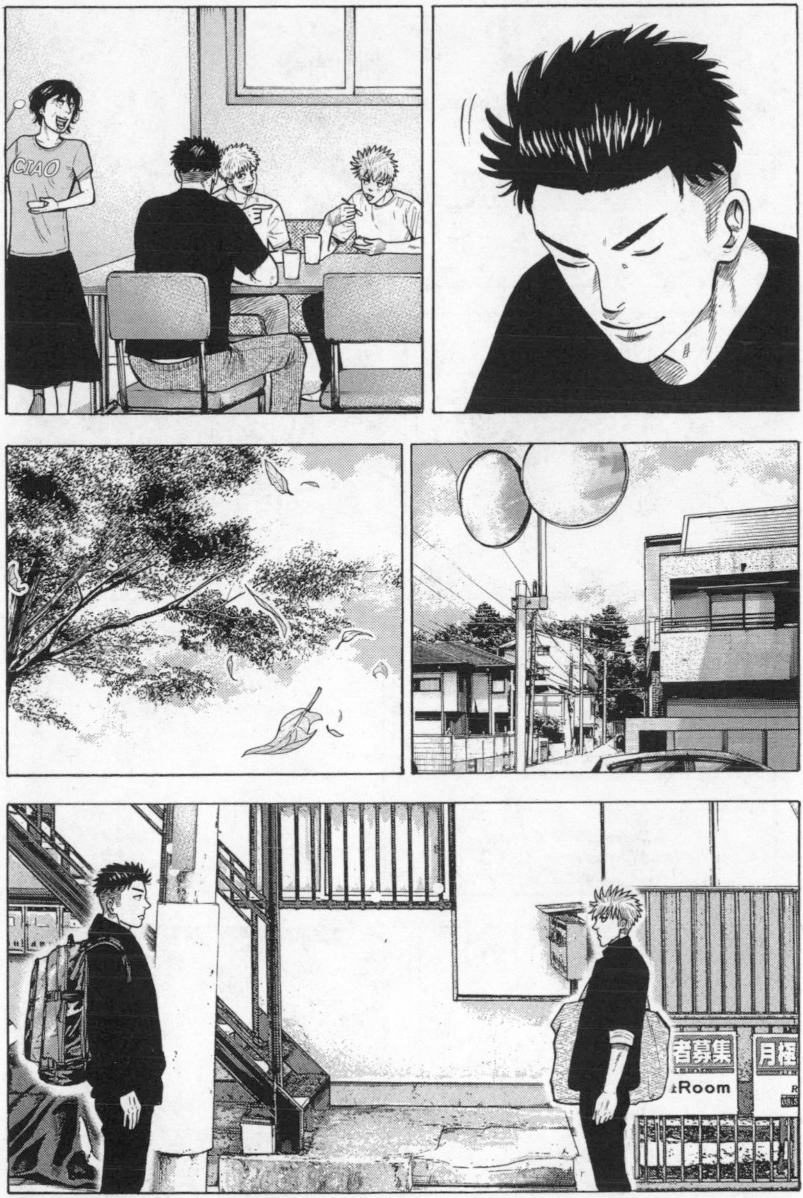
CIAO
者募集
月極
Room

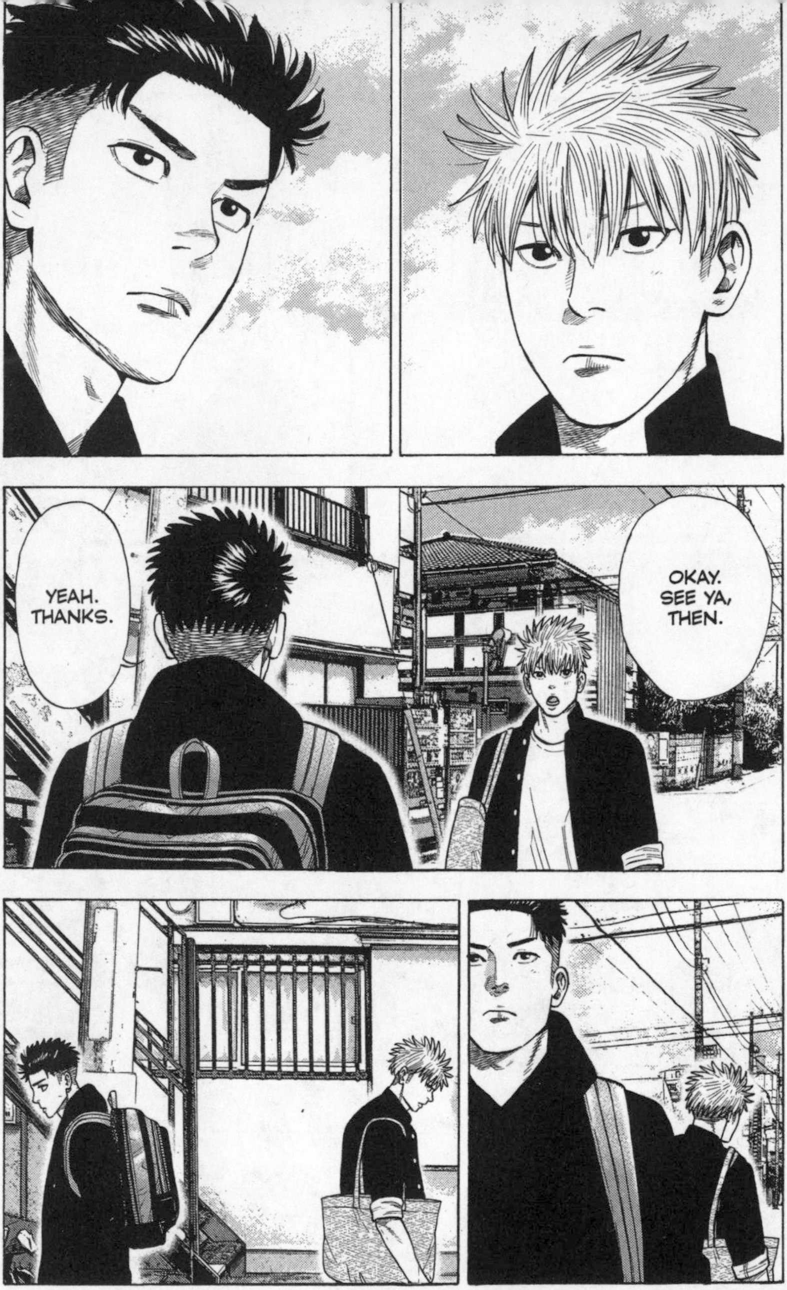
OKAY. SEE YA, THEN.
YEAH. THANKS.

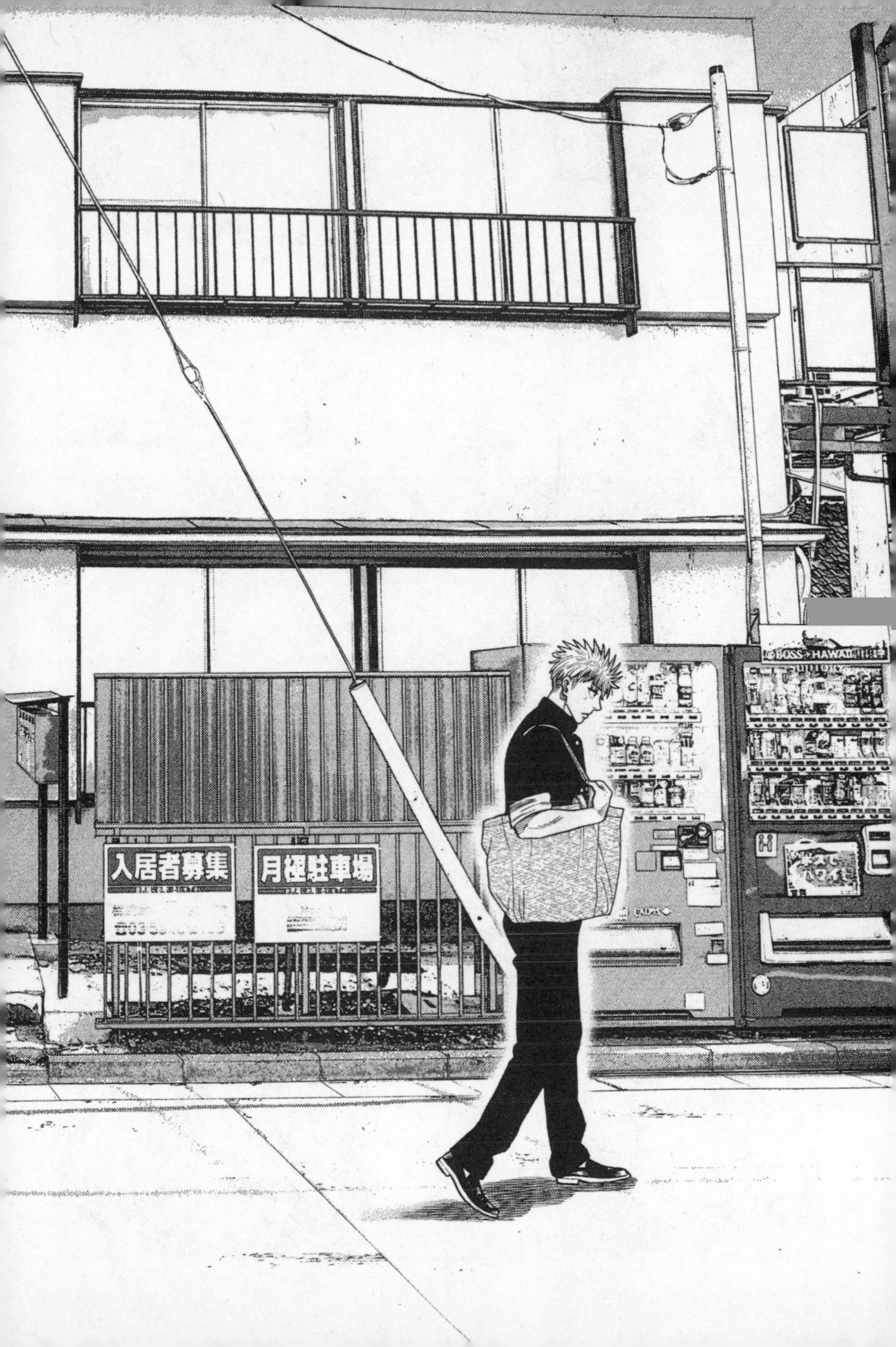
入居者募集
月極駐車場
BOSS HAWAII

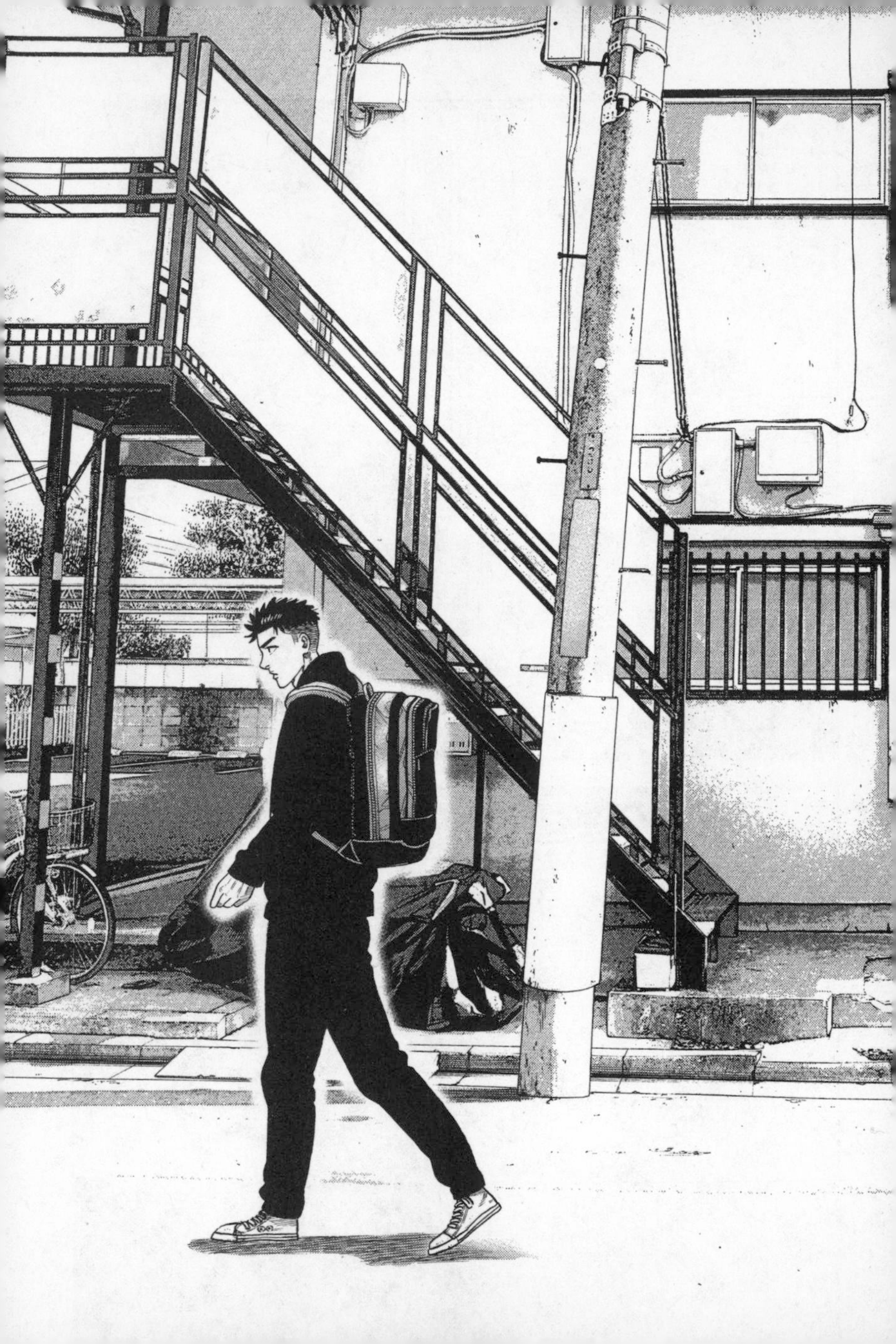

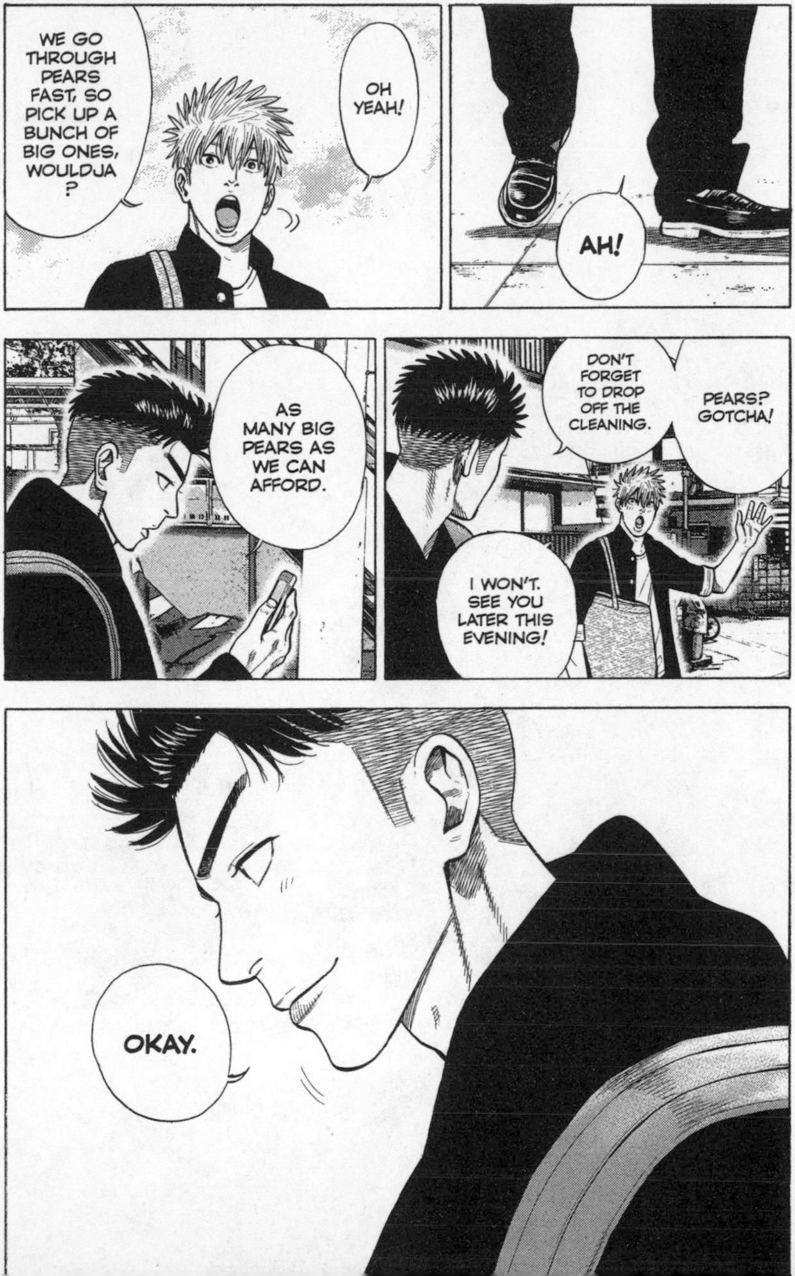
AH!
OH YEAH!
WE GO THROUGH PEARS FAST, SO PICK UP A BUNCH OF BIG ONES, WOULDJA?
PEARS? GOTCHA!
DON'T FORGET TO DROP OFF THE CLEANING.
I WON'T. SEE YOU LATER THIS EVENING!
AS MANY BIG PEARS AS WE CAN AFFORD.
OKAY.

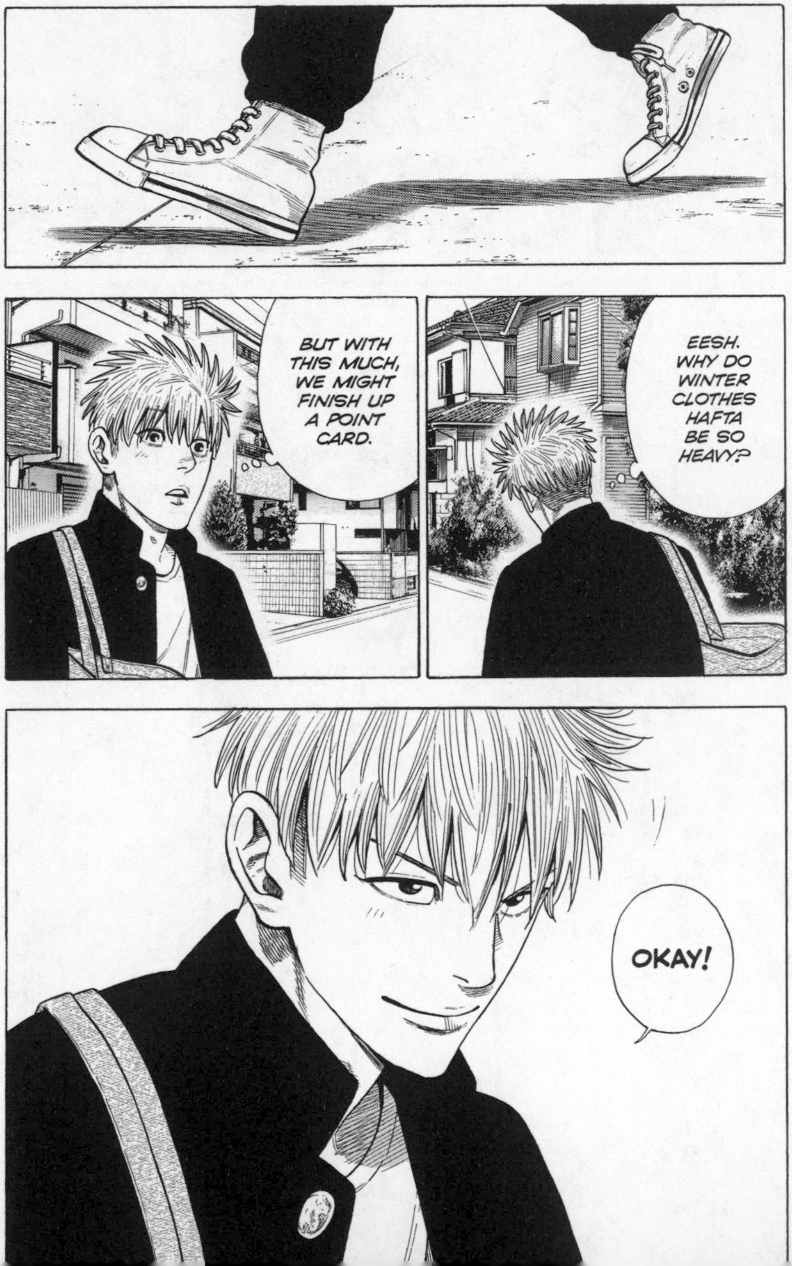
EESH. WHY DO WINTER CLOTHES HAFTA BE SO HEAVY?
BUT WITH THIS MUCH, WE MIGHT FINISH UP A POINT CARD.
OKAY!

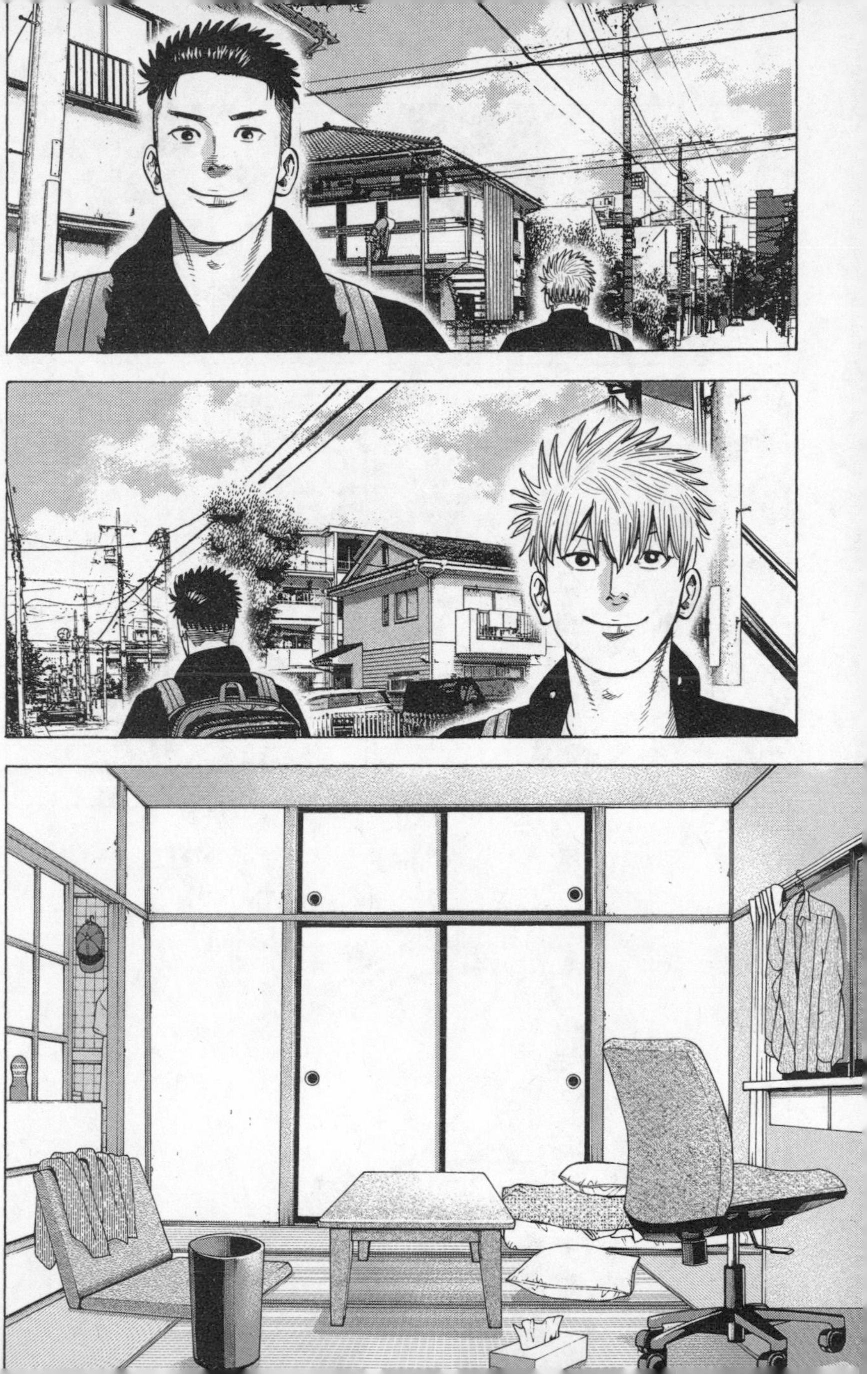

THANK YOU VERY MUCH FOR READING!

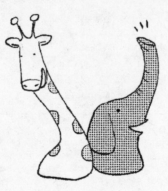

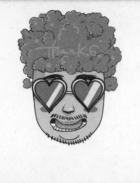

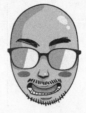

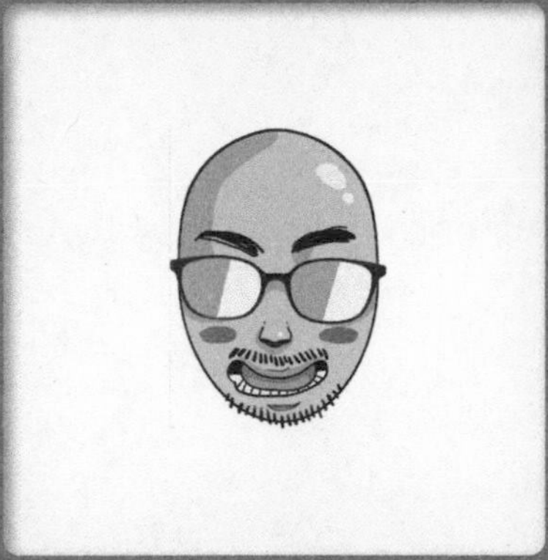

SHOOWA
Thanks for sticking around for three volumes! Mr. Okujima, thank you for making them so cute and cool all the way to the end!

Hiromasa Okujima
Thank you for watching over their lives together to the very end. Now I kind of want to live with friends again.

About the Creators

Bad Boys, Happy Home may be **SHOOWA**'s first English-language release, but she's also been published internationally in both French and Korean. You can find out more about her on her Twitter page, **@shoowa**.

Although this is **Hiromasa Okujima**'s first professional foray into boys' love, he's created many shonen and seinen manga. Some of his hobbies include martial arts and collecting secondhand clothing. You can find out more about him on his Twitter page, **@HiromasaOkujima**.

Bad Boys, Happy Home

Volume 3

SuBLime Manga Edition

Story by **SHOOWA**
Art by **Hiromasa Okujima**

Translation—**Adrienne Beck**
Touch-Up Art and Lettering—**Deborah Fisher**
Cover and Graphic Design—**Julian [JR] Robinson**
Editor—**Jennifer LeBlanc**

DOUSEI YANKEE AKAMATSU SEVEN Volume 3

First published in Japan in 2021 by Akita Publishing Co., Ltd., Tokyo
English translation rights arranged with Akita Publishing Co., Ltd.
through Tuttle-Mori Agency, Inc., Tokyo

秋田書店
AKITA SHOTEN since 1948

Printed in the U.S.A.

Published by SuBLime Manga
P.O. Box 77010
San Francisco, CA 94107

10 9 8 7 6 5 4 3 2 1
First printing, January 2022

M
MATURE
PARENTAL ADVISORY
BAD BOYS, HAPPY HOME is rated M for Mature and is recommended for mature readers. This volume contains graphic imagery, mature themes, and cute guys cohabitating.

SUBLIME
www.SuBLimeManga.com

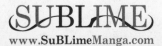

For more information

on all our products, along with the most up-to-date news on releases, series announcements, and contests, please visit us at:

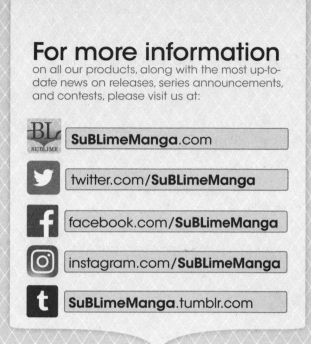

SuBLimeManga.com

twitter.com/**SuBLimeManga**

facebook.com/**SuBLimeManga**

instagram.com/**SuBLimeManga**

SuBLimeManga.tumblr.com

SUBLIME
MANGA

D0595586